Growing Up on the Set

Growing Up on the Set

*Interviews with 39 Former
Child Actors of Classic
Film and Television*

Tom *and* Jim Goldrup

Foreword by Diana Serra Cary

McFarland & Company, Inc., Publishers
Jefferson, North Carolina, and London

Library of Congress Cataloguing-in-Publication Data

Goldrup, Tom.
    Growing up on the set : interviews with 39 former child actors of classic film and television / Tom and Jim Goldrup ; foreword by Diana Serra Cary.
        p.   cm.
    Includes index.
    ISBN 0-7864-1254-2 (softcover : 50# alkaline paper) ∞
    1. Child actors—United States—Interviews.   2. Children as actors—United States.   I. Goldrup, Jim. II. Title.
PN2285.G65   2002
791.43'028'0830973—dc21   2002002396

British Library cataloguing data are available

©2002 Tom Goldrup and Jim Goldrup. All rights reserved

No part of this book may be reproduced or transmitted in any form or by any means, electronic or mechanical, including photocopying or recording, or by any information storage and retrieval system, without permission in writing from the publisher.

Cover photograph: Teddy Infuhr

Manufactured in the United States of America

McFarland & Company, Inc., Publishers
  Box 611, Jefferson, North Carolina 28640
    www.mcfarlandpub.com

This book is dedicated to all the children,
past and present,
who have graced us with their presence on celluloid.

Acknowledgments

We would foremost like to sincerely thank the former child performers whose stories are found within the covers of this book for granting us interviews and permitting us to use their stories. Secondly, we wish to thank our brother Ray Goldrup, author and screenwriter, for proofreading the manuscript and helping with the grammatical structuring of the text. Also, thanks to Boyd and Donna Magers and Michael Fitzgerald for all the help they gave us on this project in so many ways. A note of gratitude goes to Eugene and Fernita Goldrup, Leona Chaboude and to Walter Reed. Without their aid this book would never have come to fruition.

We would also like to thank the following for helping us locate some of those included in this book: Mary Badham, Patrick Curtis, Edith Fellows, Gary Gray, Jimmy Hawkins, Billy Hughes, Whitey Hughes, Marcia Mae Jones, Jan Merlin, Ray Nielsen, Marvin Paige, Bryan Russell, Screen Actors Guild, and Delmar Watson. Diana Serra Cary also receives our gratitude for volunteering to write a foreword for the book. Thanks also go out to Tom Bupp, Kevin Daniels, Michelle Donohue, Bill and Loyce Goldrup, Marilee Goldrup, Matt Goldrup, Ron Hunt, and Laurie Provost for their aid.

Contents

Acknowledgments vii
Foreword by Diana Serra Cary 1
Introduction 3

Lee Aaker 5
Phillip Alford 13
Baby Peggy 20
Mary Badham 30
Sonny Bupp 38
Michael Chapin 47
Ted Donaldson 57
George Ernest 67
Richard Eyer 76
Edith Fellows 83
Billy Gray 94
Gary Gray 103
Jimmy Hawkins 113
Billy Hughes 121
Jimmy Hunt 130
Teddy Infuhr 138
Tommy Ivo 143
Eilene Janssen 153
Claude Jarman, Jr. . . 161
Marcia Mae Jones . . . 169

Mickey Kuhn 178
Gordon Lee 186
Sammy McKim 191
Shirley Mills 200
Roger Mobley 210
Larry Olsen 218
Gigi Perreau 226
Jon Provost 233
Gene Reynolds 242
Bryan Russell 251
Jeanne Russell 259
Mickey Sholdar 269
Frankie Thomas 277
Leon Tyler 286
Beverly Washburn . . 294
Bobs Watson 303
Delmar Watson 314
Johnny Whitaker . . . 324
Jane Withers 334

Filmographies 347
Index 363

Foreword
by Diana Serra Cary
(THE FORMER "BABY PEGGY")

Persons outside the motion picture industry tend to view child actors as a group quite apart from those that lead a "normal" childhood. They also regard them as being almost carbon copies of each other in all the other aspects of their lives. This book will dispel that false concept. All kid actors, even those from the golden age of film, did not earn mind-boggling salaries or become world famous. For every major child star such as Shirley Temple there were a dozen hard-working, highly professional youngsters whose names and faces moviegoers hardly recognized, but whom directors knew they could count on to give a solid performance every time. Bobs Watson was one of nine Watson children who started out playing bit parts in movies to help support his family. All the Watson kids mastered the art of crying on cue, which made them popular with every director in Hollywood.

What *Growing Up on the Set* reveals is a remarkable diversity of character, temperament and career experiences among the contributors, even when they were children all engaged in similar day-to-day work. Earning the respectful recognition of adults as a working professional is not a common experience in any other childhood but a movie actor's, unless the child is a violin virtuoso or concert pianist at eight, or a chess genius at six. But different children in Hollywood handled it differently. The overnight global fame accorded Jackie Coogan, the silent screen's first child star, left a remarkably deep impression upon him, creating a lifelong dependence upon public adulation. When crowds of fans did not surround him he felt incomplete. "It is something you feel you need," he told an interviewer in later life. "When you don't get it, *you feel unwanted.*" In my own case, I was delighted to be able to "retire" at age ten, and no longer have to be ushered into theaters everywhere with a police escort to keep the crowds of "Baby Peggy" fans at bay.

An addiction to childhood fame is one of the worst scenarios resulting from overexposure to it in early childhood. "Fame is a dangerous drug," former child actor Paul Petersen has wisely said, "and should be kept out of the reach of children."

More commonly, though, it is the parents and not the performing child who become incurably hooked on both the big money and fame accruing to the family. It comes to them so easily it is quickly habit-forming, and with it goes the blind delusion that this child wonder will remain five years old and the family's meal ticket forever. Most common is the "stage mother" who wanted a theatrical career for herself but was thwarted by her parents or an early marriage. In this manner Gertrude Temple fulfilled her dream by pushing Shirley, and reveling in her reflected glory. But such mothers staunchly deny this truth. When one successful child star was an adolescent struggling to adjust, he asked his mother, "Why on earth did you put me in movies when I was only four years old?" She replied with what she had convinced herself was the gospel truth: "But dear, *it's what you always wanted.*"

While there have been many infamous parental thefts of child stars' earnings—Jackie Coogan, Gary Coleman and Macaulay Culkin come to mind—which rank right up there with a Brinks robbery, many other parents took care to put aside a clever youngster's movie or TV earnings. The little boy who became famous as "Mikey," who "hates everything" in the hugely popular cereal ad, earned a cool million in residuals from that one commercial and it was all safely stashed in the bank when it came time for him to go to college.

This book is a wonderful group portrait of the many faces of childhood fame and how different people handle it. One former boy actor answered a "call to the ministry" when he was 33 and at the peak of the successful *adult* acting career he had carved out after he grew up, in itself a rarity in Hollywood. Only a handful of child actors such as Roddy McDowall, Natalie Wood and Elizabeth Taylor made this difficult transition to become major adult stars. Others gladly gave up the glitter and glory of child stardom for a more rewarding private existence. Former child actor Gene Reynolds found his niche in the same industry, as a director and producer for such major successes as TV's long-running shows, *Bonanza* and *M*A*S*H*.

Those who read the following pages will never again have an imperfect cookie-cutter concept of what it means to be famous at an early age. The authors provide a wide-view panorama of this once-distant galaxy that brings the bright talents sparkling there truly up close and personal—good friends for the rest of your life.

Introduction

From its earliest beginnings, children have played a part in the world of film making. They continue to do so today, especially with the advent of television. What is it like to be a child performer? That is what this book attempts to answer through the lives of 39 actors and actresses who started working in this profession by the age of 13.

Based on personal interviews with the authors, the former child actors discuss their careers and their lives following their work in front of the camera. Questions like, "Do you feel it interfered with your having a 'normal' childhood?" "How did you get into the business?" and "What have you done since you left the world of acting?" are answered by them. From experiencing their world, one can better understand what it was like to be in the movies as a kid.

We feel it is important to leave a tribute to the child actor, and the purpose of this book is to accomplish just that, not only to the 39 included within its pages, but to each and every one who has followed that road. In many of the older movies, the child actor (unless they were a star or top featured player) received no billing in the screen credits, even though their role should have merited it. A good example is in the picture *The Sullivans* (1944). In this film the parts were equally divided between the adult and child actors playing the five brothers who were killed on the same ship in the South Pacific during World War II. All the adults received screen credit; none of the children did. For this reason it is very difficult to find a complete list of a child actor's film credits. Thus, the filmographies at the back of the book are as complete as we have been able to make them, although in some cases (i.e., the two Watson brothers) they are far from complete. In the filmographies, the dates given are the years of release.

Introduction

Most of the child actors included herein made the transition fairly easily from movies into another career. Many other child actors did not. Some left the business of their own choice; others were left behind by the business and could not find work as older actors. There were tragedies along the way, such as those which afflicted Bobby Driscoll, Jackie Moran, Rusty Hamer, Larry Nunn, Scotty Beckett and Anissa Jones. Others found the road of life afterwards difficult, but survived. Many moved on into other pursuits, such as teaching, real estate, engineering, medicine and business-related fields of endeavor. Some continued in the arts, not only as working actors or returning years later as prominent character actors (as Roddy McDowall and Dean Stockwell), but as musicians, writers, artists, directors and producers. There were even a very few who went on to become big stars in the motion picture industry (i.e., Elizabeth Taylor, Mickey Rooney, Kurt Russell and Jodie Foster).

One common theme in the child actor's emotional adjustment is the guidance—or lack of it—of the parents. When child actor Rickie Sorensen was asked what he thought was the very most important thing that a child actor could do, he responded, "Pick your parents well."

Most, if not all, of those included in this book stated that now, after their life in show business is over and they can look back on it, they are glad they had it even though some may not have been happy with their career at the time. So here it is, the good, the bad, and the ugly of being children on celluloid.

Lee Aaker

Lee Aaker was born September 25, 1943, in Los Angeles, California, and lived in Inglewood. "My mother owned a dancing studio called Gladora School Studio," Lee reflected. "My brother Dee and I started doing tap dancing when I was about five. We started doing little song-and-dance band routines at fairs and amateur shows throughout the city. We got pretty good at what we were doing so my mother took us to a dancing school up in Hollywood by the name of Reuben's Dance Studio. They had a TV show in the late forties and early fifties on one of the early stations here in the L.A. area called *Sandy's Dreams*. We were on that for about a year. The producer who was doing it split off and went to KTLA (Channel 5) and took about 20 of us kids, and started doing a half-hour TV show called *Fantastic Studios*. It was on every week and I remember we were right after the puppet show called *Time for Beanie* with Bob Clampitt, and right after us was Tim McCoy."

Lee recalled a few instances from that early television show. "I was eight years old and doing Marc Antony. It was live TV and I drew a blank, so the gal across from me fed me the lines. I also remember doing a live TV commercial for the same show. Mighty Fine Pudding was our sponsor. I love banana cream pudding and strawberry and lemon meringue pie. Well, they gave me some and I took it and threw it in my mouth. It was coconut cream pie, and phooey, I spit it out and said, 'I hate that!' and that was on live TV. I don't remember doing any more commercials," he laughed.

Lee continued on this show until Paramount Studios produced a documentary titled *Benjy*, directed by Fred Zinnemann. "I got the lead and played a little crippled boy with a bent spine. It won the Oscar for best documentary." Lee's work in *Benjy* led to his first real movie role

Lee Aaker as "Corporal" Rusty with Rin Tin Tin from the Screen Gems production *Adventures of Rin Tin Tin* (ABC TV, 1954–59).

in Paramount's *The Atomic City* where he played the son of an atomic scientist. "Foreign agents kidnap me and threaten to kill me if my father doesn't give them the atomic secret," Lee explained. "It was a pretty good movie, and that's where I started."

A bit in the Academy Award–winning western classic *High Noon* followed. "The director was Fred Zinnemann. When he directed *Benjy*, he said, 'The next picture I do you will be in.' So I got called. It is just a 20 second run-on. I ran around the corner and into Gary Cooper who's exploring the town. I was only three feet high and look up at him and he looks down at me and he seems nine feet tall. I made a little gulp and was a little scared. I worked a couple of days doing that and met all the cast, but I was nine years old and don't remember working with them. Looking back now I wish I really knew all of these people that I have met. Audie Murphy, John Wayne, Ronald Reagan."

Lee's next film was MGM's *Desperate Search* in which he and his little sister, played by Linda Lowell, are stranded in the wilds after surviving a plane crash. They are stalked by a mountain lion that traps them in a tree and Lee must fend it off with a gun he found amongst the crash victims. "They had the head of a stuffed mountain lion (down to the forepaws of the chest) on the end of a ten-foot stick. They put us in the tree and did the closeups as they kept jabbing this head up. Linda was scared to death and was a great crier. We went on location to Idyllwild, up from Palm Springs, and to Hemet Lake, but it was mainly shot on the backlot of MGM in Culver City."

Two other early films Lee worked in were *Destry* with Audie Murphy and *No Room for the Groom* with Tony Curtis. "During the movie [*Destry*] I followed Audie Murphy because I looked up to him. He was a nice person who took time to talk to me. I remember the same thing about Tony Curtis. He was one of the nicest people I remember being on a set with."

Of his motion picture features, it is John Wayne's *Hondo* that Lee will probably be best remembered for. The story concentrates on the relationship of the boy and his mother with Hondo, as well as with the Indian warrior chief. In addition to Wayne, the film featured another movie star few in the audience would recognize. Lee stated, "Rudd Weatherwax was in Mexico with Lassie who played Hondo's dog. I remember that dog in the hot desert, with all that cactus. It was really getting beat up in terms of stickers in his feet and having to do the stunts itself. Rin Tin Tin had a double, Lassie didn't."

The scene Lee is most often asked about is where John Wayne, learning the boy can't swim, throws him into the water. "We were in a little town in Mexico called Camargo which is about 400 miles below the border of El Paso. I was nine years old and weighed about 50 pounds. Wayne picked me up like a top and flung me out in the water. A lot of people remember that scene and I get asked quite a bit about how John Wayne was to work with. He was a real wonderful guy. Pat Wayne and I blew up a swimming pool at the hotel we were staying at with skyrockets on July 4th. Real skyrockets, not the stuff they sell here in the States. We lit one and it went off, but it didn't go up. It was kind of a dud and went over into the swimming pool and blew out the bottom of the fountain where the water went into the pool. We got grounded. We were kids and just having fun."

Lee spoke of working this location, saying, "I had a great time, but you know food is kind of rough down there. I don't remember getting sick, though we had to watch the water we drank and the food we ate. I ate corn and fruit, but not any staples. They had some private planes, and every day they flew out the film from Carmago to El Paso. My mom asked, 'Can you bring us some milk to drink?' So they'd bring some for me so I could get nourished."

Shortly after returning home Lee interviewed for the role of Jeff in the television series, *Lassie*. The competition narrowed down to two boys. "I had just come back from Mexico and went out to Rudd Weatherwax's house and there was Tommy Rettig and I. They had the photographers there and had us playing together with the dog. A few days later we found out Tommy got the lead in the series. Fate worked out the way it was supposed to because six months later I got the *Rin Tin Tin* series."

When asked if there was much competition for the part of Rusty on Screen Gems' *Rin Tin Tin*, Lee responded, "I was told there wasn't. I had made several episodes of *Ford Theater*, *Schlitz Playhouse*, and several other shows for Screen Gems. Bert Leonard, who produced *Rin Tin Tin*, saw me and said that's who I want. I can't remember ever doing an audition per se. I just went and knew I had the part."

Lee shared the story of how the ancestor of J.R. (J.R. being the dog who played Rin Tin Tin) had come to America. "While Lee Duncan was in the Air Corps in France in World War I a bomb blew up a subway. A couple of hundred people were killed in this bombed-out crater. A young Frenchman named Rin Tin Tin and his girlfriend, Nanette, were the only survivors. They started making good luck dolls and selling them to the troops there. One doll was named Rin Tin Tin and the other Nanette. Lee Duncan was at the air base where the bomb had blown up the subway. He found two German shepherds—a little male and female—and named them Rin Tin Tin and Nanette. When Lee came back to the States he brought Rin Tin Tin with him, and trained him. He was such a phenomenal dog Lee ended up getting him into the movies, and the rest is history. That's how Rin Tin Tin originated. The dog we used was named J.R., which stood for Junior being the son of another dog named Flame."

Lee learned to ride for the movies. "I had never been around horses much, but I was pretty athletic and coordinated. When I started doing several movies my agent suggested to my mother I take riding lessons. A few minutes from my house was a riding stable in the Baldwin Hills, so I started taking riding lessons. But it wasn't any problem for me. I never became a great rider, but I was competent. On the *Rin Tin Tin* show I did a lot of my own riding, but obviously they wouldn't let me do any of the real dangerous stuff. One time when I was supposed to jump and do a race sequence on a race horse they hired a girl. The Epper family had a daughter about my same size who was an expert at horsemanship. She'd come in and do the double riding for me. I was about ten years old, and all the guys would say, 'You'll let a girl double for you.' They all used to tease the hell out of me for about a year."

J.R. was not the only dog that played Rin Tin Tin on the series. "In the action scenes where you see the dog running and then leaping over the camera—usually when he attacked somebody—and then the camera turns around and you see the bad guy getting hit by the dog: it was just

Lee with costars Gig Young and Jean Hagen from the 3-D western feature, *Arena* (MGM, 1953). For a couple of years, a Lee Aaker impostor attended several western film conventions and autograph shows. Notice in the lower right-hand corner the signatue of Lee Aaker. This was the impostor's. On the left-hand side of the photograph, the actual Lee autographed it as "Lee Aaker, Rusty. The real one."

a stuffed German shepherd. It weighed about 20 or 30 pounds. They would throw it at the actor and he'd get hit and do a fall, and then they'd go back to the long shot and use the fighting dog. I named him. They had no name for him so I said, 'Let's call him Hey You.' J.R. did the close-ups and the acting, and the real Rin Tin Tin, a fourth generation from the first one, was mainly in the scenes with the horses because J.R. wanted to play with them and they were afraid of him getting stepped on or kicked. I remember J.R. as being a real trouper. A lot of times they wanted him to lick me and he wouldn't. He wasn't into licking, so they smeared hamburger meat all over my face and then he would do it."

Lee went on personal appearance tours to various cities with his costars during the filming hiatus. "We flew back East and played Madison Square Garden with the World Championship Rodeo for three weeks and then went with the same rodeo and did Boston Gardens for two weeks. There was Rand Brooks, Joe Sawyer, Jim Brown, myself, Lee Duncan, Frank Barnes, and J.R. Also traveling with us for a while were Wally West, Doyle Brooks and Joe Hooker, who were stunt men. They did falls off the horses and fought the dog. I came out and did a little skit with Jim. We talked and did some tricks with J.R.—we called him Rinty. Then a bad guy would come and grab me and Rinty would run a couple of hundred yards across an open arena, jump off a ramp, attack the guy and save my life. Jim or Rand would do the background narration and say, 'Rusty's in trouble and Rinty can't hear him. Come on kids, let's give him a Yo Rinty,' and 10,000 kids would scream 'Yo, Rinty.' He would come running across this arena with the spotlight on him and leap in the air. The kids loved it and we had a lot of fun doing that.

"We stayed in a hotel about a ten-minute walk from Madison Square Gardens. I got to do stuff that I would never have been able to do, like going to see all the sights and then going up to Boston and spending three weeks there in the fall; it was just beautiful. Joe Sawyer and I went to the World Series together. We were rained out and I was so heartbroken; it was the only World Series game I ever attended. Joe brought me out and bought me a soda. All the guys treated me like a son and took care of me. You hear all the horror stories about child actors, what they were doing and how they were getting taken. Well, I have no complaints. Which is good." Reflecting on the other stars of the series, Lee said, "Jim Brown, what a great man to work with. I remember him on tour, the patience and tolerance. I didn't have the patience to sit and talk. I hated it. I wanted to be a kid. I wanted to go to work and then leave it, but Jim signed autographs and treated all these people with love and respect. Rand Brooks and Jim Brown were kind of like fathers to me."

Since Lee worked five years on *Rin Tin Tin*, as well as the action features, occasions arose where his personal safety could potentially be in danger during a scene. On the series, he noted his costars were very protective of him in these instances. "So I don't remember anything dangerous that I did. In a scene in *Hondo* where John Wayne is breaking a horse in the corral I was leaning on the fence watching him and a red ant crawled up my leg and bit me. I was in pain for about a week. But there was a movie called *Jeopardy* that I did with Barry Sullivan and Barbara Stanwyck. It was a very good movie, high rated. We did it off the cliffs at Dana Point, in the ocean." In the movie, Lee walks out on a rotting pier, and Sullivan, who plays his father, tries to rescue him and gets tangled in the decrepit timber as it falls into the sea at low tide. "As the tide goes up, Barbara Stanwyck runs off to try and get help, so I'm with my father trying to console him while the tide's rising. We did some scenes which were pretty hairy, both the wave-making stuff that they had back in those days and actually doing it in the water. The waves were breaking in, and I remember Billy Curtis, who was my double, did a lot of stuff for me in that one because the social worker said, 'Lee's not going out there.' That was her job. That's what she was supposed to do. But I can't think of anything where I was in real danger."

Lee worked under Howard Hawks' direction in *O. Henry's Full House* in the episode of "Ransom of Red Chief." "I can't remember who doubled me in that, but there was a bear scene they wouldn't let me do. They don't let kids do anything fun," Lee laughed.

When asked if he felt working in films got in the way of a normal childhood, Lee responded, "Oh yeah. I mean I don't know what a childhood was. Yet the things I did and got exposed to most kids dream about. So I have mixed [feelings] about that today." What would Lee's reaction be if a parent came to him and asked for advice on how to get their kid into films? "If the kid wants to, then go for it. But I would say find something else they can do because there are going to be hard times in that business. But if the kid wants to do it, go for it. I saw kids in the business who didn't want to be there. They would screw up a scene and the parents would drag them out and beat them. The kid was scared to death. He was just there because of whatever. I wanted to do it, and I liked it. I look back on it today and I don't think if I had a choice now that I would have done anything different." When *Rin Tin Tin* ended its run in 1959, however, Lee confided that "I wanted it to end. I wanted to be a teenager. I remember talking with Tommy Rettig about this. When his part in *Lassie* came to an end he was saying, 'Thank God, now I can go and be a teenager.'"

After *Rin Tin Tin*, Lee didn't work as much as he had while on the series. "I didn't want to do it. I'd go on interviews and instead of wanting to be there I just wanted to get out. I was 15 years old, had a brand new Corvette and money in my pocket."

Lee decided several years later he might want to work on the production side of the camera. Most of the crew members from *Rin Tin Tin* remained together, working with Bert Leonard on other shows. "Bert asked if I would come to work with him as his assistant on *Route 66*. So during 1961 and 1962 I traveled around the country with that show. They called me a gofer, go for coffee, go for cokes, go for whatever."

Lee returned briefly to acting for a final appearance in a small part in *Bye Bye Birdie*. "I was 18 years old and thought about where I was and what I was doing, and said this is not what I want. I don't like it, I'm gone, and I left Hollywood. That was it. Whether or not I could have made the transition, who knows? I was working a few TV shows, but it wasn't like it was when I was age nine to 15, when I worked 20 to 30 weeks a year. I just wanted to distance myself. I didn't want to be Rusty. I didn't want to be a has-been. I wanted to go and be a young adult. And that's what I did. I walked away, and I didn't know what to do. Lauren Chapin says it best, 'What do I do now?' I moved in with a long-haired musician in Hermosa Beach and he turned me on to marijuana. That was 1964 and I stayed with that until the early seventies. Then a friend of mine who was a carpenter asked me to come to work for him so I started learning about remodeling. In 1973 I got into the union and worked as a union carpenter for 20 years."

In addition to his carpentry, Lee also was a ski instructor. "I'm a professional ski bum now," Lee smiled. "I moved here [a town in the Sierra Mountains] a couple of years ago and love it. And they have a long ski season. I like what I'm doing now. Finally I'm comfortable in my own skin, but it took me 50 years to get there." Lee's love for skiing began when he was working on *Rin Tin Tin*. "There's a funny incident. Bert Leonard gave me my snow skis for Christmas when I was 11. I learned to ski and a month later broke my leg doing it. My mother was on the phone talking to him, saying, 'Hold yourself Bert, Lee's in a cast. He broke his leg snow skiing.' He said, 'What are you doing taking him snow skiing?' She said, 'Well, you gave him the snow skis for Christmas.' He didn't know. His secretary had got the skis," Lee laughed. "So we worked around it and had a double for the running shots and long shots. I did all the shots from the waist up. But that's what I learned to do as a kid. I loved snow skiing. I skied from the time I was 11 until I was 25 years old. Then I quit, and when I was about 38 years old I started again and now I teach skiing here."

Looking back over his acting career, Lee summed up his feelings about it, saying, "It was something I would do over again, but there's a lot of things I would do different. I had a great career. I went a lot of places and met a lot of great people. I just look back and wish I had been more outgoing and was into helping more. I look at Jim Brown and the way he was always going into hospitals and helping the kids. As I mentioned, I was a ski instructor, and when I was in Los Angeles I taught disadvantaged development and disabled kids who weren't fortunate enough to learn to ski. I taught some kids without legs to ski in buckets; and kids without arms and kids that couldn't see. I wish I had done more of that. I get a warm feeling out of that now. Professionally, I did more than I wanted to. I wanted to leave earlier. I made a lot of money and ended up broke," he laughed. "But that's the way it was. It was a positive influence and something that I would do again. If I got offered a good part in a good movie I would do it today. I say I wouldn't, but I would."

Phillip Alford

Phillip Alford was born September 11, 1948, in Gadsden, Alabama. "When I was about three my parents moved to Birmingham because my dad followed the blast furnace work." Phil grew up in Birmingham, where he appeared in a couple of plays as a child. One was at Birmingham Southern College; the other, *The King and I*, was performed at a theater in downtown Birmingham. "The only reason I did it was because it was different, it was fun, and I was a boy soprano. I had a good voice. One of my teachers at Lakeview Grammar School had told them about my voice."

Phil went into eighth grade in September 1961. "I had just started when my mother asked me if I wanted to go interview for a movie. The director of the theater, James Thatcher, had asked my mother if she could send me down to this cattle call interview they were doing. I said no. I had no interest whatsoever in doing that. Then she said I could get out of school for half a day. Okay fine, five minutes, I'm done and I could play. When I was a kid I didn't want to be an actor. I wanted to be Tarzan, not Johnny Weissmuller. We went and I met with Bodie Boatright. I don't know how many kids were there, but there were hundreds of them. We met for about five minutes and then I went home. A couple of weeks later we got a phone call. Alan Pakula and Bodie came back and invited five or six of us, Mary Badham and I being two of them, to a theater where we were to do some readings from proposed scripts. We stayed for a couple of hours and went home. I thought, 'Okay. That's it.'

"About three weeks later we get a call asking us to come to New York for a screen test," Phil continued. "My mom and I got on a train (my mom was terrified of flying) and they put us up first class at the Drake Hotel in New York. We stayed three or four days." At this interview, Phil was the only person up for the role of Jem Finch, the son of lawyer Atticus

Phillip Alford

Finch in the screen version of Harper Lee's *To Kill a Mockingbird*. "I did a screen test and did some more readings. They said, 'We'll be in touch,' and I went home. My mom was talked into flying home, so this was her first flight and my first flight. It was wonderful."

Phil didn't hear anything back from the producer until New Year's Eve. "I was at a party with a bunch of other 13-year-old boys and girls, and my mother was one of the chaperones. They called the house and told my dad we had to be in Los Angeles on February 3rd or 5th to start filming the movie. And that's how it happened."

Phil commented on his reaction to receiving this news. "I was glad because it was going to be something new. I wasn't afraid of it. It never occurred to me that I couldn't do it. It was a totally new experience. This was 1962. I was a 13-year-old kid from Alabama that had never been anywhere other than Panama City, Florida, with the exception of the trip to New York. I was fired up about the whole idea. I didn't know *To Kill a Mockingbird;* I didn't read the book until later; I didn't even know what it was about."

Phil related some of his reflections on filming this movie that went on to become a Hollywood classic. "Did Mary Badham tell you about the time we tried to kill her?" he asked. "John Megna and I hated Mary. She and I are very close now and we love each other, but I was 13 and John was nine and Mary was nine, and we despised each other. At least John and I despised her, which you have to expect at that age anyway. We fought pretty constantly because Mary did things, like repeat our lines. If we were doing a closeup of Mary and I was off camera, she would mouth my words back to me. In the dinner, breakfast and lunch scenes, I had to eat lunch 26 times and breakfast 22 times because of Mary, so we just basically hated her. So when we came to the scene where we put her in the tire and roll her down the street, we tried to kill her, but we were too small and couldn't get the tire going fast enough. So when it hit the piece of equipment off camera it didn't hurt her."

Phil had, and continues to have, a high regard for the man who played his father in the film. "What a wonderful man Gregory Peck was, and still is. Not only a gentleman, but a fatherly figure. I mean this man had a tremendous influence on my life for 35 years. I see him now as just as much of a father figure as my own father was. He's wonderful; he's marvelous; I just can't say enough how I feel about him.

"The director, Robert Mulligan, was great. When we were rehearsing a scene, before we'd shoot it the camera would be off and the crew would be off. But as we rehearsed they would start moving things closer to us. We weren't aware of that, so by the time we were ready to shoot the camera was at us. Yet it had been there for a few minutes already so it wasn't an intimidating thing to suddenly yank everything up in our faces and tell us to go to work. It was all done gently and kindly and they took their time. We had a lot of fun on the set; we had lots of water fights. It was just a ball."

Phil and the other children in the picture had to attend school three hours a day on the set. "We had a lady on the set from the State of California Education Department who taught us. Not only was she our teacher, but she was the one that governed when we could come in and when we had to leave. It didn't make any difference how much time they had invested in a scene, at five o'clock she walked in front of the camera and said, 'That's it, guys. We'll see you in the morning,' and yanked us out of there."

Phil's family accompanied him to California during the making of *To Kill a Mockingbird*. "My mom, dad and my sister came with me. In fact, Eugenia did some stand-in work for Mary. They were both the same age and about the same size."

Phil concluded his recollections of working in this picture, saying, "I spent all of my summers growing up at my grandmother's in Piedmont, which is a small town in northeast Alabama. Every small town in the South back then had a haunted house, and also the odd guy. As an adult you find out he wasn't really all that odd, but just slow in some ways. So as a kid in the movie I could identify with just about everything we were doing. I had a tire swing, I had a little sister who was nine years old; I played the same games and did the same things. This was no stretch for me. I didn't have to be Shakespeare, all I had to do was be a normal 13-year-old kid from the South.

"When I got finished we went home. I don't know the circumstances behind how I got with William Morris, but they signed me. After I did *To Kill a Mockingbird* I did a pilot for a Lloyd Bridges anthology, and then I did *Bristle Face* with Brian Keith, for Disney."

Phillip Alford as Jem Finch and Mary Badham as his sister Scout examine carvings made in their likenesses left at the old tree by the mysterious Boo Radley in *To Kill a Mockingbird* (1962, Universal International).

Phil went on to speak of what it was like working for Walt Disney. "A totally different experience. On Disney's lot you weren't allowed to drive so everybody walked. It didn't make any difference who you were or how big a star you were, you walked just like everybody else. Mr. Disney walked. You'd be working and look around and there he'd be sitting off to the side somewhere watching. It's not like he drove up in a 38-foot limo and everybody announced that Walt Disney was coming on the set. He walked the whole lot every day and checked on the progress of the work. So, like I said, you'd just get finished with a scene and look around and he'd be sitting in your chair. I watched Dick Van Dyke and Julie Andrews rehearse *Mary Poppins* while I was working there. There was always something going on, and for a kid it was wonderful. During lunch I would go sit in back of one of the theaters and watch them dub in the music for *Sword and the Stone*. It was just a great place to work. For the first time since we made *Bristle Face*, I talked to Brian Keith about a month before he killed himself [in 1997]. I got to feeling bad that I had not talked to him so I got his phone number from a friend and gave him a call, and we had about a half-hour conversation. Thirty days later he was dead. So I'm glad I had a chance to talk to him."

Phil's next feature film was *Shenandoah* with James Stewart. He reflected on this film by stating, "Guys that are in the league with Peck and Stewart, they were so secure in what they were doing and who they were that nothing worried them on the set. If it did, you'd never know it. Stewart was the consummate professional. When he got to the set every day he was prepared and knew what was going on and had his lines down, and it made everybody else work the same way. He was just such a down-home, nice guy.

"The battle scenes, and the scene in the forest where I find the hat in the beginning of the movie, were all filmed near Eugene, Oregon," Phil said. "The rest of it was filmed on the Universal lot. We had a great time in Oregon. It's such a beautiful place. We'd go out in the afternoons after we finished and fish these wonderful cold streams and catch enough trout to feed the whole crew. We'd take it back to the hotel and they would clean it and cook it and serve it to them. It was hard not to enjoy it.

"You know the fight scene when I get knocked in the water trough?" Phil asked. "That was not part of the original filming. We finished filming late spring or early summer and came back in the winter and filmed some more scenes. I don't remember what month it was, but they had to knock the ice off the top of the water trough every morning. It was so cold that I had to wear a wet suit under my clothes. The whole time I was there I was soaking wet from being in that water trough."

The next show he did was a *CBS Playhouse* titled "Appalachian Autumn" in 1969 with Arthur Kennedy and Teresa Wright. "I was lucky," Phil added. "I was in the business for eight or nine years and didn't do anything I was ashamed of. I did good work and I worked with great people. As a matter of fact, I got a concussion while doing that show. In one of the scenes I get thrown up against the wall, and by the sixth take I had hit my head so many times on this set wall inside a coal mine that I had a concussion," he laughed.

Phil next appeared in a television movie dealing with Jesse James and the Younger brothers titled *The Intruders* with Edmond O'Brien and Don Murray. "It was shot on the Universal lot. All of my motion pictures except for Disney were shot at Universal. Harrison Ford had a bit part in the movie." The last production Phil worked on in California was TV's *The Virginian* in an episode titled "A Time of Terror."

"I did one more film afterwards that was never released," Phil confided, "but I don't want to tell you the title. It never came to fruition. A wealthy building contractor in Dallas, Texas, decided that he wanted to be a movie maker, so he brought Paul Ford, myself and Richard Webb to Dallas where we spent about eight or nine weeks. Everybody got disgusted with it because it was such a mess.

"By this time I was 22 years old. I was being asked to read for things that I was really uncomfortable reading. This was during the drug culture back in the late sixties and early seventies. Everybody was smoking pot and people were doing a whole lot more than that. It seemed that everything I was being asked to read for concerned drugs in some way. I didn't do drugs and I didn't really know how to react to it, so I got uncomfortable and came home after I did *The Virginian*, and just never went back."

Phil joined his father in his construction business. "I had already done it off and on all of my life. I started about the time that we did *To Kill a Mockingbird*. I worked with my dad during the summers. I mixed mortar and carried bricks all during my teen years, and when I decided that I was probably not going to go back to Los Angeles that's what I went into, and I'm still doing it today.

"I was in Kuwait after the Gulf War helping to rebuild the country. Oh man, it was hot there. A hundred and forty degrees in the daytime, a hundred and three at night. It was smoky, we were there every day of the fires. We watched them put the last one out. It was dangerous. There were three million pieces of unexploded ordnance on the ground, so the first rule you learned the day you stepped off the airplane was don't step off the concrete or asphalt because the sand was full of explosives. We had to rebuild the infrastructure of this country so they could open it back up. I had the American embassy and 17 schools, and on November 1st when school started all 17 of mine opened. It's an experience I would not have traded the world for now, but I was glad to get out of their alive.

"You know, when I quit acting, I quit acting. I didn't do theater, I quit. I know there are kids who were actors as children that are lost. They are totally lost. They want to be actors, but when they got past the cute stage nobody wanted them anymore. Here they are, 17 or 20 years old and they're has-beens. It takes them a few years to realize that it's over. They may do a *Love Boat* or little theater in Cleveland and finally realize that their career is over when they're 25. By then they don't know how to do anything else so they drift into the wrong directions. They get bitter, get into trouble, go into alcohol or drugs, and basically ruin their lives. Then they make a career out of being recovered alcoholic child actors. I didn't want to be that way. So when I quit, I quit. I wouldn't even let people talk about it around me for 15 years because I had to make my way in *this* earth, not *that* earth. That business is not real. The money's not real, how you're treated is not real, that's all on another plane, another existence. If I tried to stay I never would have met my wife Carol (we have been married 29 years) and I would have never had the two most wonderful children in the whole world. I can't imagine what my life would have been like if I stayed. Certainly not like it is now."

In summing up his feelings as a child actor, Phil commented, "I had a great time, and I think from the reaction I get from other people that I had a good career. I did stuff that people remember, certainly *To Kill a Mockingbird* and *Shenandoah*. I could look back with satisfaction on those years and say to myself, 'I made a couple of films, particularly *To Kill a Mockingbird*, that will be here a long time after I'm gone.'"

Baby Peggy

Peggy Jean Montgomery was born in San Diego, California, in October 1918. Her father, Jack Montgomery, was a cowboy by profession. When the big spreads went under he got a job as a carpenter during the war on an army post in San Diego. After the war there was a large building boom in Los Angeles so Montgomery took his family there. "We lived in an apartment in downtown Los Angeles and for three months my mother didn't know anybody. One day my father was hailed by an old cowboy he had ridden with who had come to town delivering a load of cattle. The man said, 'I hear there's a saloon in Los Angeles that hasn't been locked up yet.' This was right at the beginning of prohibition and they still served the real stuff at a place called the 'Waterhole.' So they took the trolley to Hollywood and met other cowboys there who were working in films. This was the beginning of his movie career."

Peggy's dad found work with both Neal Hart and Tom Mix. "He became Mix's double and did very well. One day while he was at work, a neighbor across the hall from us came to see my mother and said, 'I have to go to Hollywood to the studio to pick up a check. Why don't you come with me and get out of the house?' My mother said, 'I can't leave the children.' The neighbor said, 'Bring them along, you know how well-behaved they are.' We went to the studio and while there my mother put me up on a high electrician's stool. This director, who had been looking for a small child to work with Brownie the Dog, saw me and I was just exactly what he wanted, and that is how I got into pictures."

Peggy and Brownie starred in a succession of two-reel shorts. "I was called Peggy Jean Montgomery, but the director thought that 'Baby Peggy' was a good short name for the marquee and it turned out to be so. These shorts were successful because Brownie and I worked very well together.

Every five days they made a new movie, so I got lots of exposure. They started putting me in other things, and when Brownie died they put me in my own starring films. I was only 19 months old when I was discovered so I had a pretty good head start. By the time I was 2½ I was on my own, and by the time I was 3½ I had about a hundred two-reel comedies under my belt."

Peggy then began starring in features at Universal, and from there she went on to Sol Lesser's productions and made *Captain January* and *Helen's Babies*. "That's when I went on lengthy personal appearance tours because Lesser was a real promoter and had merchandise tie-ins of every conceivable thing. This was the first tour by a child performer on that scale. Lesser did something like that with Jackie Coogan, but he really pulled out all the stops with me. Everywhere the pictures played there were Baby Peggy sundaes served in the sweet shop next to the theater; there were Baby Peggy look-alike contests; there were Baby Peggy stockings, coats, jewelry, handbags—a saturation campaign really."

Baby Peggy, *The Flower Girl* (1924, Century Films).

When Peggy was away from the set and not working, she enjoyed horseback riding. "My father taught me to ride when I was about two. I used that as a skill also because I rode a horse in the pictures, but it wasn't much for fun. I didn't play with other children—I didn't know any other children. If I did it was children that I worked with. My sister stayed home and played but she didn't know any other kids because my parents were afraid she'd get children's diseases, so she couldn't ride a bicycle or use roller skates. Nor could I. So I didn't have much of a handle on just playing. I was very serious and had a sense of responsibility because early on I begin to realize I was the breadwinner, although my mother and father, like most parents of child performers, fooled themselves and fooled reporters. My mother used to say, 'Peggy only works three or four hours a day,' and 'She doesn't know that it's movies; she thinks she's just playing.' Mrs. Coogan said exactly the same thing about Jackie. So they are fantasy stories of parents."

We asked whether she did work more than four hours a day then. "Of course. I worked nights; I never took a nap. Once in a while when I stayed home and was put down for a nap I'd get nervous because I felt like somebody was going to call me for a scene. I didn't mind the work, I rather enjoyed it. But it was sort of constructive and there was nothing la de da about it."

Peggy has been termed by some historians as the Shirley Temple of the silents. What does she say about this? "Yes, I was. There were several groups of children before Our Gang. With me, as I look back now, they were very clever to push me, and they got awfully good reviews. It seems that early on comedies were often kind of dirty, so the Century Studio kept pushing theirs as good clean comedies. They said 'Baby Peggy is adorable and you'll pack the theater,' and they did. The audiences loved me, especially after I started doing imitations of grown adult actors and actresses because in those early days the audience would get so engrossed in the film and they would be in tears, emotionally overcome. They were just rung out, so as the 'chaser' they would put me on as the Sheik or as Pola Negri or doing all four roles in *Carmen Jr.*, both male and female. People just began to laugh and it shored them up for going outside. So that was the secret of my success. I was unique. I was extremely popular and got over two million fan letters a year when I was two years old, from all over Europe, France, England and Australia. *The Kid Reporter* was a classic example of a Baby Peggy type comedy. It was directed by Alf Goulding who later directed Laurel and Hardy."

Baby Peggy was often placed in potentially dangerous situations for a movie. "I did most of my own stunts. When I was in comedies one of my earlier memories consisted of me being wired to a goat. The goat was wired to the bed of a pickup truck. They hired a kid off the street to drive it while the camera car drove alongside. They shot me from the waist up because I was supposed to be a cowboy riding a horse. This guy was told to drive no more than 15 miles an hour over a bumpy field, but once he got in that car he put his foot to the floor. He was going 50. The goat lost its footing and went down and threw me over the side, and all I had to keep me from falling was a wire around my ankle. I ended up looking at the back wheel of the truck turning right in my face. My father was screaming at the kid to stop. Then he started screaming at me to put my hands up to my breast and not wave my arms or move. I was hanging upside down by my leg and he was afraid I'd tear my arms off. I did exactly as I was told, which I always did, and it took them about two minutes to finally flag the car down. I remember that quite vividly.

"Another time when I was three we were at Universal on a burning set. They fired all the window sills in this tenement apartment, but had instructions not to fire the door sill because that was my way out. The director said, 'We can't take this twice. It has to be one take because the set is going to burn down.' I was supposed to run around and see all the windows afire and then head for the door, but when I opened the door (it was out of their line of vision completely) I found that they had unwittingly fired the door too so I didn't have any way out. I thought real fast and remembered the window that was burning least was facing the camera. I got up on a chair and climbed over the window sill right into the camera. My father was saying all the time, 'Go back! Go back to the door!' I just thought, 'Don't say anything, just let them yell because they didn't know.' After the scene I showed them the door. They were shocked. As a child I was told to do these things, but I had to find markers and ways to see where I was and protect myself. That was something they couldn't understand because I couldn't even read yet."

Peggy's career crashed in 1925 when her father broke the contract with Sol Lesser. "Sol kept two sets of books and he used the old technique of block booking, so in order to get a Baby Peggy feature you had to buy five 'dogs.' Then he'd split the receipts amongst the five 'dogs' and Baby Peggy. We were supposed to get 50 percent of the film and the house returns from personal appearances. We didn't get any money and my father couldn't figure it out because we played standing room only in every town in the country. He confronted Lesser, and Lesser claimed, 'What?' Father didn't have much business acumen but I guess it was pretty transparent. They had a big falling out and I went into vaudeville as a headliner.

"Vaudeville was much harder than films. There were three or four shows a day and it was monotonous. You could add an encore occasionally, but it was very basically the same thing. We traveled all over the United States and Canada. Four or five times, back and forth."

Peggy did not receive much formal schooling during all these travels. "I was supposed to get three hours on the set every day. I had a tutor in Hollywood when I was about four. She stormed onto the set a couple of times and wasn't welcomed. So I got a little bit from her when I was at home, but I didn't have much. On the road my father found a tutor that volunteered to teach my sister and I. She went along with us for about six weeks and then threw in the sponge; it was too tough for her. We went for another two years without any further education. My great aunt Emma who was a professor at a university in Wyoming, and her sister, who was a professor at a university in Nebraska, were accessible to my father but he never sought tutoring help from them. We met my aunt Emma during summer vacation and she was horrified to find that my sister and I were traveling around like seasonal workers and were getting no education. We knew hardly anything. I knew about George Jessel and Al Jolson, but I never heard of Napoleon. She was really outraged. Finally that fall she wrote my father and said, 'I'm coming East and joining you.'"

Baby Peggy at 2½ years old, playing Pola Negri in *Peg o' the Movies* (1923, Century Films).

They were living in New York at that time. "We were centered there, so all we had to do was drive around to get to the theaters instead of riding trains. So Aunt Emma came and lived with us and really put us through the mill. There was no more sleeping in the morning. As soon as she got us up she took us to the museums and we got a royal education. At the Metropolitan Museum she took us to the Egyptian section, the Roman section, all the art—then she made us take these little stamps and stick them in an album and find out which artist painted it. She was really intense, and that is the only reason we got any education at all. From the time I was seven years old until I was 11 I didn't go to school except for those two little episodes with teachers that weren't very successful."

One of Peggy's favorite films that she appeared in was *Captain January*. "I was just four years old when I made that. I had been working by that time for 2½ years and this was a different kind of movie. It was very serious. I was fond of Hobart Bosworth who was a real pioneer. He played the old captain. He was a good actor and it was a very melodramatic film. I remember being very engrossed in this because it was a very big production and I was in almost every scene."

Peggy reflected back to the time when she was chosen as a mascot for the 1924 Democratic Presidential convention where Franklin D. Roosevelt was the keynote speaker for Al Smith's nomination. "I was in New York on tour for *Captain January* and that's how they got me in as a mascot. I remember it because it was a wild and woolly convention. They had an army of Irish policemen who were called the pride of the city. My father had me on his shoulders walking around leading the parade. There were drunks all over the place and every time somebody got in our way the policemen hit him over the head and threw him away. By the time we got to the podium where Roosevelt was seated somebody looked down at my father and said, 'Don't bring her up here, this platform is overloaded now.' Somebody grabbed me and took me up anyway. I sat down next to Roosevelt and he smiled at me and was very nice. That was my introduction to him. When he was elected a few years later I wrote him a letter and told him I was very glad he was elected because I didn't like Hoover. He sent a very nice letter back."

Years later, during the war, a USO in Carmel wanted to have a Baby Peggy night. "They ran a print of *Captain January* and it snapped in my head the moment I saw myself come on screen how old I felt. I felt so old in that film. I felt as though I had been working forever, and I felt such a responsibility because I think somehow it penetrated me that Lesser had put all of his blue chips on this, and I was impressed by the fact that this was serious heavy-duty business. So when I saw that film it was the first time it came back to me. And every time I have seen it since that is the first thing that hits me, how old that little girl is.

"As I said, I adored Bosworth. He was a very interesting man. He told me a lot of stories about trouping in the old West in the 1880s when he was a young man. I think I was born a historian because I listened to everyone from the time I was that old. I listened to the cowboys on the set because they worked with me a lot. When I got into vaudeville I listened to all the vaudevillians, a lot of Russian refugees—dancers and ballerinas. They would talk about their escape over the ice on the Volga River. I just thought it was fascinating how people survived. I think that is what impressed me because even early I didn't know how I was ever going to survive vaudeville. It was such a grind. I think I was reaching out to learn 'how do I survive in this business?' from seven years till I was ten, in vaudeville."

After vaudeville Peggy's father took what little was left of her money and spent it very imprudently. "I lost everything. I had earned over $3 million in Hollywood. Lesser paid me $2 million for those two movies and I had been making $10,000 a week at Universal. Then when everything crashed we got this rare break to be a vaudeville headliner at $2,500 a week. And that's pretty good money. I didn't take any time off. We had one vacation and I got the mumps. That's about the only time I was sick except for tonsillitis, but I always went on. Sick or well. So I figure in looking back that I earned another $650,000 in vaudeville. My father bought a ranch in Wyoming, and I thought the ranch was paid for. But he mortgaged it the first summer and remortgaged it the second and we lost it in a sheriff's sale, so we were busted a second time around when I was only 13."

The only thing Peggy's parents could think to do was take her back to Hollywood and try to start her over again in pictures. "At 13 years of age I was hardly in the position to be starring in adult roles and there were no roles for teenagers. We almost starved to death in Hollywood. I worked extra and did bits, but I never really cracked it. But every penny counted. My mother worked extra, my sister worked extra, and after giving up on trying to get another ranch, my father went back to riding with the cowboys again."

As parts slowed down and it became hard to find work, Peggy discovered life to be very grim. "I went through a terrible identity crisis. What happens to child stars is that they are so well known as children and then when they change they are not the same people to their fans. The Shirley Temple doll and the Baby Peggy doll are the same forever, but the real thing changes. You're born to be an adult. One woman came up to me at Universal after Deanna Durbin got married and went to Paris. She said, 'I think it was positively wicked of Deanna Durbin to grow up.' People were so blind, and they are still so blind to performing children. They see them as different.

"I've tried to set up a group of psychologists and family counselors to help with performing children's families to see that they get a fair shake, that there was somebody in their corner, because everybody's out to fleece you and you have no one to turn to for help. No one. I went through that and know how isolated you are; it's like being a hostage. This one psychologist was very sympathetic. He went to a colleague of his who was very well up in business and said, 'You've got to join us in this work. It's marvelous work.' And the guy said, 'Forget it. Any kid that's making $100,000 a year doesn't need any help from me.' There is so much jealousy on the part of adult males against children who are making big bucks. They resent it. They say they are so young and making so much money and can't be worth it and must be spoiled rotten."

We asked whether she felt that she had been cheated out of a childhood? "I don't dwell on that part of it. What could I do? I played the cards that I was dealt. But I advise parents who have a talented child or a child who really wants show business to spare them the big arena—don't put them in with the tigers. Let them play in a smaller area where they can perform and polish their skills, but do it in little theaters or put them in a target school where they put on shows in a safe environment. When you throw a 2½ or three-year-old child into the major world of work where you are competing with adults, it's cruel. You don't get any childhood and the family goes to hell. It chews the family up because the siblings never have a childhood either. They become extremely jealous and hateful because the child star overshadows them. Every child actor I know that has a sibling has exactly the same experience because it turns you against each other. My sister and I had the same problem. She was shunned ... and she couldn't perform. That's another problem—the parents get spoiled and they become addicted to the money and it's terribly difficult for them to go back to work."

Rejection was hard for Peggy and the transition to adult roles did not happen. She decided she needed to break clear of her family and have a life of her own. "They were dead set on my staying in films and by that time I had had it. The rejection was just too much. I just didn't want to be an actress. I wanted to write and be a historian. I started writing short stories when I was eight years old to fill in those long hours backstage. They had no interest in my doing that, so finally I wrote, staged and appeared in a musical comedy in Hollywood, in 1938. I thought I was going to make it there because I was good with music, but we couldn't pay the second night theater fee so we closed the same night. I just about gave up. My father came over to see me (my sister and I had left home to live with another family) and he insisted I come back. By then my sister was married. So I came back home with them, but it didn't work out at all. He became tyrannical and very demanding. I had been going with a boy, Gordon Ayres, whom I met on the set of *Ah! Wilderness* (I played a girl in a graduating class). He was the only boy I ever dated. My father didn't approve of him, and said, 'Either you go with him or you stay here.' I said, 'You're not going to do this to me anymore.' So I left and got married. I hung on to that marriage for nine years."

Peggy began studying with the head of the Western History Library in Denver. "He offered to take me into the library and teach me to do research. Then he promised to take me on as a graduate student and teach me how to do western history research. I did all of my research in my spare time while I worked as a chambermaid at a rooming house. He was one of the people who got me into a position where I could function." In the meantime Peggy's husband (who aspired to be an actor) had left her for an actress he had met.

Several other people took Peggy under their wings, to one degree or another. "The Franciscan priest in Santa Barbara took an interest in me because I was about to come apart in a nervous breakdown. I just couldn't handle the identity crisis and the problems. I always thought I had to perform for my parents to get anything. I didn't think there was such a thing as gratuitous love. If I didn't earn it, I didn't get it. It was the kind of thing where if I gave them money I got love, and that's where a lot of kids have the same problem. I thought Gordon was the only one who had given me this free gift, and when I found out that that wasn't true either and that he was using me because I had been Baby Peggy, I said, 'If it wasn't worth anything to me how could it be worth anything to you?'

"This priest met me when I was working in a Catholic bookstore in Los Angeles. I interviewed a convert of his who was the vice postulator for the Serra cause, for a magazine article I was writing. Father Gracian sensed something was wrong. Finally I went to him and said, 'It is. Very wrong.' He said, 'Why don't you leave Hollywood?' because I had to get out of there. At that point all the kids I had grown up with were in deep trouble too. And I felt so much empathy and so much impotence that I couldn't help anybody, I couldn't help myself. So he said, 'I can get you a job in a bookstore in Santa Barbara, and I'll give you an appointment once a week and counsel you in any way I can.' So for 90 minutes every week I got to talk to him and I got plain common sense answers.

"About six months later the girl who had been running the gift shop at the mission left and Father Gracian said, 'You got the job.' I ran the store and had five employees under me so I developed an identity as an adult. From there I became a professional book seller and while there I met my husband, Bob Cary." After they were married, Bob and Peggy moved to Mexico where they lived for ten years. "When we came back to California, I got a job as the trade book buyer at the University of California San Diego and it proved to be a very good job, with benefits and retirement." Peggy wrote two books while there titled *Hollywood's Children* and *Hollywood Posse*. The first concerned children who worked in the movies and it was later made into a documentary narrated by Roddy

McDowall. The latter book was about her father and the other cowboys in the early movies. "I do a lot of articles now for *American History* magazine, *American Heritage, Military History,* and *Wild West* magazine. I also give lectures on film history, the cowboys, and on the subject of performing children because it's such a little known subject." After moving to northern California Peggy wrote an autobiography titled *What Ever Happened to Baby Peggy?* "The reason I titled it that was because after I left Hollywood as a child star the people who were adult silent stars had a famous saying, 'What ever happened to Baby Peggy?' This was an ironic play on the fact that if a kid of seven years of age was washed up what's going to happen to us at 30?"

Peggy changed her name to Diana when she was seeking a new identity. "I was offered a job writing some scripts for a radio series and I didn't want to sign them Peggy. I looked very young at 23 years old and didn't look any different than I had before, so every time I told anybody I was named Peggy they'd say, 'You're Baby Peggy?' And then it started, 'What ever happened to your money?' 'What ever happened to you?' 'Why did it all happen, you were so cute?' These things are all just traumatic so I changed my name to Diana Ayres. The minute I told the man that wanted this script that my name was Diana Ayres I didn't get any feedback which was delightful. After my divorce and when I became a Catholic I took Serra as my confirmation name. When I married Bob I became Mrs. Cary."

Looking back over her career as a child actor, Peggy said, "I think it is remarkable that I have survived. I was very blessed in having people take a very great deal of interest in me later on trying to salvage my life. My aunt Emma who was critical to my development; the man in Denver who practically gave me my career as a writer; and Maynard Geiger who was an historian with the Serra cause took an interest in my interest in California history." So Diana Serra Cary has survived her Baby Peggy fame of her early years in Hollywood and continues working in her career as a writer. She has recently completed a biography of her Hollywood contemporary, Jackie Coogan.

Mary Badham

Mary Badham was born in 1952 in Birmingham, Alabama. Asked what were some of the things she enjoyed doing before being cast in her first film, *To Kill a Mockingbird*, Mary answered, "I would say horseback riding would come right up at the top of the list, along with ballet. Those were the two main things I enjoyed."

Reflecting on the time she was chosen for the role of Scout in *To Kill a Mockingbird*—the movie directed by Robert Mulligan, produced by Alan Pakula, and starring Gregory Peck—Mary mentioned, "They had this big audition in Birmingham and we received a phone call to come down for it. I had never done any acting before but my mother was very active in little theater. Evidently the owner of the theater was the one who called my mother and told her to bring me in. By some fluke I got the part." We asked whether, when she obtained the part, she was nervous at all. "How do you know to be afraid when you don't know what's going on? I was not a child of the movies and I had had very limited contact with much of anything at nine years old. I was kept in private schools and was very quiet. I was very limited as to my knowledge of things."

Mary spoke of some of her memories of making this film classic. "The main thing I remember about it was that it was so much fun. It took five months to make and I really had a lot of family support. My mother stayed with me the whole time and my father's sister came out to visit. We took one of the maids, Frankie, who had helped raise me, with us to take care of me. Daddy would come and visit, which wasn't very often. The Pecks would have me over to their house occasionally. It was great fun. It was all filmed on the back lot of Universal Studios.

"They had this marvelous street that was created from houses that were being cleared for the freeway. They were all period houses that would have been razed had it not been for the studio looking for them to do this particular film. They moved them onto this street and they created Mockingbird Street. Unfortunately that's no longer there, it was destroyed in the big fire when one of the guards had became disgruntled and burned half the studio down. It was so sad and rather a shock for me because when my brother John was making *Bird on a Wire* with Goldie Hawn, I had gone to the studio to go out to lunch with them. I pulled up at the gate and heard a familiar voice say, 'Mary Badham,' and I looked up and lo and behold, there's Scotty. He had been the guard at the gate when I was a child. I got out of the car and said, 'Oh Scotty, how are you?' It was really wonderful. I told him that I was thinking about going to the back lot, and he said, 'No, leave your memories where they are.' I said, 'Thank you Scotty.' I followed his advice. I didn't go back because evidently he knew that it would just break my heart."

In 1996, Mary returned to Universal for the *Vanity Fair* shoot in commemoration of *To Kill a Mockingbird*. "Brock Peters, Gregory Peck, Phillip Alford and myself were there for this shoot that they wanted to do on the back lot. The limo driver that brought me had been a tour guide there at Universal and he was excited about bringing me home. We drove up to the street and he said, 'How does it feel to be home?' I looked around and didn't recognize anything. I got out of the car and my eyes filled with tears. And this man came up and, recognizing instantly that no one had told me about it being burned, put his arm around me and asked, 'Are you all right?' I said, 'Well, I'm just in a bit of shock right now.' 'They didn't tell you?' 'No,' I answered, 'I haven't been told anything.' He said, 'It burned in the fire,' and then he told me the whole sad story and, of course, it was such a shock. They had brought in other buildings and created sort of a street, but it certainly wasn't what I had remembered. Everything was gone."

Mary worked with fellow child actors Phillip Alford and John Megna in the picture. When asked about their relationship with each other, Mary stated, "I felt closer to John Megna I think than I did to Phillip. I didn't have much contact with Phillip outside the actual filming. We lived in an apartment across the road from the studio and John and his sister were across the street from me in another apartment building while we were making the movie. John was the half brother of Connie Stevens and a very good actor. He was such a sweet, sweet guy. I've looked for John for years. No one knew what happened to him, and every time I would go on a speaking engagement or talk to anyone in the business who might know him I would give them my number and say, 'Please have him call me.' One night out of the blue I got this phone call and it was John. I

Mary Badham in Universal's 1962 release, *To Kill a Mockingbird*.

was so excited and we started this long-distance friendship that lasted up until he died. It was so sad because I knew he was ill, but I didn't know how ill. He said the last thing that he wanted was to go on this RV trip. I said, 'When you get ready to go let me know and we'll plan a hookup and I'll help you drive part of the way.' He said, 'I'll have a driver. I'm not able to drive myself. You could meet us wherever you would like and we'll just kind of do it together for part of the way.' I told him 'We can drive up and I'll be your tour guide for the state of Virginia.' We sort of had this planned and I didn't hear from him for a while and I thought, 'Well, he'll call me soon.' The next phone call I received was from his sister and as soon as I heard her voice I knew he was gone. It was very sad."

In speaking of Gregory Peck, Mary commented, "We have maintained a very close relationship over the years. He'll call me or I'll call him. He'll be somewhere and will say, 'Can you come?' and of course I can. I just cancel everything. He was so easy to work with and of course he, like most of the important people on that film, had small children at the time or had dealt with small children recently, so it was very easy for them to make it very easy for us to work. They knew how children function and Bob Mulligan is just brilliant with children. He and Alan Pakula just seemed to make our life beautiful every minute. Everyone on the crew was nice. Whitey, who was the prop man, was like everybody's kind uncle and really went out of his way to make sure everyone was comfortable and happy and had exactly what they needed when they needed it."

Mary attended school on the Universal lot during the making of the film. "If I have one of the biggest thanks to give to anybody it's to Mrs. Crotke. She was the teacher welfare worker and was absolutely brilliant. Luckily she followed me and was on every production I ever did. She was absolutely my guardian angel, just marvelous. She dealt with everything from my school and getting my grades up to where they were satisfactory for working conditions, and went to bat whenever she needed to. Between my mother and Mrs. Crotke, I had a very good working period of time."

For her performance as Scout, Mary was nominated for best supporting actress. Reflecting on the night of the Academy Awards, she said, "Oh, it was such a night. I didn't know what to expect. I was absolutely terrified that I was going to be called up on stage to have to say something and I had not a clue of what I was going to say. Somehow I felt if it did happen the right words would be there, but I felt surely they couldn't pick me for anything," she chuckled. "This confidence that nothing was going to happen and they'd leave me sit there and somebody else would get it, ... turned out very well. Patty Duke was absolutely brilliant in *The Miracle Worker*. She won it hands down. I have much admiration for her. She's one of my favorite actresses."

In between *To Kill a Mockingbird* and her next film *This Property Is Condemned*, Mary went back home to Birmingham and returned to her routine. Asked if kids at school treated her any different because of the movie, she replied, "Of course. You can't go through something like that and not be treated differently. I had changed a lot too which made it very difficult. It was a tough transition and I felt like a yo-yo. You're treated like an adult one day and like a little child the next. You have so much expected of you and then it's like nothing. You're in this limbo period. It was very difficult."

In talking about *This Property Is Condemned*, which starred Natalie Wood and Robert Redford, Mary reflected, "Sidney Pollack was the director and John Houseman produced it. It was a very tough shoot. It was shot in Biloxi, Mississippi ... seemingly forever. Biloxi's not a real fun place for a kid to be anyway. But on a shoot like that it was very tough. Nat was going through a real difficult period in her life. We had script changes daily. It was unbelievable. It was a madhouse; it was just absolutely bananas. I would get a set of script pages one day. At eight o'clock the next morning there would be changes to that. Then they would change the shoot and then decide to shoot it, and then by eight o'clock that night I would get somebody knocking on my door with other pages. Green pages, blue pages, yellow pages. They literally ran out of color for pages as to what and where changes had been made. I was 13 at that time and it's tough enough being a little kid at that age. When you're on location with a picture, we're talking thousands of dollars a minute and every minute is precious, and anything that gets in the way of that creates tension. There was so much tension on that set you could cut it with a knife. By the time we got back to Los Angeles I'm sure the studio was screaming because they've got deadlines they have to meet."

Mary shared another memory of *This Property Is Condemned*. "Nat was off that morning and they were setting up a shoot for that afternoon and her stand-in couldn't be found. Nat and I were almost identical in size as far as height goes. I was on my way to the schoolroom and saw they were trying to light the scene on the porch, so I said, 'If she can't be found, just light on me. I'm here, that's okay.' When I was present, the rules were that foul language stopped—there was to be no swearing and everything was supposed to remain very cool and calm. Well, these guys just went on about their normal routine, their tempers being rather short at that point. I didn't pay any attention to what was going on and didn't hear any of it. I just stood on the porch acting as stand-in and Mrs. Crotke came around the corner and heard things. She was so displeased and made it very clear to me in no uncertain terms that I was to go from the set to the schoolroom and not make any stops in between, and if anyone asked me to do anything I was to tell them to talk to her. She threatened to shut down the set. My mother was terrified it was going to reflect badly on me and they would get angry with me. Anyway, we finished the shoot and it all worked out just fine, but it was a very big growing up period for me. It was a major step in my growth. I learned it was real work. It definitely became business and not a very pleasant business at that. Not everything was as it had been before. I mean, before it was all kind of like a dream and we were just playing, but then it became real work, not that I would say I wouldn't want that. I'm very thankful for that experience because it was closer to reality and helped shape my feelings about the business, and helped me to make more careful decisions in the future. I think it stood me in very good stead. As much as I was sheltered, I feel like the experience was okay because it sort of helped push me into a very normal life."

Mary was approached to do *Let's Kill Uncle* during the making of *This Property Is Condemned*. "Bill Castle was the director, and he realized immediately what was going on and obviously clued them in to my situ-

Gregory Peck in his Oscar-winning performance as Atticus Finch, the lawyer father of Mary's Jean Louise "Scout" Finch in *To Kill a Mockingbird* (1962, Universal).

ation, because by the time the picture was finished I was on the verge of a nervous breakdown. I was that bad. I was a basket case, totally. Bill, knowing children and loving them, said, 'Send the kid home. We can wait. No problem.' He was an angel of mercy. God love that man, he was just like a big teddy bear. A huge man with a big cigar, just a funny, funny guy, so loving and so dear. I can't think of enough to say, because it was like falling off a horse. You know, you get off and you've got to get back on again, and he knew that. It's like, 'One down, no big deal. You had a bad experience, let's get back up and we'll do it again.' Bill said, 'You're going to have fun on this picture. We're going to have a good time. If you guys want to laugh or sing or change the script, hey, who cares?' He was at that point in his career where he wanted to sort of make a change and do something a little different, which it really was. It was a terrible picture, but we sure had a blast doing it. Pat Cardi couldn't have been nicer; he was such a nice kid. Nigel Green was terrific to work with. There was so much laughter. We laughed from beginning to end. It was just a hoot the whole way through. We had a ball. Pat Cardi made things really easy because I tended to get depressed and he just wouldn't have any of it. He said, 'We're not having that. We're going to keep laughing the whole time,' and they did. They made things so light and so wonderful. It was a breath of fresh air to do that picture. It was a lot of fun."

Mary's other credits were two television shows, one being *The Twilight Zone*. "It was a marvelous episode called *The Witching Pool*. It had something very important to say about children of divorce and it really turned out to be a good piece of work. Then the other piece that I did was *Dr. Kildare*. The episode was called *Sister Mike*. While making that one I received a standing ovation. There's a scene where *Dr. Kildare* is making a speech up on the stage and I have to run in and ask him for help. My little brother had been burned and I needed him. I come in, did my little bit, and when I finished and they called 'Cut,' I started to walk away and all these people stood up and applauded. I didn't know what was going on and my mother said, 'Oh, she's getting a standing ovation. Take a bow and say thank you.' Mrs. Crotke said that she had never witnessed a standing ovation before."

Asked what she did after her films, Mary replied, "I went home for a while and then to school in Arizona and finished my high schooling. While I was in my senior year I met the man who is now my husband. He was in his first year at the University of Arizona. I went there and when he got ready to leave I wasn't going to stay behind, so we went back to Alabama, got married and we've been together ever since."

We asked Mary whether it was hard for her when her acting career came to an end. "In a way it was. What a wonderful business, to be able to go and be somebody else for the day. I really think it was a gift God gave to me that I was able to do it. I don't know if I could do it now but it was lots of fun at the time because of the friendships you make and the good times. Thank God all I basically remember are the good times. I don't remember much of the hard times. So I've been very blessed in that I can look back on it and say, 'Wow, what an experience.' And it's still going on; it's an ongoing thing. With *Mockingbird*, I get requests all the time for speaking engagements to schools, colleges and universities, and various things with Mr. Peck.

"The 35th anniversary of *Mockingbird* was just unbelievable. I went everywhere. And next year [1999] I've got a gig in Kansas that I'm doing with a symphony orchestra where they're doing the new soundtrack of Elmer Bernstein's score and I'm going to be doing a narrative over it, so that ought to be fun. There is no one key element of that film that you can take out. It would not work. It's all so perfectly bound. It's nice in black-and-white. It could have been done in color, but the whole feel of the picture would have been different. When I go places and they ask me, 'Why do you think everything worked so well?' I have only one thing to say and that is, 'This is God's picture,' and a lot of people think that's silly. But if you think about the time period this picture was made, it had a lot of important things to say that still need to be said today and will go on being needed for ever and ever. And the way it was said, the whole feel of the thing, was so critically important to people because it made a statement that will nourish us forever. We're at a critical state right now in our society. I had talked to the powers that be about rereleasing the picture, saying that there is a need out there for people to see it on the big screen; it's taught in all the schools and they teach it in the universities and everyone's aware of it, and they all love it. And the powers that be just weren't having it. So I said, 'All right guys, I've put in my two cents worth, but I would like you to think about it because that message needs to be brought out again. And I'm saying it as I go across the country. We've got so much that needs to be given to our children to help guide them and they're obviously not getting the guidance they need, and this picture has been known to help. When we go around the country I get people coming up and saying, 'My daughter or son is a lawyer because of this picture, because of the statement that it made,' or 'This gave me guidance in my life. I came from a terrible family and this picture has given me a base to jump from.' It really can be a good tool for people to use and its message is eternal."

Sonny Bupp

Moyer "Sonny" MacClaren Bupp was born January 10, 1928, in New York City, New York. "I apparently got the nickname of Sonny because in 1928 Jolson was in his heyday on Broadway and one of his biggies was *Sonny Boy*," Sonny related. "So they hung that on me when I was a baby. I didn't use it except in show business."

Sonny's father worked in a department store in New York at the beginning of the Depression. "He had a lot of guts because in 1930 he packed up his wife, three boys, and two girls in an old car and with no promise of a job drove all the way across the country to California. We lived in the Hollywood area for a while. My mother had some influence in deciding to go to southern California rather than someplace else because she had aspirations of being in show business. When we got there she tried to get all five of her kids in movies, starting with my older sister June. She was successful in getting her into films for a while. But my sister hated it and got out. My mother got my next older sister Ann in for a while, too. My oldest brother Paul never got in, but my brother Tommy and I did and we were in for quite a while."

Sonny first obtained work onstage in the Pasadena Playhouse in the mid '30s and played Tiny Tim in *A Christmas Carol*, in 1936. He received good press on that one: "Tiny Tim is grandly performed by Sonny Bupp who stuffs the 'God bless us everyone' with so much poignancy as to cause the ladies in the audience to sniffle mightily." Another play in which Sonny appeared was *Escape From Freedom*. Amongst the cast, in a small role, was an aspiring actor named Victor Mature. Pasadena Playhouse was a source for talent to be discovered by studio scouts, and Sonny began obtaining extra work in the movies. "I did a lot of extra work. In fact, I think it was in 1936, I was in *Variety* magazine as having earned the most money as a juvenile extra."

Sonny and Fred Stone from the Warner Bros. 1939 feature, *No Place to Go*.

Mrs. Bupp engaged an agent named Julian Olynick for both Sonny and Tommy, and he began finding speaking roles for them in films. Sonny confided, "I never liked being a child actor in films. In fact, I dreaded seeing Mr. Olynick's car parked in front of our house, knowing it meant going on another interview for a movie part. On the other hand, working on the stage was really fun. I did one commercial play in downtown Los Angeles at the old Belasco Theater called *Excursion*. When you work in a stage play you worked with the people. You're reading off your script, and then finally everybody's getting their lines memorized and you begin to work it out on the stage without the props. You feel all of this coming together and you really work with each other. In the movies, you go in and shoot a scene. It could be the beginning or the ending of the movie. There is no camaraderie at all in motion pictures. You go and do your thing, and you're off and somebody else comes in. It is not that way on the stage."

In the thirties, Hollywood produced many human interest films that supplied much work for child performers. Sonny gave an example of one of these that he appeared in when he was about eight years old. *"What Becomes of the Children*, aka *Sorrows of Woe*, was about divorcing parents. He's a rich guy catting around and they divorce. I'm in the first half of the movie; then the story shifts. Now the kid is grown up. He goes bad, gets into all kinds of trouble, and the father's remorseful. That was the style."

Sonny and his brother Tommy did several films together including *San Francisco, Swing Your Lady, Emergency Squad,* and *Love Is on the Air* with Ronald Reagan in his film debut. Years later, when Reagan had been elected President, Sonny wrote him a letter and sent a copy of a movie still with them in it together. A month later Sonny received his photo back along with a personally written letter from the President. "I think that is very indicative of the kind of guy Reagan was," Sonny commented.

Whereas Tommy worked with comedians Laurel and Hardy and W.C. Fields, both brothers appeared with the Our Gang kids. Sonny also worked with the Three Stooges in *Cash and Carry*. "They were funny. They were 'on' as much off camera as when they were on, pulling their gags constantly. Moe Howard always played the straight man in the shot, but he dreamed up most of the gags. He was a real intelligent guy and did all the planning. A lot of it was extemporaneous. That's another thing I liked about theater; a lot of extemporaneous stuff in theater. The stage production, *Excursion*, was a comedy. I played a bratty kid. It was about a captain who ran a ferryboat who always had dreams of being the captain of a big fancy luxury liner. So one night he decides to take the ferry out of New York Harbor into the Atlantic. Now when you are playing to a live audience, if the audience is reacting it stirs everybody up and that's where you get better performances. They ad-lib and there's extemporaneous responses because you can feel it. Now some nights you come in and the audience is as cold as hell and you're throwing rope through your part because you're not getting anything, but some nights, man they're laughing and having a good time and you just emote like a son of a gun. Everybody does, they just turn on. So that's entirely different than movies. Movies, there is no emotion associated with it. In *What Becomes of the Children* when my parents get divorced and the kids have to say goodbye to their father I had to cry. Well, I cried. It didn't mean anything. You learn to do that like you learn to drive a car or ride a bicycle. You just do it. It isn't hard to cry if you have to. Or being mad or sad. The acting is no big deal." The year 1939 was a good one for Sonny in the movies. He costarred with William Boyd in the Hopalong Cassidy feature, *Renegade Trail*. "We shot on his property at Lone Pine, California. It was great. I didn't ride any horses in the movie although I have some 16mm film my mother took in which I was riding this big beautiful white horse Topper in those big crazy round rocks. It was a fascinating location. Boyd was an absolutely great guy. We lost a really nice person when he went. A lot of the screen personalities were not very nice, and had these egos, "I'm God, you're nobody types, but there were others. Ronald Reagan, Dennis Morgan and Jane Darwell were nice."

This was also the year Sonny was chosen to be one of the stars in his favorite feature *No Place to Go*, costarring Fred Stone. "It was a film typical of the thirties. A human interest story about a lonely old man and a mistreated orphan boy with the ever-present dog. Warner Brothers built a trailer for the movie citing a new child discovery. A real first-class build-up which would have probably kicked me off to a longer career, but the war broke out and all the human interest stories went down the drain. Warners shelved the film in favor of one they had just finished shooting entitled *Confessions of a Nazi Spy*. From that point on war movies dominated the screen and my potential career fell off very quickly." Strangely enough, Sonny's brother Tommy had a part in the film that replaced *No Place to Go*.

In 1940 Sonny appeared with John Wayne in *Three Faces West*. "I don't remember too much about it except he was well-liked by everybody on the set. Tommy had a much more interesting experience with John Wayne. Wayne saved his life in *Conflict* and almost lost his own in the attempt. Part of the story was for Tommy to fall in the river and the cowboys save him. Well the only problem was that the river was a lot more

William Boyd's Hopalong Cassidy has a talk with Joey (Sonny Bupp) in *Renegade Trail* (Paramount, 1939).

realistic than they had planned on. The kid was being pulled downstream. Wayne jumped in and now he's going down the river. That scene is in the movie, but they should have kept the real scene and kept the cameras grinding, but everyone went bananas trying to save the two of them. Tommy was about 10 or 11 and Wayne was just in his twenties. That was pretty exciting. Tommy was a freckle-faced, tousle-haired kid and that's the kind of parts he got. I always got the pretty boy parts because I didn't have any freckles. He did a lot of westerns, worked with Tim McCoy and people like that."

An actor that Sonny enjoyed working with was Jack Carson. "He was a funny guy. This was when he was first getting started. It was a B-picture called *Parole Fixer*. He gets killed in the movie and his children are left alone. Carson was not doing comedy in films at the time, but on the set between takes he kept the cast in a riot. Sometimes everybody was laughing so damn hard they couldn't shoot. They go to start the scene and somebody would start laughing and then everybody would break out. He was a riot." Sonny and Jack also worked in *Queen of the Mob* that was shooting simultaneously on the next stage. "My birthday came up, and Jeanne Cagney, who was playing Ma Barker, heard about it. She and Blanche Yurka took me out and had a happy birthday luncheon with a cake. There were some nice people in movies, and there were a lot of ugly ones."

In 1941 Sonny appeared in the Orson Welles classic *Citizen Kane*. "Welles was everything that anybody ever said of him. He was the most dynamic personality you'd ever want to meet. He was only 25 and they aged him until by the end of the movie he was an old man. When they advertise that he starred in it and produced and directed it, that's right. I remember a scene where he was running for governor and his wife and son are sitting up in the balcony of a big hall. The camera work in that movie is terrific. He was very innovative. They had the camera on a big long trolley boom that they could roll in and then bring the camera down, very dramatic. But here's this guy, he's running up on the stage and hitting his mark, and while they're setting up he runs back out and is talking to the script girl changing some dialogue. Then he's on this camera boom, up and down; leaps back up on the stage. This guy was incredible."

When asked if their was much competition for the role of Kane's son, Sonny answered, "They called me in on an interview for this job and there were about six of us sitting in the casting director's office. In walks Welles. He points at me and says, 'I want that one,' and walks out. That was it."

Sonny related what attending school was like for him as a child actor.

"What was school like being a child actor? A pain in the ass. Because in those days, for example, long hair was not in style. When you worked in films you never cut your hair. If you were doing a period picture like *Abe Lincoln in Illinois* they wanted long hair since that was the style in the 1800s. Then if they wanted you in a modern movie with short hair they cut it. You never went to the barber, you just let it grow. Of course you'd catch hell at school. A lot of teasing because you are running around with long hair and nobody else wears it that way. Another problem was that you were in and out of school all the time. When any juvenile worked in pictures the board of education was required to provide a teacher, and you had to have three hours of schooling every day. If there was a group of kids they would have a quasi classroom. If you were working at MGM they had their own schoolhouse on the property and we all went to the same place. But then, on a movie like *Renegade Trail* I was the only kid in the movie. We were on location in Lone Pine so it was like having a private tutor. You still had to get three hours in, whether there were ten of you or one of you. When the movie's over you go back to public school again. Then you get another job and you're out of school again. You're in school and out of school, in school and out of school. There was never any continuity. I was a pretty smart kid to begin with, but I was always ahead of my grade because of this virtual tutoring. I was doing things that they weren't doing in the class yet because they were trying to teach 20 or 30 kids. I was always ahead and that made it extremely boring and annoying. So schooling was not a very pleasant experience."

In referring to his feelings in regard to working in films, Sonny mentioned, "It must be really terrible nowadays. In those days all you had available was the movies, but now they grind up people in television like hamburger. You see kids that come in one season and never see them again. They just eat them up. They used to do that in movies, but not so much because they didn't need so many. But very few of the kids I worked with ever amounted to anything. A few, like Spanky McFarland, came out of it all right. My brother—it absolutely ruined him. He was the first American boy to make a movie in England. He got cast in *Hey, Hey, USA*. He and my mother went first class over to England on the *Queen Mary*. Talk about the caste system—they treated him like royalty. And he never got over it. He came back and was getting older, the war broke out and he joined up in December 1941 and was on the Battleship *Tennessee* all through the war in the Pacific. But he could never get over that notoriety. When he came out of the navy in 1945 there were no parts for people like him. I hated the business so it didn't bother me any, but Tommy just got one little hokey job after another. It was a shame. But that happened to a lot of those kids."

When not actually working, Sonny spoke of what he did on the film set. "Most of the time when you're on a film as a child, unless there are other kids, the people you associated with between the takes were the crew, not the actors. Guys who do the lighting, electrical, sound and all that stuff. I learned to play poker when I was a kid, playing with the crew. For instance, in *Little Orvie* I had a pretty good bit part, yet my actual on-screen time was probably eight minutes. But I was there for three weeks because when they want you, they want you. Many times I was there all day long. I did my three hours in school and never acted one minute. Boring as hell, especially for a kid, so you get to know the crew." Even when there were a large group of kids on the set, like when he did the Our Gang short, *Men in Fright,* there wasn't much camaraderie there either. "That was mainly because of the rogue's gallery, the mothers. The mothers were terrible. Groping, grasping, greedy. So they didn't really like their kid associating with other kids. It was a very unreal atmosphere. You would think that in the Our Gang or something where there were a bunch of kids making the movie that in between sets you would be off playing. But each kid would go back to their mother. There wasn't any association between them. Maybe there was a little interplay when you went to the commissary at lunch time, or maybe if you were at MGM where they had the schoolhouse, but not much. And as I said, not on the set."

During the golden era of Hollywood, a law was passed, referred to as the Coogan Law, which stipulated that the parents or legal guardians of a child actor had to deposit 50 percent of the child's gross income into a trust fund until the actor was 21. "That was the law because Coogan, with all the money he made, got nothing due to his old lady blowing it all. I started looking into it when a guy wrote an article about Margaret O'Brien stating she got about a million bucks when she turned 21. I wouldn't have got that much, but when you figure from about 1934 through 1941, that's seven years, my average pay was $50 a day when I worked, and in those days there was no income tax on minors. I might have been in a movie for three minutes, but I might spend two weeks there because I was on call. So $50 a day was a lot of money in 1936. My father made $35 a week managing a department store. And thanks to my greedy mother, whenever I didn't work in any one week—Monday through Friday—she'd pick me up at school and drive me down to the unemployment office where I would draw $18 a week. I always got a kick out of standing in line with all those adults. They'd look down at me, and here's this little kid standing in line. So I was drawing a minimum of $18 a week and a maximum of $250, for seven years. Now you put that in the bank at compound interest and it worked out to a pretty good little bundle by the time I was 21. But I got zippo. Mom spent it all. And it's always been a big mystery in the family just what the hell she did with it. She would never discuss it. I would try to get her to tell me what she did, but she never would. Tommy never got anything out of it either, and if I made 50 movies he probably made 100. So we made a lot of money, but never got a nickel. That was all contrary to the law. It's not that we were just being neglected, we were cheated."

When Sonny's film work came to an end he was not upset. "I never liked it. When the war broke out my mother and father had separated. She remarried an old boyfriend from many years in the past and moved to Long Beach. That's when defense work was starting up so in the summer I worked in a defense plant that made ship shafting. We moved to Taft, California, where my stepfather worked for Tidewater Associated Oil Company. I worked with them during the summers as a field repairman's helper. Then I went into the army and was in the Signal Corps in Italy just at the time they were getting ready to sign the peace treaty." After three years Sonny returned home. "When I first got back I thought I was God's gift to American industry, but after six months I would take anything I could get," he laughed. "I finally went on a job interview for something to tide me over and got a job with Ford Motor Company at the old Long Beach assembly plant. I was a messenger boy carrying mail around the assembly plant. From a messenger boy I became the senior management and managed several of their plants until I retired 42 years later. A very interesting career and they treated me very well. But I never had any desire to go back into show business. My brother, when he got out of the service in '45, kept trying to get back in but never could. So many of the kids that were in turned out bad. Drunks, drug addicts, suicides; they just couldn't get it out of their system. I had a lot of interesting experiences, but in retrospect it wouldn't bother me if I never had. It's nice, again in retrospect, thinking about being associated with the most famous movie of all time. That's interesting to be number one in something," Sonny laughed. "I've had a good life, the Lord has treated me very well."

In summing up his career as a child actor, Sonny remarked, "Having done it, it's interesting to reflect back on, but I would never recommend anybody ever subjecting their child to show business because it will ruin him. I don't think there's one child out of a thousand that can be exposed to that kind of life and not be adversely affected. Think about it. Go back ten years or so to some of the kids that were doing television and every now and then something pops up in the newspaper about their being arrested for narcotic possession or being in the drunk tank. That's still going on. The same problems. It's just a very unreal world for a child. It's hard enough for adults; they get affected by it. Don't put your kids in movies. That's the way I would sum it up."

Michael Chapin

Michael Chapin was born July 25, 1936, in Hollywood, California. "When I was six months old Adohr Farms (a very popular milk company in Southern California) ran an ad looking for a cute baby picture that they wanted to use in an ad campaign. My mother responded and my picture won the contest, so I was Adohr's official 'adorable' baby. That's where my career began. My mother ultimately became a good movie mom. She became my mentor, sponsor and promoter.

"In some respects kids are property from the point of view of a movie mom. I mean this is an asset, a property that they go out and promote. I don't see anything wrong with that. I think a very interesting sidelight is how people who do that succeed. It's rather interesting because it is very difficult. They're not agents. They don't have that status. They have to get out and somehow promote their kids. You don't get a good agent until you've worked, and you don't work until you have an agent. So again, you're back to your mom. She has to get out and learn the ropes on her own, figure out where the cattle call interviews are and get you there. The kids that we all know and love who were just brilliant, the Shirley Temples and Donald O'Connors, came through the studio system. But all of those whose talent was less apparent at a young age didn't go through this process. Their process was more representative of the journeyman actor. They needed to find a method of getting their foot in the door because the competition was very difficult. Eventually, I experienced the studio system and what it was like to be cared for. It was a very interesting experience, but I actually saw both. The other being the long difficult process of competing with 300 people on an interview for a job that will see you on the screen for 15 seconds."

Michael's film work began with the traditional extra work. "My

Michael Chapin as "Red" with his horse from the *Rough Ridin' Kids*, a four-feature western series at Republic.

mother got me registered with Screen Extras Guild. In *The Sullivans* I was one of the neighborhood friends of the youngest Sullivan brother who was played by Bobby Driscoll. We had been in a schoolyard altercation and when we did First Communion together both of us were there with black eyes. My recollection is that I was around six or seven years old when I had my first speaking part in a movie. I think *The Corn Is Green* was the first. A great movie. Bette Davis was electrifying."

Michael mentioned that the bulk of his work was in radio. "Radio was really my area, much more so than movies. For a period of time there were two kids in town who seemed to do everything in radio. There was a young man name Johnny McGovern and myself. I learned to read when I was very young and at seven I was very fluent. I had a running role on *One Man's Family*, which was an early soap. My voice didn't change until I was 15, so I was still doing seven year olds until then." Among his radio credits are *Family Theatre*, *Bob Hope Show*, *Straight Arrow*, and *Dr. Christian*.

Michael shared with us a particular experience from a radio show that he appeared in. "It's very difficult to convey as a child actor how much the people in theater, or whatever medium you are in, become instantly part of your family; they were like aunts and uncles because every time you see them they are family. Some of them treat you like a pretty mean uncle," Michael laughed, "but from an emotional point of view this is how I remember my sense of the people with whom I came in contact. Most of them were just super neat human beings who treated me very well and made me feel that familial sort of feeling. But they were grownups and had their own agenda and as a kid you don't understand what that agenda is. It's impossible for kids to really understand their parents or the adult world around them. We were doing one of those hour-long playhouses—it was a story told in flashback form by a then elderly man who was recounting his pioneering travels across the United States heading west, and eventually he hits the ocean. The ocean was a physical barrier and a symbolic sort of representation that his life as a pioneer had come to an end. He had to come to grips with that because he recognized that this adventure was over and it introduced a new plateau in his life, one that he didn't really want to accept. It was a very emotional sort of show. It introduced some philosophical ideas that I realize now are of interest to all of us, because we all have forced on us abrupt changes in our lives from time to time that we need to hopefully come to grips with gracefully."

The typical format in radio is basically the same as it is in TV shows and many movies. Reflecting on the previously mentioned show, Michael said, "The first thing we did was a cold reading, and then a couple of sit-down readings. It was a very compelling script and the first reading was done very well. Everyone got into the story and by the time we came to the end of this hour-long show there was not one dry eye around the table. I was nine or ten years old, and I was moved. Not by the story—I understood a lot of the layers of the story and so that was fine—but I was really moved by how moved my extended family was. I was touched by how much insight they had. I have fond memories of that because that sentiment just pulled us together into a really tight sort of bond that's impossible to convey or duplicate elsewhere.

"There were a lot of other experiences," Michael continued. "Jack Webb had a reputation of being a very stern taskmaster. He never swore, but he had a pretty good bark. If he didn't like you, you weren't around very long. The first time I worked for him I was literally just shaking in my boots, but apparently I did well. I worked for him many more times on *Dragnet* and came to really admire and respect him and felt very good that he had never yelled at me. Even when I made a mistake he treated me with caution and caring. He was gentle, encouraging, and this was just very contrary to the way he treated adult actors. I admire Jack Webb very much."

One director that Michael admired was Buzz Kulik. "When I was about 17, Margaret O'Brien and I did one of those horrendous 90-minute things called live television for *Lux Video Theater*. Those are frightening, but interesting. It is there, and if you blow it you'd better figure out how to recover. We did this show and we were the only two characters in it. It was a story of first love, really an unrequited love sort of situation where the girl didn't reciprocate her feelings to the same level the boy had. It was clever dialogue because he was speaking in 'what ifs' a lot to protect his young male ego, being afraid to face rejection if she were to say 'No.' He expressed his feelings, his wants, his longing for this young girl and her responses were based on feelings she had for another fellow, so the dialogue was built on that. In order to get it to play right, Buzz really had to create a lot of understanding with his two actors. He was a great director for working with kids."

Michael's godfather was Paul Price who was a radio and television editor for the *Los Angeles Daily News*. Klaus Lansberg, who was famous for having built Los Angeles' first television station, KTLA Channel 5, hired Paul to do a weekly news magazine format show titled *Who's News* sponsored by the *L.A. Daily News*. The format was that Paul would run the newspaper into my hand and say, 'Okay, three minutes to air time. Oh by the way, we're having so and so as our guests tonight.' Well, he would spring these guests' names on me that didn't mean anything to me, and I couldn't ever remember them. I did the fade-in holding the *Daily News*, and it went like this: 'Hey! Get your paper! Read all about it.' I would read the headline and fade out to Paul sitting behind the desk. We'd have a little commercial about the *L.A. News* and then come back in on

Paul who would say, 'Good evening ladies and gentlemen. Ah, Michael, I see you standing in the wings. Do we have some special guests tonight?' 'Yes, Paul, we have very special guests tonight. We have Mr. ah ... Mr. ah ... Oh, you know, the fellow who's mayor of Los Angeles.' I'm just very grateful that at least he told me their occupations. I think they found that cute and played on it because I could not ever remember the names of his guests. No one seemed to mind. I did that show for a year. That was great fun and another instance of interesting live TV."

Michael costarred with Eilene Janssen in the four *Rough Ridin' Kids* western features for Republic Studios. "When I was 14 there was a man named Jimmy Fiddler, a widely syndicated columnist, who hatched an idea with 'Papa' Yates at Republic Studio to cultivate a young Roy Rogers and Dale Evans team. It was kind of a win-win situation. If it came off, it would be great. It perpetuated the westerns at Republic and a lot of good publicity, no matter what. So Mr. Yates endorsed this idea and then mounted a nationwide search for a young boy and young girl to play these two characters. I can't honestly tell you that it indeed was a nationwide search. The publicity said it was, but they did do a lot of interviewing here in town. Eventually I got the part as did Eilene Janssen. That is where we really experienced a little bit of the studio system which by then was kind of on its way out. The studio made me dye my hair red because the character's name was Red White. We did a lot of public appearance tours promoting the concept. You do those where you can. We did charity appearances, Christmas parades and all the things that gather publicity."

Michael mentioned that doing the *Rough Ridin' Kids* shows was a lot of hard work. "Doing the personal appearances was very demanding because it wasn't rewarding to me. It was time away from school and I was a good student. It was very clear to me that to do those things was for the studio and as I was already under contract I didn't see the benefit to me, and from a childish point of view it was an imposition every time I had to go do one. I don't mean that to be a large negative at all. It's an illustration of the fact that it was hard work. I had to go in every week to get my hair dyed, and that's time away from sports and school and just being a teenager. And I caught a lot of flack at school from kids because of my dyed hair. They were quick to pick up on it, and they—as cruel as kids are—would ask me if my horse's name was Blue. But I came away from it probably no different than a kid who has a paper route and had to get up at four in the morning. That's hard work. I think we were fortunate in that we never had stardom. I never felt or acted like a typical 'star.' I understood that I was very fortunate to get a seven-year contract and work for the studio and have all these wonderful possibilities in your future. I understood that set me apart, but I guess for whatever reason my folks didn't buy into the 'you're a star' kind of thing. The truth is I don't think kids buy into it unless they're given some model. If the parents portray that then the kid can pick up on it. A kid might try it, but it's just like a lot of kids would try stealing something from the store, too. You slap their hands once and for most of them that's it."

Michael knew how to ride horseback before obtaining the role of Red in the western series. "All the stories about lying about your skills are true. One doesn't lie, one just simply projects into the future. 'I can ride,' means 'I will learn how very quickly if I get this part.' I was a fairly decent rider by the time I got that part. They had a regular schedule for Eilene and me. We went to a stable out in San Fernando Valley and they gave us good lessons."

Another western that Michael worked was Monogram's *Wagons West*. "I liked Rod Cameron. He was a cool dude. You've got to think of the way you work as an actor in just the same way as you work a regular job. When he's not in front of the camera he may well be studying his lines and getting into the mood for the next scene. So he would retire—he's not going to go and socialize with the cast and crew—to his dressing room, gets his script out and reads his lines. Some people give the impression of being more reclusive than others because they immediately go back to the dressing room. They're just professional. They go, study, come back out, and are great. It's easy to misunderstand that. Most adult actors, from my point of view as a child, didn't talk much to the kids. The *Rough Ridin' Kids* series was different in some ways because I wasn't just a kid on the lot. Eilene and I both were the stars. We had a few more degrees of freedom on the set and people were a little more deferential in their treatment of us so we did have the opportunity to socialize with a lot of the people who were there. Of the actors that I have worked with, two who come to mind that took time to talk with me on the set and were very nice were House Peters, Jr. and Tris Coffin.

"But Cameron was nice. In several scenes I was in with him we were sitting on horses waiting for the cameras to roll, and he would talk to me and treat me like a human being, which a lot of people wouldn't. I always appreciated that from him. There was one scene where we were supposed to say, 'Okay, we're leaving,' and ride off rapidly. We did it in rehearsal, and as good a rider as I was I didn't want to go off at quite a full gallop. I remember him saying, 'Don't worry about it. You just follow my lead and we'll just do it.' I remember him for being very upbeat and encouraging. I liked the man.

"I know that the B-westerns were great and they're a genre which I

Badman House Peters, Jr. holds Michael prisoner as his pals steal Trigger in the Roy Rogers feature *Under California Stars* (Republic, 1948).

appreciate more now than I did when I was involved in them. They're a real part of Americana that I admire more as an outsider than when I was an insider. I'm glad I was part of that."

Michael appeared on stage once in *Father Was President* with Albert Dekker at the Phoenix-Westwood Theatre in 1946 in Westwood, California. "It was a lot of fun, which is interesting because it's live theater also. You would think, 'What's the difference between that and live television?' Maybe there is no difference, but the role was not so demanding. That thing I did with Margaret O'Brien was so intense because it was just the two of us. With *Father Was President* you could have a whole group of people and everyone flubbing lines and ad-libbing. That's where you learn the art of ad-lib and how not to worry about it. If in theater you go overtime it's no big deal. Live TV is very tight and they're always looking at the watch."

When Michael graduated from high school he joined the service. During this time he also appeared in his final movie, a cameo role in *The Night of the Hunter*, which featured his younger brother Billy in a lead role. "I was about 18. I was one of two boys standing on a street corner when Lillian Gish brings Ruby and the two kids into town. My mother went to either Charles Laughton, the director, or Paul Gregory, the producer, and said, 'My son's going to be on leave. Wouldn't it be cute if he did this little bit here?' They said, 'Sure,' so I did that. That was the first time in my life that I fell madly head over heels with an older woman. It was very serious; it is an affection that I still have today, and that was for Lillian Gish. She was the most beautiful lady. Beauty of spirit just beyond anybody you've ever met. She and Charles Laughton would sit around when they took lunch breaks and entertain the cast and crew. They would read out of Shakespeare or the Bible and it was magical. They were so gifted, and just to have them sit around and do that was terrific. A wonderful memory."

After his discharge from the service Michael was offered a position to work as an agent in a motion picture agency, but he declined. "I wasn't interested. I like the theater; I like the business but don't need it. I have two kids who are in it now. I was interested in math and science. I had technical interests, so being an agent just wasn't what I wanted." As for having an interest in continuing an acting career, Michael said, "No. I felt my brother Billy had the charisma on film. I enjoyed acting, but I thought he looked better on film than me. There is something that real stars have that is pretty indefinable. All you've got to do is look and they just really stand out. Bobby Driscoll had it when he was younger. That person who really stands out is rare and I never thought I did. My brother could have, but he didn't have the desire. My sister Lauren had everything. She was Kathy on *Father Knows Best* for seven years."

Michael obtained work in the computer field. "I made a discovery well after my computer career had started and was under way that I was fascinated with the way people learn. I got very involved in education and ended up starting my own school. For over a decade I ran a private school in Orange County. So that was a complete change and I enjoyed it."

One of the hobbies Michael enjoys today is hiking. "I love the wilderness experience. You remember Rosalind Russell in *Auntie Mame*? She's standing at the top of the stairs and expounding to her nephew, telling him how wonderful life is, and she says, 'The whole world is a bowl of cherries and most poor slobs are starving to death.' That's just a piece of a folk philosophy that I very much subscribe to. This is a wonderful place we live in. We have a wonderful Creator who made it for us to enjoy. So I enjoy the backpacking. I enjoy getting out and getting away from the synthetic stuff."

Michael also stated that he did not have a difficult time adjusting to life after his acting career was finished. "I did not have a hard time adjusting because I chose to go in the service and I chose to go to college. I really chose the separation. I really just didn't look back. There came a time when I did. I stopped and looked back. You look back at bridges that you've gone across and sometimes wonder if that was the right one. In reflecting back, there was a certain amount of melancholy. It didn't last long, but there was a little because when you're so busy and running so hard and so fast you miss a lot of things. When you stop and you take a breath you have the opportunity to put things into perspective. One of those perspectives was, 'Jeez, I did this for 18 years and all of a sudden what do I have to show for it?' I think that's what I felt was missing—the culmination of that career. No gold watch, no retirements, no plaque on the wall, or anything like that. It was just, 'Well, that was yesterday.' But once I recognized that I said, 'Well, okay,' and just went on. Fortunately, I felt that. I didn't allow it to get under my skin. I think that there's a lot of things you learn as a human being from a lot of different places. But to me, being in the entertaining business, there were a lot of blessings there. It was a pretty neat thing for a kid to do. You have to live in the adult world and that's something which is interesting. When you're growing up it's a little bit different because you're expected to live and compete on an adult level even though you're not. You can not behave like a kid when you're on a radio or movie set."

Looking back over his acting career, Michael summed up his feelings this way: "Personally, I feel quite blessed to have been able to do that.

First of all, there was a time when my income was needed by my family and I never begrudged that. I felt it was good fortune that I was able to do it. I look at it now and I really think it was kind of a blessing. I thought it was great fun. Either by personality or by training you are on in front of a crowd of people. You're on stage, you're very self-aware, you're egocentric. So you end up, if you go into another career, a wonderful public speaker or an ambassador or a teacher; you're comfortable being stage center with people. My wife laughs because I enjoy that and there's a certain amount of adulation—it's an ego gratification kind of thing—and I don't always analyze it. I know I like it; I like interchange with people. Sometimes it's like an adrenaline rush. I mean I could really get carried away with it. You see this with a lot of people who were actors. They can become bores, but there's a lot of them that are just fun; they're high-energy people.

"Getting reacquainted with people—a lot of them were movie kids—at these reunions after so many years is just a doggone hoot. I said this in jest a couple of years ago but it was quite true: I have found it absolutely delightful to meet a whole roomful of people who are just like me and to find I'm normal. They're just high-energy, creative people. They want their moment in the sun. What is interesting about them is how gracious they are to let you have your moment in the sun. Here are two people and they both enjoy being on stage center but will allow each to do his thing. I really have enjoyed these meetings because of that. It's so fun to see God's grace pour out of people and to see how they really do reflect it. I don't think you always see that when you're younger. I've been very blessed to have been a part of this business but I don't see it as my contribution to society."

Ted Donaldson

Ted Donaldson was born August 20, 1933, in Brooklyn, New York. "My father worked in radio. My mother, Jo, I never knew. She died when I was 4½ months old. I lived in Brooklyn with Jo's sister's family for almost five years and went with my father on weekends. During that time he started going with my stepmother [the only person Ted ever called mother], Molly Pollock, who was also a composer, pianist, and worked at NBC."

Ted obtained his first job because his stepmother took him to NBC one day in December 1937. A woman named Irene Wicker had a popular 15-minute radio program on NBC then they needed a kid, and asked, "Molly, can we use little Ted?" "So I sat on Irene Wicker's lap on the stairs and said, 'Mommy, tell me about Jesus,' and she told me about him."

Ted Malone, a very popular anthologist of poetry, also had a 15-minute radio program on NBC in which he read poetry, told stories and anecdotes. He asked Ted's mother, "Could I put little Ted on the show tonight and ask him a couple of questions?" She said, "I have no idea what he will say." "So Ted Malone put me on, and I took up 12 of his 15 minutes telling him a story. And I knew that I was talking to thousands of people," Ted laughed. "That was the first indication of where some sort of talent may have lain because I was completely natural and had no nerves whatever."

At the age of eight Ted appeared as Harlan for one year in *Life with Father* on Broadway. "They wanted me to continue the second year and play the next older boy, but my parents made what I think was an extraordinarily wise decision. They said no. They didn't want me to get the idea that *Life with Father* was the only thing in the theater. I didn't know it then, but years later it seemed to me a wonderfully intelligent decision to make."

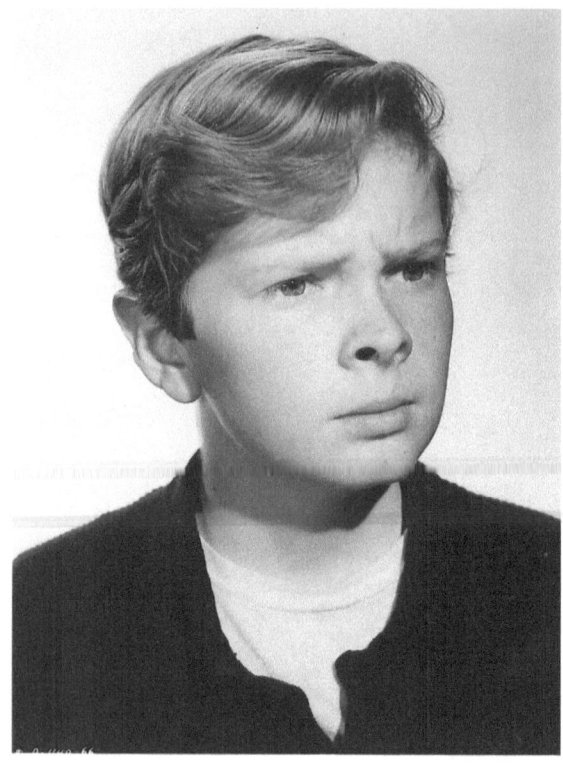

Ted Donaldson, 1947.

Ted worked on many of the soap operas and drama shows on radio. In 1943 he landed a part in Irwin Shaw's *Sons and Soldiers*, which was the final play Max Reinhardt directed. "I played Gregory Peck's brother as a boy. I was on stage for only three minutes. The reviews were kind of mixed and it lasted only three weeks, but Gregory Peck came out to Hollywood from that. I was seen by an agent from MCA who wired Harry Cohn, the president of Columbia Studio, saying she thought she had found the right boy to play opposite Cary Grant in what they were then calling *My Client Curly*. Cohn, on a visit to New York, tested me. It was all very casual. I stood in front of the camera and he talked to me. I had a terrible cold and a runny nose but he said don't worry about it. He was very gentle and charming. And I got the part." Ted, with his father, came to Hollywood in August 1943 to star with Cary Grant in the film, which was released as *Once Upon a Time*. "We thought I was going to do the movie and then go back to New York, but after it was finished Columbia said they would like to put me under contract. So my parents, who were very successful in New York, moved out here."

Ted has fond memories of Cary Grant. "This was one of the greatest professional and personal experiences that I have ever had. Let me tell you how I met him. He came to a set at Columbia to make a test for Janet Blair who played my sister. Well, I'm sitting next to my father and I see Grant standing 20 feet away talking with a representative from MCA or the studio. Grant leaves the person he's talking to and comes directly over to me. He extends his hand and says, 'How do you do? I'm Cary Grant.'

Then he turned to my father and said, 'You must be Mr. Donaldson. What a great pleasure to meet you.' That was my introduction to Cary Grant—Cary Grant introducing himself to me. I was not brought over to him, nobody brought him over to me. That's the way it started. And that was characteristic of him."

Once Upon a Time concerns a boy living with his struggling older sister. He has a caterpillar named Curly that dances to the tune of "Yes Sir, That's My Baby," and when Grant (who plays a theatrical producer who's going broke) witnesses this act he sees it as a possible fortune. "We are standing on the steps of his office. We are all dressed up and waiting for the scene to be lit. He says to me very quietly, 'Put the one foot above the other on the step. It looks better.' He instilled those little things like that."

There is a scene at the end of the film with a two-shot of Grant and Ted where the caterpillar turns into a butterfly. The photographer was a man from Germany named Franz Planer. "He was very precise and everything had to be absolutely correct. Well, Franz had taken two hours to light the final scene and Grant and I are standing there waiting. Finally Alexander Hall, the director, says, 'Quiet on the set. Roll them!' Suddenly Grant says to Hall, 'Just a moment now, Al,' waving his hand in front of his face. Mr. Hall said, 'What is it Cary?' and Grant answered, 'The setup is all wrong.' 'What do you mean?' The setup was a two-shot, and Grant said, 'It's not a two-shot. It should be a closeup of the kid.' Hall said, 'It will be fine.' 'No, no, put my shoulder in to establish that I am there, but it's a closeup of the kid. It's not a two-shot.' Al Hall implied that Franz Planer had taken two hours to light the scene, but Grant still said no. He would not do the scene unless it was a closeup. I have told this story many times and I got a lump in my throat just now as I started telling it. That's where his perfectionism lay. He was concerned with the story and the dramatic effect. He was totally unconcerned with himself and his stardom. That I think is fantastic.

"When you take all of that together, the fact that he was funny, taught me games, loved magic and was absolutely charming, well, I came to love the man. There was only one time that I ever saw him serious. The two of us were waiting for Franz Planer, sitting on a couch, and he began talking about his adopted son Lance. It was the only really serious and rather melancholy side of Grant that I had not ever seen before. He talked about how he just didn't feel he was able to spend enough time with him. It was very strange because it became a reversal of roles. I began asking him questions; I felt that I was trying to almost comfort and help him. It was a strange thing, but it gave me an insight that made me feel closer to him. I was having some difficulties with my father whom I loved and adored, and I believe that I came to substitute Grant for my father at that time. I don't know if he went as far as I did, but I think he came to have some real fatherly feelings about me. I really believe that."

After the film was finished, Ted saw Cary Grant from time to time. "In 1949 I wrote to him and asked if he would come to my high school graduation. And he did. He sat on the aisle. As a girl named Barbara in her beautiful white gown holding her flowers came down the aisle (I had not told anyone that he was going to be there) she saw him and suddenly gripped the flowers. Grant said to her as she walked by, 'You're doing fine.' It was absolutely innate in him to do that. Over the years I kept thinking I must write and tell him how I feel, but I could never think of exactly what to say. Then one day in 1979 in the middle of June I suddenly realized that it was exactly 30 years to the day that he had come for my high school graduation. That was the opening line of my letter. I sat down and wrote him, recalling some of the incidents that I have mentioned and that I thought it was long past time to have expressed the way I felt. A month later the phone rang. I picked it up and said, 'Hello.' 'May I speak with Teddy Donaldson; this is Cary Grant.' He had been traveling with his daughter and had just returned and read my letter. We talked for 20 minutes. We talked about *Once Upon a Time* and how much he had enjoyed working with me. He said the letter was terribly flattering and that he would always cherish it. It was found among his letters when he died seven years later."

Having come from the stage, Ted made the transition to film without any difficulty. "I learned a great deal by watching the rushes. I was very cold in respect to my work, even as a child. I would sit there as humanly objective as possible. I know that sounds like a great exaggeration if you're only ten years old, but I would watch myself as if it were somebody else. Very, very cold. I never saw myself upon the screen and thought, 'Hey, that's me up there.' I just sat back there and looked and watched."

Ted was loaned to 20th Century–Fox to play Neeley Nolan on *A Tree Grows in Brooklyn*, which was Elia Kazan's motion picture directorial debut. "Kazan sat us around a huge oaken table that you could imagine the Vikings having a banquet on. He sat at the head of the table and talked about the script, and for three days he established the relationships of the Nolan family. We read the script. We read it again and worked on the different scenes, and on the fourth day we started shooting. And it was not only the relationships, but the place. The atmosphere, the furniture. Early in the film Peggy Ann Garner and I come into the kitchen. We had come upstairs with pails of water, and Dorothy McGuire is at the sink washing dishes. Years later I was stunned by it when I watched it on television, I thought, 'My God, I know that sink, we know what that floor feels like, we lived there. This is our place.' That's something you sense much more in a stage performance because it is alive.

"I think *A Tree Grows in Brooklyn* was one of the greatest pieces of ensemble acting in the history of American film. Peggy Ann Garner's performance as Francie Nolan was one of the two or three greatest child performances ever given. I have always liked Dorothy McGuire, but I think her Katie Nolan was the best thing she ever did on film. Joan Blondell was always terrific, but this film gave her a chance to show a much more vulnerable side, and she really rose to the occasion. She really makes me cry in this film. James Dunn won the Oscar for best supporting actor. It was a beautiful performance. It was the role of his life. The scene in which he sings "Annie Laurie," Francie and Neeley are very affected by their father singing that, and so is Katie because she hears him, comes in from another room, stands at the doorway and recalls older times, times of more promise. Then there is this big closeup of Johnny singing that breaks your heart. It was the first time that I have ever heard this song. I've got to say that the expression you see on Peggy Ann's face and mine— we kept within the confines of the scene and the characters but that was Peggy and me reacting to James Dunn singing "Annie Laurie." We were supposed to be terribly moved by it. And we were. But we were affected as Peggy and as Ted. I'd never quite had that experience before. Yes, we were good. Damn right we were good. But that was Kazan. And that's why he produced a film—apart from Leon Shamroy's gorgeous black-and-white photography—where from the first frame on you are back in 1912. You are absolutely there all the way through and it never falters, not for a second. That is why it is a very beautiful and satisfying film."

Ted remained under contract to Columbia for about 2½ years. He played Danny Mitchell in a series of eight films for Columbia known as the Rusty movies. Flame, a famous movie dog, played Rusty in all but the first. "I was under contract when I did the first Rusty film, but not any of the others. I enjoyed working those. It's always nice to have the lead role in anything, particularly in something you knew was going to be a series because you are going to have the lead every time. Of course the dog always had the lead," Ted smiled. "The one that I remember the most making was the third film, *For the Love of Rusty*. I run away from home with my dog and meet an old English gentleman played by Aubrey Mather. This picture was directed by John Sturges who was just starting out as a director. The film had a two-week budget. Well, the reason that this film was the best of all of them was because it was the best script. A very nice relationship develops between the boy and the old man, and Sturges wanted to tell that story; he wanted that relationship. He worked with the characters. We rehearsed it and he took takes over. Normally these things were, 'Fine. Print it.' Toward the end of the second week the phone calls started coming down to the set. They're telling him, 'You're going over the budget and we can't have that.' They were telling him to wrap it up, but he absolutely resisted, and the respect that he had on that set was just enormous because he would hang up the phone, and then return to the set and do what he was going to do. He wrapped up the film in three weeks. Because of Sturges it is the best in the series."

Referring to Flame, Ted said, "Flame was a beautiful, intelligent animal, and wonderfully affectionate. He was just a sweetheart of a dog. I loved Flame. The last Rusty picture was made early in 1949, and about 2½ years later I saw Flame and his trainer. He had instant recognition of me and was tremendously friendly and affectionate."

Ted and Flame as they appear in the Columbia Production, *For the Love of Rusty* (1947).

Ted feels one of his best performances was in *The Decision of Christopher Blake*. "It's all about the kid. It's a part where you have to carry the film. The parents can be fine, but if the kid isn't any good it's all pointless. I do think that is one of the best things I did, in part because I believe there were a couple of sequences that in all modesty, I think I was the only one among all my colleagues who could have pulled it off. I'm thinking particularly of some of the dream sequences, some of the fantasy sequences, where he is imagining himself much older and quite suave and debonair. I think I did those scenes with a perspective of what a 14 year old would think was romantic and suave as an older person. He's acting grown-up, but he has to act grown-up as a 14 year old thinks a grownup acts."

Ted mentioned that the child actor's experience is a very odd one. "I think it is wonderful that I had it. I was one of the best child actors of my time. I have no false modesty about that at all. I think it is that cold, absolutely ruthless objectivity. I have had such marvelous experiences and I could have walked away from it at any time. I was never forced into it. Never. In fact, once when I was 13 or 14 my parents said to me, 'Do you really want to continue to do this? If you don't, you don't have to.' I said, 'Yes, I do. I love it.'

"The film I'm proudest to have done is *A Tree Grows in Brooklyn* because it's a classic," Ted stated. "But the single most powerful moment that I had is the scene in *Once Upon a Time* where Cary Grant takes Curly away. It was gorgeously photographed. I'm sitting on top of the bed with my legs sort of curled underneath me, and I'm a little out of focus. Then I come into focus, and I must say that I look—and this is Franz Planer's lighting and photography—absolutely beautiful. The main thing, however, is the look on the kid's face and what is clearly going through him. Finally I say, 'Once I wanted to grow up to be like you, but I don't anymore because you are a mean man, Mr. Flynn. You're a mean man, Mr. Flynn.' It is said in an almost flat monotone with almost no emotion at all. In fact, it is a very odd delivery of the line because it's almost as if the second line is less emphasized than the first one. It's almost backwards, upside down. And it's absolutely right. I don't think I have ever had a more powerful moment as an actor. I would hope someday to be able to equal that. That whole sense of betrayal the child feels from someone he once greatly loved, and his absolutely ruthless attitude. Cold, absolutely objective. He has written this person off. No tears, no hysterics, no emotion. He has dismissed him. He has turned the faucet off. I don't believe I was directed to do that, I believe I came with it. This is me. I would have chosen to do it that way. It came from my own life. If something like that had not happened in my own life I would not have been able to have done it. From the standpoint as an actor, that's my single favorite moment in all my films and, I think, the best single moment."

Ted spoke of his attempt at the transition from child actor to adult actor. "It was difficult for me. From my very early twenties I wanted to be the first male child actor to become a leading man. With all the highest respect, I do not count Mickey Rooney because he was a superb character actor. Freddie Bartholomew, Darryl Hickman, Butch Jenkins, and Dean Stockwell didn't do it. I wanted to be the first. But it didn't pan out that way. I didn't grow up in that way as a leading man and was not marketable in that sense.

"When I was 21, I was still playing Bud Anderson on *Father Knows Best*. I was the original Bud Anderson. Most people don't know that *Father Knows Best* was originally on the radio; I was on it with Robert Young from 1949 to 1954. I started when I was 16 and was still playing it when I was 21." When they were interviewing for the television series, Gene Rodney, the producer, asked Ted if he would want the role. "The only reason I bring this up is because I was 21, but he thought I looked young enough. I decided I did not want to do it. You know, we have the stupid things we have done and the stupid things we have not done. Well, this was one of the two or three most stupid things I have not done because not only would the salary have been very nice for five years, but the residuals would have also. But I didn't want to be typed. I didn't want to be a 21-year old playing a 15- or 16-year-old kid. I wanted to do other things."

In 1953 Ted had a nice role on a show called *My Favorite Husband* with Joan Caulfield and Barry Nelson. "Again, I was 20 and playing a 16 year old. After that I didn't work for 2½ years. I was still on *Father Knows Best* and finishing up at the University of Southern California, but I was looking for auditions and could not get cast in anything. From 1953 through 1955 there were a whole slew of juvenile delinquent films. There was one film after another and there were a lot of parts in those films, right? I couldn't get cast in those to save my soul. I remember going up before a casting director, and her saying, 'Ted, I would love to use you because you are such a fine actor, but you're just too aristocratic looking.' A few months later I went up for another one. 'God, Ted, I would love to use you, but you're just too patrician looking.' I may not have been young leading man material, but maybe better looking than what they wanted. My features were too delicate, too sensitive. But I don't think it's just that. I think it's attitude, the way I walked into the office, the gestures. I think that's more it."

Ted finally had two Matinee Theaters within six weeks, with excellent parts. "I'm doing okay, and then bang! The door shut again. Two years went by, and nothing."

Ted decided to go to New York. "Maybe a new face where they don't really know me. I auditioned for *A Sweet Bird of Youth* and found out I was up for one of the people who beat up Paul Newman. I was not right for that. I tried out for a production of *Henry IV* starring Burgess Meredith. I think they were looking for three people who were shorter than Meredith and never found them so the play never went on. I auditioned for *A Loss of Roses* by William Inge, for the 18-year-old sidekick of the lead. I was 25 but I looked young. I decided to be as young as I possibly could. I wore corduroy pants, a plaid short-sleeve opened shirt which I deliberately pulled down at the neck a bit like a young teenager would wear, and walked out on stage in what I thought was my jauntiest, jolliest, youngest bouncy step. I took about three steps out and I hear a voice say, 'Oh no, no, much too mature.' The voice came down to the footlights and it was William Inge. He said, 'I'm terribly sorry, I'm afraid you're too old.' The part was eventually played by Warren Beatty.

"So the transition was very, very difficult," Ted informed us. "In the mid–1950's I turned more and more to writing. I do not know what would have happened if it wasn't for the writing. It meant there was something else I could do, so maybe you don't need to feel chewed up. The writing truly, truly saved me. I've had a few things published. I have an idiotic notion that it is still possible to write plays in poetry and verse and be successful at it. I don't necessarily mean monetarily successful, but as a piece of a work of art itself. It may be a fool's errand to do it. Very few plays written in any kind of verse are ever successful.

"I have been on the edges of the theater most of my life. I act occasionally with Theater East. I always enjoy it when I'm up there, and people keep telling me that I should do a lot more. I would love to work as an actor, and I don't necessarily mean doing great parts. Give me a regular part and I will do it. But I have absolutely no eyes for auditions, and I know that's the way it's done. Either you do it or you don't."

Summing up his career as an actor, Ted said, "I am very grateful for it. I have had marvelous experiences, I met wonderful people. I enjoyed every moment of it. I think particularly with *A Tree Grows in Brooklyn* I was a part of something that more and more will be recognized as a classic film. I wouldn't have exchanged it for anything, but there are times that I would have liked to have enjoyed other things as a child. It can be a wonderful life, but I think for it to be good you need parents who have their own lives, who are not trying to live your successes or not trying to be successes through you. The parents who feel that their own lives are miserable and are failures can wind up doing an immense amount of damage to their kids. The famous stage mothers and so on. But stage mothers cannot begin to describe the damage that can be done to a child. I don't know about Bobby Driscoll. I sort of remember Bobby's mother and seem to recall her being quite nice, but I don't know what other things happened in his life. I have a feeling that because of the way in which some erred—the drugs, the marriages and constant divorces that some of them went through is rooted in a childhood that did not see that there were other things in life.

"My parents were highly philosophical. First, they had their own successful lives, and they were very artistic and had an intellectual bent. There was a world outside of the one that I was doing; not that the one I was doing was not of value—it was. But it wasn't the only thing. Just like *Life with Father* was not the only thing in theater. There were other plays, other venues, there were wider artistic and intellectual horizons and knowledge. So I had a very firm sense of identity as a child, or at least my parents did everything possible. There was something other than making money, there was something other than being a star, something other then the very success that you have. That there were values greater than that was always present. I was intellectually taught that, but mostly by example. It was all around me. When you are raised in a house with 25,000 books you know there are many worlds out there. So I think I had a very strong sense of higher values than are normally taught. It may have affected me in more subtle ways, but it would have been inconceivable for me to become an alcoholic and even more so to have ever gone into drugs. It's just impossible for me to have gone that way. The foundation was too strong. I think a lot of child actors don't have that. When the childhood ends, the acting ends, and so they are very much adrift. They don't know who they are and they have no sense of identity.

"I wouldn't give up that experience with Cary Grant for anything. And it's not simply a professional one, but because what I partly learned from him was a professional giving that goes beyond the profession, becomes the person, and perhaps even somehow becomes an act of givingness for the sake of something greater than either one of you. And professionally that is what I learned from him. And that example has never been lost to me."

George Ernest

George's father, Ernst Hjorth, brought his wife and oldest child to America from Norway and settled on the East Coast where he worked as a chef. The remainder of his children were born in America. The youngest, named George, was born on November 20, 1921, in Pittsfield, Massachusetts.

"My father decided he would rather live in California because the weather was better. We moved into Hollywood where he opened a restaurant on Las Palmas, just south of Hollywood Boulevard. We were right around the corner from the Egyptian Theater. Sid Grauman, who owned it as well as the Chinese Theater, used to come by the restaurant all the time. I was a little kid about three years old. He saw me and commented to my dad, 'He's a cute little kid. Why don't you register him with Central Casting?' In those days to get into pictures you registered with Central Casting. You put down your height, weight, color of eyes, age, and if you could sing or dance, and when they needed someone they'd go through this file and call the kids out. My mother registered me and we started being called. I got little bit parts at first, and it went from there. I loved it."

When a part for a child came through Central Casting, they might say they needed someone about seven years old, with blond hair and not fat. "They would call in 20 or 30 kids, and say, 'I'll try you, and you and you. The rest of you kids go home.' We then would have a little screen test and from that they would select the guy for the part. Later when you had an agent it was nice because you went in for an interview and they knew who you were and didn't have to ask if you had acted before. They would just say, 'Here's the scene; do it for us.' So you do the scene, they'd said thanks, and out the door you'd go. Maybe you'd hear and maybe you wouldn't. It never worried me if I got the part or not because my family

George Ernest is taking flight instructions from Randolph Scott in the 1939 film, *20,000 Men a Year* (Fox).

was very supportive. If I didn't get a part it was 'so what?' So I had no problem with that at all."

The first time George received screen credit, the studios complained about the spelling of his name. "They said no one would be able to remember Hjorth and told us to change it to something else. My mother said, 'Why not make it your father's first name—Ernst?' So they did that. However, when it came up out on my screen credit it was spelled Ernest. They added an e in there so it was spelled wrong, but they said leave it alone. That's how I got the name George Ernest."

One of the features that George appeared in was Universal's *The Mystery of Edwin Drood*. Reminiscing on working in this film, George stated, "I had a bit part in it, but I remember that because my job in the picture was to throw rocks at this drunk every night." But what George remembers most of all is working on the Jones Family movies at 20th Century–Fox. There were 17 features of this film series, the first being *Every Saturday Night* in 1936, and the final one *On Their Own* in 1940. Asked if there was much competition for his role of the son, Roger Jones, George replied, "I have no idea. As usual they called a bunch of kids. They interviewed us, took screen tests, and picked me.

"I enjoyed the series one hundred percent. I liked the people, I liked the directors we had, I liked the writers. While I was at 20th Century-Fox—I was there for four years—I didn't go to public school. I went to the studio school for three or four hours a day, and you would get concentrated tutoring. It was great and I enjoyed it. One day Mrs. Horn, our tutor, said to me, 'Here is a book that Shirley Temple needs, would you take it over to her mother?' Shirley had a private tutor all by herself. So I took it over there and said, 'My name is George Ernest and Mrs. Horn asked me if I'd bring this book.' Shirley said, 'Thank you George, I appreciate it.' That was it. About six months later I saw Shirley and she said, 'Hi George.' Now there's a remarkable memory to me. She had only met me for an instant and she remembered me. She had a remarkable memory from the standpoint of memorizing her lines too. She would memorize eight pages of dialogue in about ten minutes, just like that."

Memorization of dialogue came easy to George, too. "It wasn't difficult because it was normal conversation. It wasn't quoting Socrates or anything like that. It was just what you would normally say. The thing you want to do is be very informal about it, not speak as though they were lines. My parents would help me, and usually I would memorize them the night before. Then I would learn to forget those lines completely. If they wanted to shoot something over again three days later I'd have to memorize the lines again. I wouldn't remember them because you say the lines and then you go on to the next scene."

George was fond of his fellow cast members in the Jones Family features, saying "I loved Spring Byington, who played my mother, and Florence Roberts (who had the role of Granny Jones) was a real nice lady. Jed Prouty, who played the father, was a super nice guy. Jed used to say, 'P.P.P.P.,' and that meant 'Poor Prouty powder puff.' That was when he needed to be made up. I never had a make-up man, I put it on myself. Not much at all. It only took me about five minutes to put mine on in the morning and be ready for work."

George explained that the Jones Family series of films were made to be shown as the second feature at the movie theaters. "We were never the first film on the bill and it went over very well. Then MGM got the idea and made their series with Mickey Rooney and Judy Garland and that was much more successful than ours. They had bigger stars. Our people, Spring Byington and Jed Prouty, were both from the New York stage. I never wanted to become a star, I just enjoyed working. It was just whatever you want me to do, I'll do it. I never did anything other than plain old acting."

George shared an experience that he had while working at 20th Century-Fox. "I remember sneaking onto a sound stage one time because I knew that Fred Astaire was rehearsing. He had a firm thing about nobody watching him rehearse. I knew a guy on the set there and he let me sneak in and I watched Astaire rehearse. He would do a tap dance and was wonderful, but he wasn't satisfied, so he'd do it over and over again. I couldn't see any difference between one time and the next, but he didn't like it and did it again and again. It just amazed me. The guy was remarkable. I never met him but he was a real professional."

The only time George did not have to interview for a part was when he was hired to do the Higgins Family series at Republic. "That was fun too. It was Republic's answer to the Jones Family, but it wasn't anywhere near as successful. Roscoe Karnes was the father and Ruth Donnelly the mother. They did them very fast. They made two films in six days. We would shoot some from one film and then from the other. We worked long hours."

Although watching his films was not a prime interest for George, he did enjoy going to premieres. "I would kind of laugh to myself because all these people would ooh and ahh about movie stars. Well, the stars are people just like anybody else. One time 20th Century wanted me to show up with a girlfriend. I said, 'I know a lot of gals and had fun, but didn't really have a girlfriend.' So they said they had a girl who wanted to go to the premiere with me. They sent a studio car and picked her up and then picked me up, and that's when I met her. A nice girl. We went to the premiere together and the paper came out saying that George Ernest was running around with such and such. What really happened was that after the premiere the car picked us up and took her home and then I went home and that was the last of it. I never saw her again," George laughed. "There was nothing there, but the studio wrote it up like there was a big love affair going on, which I got a big kick out of because it wasn't true."

George doesn't have a favorite film, explaining that "I enjoyed all of it. I don't think I ever worked on a film where I didn't enjoy doing it. I loved the people without exception in all of the pictures I worked in. I never had any problems and I liked doing the work. I loved Gary Cooper. He was my favorite. He was really a nice guy. To show how nice he was, I was in a picture with him, *The Plainsman*. There was a scene where Gary Cooper was going to go off on a boat and he met this kid, and I was the kid. We had a couple of scenes before he gets off the boat, and as he leaves and is saying goodbye to me I was waving my hat and he gives me a present—he throws this knife at me and it lands between my hat and my fingers. I knew who Gary Cooper was, *everybody* knew who Gary Cooper was. He came over to me and said, 'My name's Gary Cooper, would you mind if we rehearsed our lines?' I thought how nice can you be. I said,

George with his friends Jackie Cooper and Sidney Miller at an orphanage in the 1935 Warner Bros. release, *Dinky*.

'Sure Mr. Cooper.' He said, 'No, I'm Gary.' Another actor I liked very well was Duke Wayne. He was real down to earth, like Cooper."

Reflecting on some of the directors that he worked with, George stated that "When I was a kid Mr. McGowan was director of the *Our Gang* comedies. I was about nine years old and was in six or seven of them. He impressed me because if you had a crying scene he could take you aside and talk to you. If I had to cry I couldn't just cry. He knew I had to have a reason. He was a great psychiatrist and would say, 'Well George, think about what would happen if your dog died.' He'd get me so sad and make it easy to cry. And if you missed your lines it didn't bother him a bit, he'd just say 'Don't worry about it, we'll get around it.'

"There were a lot of directors I enjoyed. Archie Mayo had a great sense of humor. I worked with him in *Four Sons*. I also learned a lot about photography on that one because James Wong Howe was the photographer—A five-or-six-time Academy Award winner. I watched when he would light the sets because I was very interested in that. I asked him one day, 'Would you mind if I lit a set?' and he answered, 'If the electricians don't mind, I don't mind.' So when they went to lunch he asked them. They said they didn't care, and afterwards I was so pleased because Howe only adjusted one light."

George enjoyed working in *Destry Rides Again* because he was able to ride a horse. "The director didn't like my riding because he was afraid I'd get thrown off. I loved riding, I really did. I don't know where I learned to ride, but I never had any problems staying on a horse. I was a fairly good rider. I enjoyed horses; I enjoy all animals."

Besides *The Plainsman* and *Destry Rides Again,* George worked in feature roles in several other westerns, including *The Deadline* with Buck Jones, *Song of the Saddle* with Dick Foran, and with Gene Autry in *Stardust on the Sage.* "With westerns everything was much more casual than it was on a studio set. It was outside and with horses, much more of a relaxed atmosphere. In contrast, when you are playing a serious picture like the one I did with Lionel Barrymore [*Looking Forward*] it is very tense and you are under pressure to make sure you are exact."

Humorous incidents abound while filming on a movie set, and George shared an example with us. "Millions of things happen. That opens a whole book. We were doing a scene in one of the Jones Family pictures where this comedienne is coming down the stairs and she accidentally falls and rolls all the way down and over her luggage. The director said, 'Hey, that's a pretty good gag,' and then they had her do it for real. It was hilarious to see her do that and not get hurt. She was so athletic, but you wouldn't know it to look at her," he smiled.

"There's scenes you would do when people messed up their lines and we'd get to laughing about it," George continued. "Once you're laughing about something and the person goes to say the line again, you start thinking about how they messed up the first time and you start laughing even though they don't mess up now, but *you* mess up. Pretty soon the director says, 'Let's take an hour off and go to lunch and come back and do the scene later.' By then everybody got over it. We had a lot of stuff like that go on."

George did a Christmas play for radio with the legendary John Barrymore. "He was Scrooge and I played five parts including Tiny Tim. We were standing on the stage in this empty theater and they were recording us. I was standing at my microphone and got into maybe the first half-minute of it when Barrymore said, 'Hey, cut it off!' He didn't like my microphone closer to the audience than he was, and there was no audience there! They made me move my microphone back about three feet so I was behind him. We started over again and it was okay. I thought that was kind of funny. I liked radio, but it was not as much fun as working in films. I enjoyed films a lot more because it took longer and you had more contact with the people. In radio you memorize your lines and stand there with the script in front of you and look at it."

George has no unpleasant memories of working in films as a child, and being a child actor did not interfere with his having a normal childhood. "I'm kind of an optimist. I remember the happy things and the pleasant people. So unless it was really horrendous it doesn't stay with me. I really don't remember those unfortunate things that might have happened. I had a fine childhood and had a lot of friends and enjoyed going out to the beach. I loved all sports. I was never a football or basketball player per se, but I loved playing all those sports. I loved to swim and dive. I also enjoyed photography as a hobby. On the set of *The Four Sons* I admired Archie Mayo. I told him I'd like to get a picture of him. He said 'Sure. Why don't you take a picture of me milking a cow.' There was a cow on the set and I didn't know that he knew how to milk one. I got my camera and just as I took the picture he squirted the milk right at me. So I have a photograph of Archie Mayo milking a cow with squirt coming right at the camera," George laughed.

George's career in pictures came to an end with the advent of World War II. "I was in the OSS (Office of Strategic Services). For 50 years I was sworn to secrecy; I couldn't talk to anybody about it. I was a photographer. I made nine jumps behind the lines during the war into France and also Germany to photograph bridges, rivers, dams. On most of these assignments I knew what I was doing. But on June 3rd, 1944, all I knew was where I was to drop and that the French underground would pick me up and take me to the place I was supposed to go and tell me what to photograph. They flew me in, the French underground picked me up and hid me, and then we got word that whatever was to happen was being delayed one day. Then they took me to a place with bushes down by the beach on the 6th and said, 'Hide here.' It was two or three in the morning and cold as hell. I heard this noise and could tell there were ships out there but I couldn't tell what they were doing. Well, it turned out they were mine sweepers clearing the area for the invasion. When it started to get light I could see what I thought were little islands. Then suddenly I realized that those were not islands, but ships. Hundreds and hundreds of ships. Then it dawned on me that this was D-Day. I photographed the troops coming in and getting shot at. The Germans were behind me on a bluff shooting on the troops. My instructions were that when I got done photographing from shore I was to board one of the landing crafts, either the *Cory* or *Hobson*, which I did. Then I photographed from there to the shore. I watched our airplanes flying overhead dropping bombs like you wouldn't believe. The main thing I remember is the noise. Oh my God, it was just horrendous. The concussion of sound on shore and aboard ship was really mind-boggling. Our planes would fly overhead and you could see the bombs landing on shore where the Germans were, almost like a piano being played; explosions going off back and forth. It was tremendous. When the ship I was on was down to about ten percent of their ammunition, they said, 'Okay, we're going back to England.' When I got back to London I turned the film in and that was it. I was 22 years old."

After returning home from the war George tried to decide what he wanted to do with his life. "Before I went away, Bill Michaeljohn was my agent, and during the war he became an executive at Paramount. I went over to see Bill and asked him what he thought about me going back into pictures. He said, 'There's a thing coming along called television, but don't expect to go back into pictures. If you're willing to starve to death for about five years I think you'll do real well in television.' I thought about it and decided no, I won't go back into films, I'll go back to school. So I went to UCLA and never did go back to the business. I never regretted it. I mean I liked pictures when I could do it, but I'm happy with what I did."

George took Business at UCLA. After graduation, he opened a camera shop in Studio City. He later sold that and was offered a job in Texas where we worked for about nine years. "Then I came back to California and went to work with McDonnell Douglas Aircraft for about 25 years, then retired from there."

George summed up his feelings on his work as a child actor. "I loved it. Even today I have people come up to me and ask, 'What do you do to get into pictures?' I recommend they don't try it because even when I was working in pictures about 95 percent of the people earned less than $5,000 a year. When you work you make pretty good money, but you didn't work very much. The best deal is to get under contract, and that's the luck I had. If my sons wanted to go into pictures I'd suggest they don't do it. I think it is much better, and a lot safer, to go into business in a big company, and work there. Sure, you don't make millions of dollars, but there are damn few people in the motion picture business who make that much. I was offered stardom at one time. I had a good friend by the name of Emmett Vogan, an old time character actor who made a good living in pictures for 30 years. He told me, 'Don't star, because when you do there is only one way to go and that's down.' So when I was offered a starring role my mother said she would leave it up to me if I wanted to make the picture. I decided not to do it. I didn't want to star. That may sound dumb, but I never regretted it. It was nice of them to offer it to me, but I didn't have the talent of Jane Withers. When you are in pictures you have no retirement and when it's over, it's over. You go to work for a big company, when it's over it isn't over. I worked for Douglas for 25 years and have a nice retirement from them, so I have no financial worries. I don't live in a big fancy house. I don't want to live in a big fancy house and neither does my wife. We're happy with what we do. That's all there is to it."

Richard Eyer

Richard Eyer was born May 6, 1945, in Santa Monica, California. "My mother was responsible for getting me into the motion picture business," Richard began. "She signed me up for a contest at the Hollywood Bowl when I was six years old called a personality contest. Hundreds of kids showed up at this event. I think I won first place. I had curly hair and freckles—the look that they thought was real cute. I believe it was from that exposure that other things happened, like little commercial offers."

Richard's first film role was as Bobby Peterson in the 1953–54 season of the television series, *My Friend Irma* with Marie Wilson. "That was live television. If you made a mistake everybody saw it. After that I did lots of stuff." Many actors were intimidated by live television, but Richard informed us, "It wasn't at all [intimidating] for an eight year old; I didn't know any better. I remember one time when I was about that age that I did blow it. It was a commercial I was doing for Chrysler. I couldn't think of what I was supposed to say and a lady—she was a famous singer—sort of pulled me through it. Normally, though, I worked pretty professionally and didn't make any mistakes."

Richard worked opposite such legendary stars of Hollywood as Humphrey Bogart, Gary Cooper and Fredric March. When asked if he had any reflections on working with them Richard replied, "I don't have a whole lot of specific memories because I was pretty young. In general I just remember all of them being gracious, fun people to work with. I remember I was in a scene with Bogart in *Desperate Hours* and he rescued me, because there was an instant where one of the arcs exploded and the hot glass from the light shot across the set. He grabbed me, threw me on the floor and covered me. He was a great guy."

William Wyler, the director of *Desperate Hours*, liked Richard's work, and from there chose him to play Little Jess Birdwell in his production of *Friendly Persuasion*. "I don't know if they had even interviewed for the part because he wanted me for it. It was quite a compliment to me. I was flattered because many years later William Wyler was having a birthday party, his 70th or 80th, and invited me. It was a gala event. Bette Davis and Barbra Streisand were there. When I arrived he left everybody and came over and said, 'Dickey.' He remembered me. He was just a very gracious man."

Richard Eyer

Friendly Persuasion was the longest Richard worked on a motion picture. "It was monumental for its day. William Wyler was known as being a perfectionist. I think they initially lost money on the film because he just went so long on it and way over budget. I think we filmed for three months, which in those days was outrageous. Most of it was on location out in the valley at the Roland V. Lee Ranch in Conejo, which in 1955 was super rural. The film's setting was supposed to be in Indiana, and it looked like Indiana. It was green and hilly, and there was a lake. I got to go fishing, so that was fun. I think that's my favorite piece of work. I can look at that film today and be proud of it."

Another prominent character in the film was Samantha the Goose. "Wyler's idea was to train it so that it would bite me. About two weeks prior to the beginning of the production there was a goose wrangler who brought the goose out and tried to train it to bite me where I'd have leather sewn on the inside of the seat of my pants as protection. We tried to train the goose by my bending over holding lettuce through my legs, but it didn't work. I don't think a goose learns much, and if it did learn anything it wasn't cooperating when they finally got to those scenes in the movie. Thus many of the scenes were done with gimmicks. In the opening scene I'm leaning over the well and the goose looks around the corner and sees my butt and takes off. Well, they had a wire attached to the seat of my pants and then extended it all the way around the other corner of the set, maybe 75 feet. The goose was on a pulley and the wrangler gave it a little jolt. I don't know if the SPCA would allow that today, but they goosed the goose and it shoots down the pulley and winds up on my butt. They had to resort to things like that because the goose was not Lassie."

Richard spoke of William Wyler with admiration. "He treated me beautifully. There was a scene in *Friendly Persuasion* where I make a face at the goose. A week or so before that scene was going to be done he said, 'Dickey, can you make a funny face that will make me laugh?' I made a few faces and he didn't laugh. He said, 'You work on it. If you can make one that will make me laugh when you come back I'll give you a dollar.'

Richard facing his nemesis, Samantha the Goose, in the William Wyler film classic about a Quaker family during the Civil War titled *Friendly Persuasion* (Allied Artists, 1956).

So I worked on that and came up with that face that's in the movie. He laughed and gave me a dollar. In the movie it does get laughs."

Richard worked with Robby the Robot in *The Invisible Boy*. "I thought it was pretty neat to get to work with that robot. Any kid would think that was really cool. In fact, the two or three film festivals I've been to I've had many men about my age tell me how envious they were of me because I got to do what they wanted to do. They'd say, 'God, I wish I could have been playing with Robby the Robot or have done that genie thing [*Seventh Voyage of Sinbad*]. You got to do my fantasy.' The robot used to operate under two different modes. One was with a battery pack (it needed power to turn the dials) so if there was a long shot the camera wouldn't see a power cable going to it. If the camera angles were such that the power cable couldn't be seen they would plug it in, but they needed somebody to feed the cable. What stands out in my mind was a couple of times when the man who was feeding the cable wasn't paying attention and it would get hung up somewhere and the robot would fall and smash face down. The man inside it obviously got his bell rung, and when they got him out he'd come out swearing and they'd rush me off the set so I didn't hear the language."

Richard shared a humorous incident that occurred while working on *The Invisible Boy*. "There was a scene where the police and state authorities are converging on this residence. They wanted to make sure they got it from a couple of angles and only had to do it once because this take was so difficult to orchestrate, so they filmed it with several cameras at the same time. When it got time to do the shot, my brother and I were playing baseball behind the house they were all driving up to. As all the cars come up to the house one of us hits the ball over the roof onto the lawn and it rolled through the scene while they were filming. It ruined the shot so they had to do it all over. They really couldn't get too mad at us because it was an accident. We didn't know what was going on in the front yard, but it was kind of funny. In fact Scott Dunlap, the producer of that show, must not have had any hard feelings about that episode because he gave me an autographed book from Babe Ruth that he had obtained. He said, 'Dickey, I know you're such a baseball fan I want you to have this.' It's one of my treasures to this day."

Richard reflected on *The Seventh Voyage of Sinbad*. "I felt a little rooked because the studio decided to try to cut some costs and so I didn't get to go to Spain where the film was done. If they had sent me, they would have had to send a tutor as well as my mother. So as a result I didn't get to work as much in the film as it looks. Much of it was filmed with a double on location. In fact, the last scene in the film is over the shoulder of the genie. Kerwin Matthews and Katherine Grant are speaking to the genie and it's not me. It's the Spanish double. When they were all through filming they came back to the studio and did my stuff in less than three weeks."

Richard also worked in westerns. Two features were *Canyon River* starring George Montgomery and *Fort Dobbs* with Clint Walker. "I have strongest memories of *Fort Dobbs* because of the location. We filmed that near a lake at Kanab, Utah, and I remember catching fish in that lake. I also remember Clint Walker pumping iron in between the scenes. He didn't have his weights with him but he would go over and get light standards from the lighting crew and use them as bar bells. He was a bodybuilder. I thought that was kind of odd, but I was impressed by it. And he was a good guy."

Richard mentioned that he had a difficult time on *Johnny Rocco*. "That was hard for me because I had to stutter. The premise of the movie is that I witnessed this gang-style murder, and I'm so horrified by it that it causes me this emotional distress that's manifested by a stutter. So I had to stutter and it was difficult to pull it off and make it seem believable."

Richard mentioned that school was his least favorite part of working as a child actor. "It required being with the tutor three hours every day, and usually I was the only kid in my class. It wasn't really much fun, and it meant me being away from my regular school. I liked my regular school so never looked forward to going to school on the set at the studio. Most of my early years I went to private schools because they were more flexible in working with someone who was going to be absent most of the year. My regular school would write me assignments and give me the books so I could stay with the normal curriculum of the other kids. Anytime that I was in between shows I went back to my classroom."

When not working, Richard enjoyed sports. "I was a baseball nut. Any free time I had I was playing baseball. I had a younger brother Bob who used to play with me. He later became a professional baseball player and played in the Chicago Cubs organization."

In addition to his feature film work, Richard remained busy appearing on numerous television shows, many of which were westerns. His credit list includes *The Roy Rogers Show*, *Wagon Train*, *Rawhide*, *Gunsmoke*, *Wanted Dead or Alive* and *Lassie*. "I was also on a series called *Stagecoach West* with Bob Bray. It kept me busy and was usually always fun. I think we did 39 episodes, and it was a very positive experience. When they hired me it was sort of a transitional point in my growing up because when we did the pilot I was 13 and quite young for my age; a real little kid. The pilot sold, and when we started production eight months had elapsed and all of a sudden I was into puberty and adolescence. I think the producer thought to himself, 'Wait a minute, where's the little kid I thought I hired.' But I think it was fine for the role and when I look at it now I'm impressed. It was a pretty darn good western."

The series was a Four Star Production, and most of it was shot at the studio. "There were just a couple of times that we went on locations. We went to Arizona, to a place called Apache Junction where they used to make a lot of westerns, and filmed several weeks there. We would film lots and lots of stock shots of the stagecoach running and then they'd intersperse those throughout the series."

Richard enjoyed the westerns, saying "It was cool for this city kid to do these westerns and I always got to ride horses, so that was fun. I do remember there were times on some of the westerns where people got hurt. That was not uncommon, but they were always very protective of me. Even on *Stagecoach West* when I was 14 many of those shots of me riding in the stagecoach are with a double. The double, most of my time growing up, was a midget named Billy Curtis. He was my stand-in and double on *Friendly Persuasion* and on many of the shows. As I grew, Billy would have to wear little lifts in his shoes so he would still be as tall as me. There was a great photograph where we were both dressed up as Little Jess. We both have the little Quaker uniform and black hat on and are standing back to back, exactly the same height, except Billy's got a big cigar sticking out of his mouth," he laughed.

Asked if he thought his career as a child actor ever got in the way of being a normal kid, he answered, "Well, it did get in my way in terms of regular school. Especially sports. I was always trying to be on the high school baseball team; we'd have a game and I'd have to go on an interview. I really resented that. But there weren't that many of those conflicts, and other than that it was fine. I did start at such an early age that I really didn't think of it as unusual. I just started working and didn't feel it a big deal. Now, in retrospect, I look at it and think it was a very positive experience. I'm glad I did it: no regrets."

We asked Richard why he stopped working as an actor. "When I did *Stagecoach West* I was 14 and my agent died that year. Milt Rossner was very instrumental in my career up to that point. One thing that I do think about is had Milt not died perhaps my career might have gone differently. When he died I was under contract for a year, so I was sort of handed over to another agency and they didn't have to do anything for me that year, and then when I did come out of the contract I was just not a priority among their clients. So I started working less and less and didn't do many things after about 15. I just sort of outgrew it. I was not really aggressively seeking parts and was changing to a young adult. In fact, I started college and sort of gave my agents the perception that I wasn't really interested. Then when I was interested I went back and asked, 'Hey, can you get me a job?' and there weren't any. But it was no rejection, no bad break-up. The last thing I did was when I was 21. It was an episode of *Combat* in which the Nazis killed me. I did a very convincing dying scene and that was it. I guess that I did it so believably everybody assumed, 'Well he's dead.'"

Richard decided to work in the education field. "First I came to the Mammoth Lakes area. I was skiing and being part of that lifestyle. I really enjoyed it. I became very enamored with the small town life style so I looked around for ways to occupy myself in this area, and teaching attracted me. At about the age of 30 I went back to school and got my teaching credential and I've been teaching since then. I've taught all grades, but I'm teaching fourth grade right now. I enjoy it, but I enjoy my free time also. Especially fishing, hiking and all the things that are around here. I'm almost looking forward to backing off on the teaching pretty soon so I can make more trips to Mexico and catch dorado and things like that."

Looking over his career as a child actor, Richard said, "In my case it was a positive experience that I could look back at now and think there's no regrets. I'm glad I did it. It was lots of fun most of the time and it opened many doors. As a kid I enjoyed traveling. I have many memories of going to New York to do promotional things or riding in the Macy's Thanksgiving parade as the genie. I got to go to Yankee Stadium to a World Series game. Many of those things most kids didn't get to do, and so I look at it and say I was lucky."

Edith Fellows

Edith Fellows was born in Boston, Massachusetts, in May 1923. Her mother had disappeared when Edith was a couple of months old and her father's mother, Elizabeth Lamb Fellows, moved in to help raise her. "When I was about a year old my father got a job offer in North Carolina, so we moved there. I had a bad problem with my feet. I was so pigeon-toed that I kept falling over myself. My grandmother took me to an orthopedics man who suggested that she get me some dancing lessons. Because I was so young, he felt that those positions of turning out the feet would really help."

Edith started dancing lessons at Henderson's School of the Dance in Charlotte. "I used to sing and recite, so they put me on a one-woman show when I was only 3½ years old. After the show a talent scout introduced himself to my grandmother. 'You know, Hal Roach is always looking for talent like Edith. I can open doors for you and pave the way if you come out to Hollywood. You give me $50 and I'll go on ahead and use it for publicity. Here's my card.'

"Daddy wasn't to go. I was standing on the observation platform at the back of of the train looking for my daddy and remember crying so much because he hadn't come. The train started to slowly pull out. I was looking down the track and I could see a small figure on a white horse. It was my father. The train was picking up speed as well as it could in those days and he rode alongside. I leaned over and got to kiss him, and then he faded as we faded away."

Edith and her grandmother arrived in Hollywood with only a small amount of money. Her grandmother thought that Hal Roach was going to sign Edith up right away. They were looking for the address on the card which the man had given them and asked someone for directions.

Edith Fellows

"That's just down the street, but there's no building there, just an empty lot." "So Grandma and I had been taken," Edith said. "Grandma knew somebody from her younger days who lived out here and we were able to stay with them. She got herself some day work cleaning people's houses and we were able to rent our own little apartment for $25 a month. There was one woman that Grandma cleaned house for who didn't want me coming because she had a lot of bricky-bracky stuff and didn't trust me being there. So I was left with a neighbor lady that had a little boy who happened to work as an extra in movies. One day he got a call to an interview at Hal Roach Studio. The boy's mother couldn't leave me alone so she had to drag me along. I must have been very bored and maybe danced or sang because I apparently made an impression. The little boy got the part. A day later he came down with either the measles or the chicken pox and was unable to go, so Hal Roach Studio called and said, 'Send the little girl.' I went and they changed the part. That was my first film. It was with Charlie Chase in 1927, called *Movie Night*. I played his daughter."

Edith did extra work in *Fra Diavolo* (*The Devil's Brother*), a period piece with Laurel and Hardy. "It was just a small scene, and they were adorable. Thelma Todd was in that film also. She had these gorgeous gowns and couldn't sit down so they had what was called a backboard, which was slightly tilted with arm rests; she'd lean against it to rest without disturbing the gown. It was a French street scene inside Hal Roach Studio and all over the top they had big sun arcs to light the set and make it look like daylight. They had a lot of tame doves flying around and one came onto the arm rest of the chair I was sitting on. I picked it up and was playing with it. Apparently my grandmother knew someone related to Thelma and they were talking. I could see them across the room. My grandmother said, 'That's my granddaughter,' so Thelma called me to come over. I picked up the little bird (I thought I would show it to her), and no sooner had I got up than the sun arc fell right where I had been sitting. Thelma Todd cried and hugged me. I'll never forget that she saved my life. Thelma had a restaurant down in Santa Monica when she died in 1935, and these mobsters tried to move in on her. They wanted her to have gambling and she wouldn't do it. I think that was the reason she was done in. I was going to be like Nancy Drew, the girl detective. I was going to get at the bottom of it. So my grandmother and I drove down to the restaurant. I was surprised that they hadn't closed it. We went in and had dinner. Upstairs was the office. I was going to go up there and start interrogating. I knocked on the door and this big burly guy opened it, and I said, 'Oh, I just came by to say that I'm sorry about Thelma Todd. Bye,' and I ran. He scared me to death," Edith laughed. "So, some big detective I was."

Edith worked in a couple of *Our Gang* comedies. "Bob McGowan directed all those. He was a wonderful director and wonderful with kids. I made friends with Spanky. In fact, I'd see George and he would say, 'Call me Spanky.' You would think he wouldn't want to be known as Spanky when he was 50 years old, but no, 'Call me Spanky.' I knew little Darla, and Joe Cobb. I did one *Our Gang* called *Shivering Shakespeare*. It takes place at school. Everyone is dressed in togas and gowns and we're doing Shakespeare. You can see Jackie Cooper in the background holding a spear. Edgar Kennedy was in it, playing Big Bug. He had an elephant's head or something and I looked right at the audience and screamed, 'Mama! The big bug! The big bug!'"

Edith's father was finally able to make a move to California. "He was a great rider. He did some horse stunt work in films. He was in a lot of the Gary Cooper pictures. Then he started an all girls polo team out in the valley. I must have been nine or ten when he decided it was time for me to ride. He put me on a horse and whacked it and off I went, holding on. So I learned the hard way, but I stayed on."

Edith reflected on working in *Mrs. Wiggs of the Cabbage Patch*. "It was interesting. W. C. Fields was quite a character. I don't think he hated children; let's say he just didn't care about them too much. ZaSu Pitts was in that and a wonderful actress named Pauline Lord. Norman Taurog, who is Jackie Cooper's uncle, directed it. We were at the old Paramount Ranch out past Calabasas in the heat, and it was murder. They had the whole place cordoned off to remind us all not to go outside the perimeter, because they said this was a dangerous time for rattlesnakes and we had to be very careful. They had a huge tent for our schoolroom and smaller tents for the dressing rooms. I was on my way to school when I heard, 'Ah, girl.' It was Mr. Fields. He was in his tent. 'Come here. Come here.' I had not talked to him, in fact we hardly had any scenes together, but I had seen him around and we'd say 'hello,' so I wasn't afraid to go into his tent. There was a cot there that he was sitting on and a chair and an end table. On the end table was a bottle that looked like it was full of water, and Dixie cups. He said, 'Little girl, I've been watching you and I think you're a very nice little girl. I don't care for the others, but you are very nice and special and I'm going to do you a favor. There are a lot of rattlesnakes around. You never know when one will come up, but I have something that I'll give you. It's a medicine. Drink some and their bite can't hurt you. Nothing will happen.' He poured the stuff into the cup and I took a swig of it and screamed. My mouth was on fire. I ran out. He had poured gin. The teacher went to him and really raised the riot act, and scared him. So that was my experiences with W. C."

In reference to what school was like for her as a child actress, Edith said, "I wasn't very interested in school and looking back it was the wrong attitude to have. But I kept thinking, 'Why do I need to study? I'm earning a living.' So I sort of played it by ear. I wasn't that great a student although I was good at spelling, but my math was terrible. I read well; I had to. The teachers finally said, 'Oh, forget it. Let her alone.' It was true I was earning a living but you don't know how long that living is going to go on for. That's the thing you don't know, but you never look that far ahead.

"A lot of the studios knew that when you're not under contract you had to go to regular school, so they would arrange interviews in the afternoon after school. I had long curls and my grandmother would put them up in rags. So I'd go to school in rags and the teachers were very upset about it. After I was kicked out of one school and then another, my grandmother heard of Hollywood Professional School which only goes from eight to noon, so I started going there. Judy Garland went there and so did Mickey Rooney when he was very young. In 1935 I got my contract with Columbia and went to school there. I had a wonderful teacher who was more my psychologist than anything else. I could talk to her and I had a lot to talk about because I wasn't happy at home. She was my Rock of Gibraltar; I mean she kept me from really going off the trolley. She certainly was my favorite teacher because she helped me through some rough times with Grandma. Her name was Lillian Barkley. Whenever anyone asked me where I went to college I would say, 'Columbia.'"

In 1934 Edith appeared with Richard Dix in RKO's *His Greatest Gamble*. "I adored that man. He asked for me to be in it because he remembered me having a small part in *Cimarron*. I didn't have an agent and when it was over he felt I should have representation. He was with one of the big agencies at that time, Byron MacArthur, who would never have thought of taking me on. I mean they would have taken on Jaws before they'd take me on; they never took kids. When Richard Dix, who at that time was the number-one-box-office draw, said, 'I want you to handle Edith,' they handled me."

Edith spoke of working on a film for Monogram called *Keeper of the Bees* with Neil Hamilton and Betty Furness. Hobart Bosworth played the keeper. "What a lovely gentleman. He played my grandfather. I had two pages of dialogue about showing Neil Hamilton how you worked with the bees; the hot iron, the honey, the whole step-by-step process. They used drones because they don't sting, so I was safe. But before they began filming they took me out to this farmer who had a beehive and let a bee sting me in the thumb so I would know what it was like in case I should get stung. That was really tempting fate. Luckily I wasn't allergic or I could have been a goner right then and there. I pretended to be a boy in the film and had to cut my hair. My grandmother cried at each curl that went. I was thrilled because I was so tired of rags in my hair and having to sleep on them.

"Then I had an audition at Columbia. There were 200 kids for the part of Annabel in *She Married Her Boss* which was starring Claudette Colbert. She was a dear lady. Melvyn Douglas played Annabel's father. The director was Gregory La Cava. When it was my turn, I walked into the office. Mr. La Cava was sitting, and standing there beside him was Benny Rubin, that wonderful comic. Benny leaned over to Gregory and said, 'This is your kid.' Gregory La Cava was the dearest man in the world. I was studying voice at the time. I had an operatic voice and did arias. They gave a wrap party after we closed down and I sang. Mr. La Cava was very impressed. He said, 'I had no idea that you could sing. Who's your teacher?' I said, 'I don't have one.' At that time he was dating Pert Kelton who was studying and taking voice lessons from Jane MacArthur. He said, 'You have to go to her teacher. I'll pay for the first six months.' So I studied and worked very hard. Finally, I got Columbia to listen to me. They put me in a film called *Little Miss Roughneck* with Leo Carrillo. In it I did *Caro nome* from *Rigoletto*, and another concert piece. I was so hurt by one review I got. The reviewer said, 'I heard studios going far with their voices, but they give that kid a phony dubbed in voice.' I looked at this and said, 'It's not. It's me! It's me!'

Edith appeared in *The Little Adventuress*, originally titled *Little Miss Thoroughbred*. "My character always felt that my horse could win a race. I called him the poor man's National Velvet. They trained him before the film and then they let me go out and work with him, so he got use to me. I really fell in love with him. We shot this at Santa Anita and it was great fun; I enjoyed it. I can always say that I rode at Santa Anita."

In 1939 and 1940 Columbia produced four *Five Little Peppers* films which starred Edith. "There were five little Peppers. Myself, a little tiny girl, and three brothers. We'd get in and out of mischief. In one of these films I'm going blind, but then I'm okay. In another one we're caught in a mine and we're saved. In yet another I sang *The Blue Danube*. The *Andy Hardy* series was going at that time and I think the boss thought it was time for another series, but it wasn't as good as *Andy*. A lot of people remembered the *Five Little Peppers* from reading the books while growing up. I played Polly Pepper. I enjoyed them and liked the kids on it. They had a wonderful director by the name of Charlie Barton. He loved the kids, we loved him, and it was terrific."

In 1940 Edith left Columbia and starred in *Her First Romance* (later rereleased as *The Right Man*). "I starred with a wonderful concert singer by the name of Wilbur Evans. We sang together. Julie Bishop and Alan Ladd were in it and Eddie Dmytryck directed it. He got into that trouble with the blacklisting. That idiot Joe McCarthy. They find ways to try to kill people. Not with a gun, but innuendoes and nastiness."

In 1942 Edith worked in two films with Gene Autry. They were titled *Heart of the Rio Grande* and *Stardust on the Sage*. "Gene was a lot of fun to work with. He was very different from what you see on the screen. He was a devil," Edith laughed. "He wanted to see how far he could go with his kind of humor. He didn't do it the first day; we had just met. The second day he figured, 'Well, maybe she's okay. Maybe she can take it.' The first thing he did was pour a cup of ice water down my boot. So I thought, 'Okay. That's all right.' I laughed and said, 'Very funny, Mr. Autry.' Then a day or so later it wasn't ice water that went down my boot, it was from Champion. I figured now I know where he's coming from and I'm going to dish it right back. On the set he had this huge beautiful rawhide make-up case. When you open it up it goes out in tiers and he had all these cold creams and make-up in it. So I got a pair of gloves, a little shovel and a little bag, and I went over to Champion and said, 'May I?' He snorted 'Okay,' and I put a little bit in the bag and managed to get it into his cold cream, his make-up. He loved that I came back at him!

"I was about 17 and I played a real snotty wealthy girl. Mr. Autry was running a dude ranch and we all came from a girl school. I didn't like

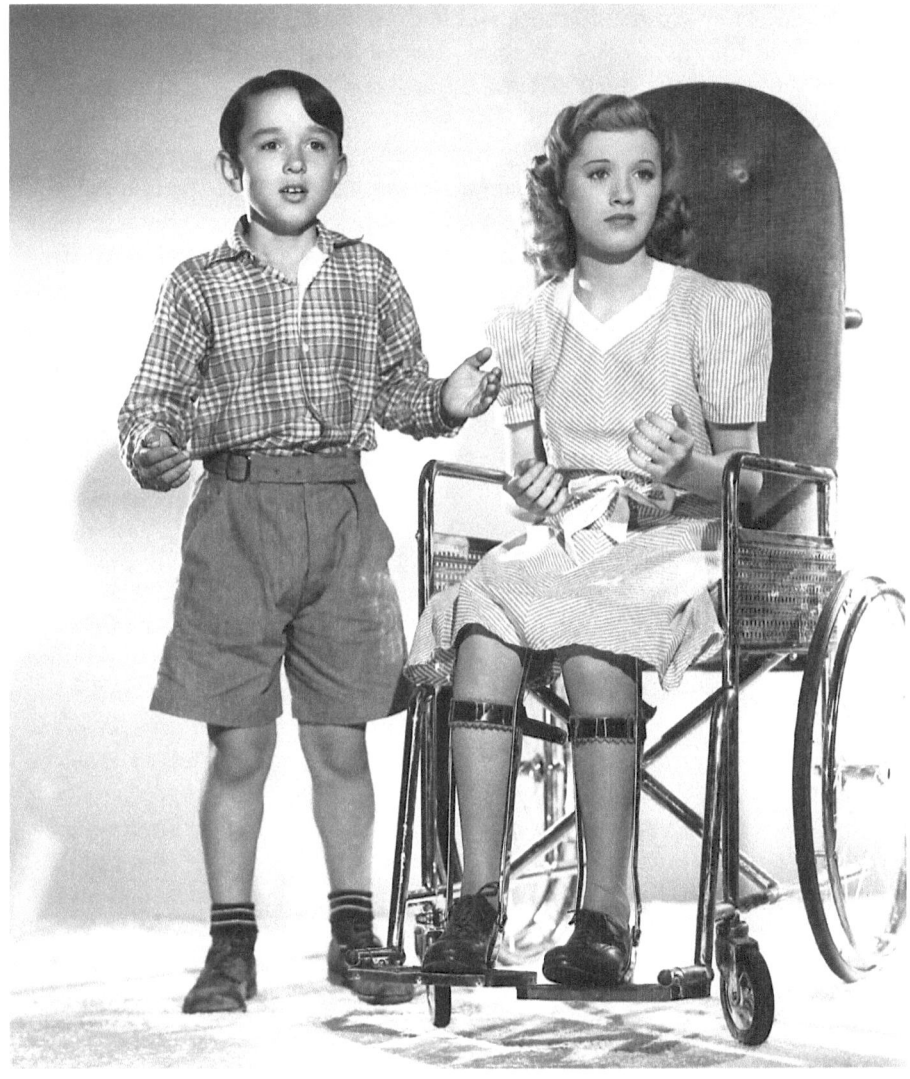

Edith and Billy Lee play brother and sister in an orphanage in *Nobody's Children* (Columbia, 1940). Lee turns down opportunities to be adopted because he wants his crippled sister, Edith, and himself to be adopted together.

the girls and I hated him. So I was being smarty and got up on this horse and he said, 'I wouldn't get on that horse.' I said, 'What do you know? Mind your business.' The horse starts bucking me and throws me off. To get a closeup of me falling into this scene and my reaction, they had us just off-camera on a two step. I was on top of it and was to fall to the ground. They got the dirt nice and loose so that it would be a soft fall. I was used to falls, I could do them. Just as the director was ready to say 'Action,' the make-up man turned me around with my back away from where I was to fall, and said, 'You're very shiny.' He was powdering my nose, and the hairdresser came; they were all in on it because Mr. Autry proceeded to put some of Champion's 'gold dust' in the dirt. So when I turned around and the director said 'Action,' I couldn't stop my fall when I saw what was coming. They all thought it was funny. It *was* funny. After all, it was Champion's."

Another western which she made in 1932 was *Law and Lawless* with Jack Hoxie. "I liked cowboys, but I would never go see cowboy films. They scared me to death. I could see *Dracula* or *Frankenstein*, but not cowboys. I cried when my grandmother wanted to take me to the movies and it was a cowboy film. I don't know what it was; maybe it was the guns. At least Dracula was pretty quiet about what he did," she laughed. "He didn't go around shooting everybody."

Edith mentioned that each year a group of actors would go to San Francisco and would perform for the union label show. She did so at the Fair in the late thirties. "I met Boris Karloff, Buck Jones, Eddie Quillan and just a whole bunch of wonderful people. It was my birthday and they knew it. They had a little luncheon for me at the Mark Hopkins, and Buck Jones brought me a corsage. Boris Karloff, who was such a sweet man, brought me a little Lancome perfume. It was the best birthday I can ever remember."

After doing the Gene Autry films, Edith told herself, "I'm not going to do any more westerns. There must be something else." Because she could sing, Edith did a lot of vaudeville, personal appearances, and nightclubs, and finally landed a job in a play on Broadway called *Janie*, which was closing and going on the road. "I auditioned for a wonderful producer named Brock Pemberton for the road company. They hadn't wrapped the set yet. It was still there, which makes it nice because most of the auditions you do in New York are just on a dark stage with one light. But the furniture was all there and that works for you when that happens. I read well and he came up to the edge of the stage and said, 'Janie, where have you been?' I went on the road with it and it was wonderful."

After *Janie* closed, Edith went back and did a lot of work in radio, night clubs, vaudeville and summer stock. "I did *Naughty Marietta, Rosalie, The Story of Robert Burns*, and I did live television—oh God! It was so scary. You can't make a mistake. You can, but they'd rather you wouldn't."

Edith spent almost 29 years working in New York. "I got married there and I had my baby there. I took over for Joan Roberts in the musical comedy *Marinka*. Then I did a show a couple of years later with a wonderful Yiddish comic named Menasha Skulnik. He was a very funny man and his timing was brilliant. I learned so much from watching him. He wasn't much taller than I was and we got along fine; we saw eye to eye. The show we were in was called *Uncle Willie*."

Edith mentioned that she preferred stage over film, saying, "You can feel an audience. There's a lot of love that comes over; and you can feel if they don't like you. In *Uncle Willie* I played an Irish woman who hated Menasha Skulnik, couldn't stand him. She was a bigot. A lot of times at the matinee they bussed in a lot of these little old Jewish folks from down in the east side who loved Skulnik. He had a following like you wouldn't believe. I'll never forget one matinee and I'm telling him off in the play, and this little old lady with a babushka on came running down the aisle, saying, 'Will you stop being mean to Uncle Willie! You bad! You bad!' I looked at Menasha and he just motioned for me not to worry about it. He told me afterwards, 'That means they love you. They hate you, they love you. You won them over because they hate you.' I said, 'Well, that's a new one.'" This was her last stage performance back east. Edith later went on tour with *The Hit Parade* to the Far East, to Japan and Korea, to entertain the troops.

Edith returned to Los Angeles in 1970 and appeared in a play that a friend wrote for her titled *Dreams Deferred*. "But for the most part I really didn't come back into the business because I had been out of it so long and I was kind of tired. It had changed a lot. It's like night and day from what it was even 15 years ago."

Amongst her hobbies Edith enjoys doing crosswords, a little painting and reading. "You know what I have? It's the most important thing, other than my family, in my life. Thirteen years ago I decided to get my last friends together and we formed a group of ladies called the Show Buddies. We meet once a month. I'm close to all of them. They're so loving. So many people have tried to see if we couldn't get a script written or a TV show or a movie about this group. I think a film could be saying to older people that this isn't the end, you don't have to quit, there are things to do."

Asked what she would say if a parent came to her asking for advice about getting their child into the business, she replied, "No. Keep them out. Take care of them, give them a good education, give them something that they can rely on. This business is too fickle. It's not a living in that sense. Half the parents, maybe more, piddle away the money and the kids wind up with nothing. You hear these stories all the time. Growing up in

England as a young girl, my grandmother had a lovely voice and wanted to act. She had a very strict English family and a wicked stepmother, so she had to submerge all that stuff. It was evil for a young girl to want to go on the stage in England in the 1800s. So when I came along I was the perfect vehicle to extend her dreams. I knew what she had gone through and I was happy I could buy her a house and that she could have some creature comforts and travel. What burns me up are the fathers. They give up their work and they retire and let the kid do it, and that's a bummer. That's why so many kids wind up as drunks, on dope, because they finally wake up and realize they have nothing and they don't have a second career. They hadn't been trained that well. Some are smart. Roddy McDowall and Elizabeth Taylor got through that age great. Not many made it. Not many could and they had nothing to fall back on."

We asked Edith if she felt that her career had any negative effects on her childhood in any way. "Oh, it left scars, but you can't let it interfere with your life. There are so many that live in the past and just think of the past. You have got to shut the door and go on or you won't grow. You'll stay stunted in an era that was lovely, but that's gone. The past is wonderful, but you have to keep it in its place. I love it when so many young people come up to me and say, 'Gee, I would have loved to live in the golden age of films.' It's nice to hear that young people appreciate it."

Summing up her feelings on her career, she said, "It did afford me wonderful opportunities to meet and work with different people. That was an education in itself. To travel and to have money to buy little creature comforts, a little car, a little house. Naturally, it wasn't all perfect; it would never be perfect. Growing up was a little hard only because out here Columbia didn't know what to do with me. I was at that awkward age and I was tiny. I wasn't a big girl; I didn't grow into a big wonderful woman, and I was the first child actress they ever had under contract. But going back East did a lot. That's where I really had a chance to grow up, because I was in the big sophisticated theater and in the big sophisticated New York and I met all these great people. And of course, getting married and having my daughter Kathy. She married David Lander who played Squiggy in *Laverne and Shirley*. That's my son-in-law and I love him. I have a darling, wonderful 15-year-old granddaughter and she's talented, and while I sit and watch her dance and sing, quietly I'm saying, 'No, no, no.' But you can't direct anyone's life. You mustn't, because you could smother them, overdo it, like I always felt my grandmother just pushed too hard. Neither can you deprive them of their own choice. It's a choice. I didn't have a choice. I don't know what I'd have been had the circumstances been different. I might have been a good waitress. Nothing better than a good waitress. But this is the hand that I was dealt, so be it. So whatever my granddaughter feels is right for her then she should do it. I would never tell her not to, but I can quietly say to myself, 'Oh, I hope she meets a nice man.' But if she does it we are all supportive, and she comes by it naturally: her mother was talented, Squiggy is talented, and her grandma wasn't too bad."

Billy Gray

Billy Gray was born January 13, 1938. "My mother was Beatrice Gray, an actress. When I was about six years old she took me to a play. I was running up and down the aisles and her agent who was there saw me and thought she could get me some interviews. Well, I started going on the interviews and phenomenally I got the part on almost every one I went to. I worked constantly as a bit player, and then when I was about 11 or 12 I started getting larger parts. I don't remember the names of all the movies I did bits in because I did the paper boy on the street or the kid next door. I would just have a line or two to say."

One of these early pictures was *Abbott and Costello Meet the Killer*. "I just had one cute scene where I was a little boy playing Indian and shot an arrow into a verandah next to Costello. I come up to him and say, 'Give me my arrow back!' Costello tried to get the arrow out but couldn't so I reached up, grabbed it, gave him a scowl and headed off."

The first important role for Billy was in *On Moonlight Bay* with Doris Day and Gordon MacRae. "That film was very successful so Warner Bros. quickly made a sequel, *By the Light of the Silvery Moon*. After *On Moonlight Bay* I started getting larger parts."

Shortly thereafter Billy worked in the science fiction classic, *The Day the Earth Stood Still*. "That is my all-time favorite. I remember Michael Rennie was very attentive to my mother. I guess he was a lady's man and was forever getting her coffee or arranging a seat for her." Why does he consider it his favorite film? "Mainly because the message was about the importance of dealing with society in a positive way and attempting to correct some very ill behavior on the part of human beings. It did it in a way that wasn't preachy, but it preached. It did lay down the law, but in an entertaining and thought-provoking way so the audience wasn't put

Billy Gray as he realizes Michael Rennie is the spaceman the authorities are seeking in *The Day the Earth Stood Still* **(20th Century–Fox, 1951).**

off by being told that they didn't have their act together. That was certainly the message, that we human beings still have a lot of evolving to do."

"I've seen the picture a number of times since then because Robert Wise [the director] is up in years and is being honored all the time. One of the things that is usually talked about is *The Day the Earth Stood Still* and they show the film. I had an occasion to go and do a symposium with him and producer Julian Blaustein afterwards. I'm really grateful that I had a chance to be involved in something that actually had some import beyond just the footholds. It still holds up amazingly well."

Billy mentioned that the film had an unintentional humorous side in one scene for later audiences. "There's a couple of little laughs in it. One is when Michael Rennie is taken to the hospital and as the doctors are talking about how he recovered from his wounds astonishingly well they are lighting up cigarettes, and the audience got a kick out of that."

The Winfield Family (Doris Day, Leon Ames, Rosemary DeCamp, and Billy) relaxing on their front porch in *On Moonlight Bay* (Warner Bros., 1951).

Hugh Marlowe costarred in the film as the boyfriend of Billy's mother in the picture. "Actually, he played Judas. People have analyzed the film to the point where they make it an analogy of the Christ myth. He is dating my mother in the show and felt that Rennie kind of usurped his place so he turned him in to the authorities when he found out who he was. He got his 30 pieces of silver for being the guy who turned in the spaceman."

Another actor in the film was Lock Martin who played Rennie's robot, Gork. "He was seven foot something, but very frail. He could only be in Gork's suit for ten or 15 minutes at a time before he just couldn't handle it. There were several different versions of the suit. From the front view they could let air in the back, and then they had a back view. I remember they had Patricia Neal on wires so he could pick her up."

Billy mentioned one particular scene in the film where Michael Rennie gave him some diamonds in return for cash. "I was kind of aware that I was getting the better part of the deal. I remember hanging onto those diamonds. I didn't give them all back to the propman. I kept them for a while. I wish I still had them. They were just glass costume jewelry, but it was pretty impressive. They were about the size of the tip of your finger."

Billy's first actual starring role was in *Talk About a Stranger* in 1952. "My dog was supposed to have gotten killed and the director wanted me to have a full-grown emotional response to it. Apparently I wasn't coming forth with what he had in mind. The way he described it was that he needed my stomach to heave and he was showing me how he wanted it. Well, the teacher on the set saw him doing this to my stomach and thought that he was being abusive. She made a big stink about it and took me off the set. We went back after and finished up the wrap, but it was a bit of a nightmare. It was a misinterpretation and I don't think the guy was hurting me."

Billy had one of the lead roles opposite Phil Carey and Dorothy Patrick in *The Outlaw Stallion*. "That damn horse was a real stallion. He was way more than I could handle. He ran away with me one time out at Iverson's Ranch, going under trees with low hanging branches. I held on to him, but I was just along for the ride." Billy also reflected on an earlier western he had worked on. "I did *Sierra Passage*, and the darn horse stepped on my foot while I was standing next to it and broke one of the bones. We had to finish shooting everything at that location before leaving, so I finished my closeup with my foot in a barrel of ice water to keep the swelling down before I went to the hospital to get it x-rayed."

When asked if he could think of any humorous incidents that occurred on the set while he was working as a child, Billy answered, "I was apparently a bit of a handful and I got nicknamed 'the Gremlin.' People were always being told, 'Nail him down' and keep me in one place because I would wander around all the time. I would be up in the catwalks somewhere, so 'Nail him down' got yelled out more than once," he smiled.

Billy is probably best remembered for his nine years as Bud Anderson on *Father Knows Best*. Asked if there had been much competition for the part, he said, "I think they interviewed most everybody that age in town. I went back for two or three more interviews and then they did a test scene with us around the kitchen table, and then I got the job. It was all new to me because I had only done an occasional television show before that and didn't have any idea of what I was getting into. I had no idea it was going to turn into such a big deal."

On the show, Robert Young played the father and Jane Wyatt the mother. The three children were Billy, Elinor Donahue and Lauren Chapin. Billy recalled his screen parents, saying "Robert Young was a real gentleman. He was the personification of a professional actor. He and his partner owned the show so he could have been a jerk if he wanted, but he always let his partner do the producing part of it and he just did the acting. He never gave the director or anybody else a bad time. You couldn't come up with a nicer person. He wasn't particularly warm, but he was cordial. You didn't have the feeling that you had a personal relationship with him; it was a working relationship. That was fine because I wasn't looking for a father and he wasn't looking to take over that position in my life either. Jane Wyatt was lovely. The only thing that we would get into occasionally would be discussions of religion. She was Catholic. I went to Catholic school early on but didn't have much time or patience for it. In fact, to get right down to it, I had downright hostility toward it. We would go round and round about that until we just decided that we agreed to disagree on that. We kept in touch over the years and she is really a gracious, lovely person."

Of all the directors that Billy has worked with, Peter Tewksbury, who directed *Father Knows Best*, was his all-time favorite. "He was really a hard worker and would prepare everything the night before or when he broke down the scripts earlier on. He would come in the morning and have all the moves and business written out, and we always had business to do on that show. He worked it all out—the props and blocking—and timed it with the various staging. We had to adjust a little bit here and there, but invariably he had it right on."

Billy received an Emmy nomination for his Bud Anderson role. "It was my third or fourth year in the show so I would have been about 18. I didn't really give it much thought. One of the things that was kind of peculiar was that their categories were all screwed up for the Emmys. I was up against Jose Jimenez and the little fellow who played on the *Tonight Show* with Jack Paar. These guys were out-and-out comedians and I was trying to be a serious actor. So here I am up against these guys for best performance in a comedic series. I didn't get it; one of those guys did."

Billy also continued working in such pictures as *The Seven Little Foys* and *Some Like It Hot* during the run of his television series. Other TV shows that he worked on during this period included *Peter Gunn*, *Cheyenne*, *The Deputy*, and *Alfred Hitchcock Presents*. Before *Father Knows Best*, Billy appeared in such early television shows as *Gene Autry* and *The Adventures of Superman*. The episode of *Superman* was one of three chosen to be edited together and released as a feature titled *Superman and the Jungle Girl*. When he was in his late twenties, Billy appeared as Hansel in a play titled *The Candyed House*, written by Jack Larson (the actor who played Jimmy Olsen on *Superman*). "He talked me into doing it. It was actually the Hansel and Gretel story written in heroic couplets. He did it in a little theater at the La Brea Tar Pits, on the museum grounds. Jim Bridges directed it and I'm sorry that I never got to work with Jim after that in any of the movies he did, like *China Syndrome*."

In comparing working on stage with working in film, Billy mentioned, "I didn't like theater very much. The repetition. I don't mind rehearsing and rehearsing and doing it enough times until we get it right, but then once you get it my whole background has been that you're on to the next scene. That isn't the way theater works. You do it all over and over again. The small amount of theater I did was probably because towards the end of a five or six week run I was really sorry that I had gotten involved. I would be x-ing out the days on the calendar." Billy's other theater credits were *Come Blow Your Horn, Enter Laughing, Look Homeward Angel* and *Oh Mistress Mine.*

Billy worked in live television on shows like *Matinee Theater*. Speaking of this he said, "That was a challenge. You rehearse and rehearse and you get it and do it right, and if you don't get it you don't get a second shot at it. That was a bit of a panic and a little more pressure than I really enjoy being under. Exciting, that's for sure."

Most actors at some time in their career face the inevitable dilemma of "going up," a term that is used to signify a sudden lapse of memory in regards to one's dialogue. Billy had this experience while filming an episode of *Father Knows Best*. "I went up once and it was really awful. Frequently you can't remember a line, but this one time I had to come in and read a big piece of dialogue, and apparently I hadn't really studied it enough the night before to have it. What I usually did was get most of it down and then let the rest of the learning take place in the rehearsing that we did. That didn't work that time for some reason and it's the only time I can remember that happening. I'd get about two lines into it and it was gone; I'd do it again, and it was gone. I tried it and tried it, literally sweating bullets. Perspiration was pouring off me because one of my nicknames was 'First Take Gray,' so this was horribly embarrassing. We finally just gave up on it and had to break the set and go do something else and come back and get it another time."

After the close of *Father Knows Best* Billy's career hit a low point. "I got into a bit of a problem with reputation. Shortly after the show I got busted for grass. I was in possession of some seeds and stems in a little baggy under the seat of my car and got a one to ten-year sentence. I did 45 days and then a probationary period after that. Apparently the better story was that I was a heroin addict. It made a much more 'poetic' story that Bud, the all-American boy, was a heroin addict than if he had just smoked some grass. At the time I was tired of playing that character anyway, so I wasn't really looking for more of the same. Yet the kind of jobs that were available to me were just Bud Anderson—in-different-clothes types of roles, so I wasn't really pursuing it that much. And then on top of that to get this bust and that label it became almost impossible to get an interview, let alone jobs. So for the last 30 years or so, every five years I get an agent, get some pictures and hope to get some work."

Billy has managed to land an occasional role, but not many. He worked on television in *Rawhide*, *Custer*, and *I Spy*. His later motion picture credits include *The Last Movie*: "I had a rearing horse in that one, which was great. I loved it because you could just pull back on the reins and he'd come right up"; *The Werewolves on Wheels*: "The producer of *The Last Movie* did a biker film where we drink this substance and turn into werewolves on wheels. Talk about being involved in some stinkers," he laughed; *The Navy vs the Night Monsters*: "It was about trees that had grown up in the Pacific where nuclear tests were done and they turn into vines that grab and strangle you. I had a little squib filled with a red fluid, so when my arm gets torn off by these vines I push it and the blood pulses out. Really, that was the stinker of all times. At that point in my career I had said, 'I'll do anything.' That was not a very good idea, but I did it because someone had given me the advice that I should be working, no matter what."

With any offers of acting practically nil at this time, Billy found something else that he described as "the absolute best thing that ever happened to me." It was called speedway. "It's a type of motorcycle racing that's very exotic," he explained. Billy did that for three out of five nights a week for 23 years. "I just couldn't get enough of it. It's very theatrical because you're surrounded; it's a very small arena. It's so elegant and dynamic, so I was able to take care of my performance needs just fine." The frosting on the cake for Billy was when he won the 1977 National Long Track Speedway Ascot one half Mile Dirt Oval Championship.

As Billy participated in speedway motorcycle racing, he continued his acting pursuits. "Like I said, every four or five years I'd get pictures made and get an agent. In 1971, Billy did a movie about heroin addicts called *Dusty and Sweets McGee*. "I played a dealer named City Lights that didn't take any drugs at all, just sold them. In 1974 Leonard Maltin reviewed the movie and accused me of being a heroin addict in his book in which he reviews all the movies. Actually it is a very good book and I'm sure a lot of people use it, but he wrote of the film, 'Unconventional no-holds-barred documentary detailing day-to-day life of various heroin addicts in the Los Angeles area. Among real-life addicts and pushers shown is Billy Gray of TV's *Father Knows Best*.'" The movie itself opens with a screen disclaimer stating that eight of the characters in the film are real people and not actors, and that the dealers are portrayed by actors. Billy filed a lawsuit and by the 1998 edition of Maltin's *Movie and Video Guide,* the portion referring to Billy was taken out. Maltin also was made to make a public apology to Billy in 1998 as part of the lawsuit settlement. He gave the following statement: "I did not intend to convey that Billy Gray was a heroin addict or pusher in my review of the film *Dusty and Sweets McGee*. If any damage has resulted from the publication of the review, I apologize for that. I grew up watching and enjoying Billy Gray on the television series *Father Knows Best* and wish him success in his future acting career."

In addition to his acting and speedway racing Billy is also highly committed to safety in sports and other pursuits. In his youth he prototyped much of the safety equipment worn by motorcycle riders today. Thanks to Billy, every Halloween millions of Safe-2-Lite Safety Candle Holders are purchased and it has helped to make that a safer time. "I invented a means of holding a candle in a jack-o'-lantern. You know how difficult it was to make a candle stay up? Well, I solved that problem." Also, Billy is the inventor of the Love'n Thumb, a simple, economical metal device that allows you to rub the tension spots on your own shoulders. A more recent invention he designed is a new ergonomic guitar pick called the F-1 which is being used by rock, country and jazz guitarists.

Billy's most recent acting part to date was a film produced in 1996 called *The Vampire Wars* with Chris Sarandon, Amanda Plummer and Maximilian Schell as the patriarch of the vampires. "I got a call out of the blue saying they wanted me to play Chris Sarandon's handyman and supply him with blood whenever he needed it in this little weird movie. I said, 'Great.' I was really blown away watching Maximilian Schell at work. He was so off the wall that I was in awe. I couldn't take my eyes off of him. It was a real acting seminar to just be on the same stage with him. But then it all turned to shit. The movie got hung up in some kind of lawsuit, so it has been put away in a vault somewhere until the lawsuit can be squared away. There it sits; it hasn't moved in a couple of years. I can't even get a still or clip from it."

Billy was asked what his schooling was like as a child working in Hollywood. "That was a big problem. The school was pretty much a farce. The deal was you had to spend three hours in school each day. The schoolroom setting was like a canvas tent, and they could take it in 10- or 15- minute segments at a time. So it was not anything that resembled a real education, and the fact that I worked a lot meant that I really got short-changed in the school end of things. Then by the time I got to high school I was in *Father Knows Best* and it was pretty much the same thing. There was no attempt at pushing it on you like how they would at a regular school where you have tests and report cards. We didn't have anything like that. In fact, when I graduated from 'high school' the teacher at Columbia gave me the answers to the test that I was going to take when I went to the board of education. She said, 'Don't get them all right.' I liked it fine at the time. I wasn't interested in learning and consequently didn't. But in retrospect I think I did get short-changed because I would liked to have had some kind of a more formalized education."

Does Billy feel in any way that his work as a child actor got in the way of being a normal kid? "Notwithstanding the education deficiencies, it was by far a very fortunate experience and I wouldn't change it for anything. Absolutely not. I've got so much more richness out my understanding of life in general. I've had a really good break. My mother wasn't like a typical Hollywood mother. I was very fortunate in that she was an actress herself and knew that I was very willful as a kid and wouldn't do it if I didn't want to. That's all there was to it. She hadn't forced me into doing something that I didn't want to do. If that had been the case I am sure it would have been a lot different. I've known kids that had that experience. It's such an important part of a person's life—presenting himself. If it has kind of an uncomfortableness to it early on it can be very traumatic and very damaging to the rest of your life. It doesn't have to be, but it seems like it has been on many occasions. Bobby Driscoll comes to mind. He had horrible memories of his early childhood. But I find it to be a real blessing. I couldn't be more happier about it."

Gary Gray

Gary Gray was born December 18, 1936, in Los Angeles, California. His father worked as a business manager for film stars, paying their bills for them, advising them where to invest their money, so on. "Two of his clients were Bert Wheeler and Jack Benny. Both of them told my dad, 'You ought to put Gary in pictures.' I was two years old, so dad took me down and registered me with Central Casting and the Screen Children's Guild. I started going out on calls, and doing some modeling."

The first movie Gary worked in was *A Woman's Face* starring Joan Crawford. "I had a silent bit. She was a criminal with a big scar on her face, and when she walked in the park kids would run from her. She had plastic surgery, and afterwards while walking in the park she looks down at me and I look up at her and give her a big smile, and that was about it. An interesting note, during the making of that movie I was playing hopscotch and fell down and hurt myself. By the time my mother could get to me, Joan Crawford had picked me up, taken me to her dressing room, and was feeding me chocolates. That's how I got started. I just continued to do bits and extra work."

Another bit in an early film was as a leprechaun in *Three Wise Fools*. "We had to go in every morning and have these pointed ears put on and the nose that came up. That was the neatest picture; it was with Margaret O'Brien. She played an Irish girl whose parents had died and was put in the care of these three wise fools. In one scene she chains herself to a tree and sees all the little people. We're the little people, the leprechauns nobody believes in. It was a cute movie."

Gary continued working in bit parts, one of the films being *Whispering Smith* with Alan Ladd. "There's a scene in that film where J. Farrell MacDonald, who was playing my grandfather, is walking me down

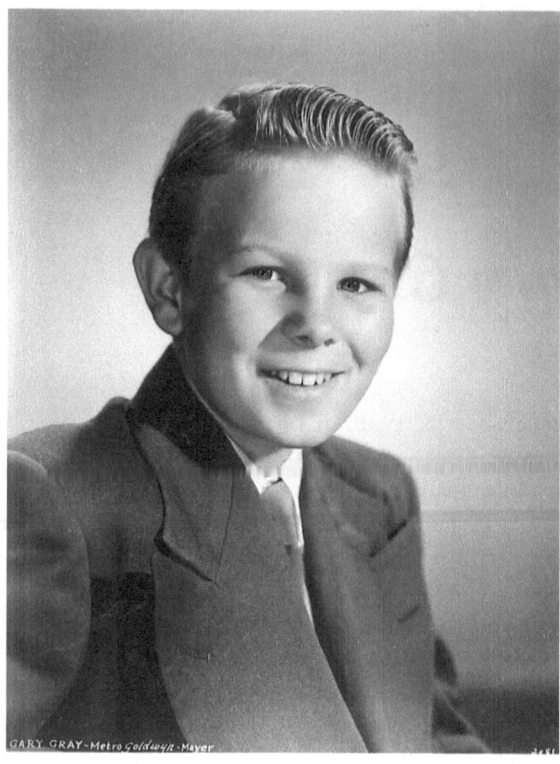

Gary Gray

the street and I meet Whispering Smith. He reaches over to the dog I have and pulls a dollar out of his ear and gives it to me. It was just a small part. That was my first role after I went under contract to the Mitchell J. Hamilberg Agency, my agent until I retired from the business. Before that I'd been with Lola Moore, who was really the agent for most of the children in Hollywood at the time."

Gary's next film role was a much larger part in *Return of the Badmen* which starred Randolph Scott and Jacqueline White. It was this film that really launched his career. Jimmy Hunt initially had the part, but he was a couple of years younger than Gary, and the studio decided they needed somebody a little older. "I'd been at RKO in the morning for something else and didn't get the part. I went home and started playing baseball. Two of the casting directors called me to come back and interview for this part in *Return of the Badmen*. My folks went running all over to find me because they really hadn't known where I'd gone. They finally found me and we got over to RKO around six or seven at night. They interviewed me and gave me the part."

Gary's memories of Randolph Scott were that "he was a very nice guy, the term Southern Gentleman really fit him. He always seemed very polite and quiet and seemed to keep to himself. Most of the time if I wasn't working I was at school. From what I remember hearing when he wasn't working he was playing the stock market and making money. What I remember most and what really impressed me was when he would throw the reins over his horse's neck and walk off, the horse would follow him around like a puppy dog. Jacqueline White was absolutely beautiful. In the last few years I've been able to see her at several different functions. She is still a very beautiful, nice lady."

Reflecting on George "Gabby" Hayes, another of Gary's costars in the film, he said, "Gabby was a neat guy. One of the first things I did in the film was the scene in the buckboard, and Gabby said, 'You make sure you can see the camera. Lean out, because if you can see the camera, the camera can see you.' Heck, I didn't know that. I wouldn't have even thought about it. I never forgot that lesson. They always say dogs and kids steal scenes from adults, well nobody ever stole a scene from Gabby Hayes, so obviously he was not concerned at all," Gary laughed.

Gary's next film was as one of the stars in *Rachel and the Stranger*. Gary reflected on how he obtained this choice role. "It's funny what gets you parts. If Jimmy had been a little bit older, I would never had the part in *Return of the Badmen*. The very next thing I did was *Rachel and the Stranger*. They'd seen a kid by the name of Dick Tyler in a play in New York, and had hired him to come out and do the part. He was at that age where he started growing real fast. By the time he got out here he had grown so much he was too big for the part. So now what do they do? Well, there's this kid doing *Return of the Badmen* and they came over and watched, and then I was asked to test for the part. That was the first time I ever had to do a test. I tested against Bobby Driscoll, *the* big kid in Hollywood at the time. Loretta Young did the test, and Norman Foster, who was her brother-in-law and director of the show, did the actual test also. Bobby did his test and I did mine. At the end of the test Loretta Young gave the okay sign, and it was kind of given that I had] got the part.

"*Rachel and the Stranger* was the favorite of all the movies I've worked in. Loretta Young was so neat. She helped me with my scenes. There were so many neat things about Bill Holden. One of the things is, and I still have it, the Winchester 22 rifle. On the last day of production we were at the old RKO Pathé studio. Bill came in with this rifle and asked my mother if it was all right if he gave it to me. There wasn't much my mother could say. She wouldn't even let me have a BB gun at that point," Gary laughed. "But he gave me that 22. I also got to work with him in one other picture, *Father Is a Bachelor*. Prior to his untimely and tragic death, his girlfriend Stefanie Powers was one of my dad's clients. Whenever Bill would come to my dad's office with Stefanie he would always ask about me. He always wanted to know how I was and how my family was. He was just really a nice guy. So was Robert Mitchum. He always seemed like a big friendly guy. I remember this older guy attempting to chop wood and wasn't doing too good a job. Bob said, 'Here, let me have that axe.' He ripped his shirt off and had chips of wood flying all over. He was chopping that wood up like it was going out of style. Just a regular guy; most of them are regular people."

Rachel and the Stranger was filmed on location in Eugene, Oregon, where Gary has fond memories of working. "There were a lot of instances where we had the key to the city. It was unbelievable. We had autograph parties; I had a pass to go anytime I wanted to the theater. In fact, the owner of the three theaters and his wife took my mother and I to see Crater Lake. I became friends with some of the kids who came up to watch the movie being made, and was invited to a birthday party. There were just a lot of friends. One of the guys sent us a fresh cut tree the next Christmas. I got to run the elevator; these were the old days when you had an elevator operator at the Hotel Eugene. Boy, anytime I wasn't working I was running the elevator up and down," he laughed. "It was kind of funny; you got to do almost anything you wanted. We were there for 11 weeks. It was kind of drizzling when we got there and raining the day we left, but it didn't rain for 11 weeks, which is unbelievable. That's always been a favorite movie of mine, the people were just so neat in it."

When asked if there were any humorous things he remembered while working on that film, Gary replied, "The McKenzie River is very cold. There's one scene where I'm swimming in the river and had to say to the dog, 'Come on in Corky, the water's fine.' Well, I could hardly say 'C-c-c-corky.' The dog wasn't as dumb as I was. I'd get in the water because that's where they told me to go. The dog would take about three steps in, turn around and walk back out; it wasn't going in that water. They finally had to go out in a boat and throw him into the water to see him swimming," Gary laughed.

Gary worked in two of Tim Holt's westerns at RKO, *Gun Smugglers* and *Masked Raiders*. "Tim was really a neat guy. He had the first or second Lipazon Horse they'd imported into the United States. He had a big picnic at his ranch in the San Diego area and invited my mother, my dad, my sister and me to come. I remember him putting his horse through the paces; he was truly a horseman. It wasn't any make believe. In *Masked Raiders* there was a guy who later became quite famous, Clayton Moore. I was hitching on the corner of Wilshire and Fairfax, and Clayton Moore picked me up. He told me he had just landed this part in a television series. Of course that part turned out to be a pretty good role for life as *The Lone Ranger*."

Working in the westerns involved horseback riding, so we asked Gary if he enjoyed it. "I loved it. In fact, after I bought a horse I learned how to trick ride, which I really enjoyed. I competed in five events in gymnastics all through high school and into college, so that just came really

Gary as Little Davey Harvey in RKO's 1948 film, *Rachel and the Stranger*.

natural to me. A guy named John Hovious—Redd Russell is what he went by—taught me how to trick ride. We became very good friends.

"I did a little bit of riding in *Rachel and the Stranger*, not a whole lot, but I wouldn't say I was a horseman by any means. When I tested for *Gun Smugglers* there was quite a bit of riding in that; it came down to Alan

Dinehart III or Gary Gray, and it was which ever one rode the best. He had a horse, but my dad and I must have gone riding almost every day for two weeks. We went out to Culver City to a stable, because there used to be a lot of open space out there. The horse I learned to ride on was called Little Apples. Anyway, I tested, got the part, and I've been riding ever since. I always enjoyed horses."

Gary starred in a 20th Century–Fox, Sol Wurtzel picture, *Night Wind*, which featured a dog named Flame. From *Night Wind*, RKO made a series of shorts about a boy (Gary) and his dog, Pal, again played by Flame. "Flame is the smartest dog I ever worked with. Frank Barnes was the owner and trainer. Flame was amazing. Everybody used hand signals and some voice commands. I swear this is honest—if Frank said, without using hand signals, 'Flame, look right,' the dog would look right; and if he said, 'Flame, look stage right,' the dog looked stage right. This dog was unbelievable. When we went away for lunch there was a little carpet. Frank would say, 'You stay there.' We'd be gone for an hour and that dog would stay on that carpet. But at the end, the dog would obey me almost as well as Frank. In fact, I guess it was kind of frustrating for the dog, because Frank would say 'Stay there,' and I'd say 'Come on, boy.' Flame would start to come, and Frank would say, 'Flame, go back there,'" Gary laughed. "That was a great dog. We did some guest appearances together. I did some with Lassie too. With Flame, some of it was on TV, but with Lassie we did a guest appearance at the Million Dollar Theater in downtown Los Angeles. They had motion pictures playing, and Eddie Peabody, the world famous banjo player, performed. These guys were doing live stuff, then they'd introduce Lassie and myself. So actually, it was like the last of vaudeville."

Gary went under contract to MGM when he was signed to work with William Wellman in *The Next Voice You Hear* as the son of James Whitmore and Nancy Davis. In his recollections of William Wellman, Gary related, "He was great. He would put in little things people wouldn't even think about. It is an interesting movie. The voice of God comes over the radio; the audience never hears the voice by the way, but it says there is going to be rain and all of a sudden there's thunder, and rain just starts pouring down. Wellman could really get things out of the actors. In the scene when Nancy Davis hears the voice say there's going to be rain, and when it thunders, she screams. Of course the three of us all clutch together. Wellman had told her to scream without us knowing it, so he got a good reaction from us. None of us knew it was coming except for Nancy. We didn't do it during rehearsal, but he told her when this happens I want you to scream. She let out this blood curdling scream and, believe me, we all grabbed together. It's real. He just had a knack."

Gary not only worked with Nancy Davis, he also worked with her husband, the future President. "I made *The Girl from Jones Beach* at Warner Bros. It starred Ronald Reagan and Virginia Mayo. A few years ago, my wife Jean and I visited with President Reagan in his office. I told him at the time we were making the picture I was really more impressed with Virginia Mayo than I was him, but that I was awfully honored to be able to meet with him now. He just laughed and said, 'Yeah, she really was pretty wasn't she?'"

Reminiscing on his working with Lassie in MGM's *The Painted Hills*, Gary said, "Lassie was a very smart, friendly dog, just what you would expect. I was lucky because I got to work with the original one. Lassie, who was actually a male, had sired some puppies and Rudd Weatherwax, Lassie's owner, wanted to know if we wanted one of them. We were living, at the time, in an apartment and I couldn't have a dog, but right afterwards we bought a house. So I called him and said, 'Rudd, my folks bought a house in Encino. Is there a chance I could still have one of the puppies?' and he answered, 'Sure, I'm not going to be home but my daughter will be there. Just come on out and pick the one you want and take it.' We went and picked out this puppy and took it and played with it all day. I was about 12 and my sister ten. That evening we got a phone call from Rudd. He said, 'Gary, you took the dog I was going to use to replace Lassie,' and he wanted the dog. Naturally we had fallen in love with this dog and were in tears. Finally Rudd said, 'Oh hell, keep the dog.'

"There were a lot of things I enjoyed about making that movie. I really enjoyed Paul Kelly, an ultimate professional. A good actor. I was also very impressed because the Indian in it was a real chief and I'd never met an Indian chief before. And Little Brown Jug was in it, who I had known. Ann Doran was great. She played my mother in that picture and about three years later played my sister in *Rodeo*. I got a new fly fishing rod while I was in Sonora, which I still have. I remember my dad caught a rattlesnake," Gary laughed. "Speaking of rattlesnakes, on *Rachel and the Stranger*, if you remember the hill where the grave was, well on that hill we caught 11 rattlesnakes during the 11 weeks we were there on location. I say we—I didn't do it. Billy Curtis caught one of them with a long stick."

Continuing with his reflections on *The Painted Hills*, Gary said, "There was this colt up there, and I was fooling around with it. Well, when a colt decides he's not going to do something, he doesn't. I'm leading this colt along and all of a sudden he decided he doesn't want to go where I want to go. He reared up and came down right on top of my head. I had a beautiful bruise. There were a lot of things that happened. I remember doing one picture when I was playing around and jumped through a window and stuck a piece of glass into my arm and had to go to emergency hospital. But those things kids just do," he smiled.

"My mom was always on the set with me," Gary continued. "She was far from the typical movie mother, however. I think she's probably the only movie mother Bill Wellman ever liked. He didn't like hairdressers and he didn't like movie mothers. When my mom and I came on the set, he wanted to know, 'Who is that woman?' When he found out it was my mother there wasn't much he could do because there had to be a guardian on the set with me. However, the further my mother could get to the back of the sound stage the better she liked it. She had her needle point and would sit and do that and not bother anyone. So she and Mr. Wellman got along great. There were some of those mothers who practically got right up underneath the camera. But mom wasn't one of those. The only picture I can ever remember my dad going on was *The Painted Hills*."

Gary also costarred in a series of five comedies at Monogram about the Latham Family. Raymond Walburn played Henry Latham, the father, Barbara Brown played the mother. Their children were Gary and Mary Stuart (who left the series after the first three shows for a TV job on *The Guiding Light*, being replaced by M'Liss McClure in the final shows.) The other star was Walter Catlett as Mayor Colton. George Nokes played his son Georgie in all but one episode, in which George MacDonald filled the bill.

Gary compared Walburn and Catlett to Gabby Hayes, in the sense that, "I don't think you could steal a scene from them if you had to. They knew the lines, but they never came out the same; not twice in a row, anyway. Fortunately, a lot of these were done fast, like 'Everybody know the lines?' They'd block it out and then, 'We'll rehearse it with film.' That's the way they did a lot of it at Monogram. If it was a good one, it was a take."

The Latham Family series supposedly took place in Riverside, California, but only the exterior scenes were shot there for long shots. Walter Catlett was the mayor of the town and Ray Walburn was an attorney. "He was one of those guys always fighting city hall. Of course, every time he fought city hall everything went wrong. He and Walter Catlett are friends, but they're always having a problem with one another," Gary smiled. "There was one titled *Father Makes Good* where he buys a cow because he doesn't want to pay ten cents tax on milk. This causes all sorts of problems in the neighborhood."

Gary also worked in a number of shorts during the 1940s. He mentioned that his sister Arlene, also a child actress, had worked with Mitzi Gaynor in *The Song of Norway* at the Philharmonic, and that they'd gotten to know her. "Really a nice young girl," Gary added. "My agent contracted me to do a short for the Southern California Dental Association, *It's Your Health*. They had a new girl they wanted to play my sister. That was her first picture under the name of Mitzi Gerber. Later she became Mitzi Gaynor, who went on to be a big star. It's funny when you look back at some of the things that happened."

Gary discussed the point in his career about the transition from child roles to younger adult roles. "I was fortunate. I didn't do as much as I would have liked, but I did make the transition. I worked in television. The first show I did was a *Fireside Theatre*. After that I did quite a bit. I did *Trackdown*, a couple of *Jim Bowie*'s (Tommy Ivo was my brother in those.) I enjoyed *26 Men*. They were done at Coodia City (now at 40th and Camelback in downtown Phoenix, Arizona.) In those days it was way out in the sticks. Russell Hayden had a western town and a sound stage there. I played Billy Clanton in *The Buntline Special* on *Wyatt Earp*. Unfortunately by the time they did the actual gunfight at the OK Corral I'd gotten out of the industry and there was no going back."

Gary shared with us several experiences he had in two movies he made as a young adult actor: *Wild Heritage* and *Terror at Black Falls*. Of the first, Gary said, "Ingrid Goode was the love interest for me in the picture. She'd been Miss Sweden just previous and was very well endowed and good looking. In a scene where I had to help her down from the wagon, I had to say, 'Sorry guys, forgot my lines.' I was more interested in Ingrid Goode than I was in the lines. But those things happen to people," he laughed. "The biggest thrill on this show was that I got to work with Casey Tibbs. He was five times saddle bronc champion."

The last movie Gary worked in was *Terror at Black Falls*, which was filmed on location in Scotland, Arkansas. "Kind of an arty western, released back in Arkansas and then disappeared. Richard Sarafian had written, produced and directed this show. It was in black-and-white; the budget was nothing. The film was a lot of fun, and there were some good actors in it like House Peters, Jr. and Peter Mamakos. I remember an old guy who lived there, about 98 years old and blind at the time. He'd never been over ten miles away from Scotland. They had just gotten some indoor plumbing in some of the places. The people of Scotland, Arkansas, couldn't have been nicer."

Gary explained why he left the picture business. "Actually, I had met Jean. Nineteen fifty-nine and 1960 were not great years, so I'd gone to work selling cars. I sold Jean's dad a car and that's how we met. We went out a couple of times for about a week, and then she went away on vacation. When she came back I asked her to marry me. We waited for about six months, got married, and it's been 38 years and we've raised four daughters and just had our 20th grandchild. Anyway, I needed something a little steadier. Motion pictures, as much as I loved it, was just a job. So I bought a business and went to work and got out of the picture business. It's that simple."

Summing up his feelings about his acting career, Gary says, "I had a ball. I thoroughly enjoyed everything I did; I wouldn't trade it for anything. I got to go places other kids didn't go. I was flying on a plane when we went to do *The Painted Hills*; it wasn't a long flight, but there weren't a whole lot of kids flying in 1950. I got to meet people most people never get the opportunity to meet, and work with them. It's funny, you work with them and you don't even think anything about them. They were just nice people and I had a really good time working with them."

Jimmy Hawkins

Jimmy Hawkins was born on November 13, 1941, in Los Angeles, California. Jimmy stated, "My grandfather, Rudy Unholtz, was one of the original Keystone Cops. My mom was raised around studios and always wanted her kids in the picture business. So I just naturally followed in my brother Tim's footsteps. We would always go on interviews together. If they said, 'We need somebody a little older,' she would bring my brother in, and if they needed somebody a little younger, they'd bring me in."

Jimmy's first film was MGM's *The Seventh Cross* in 1944 with Spencer Tracy. "I played the son of Hume Cronyn and Jessica Tandy."

Asked what his earliest memory of working in films was, he answered, "Going out to MGM in Culver City, because it was a long ride from the part of L.A. where we lived. Getting up early in the morning when it was still dark and taking buses and streetcars leave wonderful memories."

Reflecting on his trips to Culver City (to the RKO Pathé lot where they filmed *It's a Wonderful Life* in June 1946), he said, "Even at the age of four I have very vivid memories of working with Jimmy Stewart. In one scene I had a Santa Claus mask around my neck and I'm sitting on Jimmy Stewart's lap. [He's pondering losing $8,000 and reflecting on what's become of his life.] I remember through the different rehearsals and various takes Mr. Stewart pulled me into him. The mask was very coarse inside and would scratch my cheek every time he did it. I kept wondering, 'Why is this man doing this?' I also remember Frank Capra squatting down and explaining face to face what he wanted me to do in a particular scene; he would direct me to say, 'Excuse me' and give me specific places to repeat the line.

"Jimmy Stewart was a real gentleman all through the years. When I put together a book on the history of *It's a Wonderful Life* [*The It's a*

Jimmy as Tagg Oakley in the television series of *Annie Oakley* **(Flying A Productions).**

Wonderful Life 50th Anniversary Scrapbook, Running Press] I sent Mr. Stewart a dozen copies to sign for various charities. A week before he died they all came back signed. He was very giving to the end."

Reflecting on working in the film *Moonrise*, Jimmy said, "The entire stage was a midway at a fair, complete with a Ferris wheel, toss games and the best of all, cotton candy. I remember getting to eat all of this cotton candy and the prop man was telling all of us kids to stop eating all the props. Here's this whole sound stage with these Ferris wheels, sideshows, cotton candy and candy apples. It was great. I went to work every day thinking, 'Wow, this is cool,' and I was getting paid to do it."

Jimmy talked about working with Lassie in *Challenge to Lassie*. "They had had several Lassies. The trainer was always nice and would let us kids play with the various Lassies. They had one that would just sit there and look pretty, another one who would just run, one who would do stunts, and another to do tricks. They had quite a few as I remember."

In 1949, television was just getting started and Jimmy was cast as a regular playing one of the twins in the television series *The Ruggles*, which featured movie character star Charles Ruggles. Asked what it was like working on live TV he replied, "It was frantic. We would rehearse all week and then do the show. Actually we'd do it twice. Once for the east coast and three hours later for the west coast. This was the years of live television, you had to be ready … this was going out live, and now. There was no 'Okay, cut. We'll pick this up later.' We were together weekly for

The closing scene from RKO's *It's a Wonderful Life* (1946) features Thomas Mitchell, Carol Coomes, Donna Reed, Jimmy Hawkins, James Stewart, Karolyn Grimes, Larry Simms and Beulah Bondi. The other two are unidentified.

almost four years on *The Ruggles*. We were doing 52 episodes. TV was new then. The networks were experimenting. It was a great experience. It was fabulous growing up with all of that. The ABC lot in Hollywood (at Prospect and Talmadge) had a variety of shows going out live. During the rehearsals I remember the girl who played my twin [Judy Nugent] and I would sneak off and visit various other shows and would just walk in on the noon cooking show in progress. We'd be surprise guests. Everyone liked *The Ruggles* (it was one of the few series out here that was national) so to see two cast members show up on local TV was a big deal. We didn't realize it at the time. We were seven or eight year old kids having fun. It was terrific. It was very special and we didn't fully realize it."

Jimmy worked with Clifton Webb in *Mister Scoutmaster*, directed by Henry Levin. "I just had a great time doing that film and going to the

Fox ranch in Malibu where we shot all the exteriors. One particular incident sticks out in my mind. In one scene Clifton Webb had to throw ice cream in a kid's face. Take after take he kept missing the kid's face and hitting him in the neck, and the kid had to keep going and getting cleaned up and putting on new wardrobe. That happened about five times and finally Mr. Levin suggested the prop man try it (they were running out of wardrobe.) I think Mr. Webb was glad and a little embarrassed.

"There's an anecdote to this story: in 1980 I produced an NBC "Movie of the Week" loosely based on *Mister Scoutmaster* entitled, *Scout's Honor* starring the very talented child star Gary Coleman. I was in the position to hire the director and immediately thought of Henry Levin ... remembering how good he was with kids. I wanted somebody who was going to be very patient with Gary. My instincts were right. Henry Levin was a real gentleman; we had a good time and a lot of laughs making the film. Then on the final day we were shooting an office scene on location in Glendale, California. Henry was setting up the shot and suddenly turned to Harry Morgan (who was costarring in the film) and said, 'I'm in big trouble.' Henry sat down on the couch and dropped dead. We dedicated the movie in his honor."

Jimmy appeared in several western features before Gene Autry's Flying A Productions signed him to costar as Gail Davis's younger brother Tagg Oakley in the television series of *Annie Oakley*. "I had been around horses before, but in order to get the part they had me go out to a Hudkins stable and ride so they could see I wasn't afraid of horses."

Jimmy was asked if there was much competition for the part of Tagg. "Oh yeah," he responded. "Quite a bit. They looked at every kid in town. In fact, they made a pilot for *Annie Oakley* the year before with Billy Gray (in my opinion one of the finest kid actors ever). He was the original Tagg Oakley. Gene Autry had a lot of faith in the project so they did another pilot (the feedback on the first was that it was too saccharine; they wanted to make it more action adventure) but when they went to reshoot Billy had outgrown the part, and that's when they hired me. It came down to me and another kid. We had to meet with Gene Autry and the heads of his studio, Mandy Schaefer and Mitch Hamilberg. The good Lord smiled on me that day. The show was great. All the other ten year old kids would talk about being cowboys and riding around on broomsticks, and here I got the opportunity to do the real thing, go out on location with real horses and real stagecoaches. It was great. I was very, very fortunate.

"We'd shoot exteriors at Gene Autry's Melody Ranch in Newhall, California, about an hour's drive from his Hollywood stages on Sunset Boulevard, and out in the San Fernando Valley at Corriganville and Iverson's

Ranch. Sometimes we'd travel and stay for a couple of weeks in Pioneer Town [in the high desert above Palm Springs, California.]

"During the summer we'd go on tour to state and county fairs. Sometimes I would go by myself or with Gene Autry. I had an act with my horse Pixie from the series. He was a trick horse. He'd say yes or no, bow, say his prayers, smile, count, and then for a finale we'd jump through a hoop of fire. The crowds were always wonderful and it wouldn't be out of the ordinary to play to 50 or 60,000 people. Gail Davis was a great gal. I loved working with her. We kept in touch after the series and, in fact, I was at her bedside the night she died. We had a nice long friendship. She was a very special lady."

When a child actor is on the set filming, they have to go to school for three hours a day. While not filming, Jimmy went to parochial schools. In addition, when a child actor becomes identified with a popular film or TV series other kids take notice. That can be a good thing; it can be a bad thing. A successful child actor can run into two types of other kids. "Either they want to be friendly," Jimmy noted, "or they harass you because of your celebrity."

Asked what some of the things were that he enjoyed doing when away from the set, Jimmy responded, "I just went back to school and associated with all the other kids. I became a yo-yo champ for my grade school, Holy Trinity. I joined in sports with other kids (little league, etc). I liked doing those kind of things; I was always busy. When I wasn't at school I'd spend the weekends with my horse or doing personal appearances."

Learning lines seemed to come easy to Jimmy. "I would just keep going over them until I memorized them," he said. "The good thing about *Annie Oakley* and other filmed shows was that you didn't have to memorize the whole script at one time. You just memorized what you were going to do for the next day and prepare for that. A lot is expected from a kid actor. They expected you to be an adult: be there, be prepared, and know your dialogue and, yet, get your studies done."

Jimmy did a lot of work on television that included his roles as Jonathan Baylor on *Ichabod and Me*, Jimmy on *The Adventures of Ozzie and Harriet* and as Scotty, the boyfriend of Shelley Fabares, on *The Donna Reed Show*. "It's ironic that I was Donna's son in *It's a Wonderful Life* and was a regular for eight seasons on her TV show and today I sit on the board of directors for the Donna Reed Foundation. The foundation gives scholarships to students to go to college so that they can study the arts and hopefully follow in Donna Reed's footsteps."

Among his other television work Jimmy acted in three unsold pilots: two for his alma mater, MGM, *Andy Hardy* and *See Here Private Hargrove*, and *The Voice of Gruber Hills* at Columbia (Screen Gems). "*Andy Hardy* was very important," he reflected, "because that was the crown jewel of MGM's library. It had made Mickey Rooney a household name and MGM TV wanted the same for TV viewers. They were going to bring *Andy Hardy* to television. I'd hear ripples that they were looking for an Andy, but they were trying to find a Mickey Rooney type. One day they called me to come and meet with them. I was very happy over at Columbia doing *The Donna Reed Show*. One of the episodes I had completed was a spin-off for a pilot and I was waiting to see if that was going to sell. I went out there and met with the head of casting, Al Tresconi. He took me to meet the producers, and they asked, 'Would you read?' I said, 'Sure.' I studied the scene and read over it with Mr. Tresconi. I said, 'Well, what do you think?' He said, 'Just do it that way.' He called the producer and said, 'He's ready to read.' So I read. The producer looked at me and said, 'I don't care who you're under contract to. You are Andy Hardy and I'm going to get you out of whatever contract you're in.' He bought me out of my contract with Screen Gems. In fact, Columbia, who owns Screen Gems, was doing a picture called *Diamond Head* and they wanted an MGM star contract player, Yvette Mimieux, for it. The story I was told is Columbia said, 'We'll give you Jimmy Hawkins to play Andy Hardy, you give us Yvette Mimieux for *Diamond Head*.' Ah, deals."

NBC offered a time slot for *Andy Hardy* at seven o'clock on Sunday and the producers turned them down, saying, 'No, we want a nine o'clock time slot. The audience that knows Andy Hardy is a nine o'clock audience.' MGM waited for a later time slot, which they never got, so it went by the wayside. Ah, deals."

Jimmy appeared with Elvis Presley in two films: *Girl Happy* and *Spinout*. Reminiscing on working with Elvis, Jimmy said, "It was great. Here you are with the king of rock and roll and your bipping and bopping. It was nostalgic to go out to MGM, where I started in the forties, and here I am in the sixties still working there. Shelley Fabares was Elvis' leading lady and I was his sidekick. It was great working with her again. And we doubled that pleasure the next year in *Spinout*."

During the Vietnam War Jimmy took a USO tour to visit the bases over there. He reflected, "It was an experience to be able to drop into a war and talk firsthand to the guys and hopefully get their minds off the war and bring a little bit of home to them. It took us 33 hours to get over there and we spent 20 some odd days entertaining. I lost 20 pounds. They just had you go, go, go. But it was nothing knowing what they were going through. I think we helped make a difference."

The idea of working on the other side of the camera always held an interest for Jimmy. "I wanted to try something else so in 1968 I went into producing. I lucked out on my first film. I found a great story and put together the financing for a movie called *Evel Knieval*. It cost $750,000 to produce and grossed over $25 million. Like I said, I got lucky."

Asked if he'd written any of the stories he has produced, Jimmy answered, "Sometimes, like on the Disney film *Love Leads The Way*, but usually I have a vision of the way I want the story to go and talk it out with the writer until he understands that vision."

One of the many shows that Jimmy produced was a PBS special. The Lux Radio theater version of *It's a Wonderful Life* with an all-star cast: among others, Sally Field, Christian Slater (both former child stars), Martin Landau, Nathan Lane, and Bill Pullman. "That was quite an experience coming full circle with *It's a Wonderful Life*, but the big plus was that it was a charitable event that ended up raising $150,000 for a children's charity."

If a parent came up to Jimmy and asked for his advice on how to get their child into films or if they should, what would he answer? "Well, I'd just tell them what my folks told me. 'As long as you enjoy it then you can keep doing it, but if you become a wise guy or a smart aleck then we'll take you out of it.' Any time you see a kid that has a bad time in later life after being a kid actor, the problem will most likely be their parents. A lot of parents let the studio run their kid's life. The parents should look at it like being in little league, cub scouts or whatever—you've got to take control of your child. You just don't send them off and say, 'We'll come back later.' Parents think the studio's going to do right by them, but they're going to do right for the studio. There's got to be a time when the parent takes control and tells the kid that this is a job and as long as you're having a good time then do it. Because one day the job is going to be over and they're not going to need you anymore, so you have to psychologically explain to the kids what to expect in the real world.

"I know in talking to other kid actors they sometimes feel the industry owes them a living, even today. And I say, 'No, they don't. They paid you for your job. Your parents put you in that business. If you're ticked off at anybody, it should be your parents'. It's up to the parent to instill in the kid what to expect; it's a nice job while it's going on, but it's going to end one day and then you'll have to go on with your life. A good parent prepares their kid for real life. That's what it's all about. I'll guarantee you anytime that a kid ends up having problems, just look to the parents. When you read about a kid getting into trouble, remember they aren't all former kid actors."

In talking about child actors making the transition to adult actors

Jimmy said, "Kid actors (if they want to stay in the business) have to make it. What was cute at ten isn't cute at 20. You've got to keep reinventing yourself. Liz Taylor, Sally Field, Jodie Foster and Shelley Fabares have done that very well. They made those transitions—re-invented themselves and keep giving the industry something they want.

"You've got to have ambition, that passion to make it in this industry—let nothing and no one discourage you. It's a do it yourself proposition all the way. You can't borrow the ambition. You've got to want it. If you have the basic talent you're going to make it."

On hobbies, he said, "I like going to collectors shows and looking at all the old toys. I have a western-themed room. All the memorabilia from my *Annie Oakley* days. The Bohlin silver saddle from the tours I did, the saddle I used on the *Annie Oakley* series, pictures, banners, placards from touring the U.S. and Canada. One sheets, half sheets, insert and lobby cards from various westerns I appeared in. I'm a big Hoppy, Roy and Gene collector (clocks, cap pistols, holsters, etc.)."

Asked if he has a favorite that stands out in all the over 500 movies and TV shows he did, Jimmy stated, "I have fond memories of all of them, but liked doing the pilot of *Annie Oakley* (I got to go on overnight location). I remember fondly an episode on *The Donna Reed Show* called *Mary's Driving Lesson* where I taught her to drive, and I liked working on *Girl Happy*. The feelings when I think back, the fun that we had, the way they turned out, the excitement of it all."

Looking back over his career in the picture business, Jimmy summed up his feelings about it. "I feel very blessed to have been a part of the motion picture industry and I wouldn't trade anything for the experience. I meet people that other people only think of meeting. I've been able to work with wonderful actors, directors, writers, and I just thank God that He let me be in this business."

Billy Hughes

Billy Hughes was born November 28, 1948, in Los Angeles, California, the son of stunt man Bill Hughes and nephew of stunt man Whitey Hughes. "I went through a rocky childhood. My mother and dad were separated when I was three. We moved to Oklahoma when I was about four and spent a couple of years there, and then, for economic reasons, moved back to California and lived in the San Fernando Valley."

In 1961, Robert Hinkle, a friend of Billy's dad and uncle, was preparing to produce and direct a film titled *Ole Rex* and needed a boy who could carry a 30-pound dog. "I had never done any acting or ever had acting lessons, but Mr. Hinkle thought, 'Why don't I look at Bill's boys?' He chose me and we went to Wichita Falls, Texas. That was my introduction to the movie business and my first feeling of finding something I loved to do."

When making *Ole Rex* the director asked, "Billy, you have no experience. Do you know what we expect of you?" Billy replied "Well, you expect me to portray this boy who finds a wounded dog and brings it home. The father kicks the dog out and the boy goes with the dog." He said, "No, that's not what I mean. Do you know how to deport yourself in the presence of the camera?" "I don't know," Billy answered. "I've never done it." But it seemed like it just fell into place because Billy had been around the studios with his dad all his life. "So after a couple of scenes it just became natural to me. I don't mean to be egotistical in any way, but I just felt I was born to act. And I was happy doing it. That was the important thing. By the time we finished *Ole Rex* I guess I had enough exposure that I felt really confident about doing anything else."

The following year Billy's dad and uncle decided to produce a movie. "They had both been in the stunt business for years and had a lot of connections so they came up with *Stakeout*. Wichita Falls, Texas was chosen

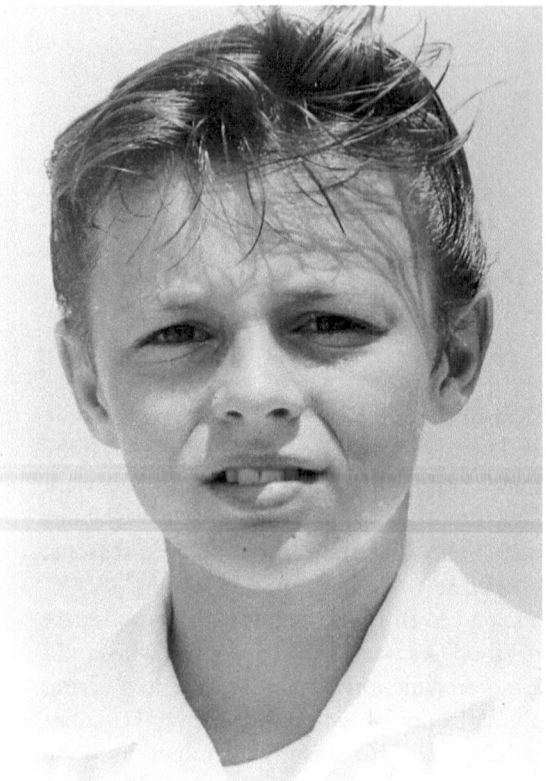

Billy Hughes

as the location because they were familiar with the area. Billy drew upon some deep emotions in portraying the son of an ex-convict played by Bing Russell. "The two of us immediately had such a chemistry that it was almost like I was with my dad. I don't mean that to be in any way disrespectful to my dad, but Bing just had that ability. The show to me was a very dramatic episode because in that movie was a part of my real life. I had lost people very dear to me when I was a child. I lost my mother when I was three. She didn't die—my dad and her were divorced—but I never saw my her again until I was 32 years old. My second loss was my grandfather. We had moved to Oklahoma where I developed a strong attachment to my dad's dad, Robert Marshal Hughes. I loved him very dearly and he died of cancer when I was six. So when I did *Stakeout* there were a lot of pent-up emotions in relation to loss. The story lent itself to that kind of life. Bing is portrayed as a character just released from prison for a robbery he allegedly committed, and I was a character who had lost his mother because of divorce and put in an orphanage. All of my emotions seemed to come out as we portrayed scene after scene, and in the end Bing gets killed. I can remember that day. Bing set the emotional mood for us because he knew it was going to be a serious time. We had a special bond that day and it was like I knew I was going to lose another person in my life, but I had to try to keep it balanced knowing we were still being actors. It was in that last scene when the police officers shoot Bing and he is laying dead and I am crying over the body. The scene ends with a blanket being thrown over him, with just his arms sticking out and his hand rolled up. All the real life things that had happened to me in the past begin to flash by me. I begin to really scream and cry because it was the final portion of the movie, and by that time I had definitely grown very close to Bing and I think he did to me, so when they shoot him and he goes down I couldn't contain myself. I really fell apart. It wasn't until I watched the movie several decades later that I began to see what motivated me to be able to show this emotion and this reaction on camera. Again, it was drawing on that psychological loss of my mother and grandfather, and it all came out at that moment. It was a tough scene and all day long I was disturbed because I knew this scene was going to be a rough one to pull off."

After the filming was completed Bing told Billy that he needed to get into the Screen Actors Guild because he thought he had good potential to work as an actor. "This very loving man picked me up at the house one day and said, 'Kid, we're going to get you into the movie business.'

Billy on the set of *Stakeout* (Crown International, 1962). Standing on his right is his uncle, stunt man Whitey Hughes. On his left is his father, also a stunt man, Bill Hughes.

He took me to Hollywood and introduced me to his agents, Walter and Hilda Herzbrun. At that point they both kind of balked. They told Bing, 'You know our policy is that we don't represent children or animals.' But Bing responded, 'I'd like you to give this child a chance. He's got something special.' At that point I was just a kid and really did not know how much this man was trying to help me and didn't know how to thank him for what he was doing for me." The agency relented and signed Billy on Bing's recommendation.

After that, Billy began to work in many of television's episodic dramas. "I was a free lance actor; I never had my own series." Billy did, however, appear in a pilot for a proposed series with Dean Jagger called *Mr. Doc's Examination* that he would have had a regular part in if it had sold. "It would have been a great series. Dean Jagger owned a little pharmacy at the turn of the century and I played his son. I was very properly dressed with the white stiff collar. We had gas lights, a beautiful stage and a wonderful format in my assessment, but it just didn't sell."

Billy worked in a number of westerns on television. Asked how he liked doing these shows, he responded, "I enjoyed them immensely. I have wonderful reflections. I think my heart would tell you that I really enjoyed working with Chuck Connors and Johnny Crawford on *The Rifleman*. It was a very comfortable set, I had a good part, and Johnny and I were about the same age. We developed a good rapport with one another. I think one of my favorite performances was an episode [*Day of Reckoning*] when the outlaws were coming to town to kill Chuck Connors and nobody, including my father, wanted to help him because they were afraid. I spend the night at Lucas McCain's house, and Johnny and I have this wonderful scene in the bedroom. He's worried about his dad going out and being one against the outlaws, and I'm ashamed of my dad because he won't help. The director [Lawrence Dobkin] had this wonderful ability to create an image of the scene. He said, 'I want this set really quiet. I want the lights dimmed down really low and the kerosene lanterns turned up to create the environment.' Then he sat close to Johnny and I and started telling us what was going to happen. 'Tomorrow,' he said to Johnny, 'your dad is going up against five outlaws and the chance of his making it through is not very good.' Then he turned to me and said, 'Your dad doesn't have the courage to go up against them.' He had us both crying within five minutes." Then Dobkin backed out of the scene, issuing the order for the cameras to start rolling and telling Billy and Johnny to start when they were ready. "It was a wonderful scene because it was so natural and the relationship between me and Johnny was like we had been pulled together as brothers and were actually living in the 1880s. We did it in one take.

The dialogue was right on, the tears were flowing from both of our eyes. When the director said, 'Cut it and print it,' they brought up the stage lights and everybody in the studio was crying. I really admired Johnny. He was a trouper, a great guy."

Billy worked in several episodes of *Gunsmoke*. "That was my grandmother's favorite show of all shows. Everybody sat down and shut their mouths when it was time to watch it. So when I walked on the set for the first time and saw Mr. Arness, to me he was bigger than life because I'd been watching the show all those years. I thought, 'Here I am now in his presence,' and was just awestruck by him. I had a deep respect for him." Billy also worked on three episodes of *Wagon Train*. "I did one episode with Ward Bond, and then he passed away and I did two other episodes with John McIntire. They were both very professional, nonpretensious people. I felt comfortable being around them."

With all these westerns, Billy was asked what his feelings are about horses. "Dad had a magic touch, and was almost like the horse whisperer. His favorite horse that he broke from an absolute maverick he called Triple Day. He broke him in three days and made one of the best falling horses in the business. I used to love to get on him and ride out into the country. He was so gentle, so wonderful. A nice horse. Dad just had that ability. He could charm a horse. So I grew up with horses and loved them from the beginning."

Another show Billy is proud of is *Lassie*. "I really enjoyed working with Jon Provost. A sweet young man. It pains me because after the *Lassie* series, here was another fine young actor who couldn't get a job in Hollywood. I did three episodes, two of which were like a serial episode. My mother and I came to the farm where Lassie lived and I brought a big old walloping dog with me. Jon takes Lassie and I take my dog out for a walk in the woods, and a hunter shoots and kills my dog, so we had another very emotional scene. I did the Christmas show when my character comes back a year later. They have flashbacks of me from the first show showing us having fun frolicking through the woods and then the dog getting shot. We filmed it in midsummer even though it was a Christmas show. In this one we come across an overturned sleigh with an old man lying under it, and we think he is Santa Claus. He is pinned under the sleigh so we and Lassie rescue him by getting it off. That day was 95 to 100 degrees. The crew was sitting around with the least amount of clothing on. Jon and I were in Mackinaws and wool hats. I have never been so hot in all my life. The snow was like a foam that they shot out of a big hose. It didn't have the consistency of soap suds as much as it did shaving cream. It looked very real."

Billy's other television credits include *Twilight Zone, Laramie, Wide Country, 77 Sunset Strip, The Detectives, 87th Precinct, Dennis the Menace, Leave It to Beaver*, and *The Law and Mr. Jones* ("I can't give enough credit to James Whitmore. A wonderful actor and a prince of a guy"). He also worked on *General Hospital* and *Divorce Court*. In reflecting on the live-taped shows he said, "It was kind of nerve wracking. You didn't get too much margin for making a blooper. You rehearsed hard and heavy for about a week, and then it was show time. It's kind of like stage work. You better deliver the goods because you only get one chance at it."

In 1963 Paramount Pictures was interviewing for a movie called *My Six Loves*. "First we had the routine cattle call that you go through. We went weeks interviewing, sifting and sifting. Finally they said, 'Billy, would you mind if we dyed your hair? We want all you six kids to kind of look the same.' I said, 'No, I don't mind.' So they bleached it out and made it sandy colored. It was then down between two or three boys. Then I got a call from my agent. 'Billy,' he said, 'you've been cast in the part of Leo.' That was the height of joy. Getting the production on line, getting it rehearsed, landing the part, and all of this uniting as a show business family. After two weeks we were very tight people. Debbie Reynolds was absolutely the most wonderful person to work with. She was sweet, she was kind, she was caring and funny. When things got a little hectic or stressful on the set she would always break the ice with her jokes. David Janssen was a quiet gentleman but a privilege to work with. Cliff Robertson was a very professional actor. There were some great actors that had cameo parts. I felt like I elevated my career to a level where I was working with some pretty big movie stars, and had the opportunity to work with the other five kids who were just wonderful. We were just like a family. I have to pay tribute to the director, Gower Champion, who was a wonderful man and who made possible a very good movie. He was a prince of a director and such a compassionate man. He was capable of drawing out emotions and talking softly and bringing the best cream to the top. By the end of the eight weeks of shooting, needless to say, there were multiple tears that came from all of us because it was like saying goodbye to a family. The reflections from *My Six Loves* are the most wonderful of all. It was my highlight; my hour of glory. I worked on it for eight weeks and it was absolute pleasure."

With *My Six Loves* wrapping up, Billy's career came to an unexpected end. "I was feeling that I had broke the barrier and from that point on I thought good things are going to happen. They didn't. This was very traumatic for me. All of a sudden I didn't have the support of my family. My dad was having divorce problems and there was crisis going on in the family. My grandmother, who was raising both me and my brother and doing the best she could, became frustrated. She didn't want anything to do with Hollywood. She couldn't carry it alone, and so said, 'You boys need to get an education and a job to support yourselves because this is not working.' So when the agency called, saying, 'Mrs. Hughes, we've got several interviews set up for Billy and Chris [Billy's brother],' she would just say, 'I can't get them there.' He responded, 'You've got to, they're right at their pinnacle and everything's about ready to break open good for them.' But because of my grandmother's decision and circumstance, by 1964 I couldn't get a job and I became a very depressed person.

"I at least had the sense to finish high school and keep my grades up so I could go to college if I wanted. One of the teachers on the set had encouraged me earlier in my schooling, saying, 'Billy, don't let show business be your primary goal in life. Get a good education.' Well, I listened to that advice and tried to stay a B student all through high school even though I was dealing with a lot of depression, especially in my senior year."

Reflecting on his school years while working as an actor, Billy stated, "School was tough to start with because it was very regimental during that era. The hippie movement hadn't started yet so all the young men were macho, and you weren't considered macho unless you had a crewcut. Well, I had to keep my hair a little shaggy because of the westerns and different period films, and I liked it that way. That was a constant challenge because I always had to fight with my peers due to my having long hair. I even had trouble with the principal and some teachers. I think my Uncle Whitey—or it may have been my dad—went to the education department and said, 'Look, here's the situation. He's not being rebellious. He's a good student. He's just got to keep his hair long for these parts.' The dress code at that time was very strict, but they said they would accept it. I would try to pick out one person who had enough sense about him to recognize that I was just another kid. I never was pretentious about being in movies, and I never was arrogant. When I went back to school after each production I just wanted to be one of the kids, but they would not allow me. When I came back it would always be, 'Oh, the movie star's back in school.' They were picking and word throwing, and it came to the point where I really dreaded going. There was one guy who was very antagonistic about my being in the picture business. I assume now the guy would probably have liked to have been in the business himself, but needless to say he wasn't doing any favors by picking on me. He would challenge me about every day to come to the back gate of the school, stating he was going to whip me. I always found some way to get out of it and go home because I didn't like fighting. One afternoon the class was over and I came down the stairs and there he was with his talk. Well, I just had enough, and I turned around and laid into him. That was the only time I had a real fight with anybody in school. And you know, that's what it took. From that point on he didn't mess with me.

"I was pretty much a loner through high school outside of one friend and buddy that I could confide in and get along with (the one being fellow child actor Mickey Sholdar). I was just anxious to get school over with. I graduated when I was 18 and spent a couple of years doing odd jobs. One was working with my dad as a wrangler and stunt man on *Five Card Stud*. But these jobs were not satisfying or fulfilling. I was very lost and very disorientated as to where I was going because my show business career wasn't going anywhere. I started medicating myself just to keep sane. I was lost and confused during that little span of time, my heart in tumultuous turmoil, and then my loving wife came along.

"It was in 1969 that I met my lovely wife Aida. I said, 'Come on, sweetheart, I want to get as far away from Hollywood as I can get,' and we went to Van Buren, Arkansas. That's where we had family roots. My dad had more or less retired from the business and lived back there. I had saved enough money from show business to where we were able to buy a nice little house on half an acre. The cost of living was not bad at that time and living in Arkansas was even cheaper. I worked at odd jobs, but I always found myself slipping back into that depression because the job that I was doing was not what my heart wanted to do."

In 1971 Billy's father told him, "We're going to do a picture." He had put together the concept for *Smoke in the Wind*, and said he would write in a good part for Billy if he'd help with other things. Billy told him, "I'll do anything just to be in the business." Speaking of his working in this film, Billy said, "I literally worked for gratis, I never received any money for it at all. At the end there was a situation where they didn't have the money backers to finish the production so they had to start cutting it short. The film was another let-down, and that was the end of my career. No, I won't say it is the end of my career because in my heart I am still an actor. That's my profession, my career, and that's what I love. Just because the time frame is out of focus it doesn't mean I wouldn't, if given the opportunity, work again. I'd love to have that chance. Even though I haven't worked since 1971, I'm just an older man now, but there are still wonderful parts out there for a 50 year old."

Billy and Aida's son, Billy III, was born in 1973. "Now I had focus on something to do, and that was to raise my child. I wondered what we could do that had a little dignity to it, and make a living and get by until we raised our son." Billy opened a restaurant and later he and Aida operated an interior decorating business. They lived in Arkansas until 1989. "Our son was grown and graduating, so I said, 'This has been good to us here, but I would like to go back to California.' We made the move in 1990, and from then until now my life has been pretty difficult. I've been a manic depressive and have been unemployed for almost eight years because of my depression. I need to go back to work. I think the problem is that I've done everything I wanted to do, which was to rear my son. He's on his own now and has his own life and is an example of a good young man. Now I'm at a complete loss."

Three months before this interview, Billy received a phone call from former child actor Paul Petersen. "I've had lunch with him and shared my story with him. I have to give tribute to Paul Petersen because he is reuniting a lot of us together. He calls it the new version of *Our Gang*. He says he has about 500 actors and has gotten them mentally focused to let us all know that what happened to us wasn't an isolated case, and that's what all of us were thinking. We're thinking how come I went down? How come I lost my status? The problem was so prevalent, but we just thought it was happening to us because we didn't communicate with one another. Acting was our whole life, and then you are too old at 13 or 16. Doing all these programs and hitting 14, and then all of a sudden no more calls coming in. I just really got very downhearted. It was such a let-down. So now as Paul brings all *Our Gang* back together we see that it happened to all of us."

Jimmy Hunt

Jimmy Hunt was born December 4, 1939, in Los Angeles, California, and raised in the areas of Culver City and Santa Monica. "When I was about six years old I was going to grammar school about six blocks from MGM. They were looking for someone to play Van Johnson as a young boy for *High Barbaree*. They looked throughout Hollywood and couldn't find someone that they wanted, so when they came to our school they picked three or four of us out. MGM gave us a screen test, and I was fortunate enough to get the part."

Jimmy went to the studio, where the picture was in preproduction. "They put me on the lot and I went to school there with Elizabeth Taylor, Roddy McDowall and a few of the other kids which were making movies at that time. Then they put me into a movie called *My Brother Talks to Horses* with Butch Jenkins. We made that one, then came *High Barbaree*. Then they asked me to come back and make another movie called *Living in a Big Way*, and it just started to roll from there."

Jimmy reflected on his start in the movie business, saying "It was an experience I never sought for. My parents didn't know anything about the movie business at all. My dad was a tool and dye maker and my mom was a homemaker. They had no idea of what it would take to get their children into movies. I know there are children who want to be in movies so badly and are very talented. They can sing, dance and do all kinds of things and never get the opportunity because the break never happens, and I was just fortunate to have that happen. I think I just went to work in the movies like a little kid would go to play. Of course I had to memorize my lines. My dad and mom worked with me on that, and then I would go and do exactly what they told me to do. I guess with the freckles and the curly hair, that was enough to get me through those first few movies. As I look back I think I did an okay job. I now like to see some of the old movies. It's kind of fun to watch yourself when you were little and say, 'Hey, I remember doing that,'" he laughed.

When asked if he had a favorite movie that he was in, Jimmy quickly answered, "*The Lone Hand*. I was probably more involved in that movie up to that point, except when I did *Invaders from Mars* where the whole movie revolved around myself. Joel McCrea and myself were the leading players[in *The Lone Hand*]. And I narrated the movie. That was the first time I ever did any of that kind of thing." Speaking of his favorite actor that he worked with, Jimmy stated it was Joel McCrea. "He was a special man. He treated me just like his son. He was really just a nice man, so we really had some good times together." Why was this his favorite film? Besides working with McCrea, and the important role he played in the film, Jimmy replied, "It was a western. I got to ride a horse and drive a team of horses."

Jimmy Hunt from *The Romantic Age* (Columbia, 1949.)

A large portion of the movie was filmed on location in Colorado, which Jimmy also enjoyed. "My mom went with me. And my dad and grandparents came up with my sister to see me at vacation." Although the film was shot during the summer, there nonetheless had to be a teacher on the set when child actors were involved. "You still had a teacher that was there with you at all times because they were sort of like your welfare worker and made sure the production company didn't do anything they shouldn't do for the child. There were only so many hours you could work." During the school year three hours a day had to be set aside for the child actor's education. "You could get that in 15-minute increments, but you had to get three hours in. So that was one of the reasons they came up with the little midgets to do stand-in work for the kids because they were relatively the same height we were, and they could light the set without us being there."

Besides the use of little people standing in, Jimmy explained, "In the faraway shots they had a young jockey that did some of the scenes driving the wagon, especially the ones like where I get roped off the horse." In another scene Jimmy reflected, "I got to drive the wagon to a certain point, and then they'd do it over again with the jockey. This is where the wagon goes off into the river and he jumps off."

Jimmy had a few uncertain moments during the filming of *The Lone Hand*. "They got a horse this little girl had owned. They figured if she could ride it then I'd be okay. But she was the only person that ever rode this horse and he was used to her, but wasn't used to anybody else. He messed me up a couple of times; I got thrown off him, he ran away with me once, and dumped me off into a side of the hill. Then they shipped him back to Colorado, and he got into a fight with another horse in the trailer. He got kicked up pretty bad so they had to get a different horse, and they don't know how happy I was," he laughed.

Another one of Jimmy's favorites was *Family Honeymoon* with Claudette Colbert, Fred MacMurray, Peter Miles and Gigi Perreau as the other members of his family. One of the scenes has the family riding muleback into the Grand Canyon. Asked about his reflections of filming there on location, his answer was somewhat surprising. "We never went to the Grand Canyon on location for that one. They took a group of doubles. Most of it was far away when you see them riding into the Grand Canyon on mules. The close up of us on the mules was done at the studio."

Jimmy also mentioned that he did the radio production of *Family Honeymoon* on *Lux Radio Theater*. "Radio was really interesting. Completely different than doing film because they had this huge audience that would come and sit there. Of course, I had my mother sit with me because when I was little I couldn't keep up with where we were supposed to be, and she would help with that. You would go up with the script in your hand and stand in front of a mike and say your lines, and then come back and sit in your chair and wait as the scene played out. So it was very different."

Two other films that were among his favorites were *Cheaper by the Dozen* and *Belles on Their Toes*. "We had a lot of fun making those." Reflecting on *Cheaper by the Dozen*, he stated, "I can remember the two older kids, Norman Olmstead and his stand-in, and a few others below me. We were playing a scene that was supposed to be at Nantucket, and

Jimmy with Peter Miles as Charlie and Abner Jordan, a couple of annoying kids, in *Family Honeymoon* (Universal, 1948).

they made it down at Seal Beach. We stayed at Long Beach at the biggest hotel at that time. It had an elevator that we thought was really great because at that time they had the elevator operator. So we would get in and the operator would take you to whatever floor you wanted to go to. At night he'd go off. We were on the 15th floor, so we'd get in the elevator and swoosh—down we'd go and about the second or third floor we'd shut it off and that thing would come down and bounce up. We thought that was the greatest thing in the world. If they had caught us they would have killed us. But we were being kids having fun because all day we'd be working. We probably caused a lot of trouble," he laughed. "We'd go to dinner and go right down the menu and, of course, you'd follow what the older kids would do. They'd order what was most expensive, and we'd do the same thing. The studio's paying for it. My mother was always saying, 'No, you don't want that—you want this.' That was a fun movie to make."

When asked what Clifton Webb was like to work with, Jimmy reminisced about him and various other stars he had worked alongside in the movies. "Clifton Webb didn't like kids," he laughed, "so he was really acting in that movie. He was pretty good. Jeannie Crain was nice; Myrna Loy was a nice lady, and most everybody treated me well. I guess if you had to say, Joel McCrea was the very best." We asked him who was the worst? "Maybe Bob Hope. I was in a movie called *Here Come the Girls*, and that was a movie I really didn't want to make. It was a small part and so I didn't get a lot of interface with him, but what I had just wasn't the greatest experience. Another one was Bing Crosby. I made a very good movie with him called *Top o' the Morning*, and we acted a lot together in that movie. But afterwards he went off to his dressing room and you were by yourself. But that was a fun movie too, because I got to learn to speak with an Irish brogue. The lady did such a good job teaching us that it got to the point where they could hardly understand us, so we had to go back and dub a lot of the dialogue. That was hard to do. I had to do the same thing when I did the narration on *The Lone Hand*. They set you down after the movie's been made; you sit there and watch the movie, and start your dialogue exactly when they tell you to so that it fits within the film sequence."

Among Jimmy's other film credits are *Louisa* in which he played Ronald Reagan's son; *All American* with Tony Curtis: "They had some football players from UCLA on the set so it was fun to see those guys"; *Rusty's Birthday* in which he plays the son of a drifter family and is accused of stealing the hero's dog Rusty. "The dog that was in that movie was called Flame. He was pretty famous, kind of like a Rin Tin Tin. He was the father of a litter of puppies and I got one for being in the movie. We got the dog, brought it home and this dog got distemper and we had to put it to sleep"; *The Fuller Brush Man* with Red Skelton ("I played the part of a mean little kid. Red Skelton was good. What I understand now is that when you were on a set and he told a joke you needed to laugh, whether you thought it was funny or not. But he was good"); and several westerns: *Rock Island Trail* in which he plays a boy fishing with Abe Lincoln; his testimony in court recounting his knowledge of the river currents saves the railroad; *Return of the Badmen* where he worked the first couple of days with Gabby Hayes, but it was then decided he was too young for the part and was replaced by Gary Gray; and finally *Saddle Tramp*, again with Joel McCrea in which he was among a group of orphans that McCrea had to care for.

Some directors in Hollywood had a reputation of being really nasty on the set, where others had just the opposite. Jimmy spoke of his experience with directors, saying "I'm sure they were a little more gentle with us and they had patience with children. I think with all of us kids being there on the set of *Belles on Their Toes*, we tried the director's patience a little bit. Normally when you are on a movie and it's just you, there's nobody else to play with so you just do your thing and hang around. You are either in school or the teacher tries to keep you busy with some kind of a project, but when there's other kids, hey—now there's somebody to play with. Then you could get yourself into trouble, and we did that every once in a while. We'd play where we were not supposed to be. We were always hounding the prop man to see if we could play with some of the props, and of course it's 'Get out of here, leave it alone.' I enjoyed the cameraman and some of the behind-the-scenes things. I thought that was really great. They treated me very well, and most of the directors were very good too. As you got older, they expected more from you. Then it became work. *The Lone Hand* and *Invaders from Mars* became real work."

Although Jimmy's favorite film was *The Lone Hand*, he did add that "The one I'm most recognized for is *Invaders from Mars*. It was a neat film to be in because of the mutants, and those guys were unbelievable. Max Palmer was about eight feet tall, and the other guy was like seven feet nine inches. They had to put lifts on him so they'd be the same height.

"But like I said, I always thought it was really neat behind the camera," Jimmy continued. "The special effects they made for that movie were really neat. I enjoyed that. And then they had the army involved. Just the half-track and tank; I thought those were really neat. These are the kind of things that were fun. All of the rest of it was just work. You went there, somebody told you what to do and you tried to do your very best. Of course, as a child you really tried to please someone, so you wanted really hard to get everything right."

Reflecting on some of the special effects in the movie, Jimmy said, "They made up a model and had it in a crystal ball. When they showed the Supreme Being, and you could see the eyes moving and it was thinking, it was a lady by the name of Luce Potter. She was a midget. They put this head they made around her with the makeup and tentacles, and had the ball over her. She sat in this box and did all of her movements."

Jimmy's career was mostly in features. His television work was minimal. "I did a pilot for a series called *The Loving Family* with Marjorie Lord. We did several episodes but they didn't pick it up, or it wasn't what they were looking for."

Outside of the few difficulties with the horse in *The Lone Hand*, Jimmy had one other mishap while filming *Weekend with Father*. The movie concerned two divorcees getting their kids to go to camp. Patricia Neal played the mother of two boys (one being Jimmy), and Van Heflin played the father of two girls. The kids meet each other at the camp, and their parents also happen to meet each other and fall in love. When they come to the camp to pick the kids up and Jimmy is told Heflin will be his new dad, he thinks, "Oh man, what a lame guy." Jimmy explained that

that "part of the movie concerned us playing some games, Van Heflin and I. One was a potato sack race. While we were doing it he was in front and I was in back. We were hopping along and the director said, 'Cut, lets do it over again.' So instead of getting out of the bag and walking back, we started to jump backwards. We lost our balance and going over backwards I put my hand out to break the fall and he fell on top of me. He was a pretty big man, and it broke my arm right where it joins the shoulder. They took me to the hospital. If it had been a regular kid they would have put a full cast around him, but they needed to continue the movie. That's when they decided that I was going to tell Heflin that I don't want to do that game, that it's lame; so my little brother had to do it, and was in all those races with Van Heflin. They fixed up a special kind of harness for the broken arm, strapped my arm to my body, and I made the movie with a broken arm."

Jimmy's career covered seven years and 38 movies. He began at six and left at 13. Why did he leave? "I decided I wanted to play sports. I hated the fact that my mom had to come to school to get me. I'd be playing sports, and she'd say 'Come on, we have to go to an interview.' That was the worst thing I ever did: go to an interview. When I went, I didn't want to get the part. But unfortunately the other kids came and had their little suits on and had their portfolios, and when I came I had a pair of Levi's, and my mom would always give me a clean shirt and comb my hair. I went and I guess I was what they were looking for and I'd get the part. I don't think I was ever disappointed that I didn't get a part."

His parents' reaction to his leaving the business was simply that "They wanted me to know what the consequences would be. I was at the point when I was one of the top child movie stars in Hollywood at that time, because all of the big stars before me had grown up; they were either doing young adult movies or out of the business completely. So they really discussed it with me and let me know what I was going to give up. I don't care, I just don't want to do it anymore. I look back on it now and yes, it was a good decision. There were a few times, like when I'd like to have something, a possession of some kind, and think if I was still in the movies I could be able to afford this, but besides that, no, I never regretted it. Every once in a while when I was watching something like *Father Knows Best* or *Ozzie and Harriett*, I would think I could do that, but I was very happy. I played sports in high school, had a good childhood, and was able to grow up and grow up right."

After leaving the movies, Jimmy finished high school, attended college and went into the service. "I was in the Army Security Agency where we intercepted and broke codes. I was stationed in Germany and met my wife Roswitha there. I got out of the service after three years and we came home. I went back to school and then started a career in manufacturing. I was a draftsman for a short period of time and then went into sales. About 1971 I went into industrial sales and I've been doing that ever since."

In 1986, Jimmy experienced an unintentional return to work in a motion picture. He explained how this came about. "I was calling on a young engineer at Lockheed, and he was into music and movies. He read *Variety* every day. He found out that I was in movies, so I showed him my scrapbook and he thought it was great. About this time, Scott Holden and Robert Slovak did an article on *Invaders from Mars*, the original movie, and this engineer and I had kidded about the fact that it would be funny if they ever did a remake that I would be in. When he found out that they were going to do the remake, and that Holden had become the publicity guy on the movie, he kept telling me 'You got to call those guys.... You got to get in this movie.' I kept saying 'I don't want to do that,' so he called the studio and said he knows where the original kid is. They invited me to come down for an interview and asked me if I would do a cameo role and play the chief of police. I took some vacation time from work and went and did it. It was kind of fun. In that movie, as policemen, we were coming down into the basement because that is where the young boy and the school nurse had hid. We go into this boiler room and just for a second the camera pans across and you see some old files, and on top of the files is the original *Invaders from Mars* head in the round crystal ball. So they did that. And when I and another policeman were going up the hill to investigate the fact that the father had gone away and not come back, I say 'You know, I haven't been here since I was a kid.' We go up over the hill and they suck us down. When we come back we're all messed up."

In summing up his feelings about his work in the movies, Jimmy stated "There were a lot of things I got to do that I never would have been able to do in my whole life if it hadn't have been for the fact that someone came and took me out of school that day. It was a very interesting thing to do. I was glad to get out of it, like I said, but now it's fun to reminisce."

Teddy Infuhr

Teddy Infuhr was born November 9, 1936, in St. Louis, Missouri. "My parents moved to California when I was three years old to get away from the weather and at that time Hollywood and Southern California was a good place to go to. Somewhere along the line—I was five years old—my mother had me in an acting school in Hollywood and I was in some little play. An agent saw me and told me to go to an interview, and I got the first part I went for. Once you have credits you keep on working. So that's how it started—simple as that."

Asked how he enjoyed working in the movies, Teddy replied, "The movie thing was my mother's idea. It wasn't anything I was in love with. You know, show business is funny, you either love show business and acting, or ehhhh! It just didn't fit me the way I was, so that's the way that went. Probably as a little kid I'd just as soon go play. It's as simple as that."

Teddy attended regular school when not working in a picture. Asked if the other children treated him any differently because he was a child actor, he replied "Not really, I guess I didn't play the part with them either." Teddy enjoyed bowling with his school friends, but as far as other sports were concerned he mentioned that "I was just a short little runt so if I'd get into contact sports, they'd squash me." One of the things Teddy enjoyed was horseback riding. "I learned to ride pretty young. I used to ride horses all the time. I enjoyed that. The stables used to be right over at Los Feliz and Riverside Drive."

When working in a film during the school year, Teddy would get his lessons on the studio lot. Asked what that was like, he replied, "Three hours a day with a social worker. I'd get my assignments from school." What was his impression of this type of schooling? "It would depend on who you had as your teacher or social worker. Some of them were very nice and some of them were mean," Teddy laughed.

Teddy's first film role was in the 1942 movie classic *Tuttles of Tahiti*. When asked about any reflections on his first day on the set, he laughed and answered, "That's the funny part. At five years old what do I remember? I remember a few things here and there, but in general I was just a little kid."

Teddy worked with Abbott and Costello in *Pardon My Sarong*, stating that "I just remember Costello was cuckoo. Even as a kid I wondered who was this guy running around. He was a real character.

Teddy Infuhr

Just hyper all the time; doing this and doing that even when he wasn't shooting the movie," he laughed.

He does remember when he had to work in a movie where they had to shave his head. "Then I had to go to school in the fourth grade and I wouldn't take my cap off," he smiled. "And I'd get a note from school—*that* I remember." Having his head shaved for that particular film was the reason he landed the role of the deaf-mute in *Sherlock Holmes and the Spider Woman*.

Teddy also appeared in the Alfred Hitchcock thriller, *Spellbound*, in which he played Gregory Peck's brother. In his scene, a flashback, Joel Davis (playing Peck as a child) slid down a cement porch and bumped Teddy causing him to fall and be impaled on a spiked fence. "I remember that scene because those bars were made out of charcoal, but it looked real and it was kind of weird falling over on those things."

Teddy played the character of Squeaky Foley in four of the *Rusty the Dog* series and as a boy named Tommy in a fifth. Teddy has no exceptional recollections of any happenings on the sets of these films, except

"I remember doing a lot of them. The dog [Flame] was nice." But playing one of the Kettle boys in the Ma and Pa Kettle films with Percy Kilbride and Marjorie Main does hold several memories for Teddy. Asked for his reflections on these two character actors, he stated, "Percy Kilbride was a very quiet person. I remember shooting on the backlot at Universal and my brother-in-law was out from Missouri. He was a farmer. They called lunch break, and when they started to shoot again at one o'clock they couldn't find Percy Kilbride. Well, he and my brother-in-law were sitting way up on top of a hill talking about farming and just forgot about time. He was a real down to earth person. Marjorie Main had sinus trouble like you'd never believe. In fact they kept the set so hot that you could hardly breathe in there so she could function. You ever watch that movie *The Egg and I* when she opens the front screen door and it falls down and all the dust comes up? Well, somebody screwed up on that and when the dust got in her nose we couldn't shoot for two days. She was out of it. So I still remember a couple of things like that."

Teddy made a number of films away from the studio lot. One of his favorite locations was in the redwoods near Santa Cruz for *The Sun Comes Up*. "We stayed at Santa Cruz a few days and they would bus us up to the location every morning. It was a pretty area."

At the age of 14, Teddy played the role of Jonathan in the biblical epic, *David and Bathsheba*. "That was the first time I was in an airplane. We went to Nogales, Arizona, to shoot that. My mom was born in Austria. She came over here when she was 18. We went across into Mexico and to come back they wouldn't let her across the border because she didn't have any papers. The studio people came by and got her through," he laughed.

Besides his close to 100 motion picture credits, Teddy also appeared in early television shows such as *Gene Autry*, *Red Skelton* and *The Cisco Kid*. Speaking of the roles he played, Teddy said "I was typecast as a mean little kid." He then went on to reflect on several of his television shows. About his work in *The Cisco Kid* series, Teddy stated, "Leo Carrillo was a great card player. There would always be card games going." About working on live television on the *Red Skelton Show* he said: "I had a line to speak and was waiting for my cue. Well, Red Skelton never followed a script and I was sitting there waiting; finally he stopped whatever he was talking about for a second and I stuck my line in there just to get it in. Everybody cracked up because it didn't fit, but it was the only chance I had to say anything. He was just all add-lib. I stood waiting for my cue that never came," Teddy laughed. Teddy told of a humorous incident while working in a television show with Gene Autry. "Autry was climbing

Teddy played Alvin in RKO's *They Live By Night* (1949). Here he is seen with doomed lovers, Cathy O'Donnell and Farley Granger.

through this window and I'm supposed to be standing there with this big frying pan and hit him over the head with it. The bottom of the frying pan is two inches of foam rubber painted black and I guess I turned the thing sideways and hit him with the side of that steel frying pan and knocked him out. It's one of those things," he laughed.

In discussing his work with various directors, Teddy was asked if he was treated any differently than the adult actors. "Not really. As a kid you just did your own thing. With the social worker around there they had rules to follow. They could work you only so much under the light and then they'd give you a break periodically. So they couldn't do whatever they wanted."

When the studios quit calling Teddy for interviews, he stated, "I felt just fine. I was still in high school. Like I said, if you enjoy acting and show business it's the greatest high in the world—but if it doesn't really hit you that way, you'd just as soon not do it. It's like any other job. Whatever you like to do you enjoy doing it; if you don't like it you don't enjoy doing it and just as soon would not." However, when asked if he felt his acting career got in the way of his childhood, he replied, "No, not really."

After his acting career was finished, Teddy graduated from Loyola High School and then attended Loyola University where he took premed for a year. "I then decided to go into chiropractics and went to Davenport, Iowa; for four years. In 1958 I started chiropractics in Los Angeles."

For enjoyment, Teddy said, "I'm a fisherman. Freshwater." His favorite fishing spots include the Sierras, local lakes and the Colorado River. "Getting away is half the fun of that."

In summing up his feelings about his acting career, Teddy sat back and thought for a moment. He then said, "Well, it's hard to say because I really don't remember that much from that whole era. I hate to leave you in a void, but when you are six or seven years old it just doesn't stick in the memory. I did most of the movies when I was five to 15 and it's just history."

Tommy Ivo

Tommy Ivo was born in Denver, Colorado, on April 18, 1936. "When I was in Denver everybody sang and tap danced instead of playing guitars like they do nowadays. I went around with the tap dance school and entertained at various places. Everyone thought I was cute, and said, 'You ought to take him to New York or Los Angeles and get him in the movies or on the stage.' My mother had arthritis real bad. Every winter she was damn near in a wheelchair, so we thought, 'Let's take a run out.' When I was about seven years old my mother and I came out to California. One reason was to see what happened with her arthritis, which went away just like that. The other was to see if she could get little Tommy into the movies. Well, of course, that was pretty much of a long shot."

Tommy had a written introduction from his singing teacher and went with his mother to Warner Bros. They were told, "We don't need any blond, curly-haired, blue-eyed kids, we got them coming out of our ears." Having no luck at the studio, Tommy began taking a dancing class. "Warners was doing a movie called *Earl Carroll's Vanities* with Dennis O'Keefe, and needed a kid for it that looked kind of like him and that could tap dance. They searched all over and came to my dancing class and there I was. My front teeth were missing, I did the boogie woogie and just had the right look at the right time. And I got in. You know the Catch-22: you can't get a movie until you have an agent and you can't get an agent until you have a movie, so you've got to stumble onto the thing." After Tommy's first movie, his dad moved to California in a Model A with all their possessions. "So we were here to stay."

Tommy credits his brother Don with helping to teach him to act. "He was seven years older than me and ever since I was three years old we would play *Butch and Joey*. Butch was my pet gorilla. Don

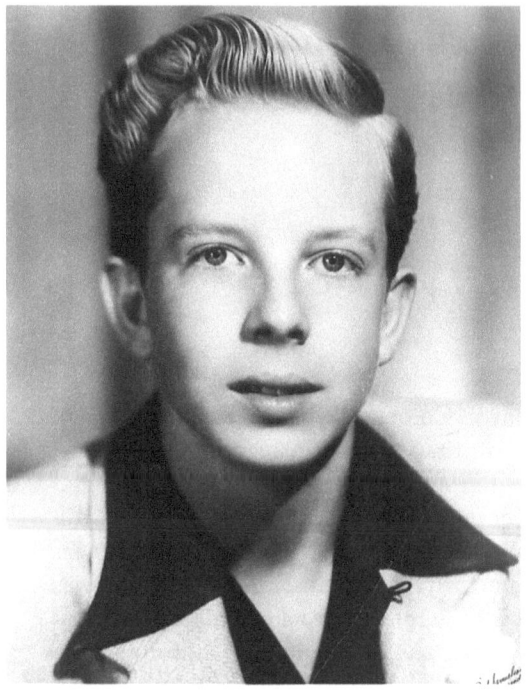

Tommy Ivo

played Butch and I was Joey, the little Superman type kid. We would go out and fight the Germans and Japanese because the war was going on. We were dead poor so we would go around after Christmas and collect all the Christmas trees and make a forest out of them and play in that forest. This ongoing series that we had going had a lot to do with helping me pretend. Don was ahead of me and sort of went his own way. He went to Korea and spent a couple of years there. When he came back home I was 17 and he was 24. We were really starting to grow together, but unfortunately he was killed in an automobile accident."

After completing *Earl Carroll's Vanities*, Tommy obtained a part in *Song of Arizona* with Roy Rogers. "Roy Rogers was my hero. I used to ride when I was in Denver on the merry-go-round and would always get Trigger. So to actually go and be with my hero when you're seven years old, that's something."

When Tommy was nine he appeared on stage as Pud in *On Borrowed Time* in Hollywood. "A lot of actors were trying to get legitimate theater out here and got together at the El Patio Theater on Hollywood Boulevard near La Brea. One would be a director one time or a stage hand. On ours, Keenan Wynn was running the production end. But they wouldn't have a kid in every show, though they needed one for that one. That's where I really got a love for the stage. I wish I had done a lot more because it was so much fun to do. That catapulted my career because with all the actors in there, everybody in town came to see the thing; when I read for it I read it with Keenan Wynn. I thought, 'Gee, he's really great,' but he said Boris Karloff was going to play the grandfather. 'Boris Karloff. You got to be kidding me?' So the first day we were rehearsing I was sitting there just glued to the door waiting for this guy with a square head and pegs coming out of his neck to come walking in," he laughed. "But of course Boris Karloff was very much different than that." We asked him what Boris Karloff was like? "He absolutely couldn't have been nicer. He used to call me his walking script because if he couldn't remember something while we were doing the show I'd whisper the line to him. I loved live audiences, but I didn't get to do a lot of plays because there wasn't a whole bunch of it around at the time."

Tommy discussed his feelings on being a child actor, saying "These kids that say, 'I ruined my childhood,' I don't know what's wrong with them because it just could not have been better for me. But I did it a little bit different because I would keep doing public school. I'd get my assignments and go to the set. When I did Cousin Arne in *I Remember Mama*, I was on that for six months. In between time I would go back to my regular school, but when I was working they had to have both a teacher and a guardian on the set and they could only work you eight hours a day. Of those eight hours you had to have three hours of school and an hour lunch, so you could only actually work four hours a day. When you're 18 they can work you all the time, so when I got to my last year of high school they had kids that were older that looked younger and they could bypass that time schedule. So I got my whole last year of high school in by just going to school. Maybe that gave me a little different outlook because I got the best of both worlds. I went to the normal life and then had the movie life all mixed in at the same time. The only time I was under contract to a studio was when I was already out of school and doing the *Margie* show."

How did Tommy's classmates treat him? "Terribly," he laughed. "In the first place, I was a runt. I didn't look my age. And then I was doing all these westerns. In those days no one had long hair. The kids had white sidewalls and here I come hustling through the hallway with my hair half way down to my rump and they would say, 'Who's that kid?' They also didn't like that I had a new car when I was 16. Nobody had a new car, not even the principal in those days. That was before Dad and the Visa card. Every once in a while they'd cut my tires. I was kind of a little geek in a way, but I had my girlfriend and that's all I needed—my girlfriend and my work. So I don't feel it was a detriment of any kind, though I was a little bit different than the other kids at school."

Tommy said that he seemed to get typecast as orphans or kid brothers on a ranch. "I did upwards of 100 movies, but a lot of them were B-westerns of the late 1940s and early '50s." Commenting on these films, Tommy said, "That was kind of a mixed bag. For one thing, I've always been a pretty late sleeper, and you had to be on the bus on the way to

Corrigan's Ranch or wherever before the sun came up. And then they had the old pancake make-up. They would warm up the water, but it got cold and they'd hit you in the face with a cold, wet sponge. As far as the things that stand out, my favorite was the special effects. I'd follow those guys around like they had a leash on me. It wasn't too sophisticated in those days. They'd shoot holes in a door and then putty them back up with charges behind them. Then you would stand there and they'd blow the charges out when someone was shooting at you. Jock Mahoney was absolutely my stony-eyed hero because he did all the stunt work for the *Durango Kid* shows, and I did a number of those. I was small enough that everybody treated me pretty good; they'd always come by and tap me on the head and say, 'Hi ya kid, how are you doing?' I heard through the grapevine that Smiley Burnette was a little tough to deal with, but he just couldn't have been nicer to me.

"The first time I did a western where I had to ride, I went out and learned. Everything worked out pretty good with the stable horses, but when we got to the movie horses Ray Nazarro said, 'Okay, come from the top of that hill and run by the camera hell bent for leather,' and I beat on that horse and it would not move. It would trot down the hill and there was nothing I could do to make it to go because I wasn't exactly a horseman. So Nazarro said, 'Okay, we'll crank the camera and see what we get.' So I got back up to the top of the hill and I hear, 'Okay, roll them!' and I saw the horse's ears go up. The clapper went off and I started to say, 'Giddy-up,' and that thing took off like wildfire. It went passed the camera, put all four hoofs out and stopped on a dime, and over it's head I went. After that I was a lot more cautious with movie horses because they were a lot smarter about the whole deal than I was. They weren't going to run in rehearsals, but when they heard the camera was rolling, 'Okay, here we go. Hang on.'"

I Remember Mama was one of the big pictures Tommy worked on. Speaking of working with director George Stevens, he said, "That's what took so long to make it. We'd sit down on the set around the table on the first day and talk about what everybody should be feeling. The next day we'd take a few run-throughs, and finally they'd get to the cameras and he'd get one scene done and say, 'That was perfect. Let's see if we can get one more just like it.' And it went on for months and months and months.

"When I did *I Remember Mama* I had lots of curls. That was the fashion, but I was getting tired of them. What they decided to do was cut the curls off so I'd have straight hair. They said to come to the make-up table, and whoop! Off come the curls and I was all smiles. I put my hat on and went over and stood in front of my mother and whipped off my hat and she about had a heart attack. But I got rid of the curls and was in seventh heaven."

Tommy's mother always accompanied him to the various movie sets that he worked on. "My mom was born in Sweden before the turn of the century. Her father was a Protestant minister and had some pretty strong thoughts about things. She came over here when she was 16 years old and didn't really have too much of a life. She lived it vicariously through me. The sad part of it was that *I Remember Mama* was really a good movie, but seeing how her father was a minister and to him films were the devil's tool she couldn't tell him to go see his grandson in the pictures. It would have been great because that was a good movie."

Tommy enjoyed working with Johnny Sheffield in a Bomba film, *The Lost Volcano*, directed by Ford Beebe. "Johnny was great. He was one of my prize people. It was fun swinging through the trees on vines with the jungle boy. We went to Santa Ana by the racetrack for some scenes. It was the first thing in the morning because they don't ever shoot anything in the afternoon when it's involved with water, right? Well, Ford Beebe said, 'Okay, just go dive into the lake.' I hit the water and it was so cold that it took my breath away. They did 90 percent of the film inside on a set at Monogram Pictures. They had all the trees on standards. They weren't really trees, but they were trees. They had ropes tied to the ceiling with little labels on them; this one for scene two, that one is for scene one. We'd swing through the tress, and then they'd move them all around and we would swing through them again. Well, they handed me a scene two rope for scene one. I started off and the rope sort of hooked over the left and I fell into the tree, which panicked them. I was hanging on for dear life, so that obviously was a great thing," he laughed.

In 1952 Tommy worked with Spencer Tracy in *Plymouth Adventure*. "That was another big one. You talk about your special effects. They had three ships: One on a pond. They had the inside of the ship as a set [the inside hull] that had elevator weights on it and would move it up and down as the camera stayed steady outside the set. Then they had an onboard ship that was set up so the end of it hung over the side of the stage, and a huge pool where Esther Williams used to do all her swimming movies. They would pull it up by sections filled with water and had a big weight that they lifted up and down to make waves for the exterior shots of the big ship. They had a huge storm in the picture that was supposed to nearly capsize the ship, and when you were in there and they were shooting fire hoses and running that wave up and down and with all the wind fans going you would think you were at sea. Of course, that was seventh heaven to me."

That same year Tommy appeared in his favorite film, *The Treasure of Lost Canyon*. "I did *Take One False Step* with William Powell, and then we did *The Treasure of Lost Canyon*. When I came on the set Powell vividly remembered me and was just one prince of a guy. I think that's my best movie. I don't say best because it was my biggest part—I've had bigger parts in smaller movies and smaller parts in much bigger movies. But they really worked hard on that one. Back in 1951 when it was made they did it in color, and when they did things in color back in those days that was really something."

A portion of the film takes place in a pool at the bottom of a waterfall. They went on location to Burney Falls in northern California for the long shots, but most of it was filmed on a studio backlot. "They had a small waterfall at Universal and just shot from the top of the fall down to the bottom so it looked like the end of this huge fall. That's where we did all of the diving into, and coming out, of the water. As far as the underwater shots were concerned, they used a huge tank filled with fifty thousand gallons of distilled water so that they could see through it, because city water isn't good enough to see through. We were in there for three days: Dive, dive and dive. I came home after that and was a dead puppy at night. They had big windows in the side of the tank that the cameras looked through.

"As I say, that is probably my best picture and it probably has a lot to do with me liking William Powell. The thing I learned in that picture was that if you are going swimming with longjohns on you'd better keep your behind away from the camera because it's a perfect fit. I looked at that when it first came out and, 'Gee whiz.' I'm really surprised it got past the censors because they were so touchy in those days. And, again, I looked so young. I was 15 in that one."

When Tommy graduated from high school, he decided that he wouldn't continue his education. He said, "Why give up a bird in hand for one in the bush. Instead of continuing on with school I continued acting. I was so hot because I was 18 and looked like I was 15. From that point on I just stormed right along." Tommy worked in many of the television shows of that period. But he had also developed a new interest. Shortly after he had worked in *Treasure of Lost Canyon* he started drag racing on the weekends. "I started tinkering with the cars because no matter how much you work, you always have time to yourself. Southern California is where hotrodding started," Tommy explained. "It was just kids racing up and down from the signals. I was getting tickets so I built a car specifically for the dragstrip which they had opened at an old airport so kids could go race out there supervised so they wouldn't have problems.

Tommy costarred with William Powell in *The Treasure of Lost Canyon* (Universal, 1952).

That was new and fresh. I had done the picture business so that was kind of old. Well, it wasn't old and it was still fun but I had been there and done that."

One summer the race car organization in the east asked, "Can someone come back here with their car for the summer. We'll give him several different tracks and $500 to stop at these various spots." At this time, no drag racer had ever been invited to travel from the west coast to the east coast. "They sent out to a list of people that they had read about in the magazines," Tommy said. "I had this show business flare in me so when I built cars I built them flashier than anybody else's. In fact, I even built a trailer that had big glass walls on the sides so people could look in, and had lights on it that I would turn on at night—it looked like a jeweled showcase going down the road. When they asked if someone could go back east for the summer I said, 'Sure, I'll go.' It was kind of hard for other people to do that because they had some sort of a business that they just couldn't close for the summer. Whereas when I was done with my job on a picture, for all intents and purposes I was out of work. I took off and went across the country. It was really the first time I was away from home with my race car and that was seventh heaven," he laughed.

When Tommy returned home after the summer he obtained the role of Heywood Botts on the *Margie* television series which concerned teenagers in the roaring twenties. "It was a half-hour show and we did one a week. That was unheard of because they always do two a week. So we had a lot of time. Cynthia Pepper was the star of the show. It was happy-go-lucky because there were no big stars on the set."

While working on the series, Tommy informed his colleagues that he did a little drag racing from time to time. "They thought it was better that I run my Cadillac at the dragstrip than race around on the signals. They didn't really pay too much attention to it until I had a car with four engines, and it was a monster. They wanted to take a picture of it on the set with me and Margie, but when I rolled that thing out of the trailer and they looked at it I could hear doors slam all the way to the other side of the lot as a guy was coming from the office with an addendum to my contract: 'There will be no more drag racing while the series is going on.'

"When the *Margie* show was canceled everyone was walking around saying with tears rolling out of their eyes, 'Ohh, we lost the series,' whereas I was doing handstands, 'Oh boy, oh boy, I get to go racing again.' Having been the first one back there I had already had a taste for it. The movies, although it was still fun, I had done for 19 years and this racing thing was brand new. And of course being all of 115 pounds, when you raise one arm in the air and 20,000 people go 'Yea, Yea, Yea,' well that's pretty nice too. A live audience. A *big* live audience. In a way it was kind of a nice catch net, because as I said I weighed 115 pounds and I wasn't exactly going to graduate into leading men parts. It was a blessing in disguise. And because the racing was so much fun I didn't miss the movies, whereas some other kids like Bobby Driscoll kind of went off the deep end. That's what I mentioned earlier—I just don't understand when these kids say it wasn't great. Well, I didn't have the big fall off. I went right from acting to the racing and it was just that much more exciting."

Tommy spent 30 years as a dragstrip racer. "Eleven years with pictures and the racing at the same time—which was amateur—and then going into professional racing for 19 years. I shocked them when I first went out with my race car because my fame preceded me. I'd drive onto the track and say, 'Hi. I'm Tommy Ivo.' They were expecting a race car driver and I look like I'm 16. They would say, 'You're Tommy Ivo?' That was a novelty because my looking younger than I was really had helped in the picture business. When I did my first movie, *Earl Carroll's Vanities*, I was seven years old. I looked to be four, maybe five if you pushed it. I was a fairly sharp seven year old, but I was a smart four year old," he laughed. "So I got a lot of mileage off that."

Drag car racing does not come without its potential hazards. "I've driven upside down and backwards faster than most people have gone on the ground," he laughed. "I ran 240 miles an hour one time upside down and backwards. The car disintegrated, but I didn't get a scratch out of the deal. The first person that got to me was a guy on a motorcycle—they would help you if your car was on fire or something until a fire truck got there, because they were quicker. Being the show biz guy that I am, I grabbed that motorcycle and ran it down to the starting line, jumped off and waved my arms in the air, ta da, 'How did you like that?'"

Tommy has not only won awards for his racing, but has also been inducted into the Drag Racing Hall of Fame. He retired at 59. "I quit racing because I was just tired of being on the road. It's fun when you're out there waving your arms and around 50,000 people are screaming, but when you're in the Piedmont of North Carolina and you have from Sunday till next Friday to sit there it does get a little boring."

In looking back over both of his careers, Tommy said, "I'm just so pleased about it. To be riding the horses, chasing the bad guys, shooting at them instead of riding my bicycle or shooting my cap gun. It was perfect. It couldn't have been better. And then when I started racing—just something to do between pictures—it turned into a business, and I did my hobby for the rest of my life. So I have been pretty lucky. I got my three wishes: the first wish was to be in the movies, the second wish was to go racing, and the third wish was to be remembered. So that's really kind of nice. I can't say how happy I am the way my life has gone. I've accomplished everything I wanted to. I started it all myself because when I was three years old we went to an auditorium at a school. I was standing

Tommy with his racing car.

on a chair watching the kids singing and dancing and said, 'That's what I want to do. I want to go up on the big stage and entertain people.' We were so poor we couldn't afford tap dance lessons. My mother's sister bought it all for me, so she was sort of my second mother. And the racing thing I just started doing myself and sort of blossomed from there, too. So although nothing was planned I was sort of at the spearhead of everything happening. Maybe I've got a rosy, deserved outlook on it. I'm kind of the glass is half full type of person instead of half empty, so if you had a good time you'll only remember the good times. You don't remember the bad times, if there are any which you'd call that. There was no downside to the movie career either; it just got better and better. On the *Margie* series I had my own chair, my own parking place, my own dressing room. All the amenities that went along with it. I had a good running part on the show, so I quit at the top of my game, which is more or less what I did with my racing."

Eilene Janssen

Eilene Janssen was born May 25, 1938, in Hollywood, California. Her father, Henry Janssen, began working at Universal Studios before the advent of sound, and her mother, Mary Ellen Thompson, was an opera singer at the Los Angeles Civic Light Opera. "My dad was at Universal for 47 years and retired at age 82. He was the one who brought me to Universal and put me in front of the camera to double for Baby Sandy when I was two years old." The picture was titled *Sandy Gets Her Man*. "The girl they had wouldn't do the stunts that she was required to do (one of which required her to jump out of a flaming building into a net), so they needed someone who would. My dad said, 'I have a daughter at home; she'll do those things.' So he brought me over to the studio and I got the job." Asked if she was scared to do that scene, she replied, "I don't remember. I did it, and that's the way the rest of my life went. I never rode a horse in my life until I acquired the *Rough Ridin' Kids* series at Republic Studio, but I told them I'd been on horses all my life, so they believed me."

Before Eilene ever stepped in front of the camera she had posed for commercial ads. "I was the Adohr baby on the milk trucks when I was about 18 months old. My picture was on the those trucks for years. From that I went into commercial photography interlaced with my movie work. I was the Weber Bread Girl; the Challenge Milk people hired me to do the milk and butter commercials on the big billboards; with my red hair and freckles I was holding a pickle for Heinz 57 Pickle Plus; I did one for Franilla Ice Cream; another for Dolly Madison; it just went on and on and on. I was at one time the most photographed child in Hollywood. No one else had done as much ads and commercial work."

Eilene also modeled for back-to-school shows. "I did those with

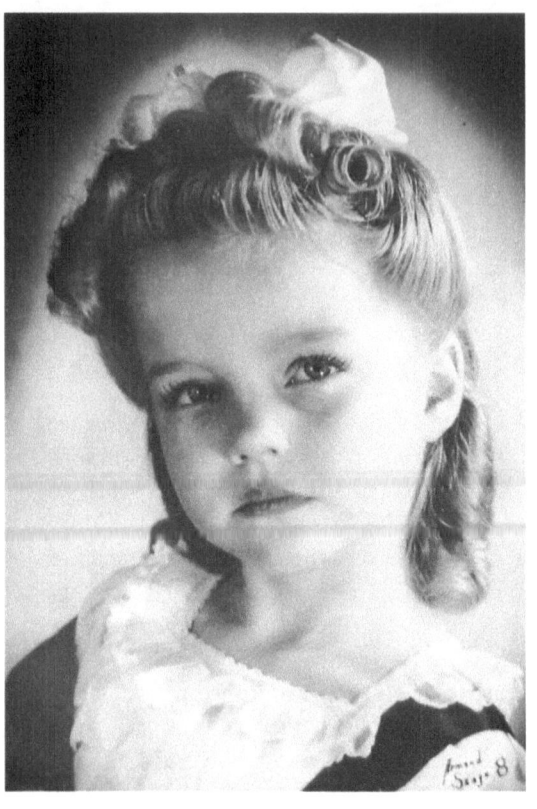

Eilene Janssen

Margaret O'Brien and Natalie Wood for the May Company and Broadway. I did a lot of theater where we would go around in troupes of performers. We'd go in army trucks in the dark because of air raid warnings going on, and perform on the docks at night to the boys that came in on the ships. I was trained to play the marimba and sang and danced. I put in over 1,000 hours of entertainment at the USOs as a child in the Hollywood Canteens along Hollywood Boulevard."

Eilene's first real film role was in *Two Girls and a Sailor* at MGM. "Gigi Perreau and I were in the first part of the picture with Jimmy Durante and we had a few lines. We played June Allyson and Gloria DeHaven as children. We had grown up in the trunks while our parents, who were vaudeville players, were out performing. Jimmy Durante was great."

The Seventh Cross was another early film for MGM directed by Frank Borzage. "He was the one that gave me my hairdo that I would carry through my whole career. He wanted me to look like a little French schoolgirl so he gave me the pigtails and the little primps. From that time on my mother always curled and braided my hair."

Eilene continued working at MGM, appearing in two films with Dean Stockwell. The first one, *The Green Years*, also featured a child actor named Richard Lyon, son of actors Ben Lyon and Bebe Daniels, who later worked behind the cameras in England. "The three of us were quite well known for that movie. After that was another MGM picture, *The Boy with Green Hair*. I remember going to MGM's school for quite a while. Elizabeth Taylor and Janie Powell were just graduating from MGM school when I was just starting. They had a physical school on the lot and so if you were doing movies you could go to school, thus we used to drive every day from North Hollywood to Culver City and I'd be trained in singing and whatever I needed to be trained in, and would go to school. That's where I went for about five years. Roddy McDowall was also there. I would eat in the commissary and see Clark Gable and all the wonderful old movie stars, which was very exciting at that age—to be sitting next to somebody who was a big star. So I grew up kind of thinking that was my family, and in a way it was because although I graduated through Immaculate Heart High School, I was not in school very much there. I was in studio schools."

A child actor was required to keep up in their school grades in order to continue taking time off to work. "The State board of education monitored what you were doing. The studio had to have a qualified teacher there who was from the board of education to keep you up with your studies from your own school. My school would send assignments and I would do those with that teacher. If you fell behind I guess they wouldn't allow you to have a permit to do another movie. I never fell behind so that never became an issue. When you went down to the board of education to get a work permit they would give you a slight physical exam to make sure that nobody was beating you to force you to be there. And it wasn't like the permit was forever, it came due every so many months. You had to go back and go through that whole routine again to make sure everything was on the up and up. It was a big deal to go there. You had to be passed by a board of people to be allowed the permit, so it was tedious, and sometimes you worried about what they were going to pick on or do."

Eilene won the 1945 *Los Angeles Herald*'s Better Babies Contest, and was chosen as Little Miss America 1948. "I won that title at the Hollywood Bowl with hundreds of young girls my age. They picked a boy too, so there was a Little Mr. America and a Little Miss America. That title was quite cherished. I remember going through lots of interviews for that, parading across the stage and being asked questions. It was quite an honor."

When she was about ten years old, Eilene was chosen by General Electric to act in a promotional film called *The Light in Your Life*. "It was a full-length movie in which I talked about how light bulbs are made. Then they sent me on tour with the film. I went with my mother, my pianist, and my marimba. I entertained and presented the film to all the big people in the lighting industry. In the film they actually put me into the light bulb. They made a shell of a light bulb and had me sitting in it. Then they talked about the filament and how it was put together. The film featured myself and a Disney animated character called Professor J. Luminim Lightly. Then they came out to our home and put in all new lighting and gave me a TV set, which was one of the first TVs around."

Eilene also worked in radio. "I did *The Art Linkletter Show*, one of those 'the kids say the darndest things.' I can't remember the other radio shows, but I do recall an interesting TV show. Do you remember Squeeky Mulligan the talking cat at KTLA? I was about ten and had my pigtails. The cat and I carried on conversations back and forth. I also played the marimba on live TV with Stan Chambers. They had to have intense lights to get a picture back on to your set and you would just perspire. I remember being in these bright lights and just dripping wet. I could barely keep my eyes open when they did those first TV shows, the lights were so bright. It was really difficult. So I have been in every aspect of the business."

Memorizing lines came easy for Eilene. "My mom and I would practice lines in the car. That was our routine. We would get the script out and while she was driving we'd do the lines and I would always have it memorized by the time I got to the studio. They used to call me 'One take Eilene' because I never flubbed. I was lucky."

Eilene worked under contract for Hal Roach in *Curly* and *Who Killed Doc Robbin?* "These were a takeoff on the series of *Our Gang* comedies. There was a lot of interviewing for the parts that went on for quite some time until they put together the kids that they felt they could work with. Larry Olsen and Gerald Perreau were also in them. That was another time when we were just a group of kids that were having a wonderful time doing movies together. Everybody was there for us, and we just had a wonderful situation of going out and being recognized and people applauding us for what we did."

Eilene mentioned one incident that happened while she was working with a chimpanzee. "We worked with a lot of animals and they would get kind of unruly. I had to hold one chimp's hand and walk through the set with him. He took my hand and took a bite out of it and that wasn't too fun. That was kind of scary. But the kids got along real well. We all had a good time doing those two films. I remember sitting on Hal Roach Jr.'s lap and signing my contract. That was quite an honor to be out at Hal Roach at that time."

Eilene may be best remembered by film buffs for her role as Judy Dawson in the *Rough Ridin' Kids* western series for Republic in 1951 and 1952. She and Michael Chapin costarred in four features for this series: *Arizona Manhunt*, *Buckaroo Sheriff of Texas*, *The Dakota Kid*, and *Wild Horse Ambush*. Reflecting on her work in these pictures, Eilene stated,

"They had been interviewing for about a year and a half, but I had never tried out for it because I was just so busy. They still hadn't cast the Judy Dawson part and I got over there for the last interviews. When I walked through the door they said, 'That's our Judy Dawson.' They asked, 'Can you ride a horse?' I said, 'Sure I can ride a horse.' Little did they know that the only time I'd been on a horse was with my grandfather in Griffith Park, riding around in a ring. But they didn't care at that point, they were pleased with what I looked like and they liked the look of Michael and I together. They gave the two of us lots of riding lessons with Ace Hudkins out at his ranch. We were there three or four days a week learning to ride properly. They gave us our own horses to ride and groom and to become cowboys. Just get into the whole role. In the movies we did all our own riding, everything."

Eilene remembers an experience she had during the filming of *Wild Horse Ambush*. "They were herding some wild horses through an area where the bad guys had tied us up and left us out in the dirt to die. These wild horses were to run by and come very close to us, and they *did* come pretty close! Everybody on the set was a bit nervous about it, but I don't remember being too shook up. I think my mother was probably sweating at the time," Eilene laughed. "It was a one-take deal, not to be done again."

Eilene and Michael Chapin from one of the Republic *Rough Ridin' Kids* features.

Nudie, who was the official costumer for Roy Rogers and Dale Evans, made Eilene and Michael's costumes as well. "He made them similar to Roy and Dale's," Eilene said. "We rode in several parades on our horses behind Roy and Dale as a junior version of them. So we did appearances with them and I still have some of those costumes.

"Michael and I had a wonderful time. It was just a dream come true for kids to have their own horses, to be in the limelight, to have everybody taking care of them, and wonderful people to work with—the wonderful old stars that were in our movies doing cameo roles—and we were stars in the movies. It was a great time. We were under contract at Republic for two and a half years for the series and had school together in a trailer. James Bell [who played the grandfather in all four pictures] was the greatest. He was wonderful. A really nice warm person who became a good friend. That's what I mean; some of the people that were actually well-established actors came to be in our movies, which was an honor. I appreciate it more now than I did then, but it was nice to do."

Buckaroo Sheriff of Texas was one of Hugh O'Brian's first movies. "He was very handsome and much too old for me," Eilene smiled. "I saw him very recently and he is still very handsome, but he denied ever doing this movie. He said Universal would never have loaned him out to Republic. But I have a still to prove it."

When television began, Eilene went into that medium, interlaced with movies. She worked on *The Stu Erwin Show, Gale Storm Show, December Bride, Mr. Ed, Perry Mason, My Three Sons, Beverly Hillbillies* and many others. "I usually played the girlfriend of the primary boy who was son of the main star. So I grew up being the girlfriend of these young men. I had running parts where I would be in one episode and then come back in another one. I started doing *Life of Riley* when I was quite young. I was in *Life With Father* with Leon Ames. I was the oldest boy's (Steve Terrell) girlfriend in that and was in and out of it for several years. At the same time I was doing *Father Knows Best* with Robert Young and Billy Gray. I played Sherry Jackson's girlfriend at school in *The Danny Thomas Show*. Donald O'Connor picked me to be his leading lady on *Texaco Star Theater*. I interviewed a long time for that part and had to dance, sing and act. I got the role and went to work the first day. My mother went with me as they [parents] were required to do. We looked around and asked the first assistant, 'Where is Eilene's schoolteacher?' 'What do you mean?' he laughed. 'She has to have school, she's only 16.' 'Just a minute, I'll be right back,' he said. He went off and came back with Donald O'Connor and a few people. They were smiling and musing, and said, 'What's this now?' I said 'I was only 16 and have to have my schooling.'

Donald said, 'Get this girl a school teacher.' They made a big publicity thing out of it, Donald O'Connor's leading lady being still in Immaculate Heart High School. He wanted to take me with him as his partner on tour to Las Vegas and do live shows, but I was legally too young to do that. In those days they didn't allow you to do such things at 16. So it was a little stretch, but he let me be in two of the shows with him for TV, and that was quite fun."

Eilene played Nancy Baker on *The Adventures of Ozzie and Harriet*. "I was David Nelson's girlfriend for many years on that series. Ricky was about four years younger than we were so was always teasing us about dating. That was a delightful series to be on. Ozzie was a real character and had to control everything and do everything his way, but once it was done it was right. I think that is why their shows were so successful because he kept control over it. David and I went out a few times. We went to cotillion dance things and school activities together. They were a nice family. A complete family."

Eilene also worked in some of the television western series, such as *Range Rider*, *Sugarfoot*, and *Rifleman*. "I also did a lot of the *Hopalong Cassidys*. [She also worked with him in the 1948 feature, *Borrowed Trouble*]. He was wonderful, but I remember Gene Autry better because I did more of his shows. We went out to Pioneer Town out near Palm Springs, and the motel we stayed in looked like the motel in *Psycho*. Gene Autry and Hopalong Cassidy were just such icons of the western industry that I looked up at them in awe and amazement as they rode off into the sunset. They were heroes, and were wonderful people. I was also on Dale Robertson's *Tales of Wells Fargo*. That was one of Michael Landon's first TV shows. He was my boyfriend in that episode."

Eilene enjoyed live television because it was like performing in a play. "I did do *Jenny Kissed Me* on stage with Rudy Valee. I was Jenny, the lead, and took over Lee Remick's part when she stopped doing the role and went on to do a movie. I was shuffled off to Phoenix and in less than a week had to learn the entire play. Rudy Valee was a really interesting man," she chuckled. "He was a little difficult and strange and you just had to be on his good side, but once he liked you you were in. He liked me and my mother and we traveled with he and his wife and his dogs across the country to New York. We did the play in Phoenix, East Hampton and West Hampton for three or four months. I was about 14 or 15. That was really my first experience with live theater, and then when we came back we did it on *Front Row Center* on TV."

Eilene continued working in features at the same time that she was very active in television. "I was in *About Mrs. Leslie* in which I played a feature role called Pixie. That was with Robert Ryan and Shirley Booth. I was the nasty teenager who told all about Mrs. Leslie and got her in all kinds of trouble. It was fun playing that. Shirley was delightful, helped me a lot with my lines, and kind of coached me."

Eilene continued her acting career until about 1980 when her third child was born. "I was mostly doing commercials at that point. In between all of that I had some children and continued working when I could get back to it, but in the last 18 years, I haven't done any. George, my husband of 32 years is a personal injury lawyer. We have daughters Jenny, Erin, Lisa, Mary and Julie."

And if she was asked to appear in a film? "I would probably visit that idea at this point in my life of going back and doing that again," she answered.

In summing up her feelings on her career as a child actress, she said, laughing,"I think it was the only way to go. It was wonderful. I can't even begin to tell my girls the whole of it because there was just too much about it. For 24 hours a day I was a movie star. I was being patted on the back and groomed and kept lovely and taught different things. It was just wonderful; a fairy tale."

Claude Jarman, Jr.

Claude Jarman, Jr., was born September 27, 1934, in Nashville, Tennessee. "I was the typical Southern little boy. I used to spend all my summers at my grandfather's farm right outside of Nashville. He was a country doctor and I traveled with him all around the area. He was my idol at that point in my life." Claude also developed a strong interest in acting at a very early age. "I was the lead in school plays and was in community theater. I went to the movies every Saturday and spent all afternoon there. So, although I didn't grow up with a family of actors or performers, the interest was there."

In February 1945 Claude was selected out of his schoolroom in Nashville by Clarence Brown to play the role of Jody Baxter in *The Yearling*. "They had started the film in 1939 and it was aborted because everything went wrong, so they revived it again with Clarence Brown who was the top director at MGM at that time. He had just completed *Human Comedy* and *National Velvet* and was really quite adapt at working with children. But he was unhappy with the way the search for the role of Jody was going. MGM was sending out a lot of talent scouts and going into cities and advertising in the paper and getting all sorts of people coming in to test for the part or to be looked at. Brown wanted to take an entirely different approach, which he did. He went into each city in the South and would go to the superintendent of schools and identify himself. He said, 'All I want is a letter from you which gives me admission into these schools. I just want to look around and don't want anybody to know that I am there, and if someone sort of sparks my interest I would like to be able to talk to them. If not, I'm in and out of that school and no one in the town even knows about it.' That's what he was doing, which was sort of an unusual way of doing it."

Claude Jarman, Jr. in MGM's *The Yearling* (1946).

When Clarence Brown came to Nashville he noticed Claude in a classroom and asked for him to come to the office. "We talked for a little while just in general terms. He wanted to know if I was interested in acting and said, 'We'd like to come out later this afternoon and maybe take some pictures.' I said, 'Fine.' Then I went home and really didn't pay any attention to it. I told my mother about the meeting and then went off in the neighborhood to play. They showed up and my mother said, 'He's not here.' They were going to leave and it started to snow. They asked, 'Can you get him home?' I came home and they took the pictures."

The following day Brown and his associates were leaving for Knoxville, but the weather was still foul so they called Mr. Jarman and asked if he could bring Claude to the hotel as they wanted to talk with him. "We went, and that's when they said, 'We're really interested in you.' They asked if I was interested in doing the movie. Had I ever heard of *The Yearling*? 'No.' Would I be interested in going to Hollywood? 'Yeah, I guess.' You have to remember that in 1945 there were no airplanes. You had to get on the train and it took four days to get there, so you're looking at a totally different world." Almost a week passed and Claude had begun to forget about the prospect of doing the movie, when the family received a call from MGM saying, "We want you to come to California."

Claude went out to Hollywood in March and found that they had also brought in four other boys besides himself. "I was the only one that Clarence Brown brought in and he was the one who made the decision.

I just went to the MGM school there from the first of March till the middle of April. My father worked for the railroad and took a leave of absence for two months. They had to start testing for the other people in the movie and I had to be in all of those tests, and then we left for Florida [Ocala and Silver Springs] in April. So then I was launched."

Looking back on working in *The Yearling*, Claude said, "Gregory Peck was wonderful. All of the people that I worked with were fabulous. When you look back and think about the patience of working with a ten year old kid who had never made a movie before, and working with animals—particularly wild animals who really can't be trained—and you just have to keep doing it and doing it and doing it and hoping that the animal does what you want it to do, whether it follows you or runs or does whatever. I've made 11 movies and it was by far the most difficult. We started filming in April and didn't finish until the following February. Ten months. In those days you worked six days a week. What made it extremely difficult for me was that you still had to go to school. You had to go to school three hours a day and you took it in increments of ten or 15 minutes. You'd do a scene and then while they were setting up the next one you'd go to school. You never got any relaxation. It's the only film that I was in where I was in every scene. So there wasn't a day off. There was never a day that I didn't have to be there. Particularly because it was such a dramatic film, it was very difficult to keep doing that and going to school. It was an extremely hard film to make. It was hard on everyone. But it was exciting, particularly since I really had an interest in it. The story holds up well because it's timeless."

"Clarence Brown was a real perfectionist," Claude continued. "If you had a scene where an animal was involved, I would say the average number of takes was probably 25. If there was just people in it, it was always at least ten or 15 times. So it just kept going. He had a saying, 'That's great, and now let's do it once more for Paris.' And you think, 'Oh my God, you've got to do it again?' So you just kept going and going and going." Claude also explained that when they finally finished, it was discovered that the soundtrack had too much noise on it. "We had filmed so much in Florida in the woods and because of the crackling of the branches and stuff we had to go back and practically redub all the exterior scenes." Claude mentioned that when he did a second film for Clarence Brown, *Intruder in the Dust*, the director said, "We're going to use an open camera and loop the whole film."

The cast of *The Yearling* included not only Claude and Gregory Peck, but also such people as Jane Wyman, Forrest Tucker and Donn Gift as Jody's friend, Fodderwing. Claude mentioned, "Donn Gift was 20 years old when he made that movie. He had a glandular problem or something. He had come out to MGM from Indiana wanting to play the role that I played but Clarence Brown immediately said, 'That's Fodderwing.' My daughter went to Emerson back in Boston and said that one of her classmates had gone to school in New Hampshire and had said that Donn Gift was a teacher there."

The other important character in the picture was Flag the deer. We asked Claude how many deer they used to play the part. "I would say four or five, but there was one that was in 75 percent of the scenes. He was also in the first scene that you see Flag. He was a yearling and we called him Bambi."

Claude was given a special Oscar at the Academy Awards for his portrayal of Jody. He was the first child actor so honored, and was followed a few years later by Bobby Driscoll for *The Window*. No other child actor has been given a special Oscar since, although several have been nominated (two have won) in the standard acting categories.

The second movie Claude made was *High Barbaree* where he played Van Johnson as a young boy. Then he was loaned out to RKO to work in his first western, *Roughshod*. "In those days you were under contract and they could loan you out. We were up in the high Sierras and at Lone Pine and Bridgeport for three months and I rode every day. That's when I learned how to ride a horse and I really enjoyed it. I ended up making three or four other westerns."

Another reflection that Claude has concerning *Roughshod* was the women in the cast. "There was Gloria Grahame, Myrna Dell and Jeff

Claude as Jody Baxter with Flag the fawn from *The Yearling* (MGM, 1946).

Donnell. I was 12 and I loved the gals. I just thought they were terrific. Myrna Dell wrote me a letter a couple of years ago and said, 'You know, I've been thinking when you were making *Roughshod* you were too young for me then, but you're too old for me now,'" he laughed.

The other early westerns that Claude made were *The Outriders, Inside Straight, Hangman's Knot* and *Rio Grande*. Claude enjoyed westerns, saying "I loved horseback riding and I loved the people. *Rio Grande* was probably the most fun of any movie I ever made. Working with Harry Carey, Jr., Ben Johnson and the Sons of the Pioneers. John Ford was a real enigma. Carey and Johnson said, 'This is the way the guy works. He's going to pick out one of us and he's going to ride him the whole film and just make him the whipping boy the whole time.' It was Ben Johnson that got that dubious honor. He just hounded him the whole time. He would use me as kind of a foil. Like when I did the Roman riding. He just lorded over those guys, saying that I could get on the horses and after three weeks of training I was able to ride on two horses standing up. He would just say, 'Look at this kid. Look at him, you guys. He can do it. Why can't you?' We were up in Moab, Utah, the whole summer and had a great time."

Claude also expressed his feelings about *Hangman's Knot*. "Lee Marvin was in it and I was 17 and followed him around. I just thought he was great. He sort of took me in as his sidekick. I'd go to Hollywood and ride around with him in his little red convertible. He was just a fun guy. But the film had an unbelievable schedule: 15 days. There wasn't much dialogue in it, just a lot of action. Randolph Scott was a good guy," Claude added.

"A movie which I didn't think was very good was *The Sun Comes Up*. It was a Marjorie Kinnan Rawlings story and was kind of like the sequel to *The Yearling*. It was with Jeanette MacDonald, Lloyd Nolan and Lassie. It was supposed to be North Carolina, but it was actually made in Santa Cruz, California. I think we did okay, but it really wasn't a *Rio Grande* or *Intruder in the Dust*."

The final film that Claude made before entering the navy was *Fair Wind to Java* for Republic Studio. "It has to be one of the worst films ever made. It was laughable. I made it in the summer when I was in college. I just got a call, 'You want to make this movie?' Herbert Yates was married to Vera Ralston so he wanted to have an all-star cast with Fred MacMurray, Vera Ralston and Victor McLaglen. I enjoyed MacMurray a lot. He was just shaking his head, 'Why am I in this movie?'"

Claude's father left his job and was the parent that accompanied him on the film sets. "He was a terrific guy. He was somebody who all the crew loved. He liked to hang out with the grips and never went Hollywood at all. He was just a real down to earth type of person." Asked if the family moved out to California, Claude replied, "We moved back and forth for five years. My mother and sister never liked California. They loved their roots. When we weren't working I'd go back to Nashville. Actually I went to school there when I wasn't working and would supplement that with the tutors when I was at the MGM school."

In between making movies Claude said "I just enjoyed being a boy without a lot of restrictions. At that point it was hard for me to go somewhere that I wasn't recognized, and I found that hard to live with. I didn't really enjoy it; I wanted to be just a normal boy and not have that trail me around."

When asked if he has a favorite movie he appeared in, Claude answered, "If I had a favorite movie to make it would be *Rio Grande*. If I had a favorite movie that I'm proud of, it would be *Intruder in the Dust* which I thought was the most interesting movie I made. I think it was a movie basically ahead of its time. The studios didn't know what to do with it because they were dealing with a subject matter that they weren't ready to deal with. In fact when I ran the film festival here in San Francisco, Albert Johnson, an Afro-American, was the program director. He was very involved in film; a film historian. He used to go around to all these different countries and talk about race relations in American films, and *Intruder in the Dust* was one he would always take with him. It won the British Film Critics Award. Had it been a different era or promoted differently I think it would have been one of the nominees for the Academy Award because it was highly regarded, but MGM didn't want to touch it."

Claude was asked if he decided to quit movies after *Fair Wind to Java*, or if the motion picture industry quit him. "I don't know," he replied. "It's the same as it is with anything. If you really want to succeed you've got to make a real commitment to it, and by that time I really didn't. I went to college and got involved in other things. In those days, after college you had to go into the service so I was in the navy for three years, then I got married and had a couple of children. I sort of came back and did a *Wagon Train* and a couple of other TV shows, but all the people that I knew were gone. So, it was like starting all over again and the business had changed tremendously. I think had the continuity been there the way it was earlier when I was there, I probably would have stayed with it, but it just wasn't the same."

Claude did work in one last film in 1956 before leaving Hollywood—*The Great Locomotive Chase* for Walt Disney. After the navy, Claude moved to Alabama for two years and worked for an advertising agency. "I came to San Francisco in 1961, Claude informed us. "This is really home. This is really where I've grown up. And I have seven children; two sons and five daughters. My daughter Natalie works in Los Angeles in the movie business, but not as an actor; she wants to write and produce. She's been involved in casting and she's got the bug, so I think that's great. My youngest children are twin girls who are 6½ years old."

Since moving to San Francisco, Claude has served as manager of the San Francisco Opera House, has been a film producer (one of his productions was the feature-length rock music movie *Fillmore*), has assisted in founding a western film festival in Tucson, Arizona, and has served as vice-chairman and treasurer of the San Francisco Film Festival. Speaking of the last named post, Claude said, "I enjoyed that because it really gave me an opportunity to stay involved without having to be involved with the production side. I got to know a lot of people. We used to have these wonderful afternoon tributes and had people ranging from Henry Fonda to Rita Hayworth to Jack Nicholson to Michael Douglas. They were all here. So that was a great opportunity to sort of be in the business. Then in 1998 I went to the Academy Awards, which was a great thrill. I saw a lot of people including Gregory Peck who I had not seen in probably 25 years. He's a terrific guy that has done wonderful things for the movie industry as well as being a terrific actor."

Claude returned for one final film role in the television miniseries *Centennial*. "I got a call from John Wilder, the producer, who I knew socially. He said to me one time, 'I'm getting ready to do this series and I want you to be in it.' I said, 'I won't play it unless I can come down and audition for it because I haven't done it in years.' So I went down and read for it and the director said, 'I want you to do it.' We went to Greeley, Colorado. It was winter and felt like it was 20 below zero. We were there for three weeks. It was funny because I really enjoyed it. I think I enjoyed it because I didn't have the pressure of wondering what I was going to do next. This was the last episode and all these people were getting very nervous, saying things like 'Oh my God, what am I going to do next week?' and I thought,I know what I'm doing. I'm going to go home,'" Claude laughed.

In 1986 Claude began his travel agency business in San Francisco. "We do meetings with companies, let's say like an insurance company, and take their top agents who qualify for awards. For example, we just had 700 people in London for five days. This takes a lot of planning. It's like producing."

Claude's hobbies include golf and traveling. "I also spend a tremendous amount of time with my kids. These little girls are just unbelievable.

I have two other daughters that live here in the city. This is my third marriage. My first wife lives in Florida with my three kids there, and then I have two daughters, one in Los Angeles and the other one here. So I just spend a lot of time with the family. We lived in the city until the little girls were born. I didn't want to raise them there so we live out in Kentfield. It's a beautiful area. Sean Penn's building a house there, and Barry Levinson lives in Marin, so there's quite a little group of people there that have moved out of LA."

Looking back at his career as a child actor, Claude was asked how he would like to sum up his feelings. "I don't know," he answered. "I'm still somewhat amazed that I was actually able to do all of that. I feel very fortunate to have had that opportunity, and I also feel very fortunate to have not let it dominate my life. I don't think I'd be happy living in Southern California making movies the way they make them now. I was in Los Angeles last week. I go there maybe once every two or three years and I feel very uneasy. It brings back a lot of feelings about why I'm glad I didn't stay involved. When I was at MGM you just worked. It may not be a good movie—that's why you see so many dog movies—like when you see Clark Gable singing and dancing it's because L. B. Mayer said, 'I'm paying you, you do it.' It was just working at your craft. Today all of these people just sit around between assignments and wait for a year and then maybe make a film, even if you're good. It's got to be frustrating. It's just a different world."

Marcia Mae Jones

Marcia Mae Jones was born on August 1, 1924, in Hollywood, California. "My father worked for Western Union and traveled, and my mother lived alone with four kids in a duplex on Kingsley. At that time *anybody* could be in pictures; they were asking people on the street to be in them. One day the babysitter didn't show up so my mother took me in the baby carriage and parked it outside of the sound stage. They were looking for someone to play Dolores Costello as a baby in *Mannequin*, and the director, James Cruze, walked by the baby carriage and said, 'That's the baby.' And that's how I started.

"After that I had a little part in *King of Jazz* with Paul Whiteman. I worked extra in pictures. In fact, all of us kids did. One minute we were extras, the next minute we were saying lines." In 1931 she was featured in *Street Scene* with Sylvia Sydney. "I was to say, 'We're going to be dispossessed today,' and they worked with me because I couldn't say the word. It was my turn to say grace at the dinner table [at home] and I said, 'We're going to be dispossessed today,' and I never lived it down with my family," Marcia Mae laughed.

Later that same year Marcia Mae played Jackie Cooper's sister in *The Champ*. "It's funny, but it seems the only things you remember as a child are things that you did wrong. I don't know why that is. In *The Champ* there was a scene which is not in the movie where we were having a spitting contest, and I couldn't spit. I kept drooling and the director was getting a little annoyed with me. I get a kick out of it, because Jackie saw me years later and said, 'You know, I've been meaning to tell you that I thought you were very good in *The Champ*.' And I said, 'I thought you were pretty good too,'" she chuckled.

Asked for any remembrances of the 1931 Clark Gable film, *Night*

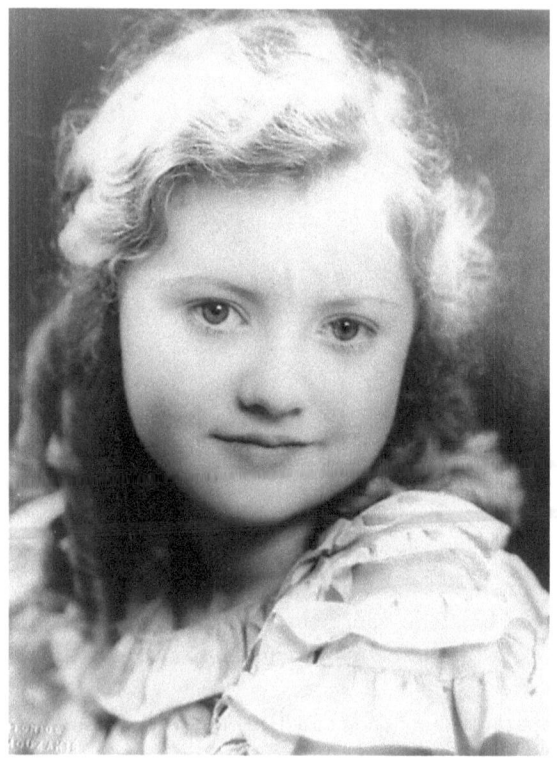

Marcia Mae Jones

Nurse, Marcia Mae laughed and explained that where she was supposed to sit was hot from the heater. "They kept telling me to sit down, and I remained standing up. Finally the prop man realized they had the fire up too high, so they turned it down. I get a kick when I see it, because I just don't move.

"I don't know how old I was, but I did a picture with Jean Harlow and Franchot Tone. They were getting married, and she was all in white: white fur, white hair, white dress. I'm supposed to be the flower girl and all I kept doing was look at her. They were getting annoyed with me because I'm supposed to be walking, throwing flowers; but she was so beautiful. And that's how I felt when I was in *The Garden of Allah* with Charles Boyer and Marlene Dietrich. I can still see them in my mind. They were both beautiful. I was just a little girl, and was so thrilled that it was Marlene Dietrich and Charles Boyer."

In 1936, Marcia Mae costarred with Bonita Granville in *These Three*, based upon Lillian Hellman's play *The Children's Hour*, and directed by William Wyler. "I remember going on an interview to get the part. I had been on a Jane Withers movie on the backlot at 20th Century and I had dirty hands and dirty clothes. I kept apologizing that I didn't have time to wash my hands, and all of a sudden Wyler said, 'That's Rosalie.' I turned around to see who Rosalie was. I had no idea what he was talking about. He was very difficult to work for, only because he wanted perfection. You did it over and over again until you did it correct. The one thing that I felt bad about was the scene I did of screaming, 'Yes. Yes. I did it. What Mary said is true.' The sound was bad so they had to make another soundtrack of it. We had to get off the set by noon because they were breaking it down. So they had no choice; they had to get it. We did it over and over again and I just couldn't cry anymore. I laughed at him and he knew I was faking it, so he said, 'You know, I interviewed 300 little girls for this part. Maybe I made a mistake.' Well, that did it. They couldn't stop me from crying. But I did like him; he was a wonderful director. Bonita and I paid strict attention to anything he said, but you did do it over and over again until he was pleased with it. He really wouldn't tell you what you've done wrong; he just said, 'We'll do it again.' And again and again," she laughed. "Oh, I would have given anything to have worked with Wyler as an adult actress. I think I was making *The Youngest Profession* at MGM, and he saw me coming out of the writers' building. He asked, 'Have you seen the remake of *The Children's Hour?*' I hadn't, and he said, 'You're not going to like it.' When I saw it I didn't like it because they had cut the two little girls out, and that was Lillian Hellman's play. I mean the two little girls were the story."

Marcia Mae worked with director Michael Curtiz in the 1937 film *Mountain Justice*. "I got a kick out of that, because Michael Curtiz couldn't say 'Marcia.' He'd call me Garcia," she laughed. "I remember being on the backlot at Warner Bros. I think it was a 110 degrees, and we did this courtroom scene over and over again." While making this film, Josephine Hutchinson had given Marcia Mae a little breakfast set. "It was pink and white. I cherished that breakfast set and the note. I still have the note. It just said 'Every little girl should have breakfast in bed once.' I carried that breakfast set with me and it was destroyed in the earthquake. I just heard Josephine Hutchinson passed away and it really made me feel bad.

"*Mountain Justice* was a true story. I played Josephine's sister. Robert Barrat played our father and he was marvelous. The father was very mean and would beat Josephine, but one night as she went to protect herself she pushed him, and he fell and hit his head and died. The neighbors accused her of murdering him and were going to lynch her so the government got a plane and flew her out. Because of the brutality in the film, the Hayes Office would not allow it to go through, so it kind of ruined the movie. It was a shame because it was Michael Curtiz's first movie."

Reflecting on her work in the 1937 film *The Life of Emile Zola*, which starred Paul Muni, she stated, "This is a funny story. First of all, it started with the dialogue man saying, 'Mr. Muni does not want to work with anybody who doesn't know their lines.' Then the director said the same thing. Then my mother said it. Then the assistant director. I was a nervous wreck. So now I am to carry this tray of dishes down the hall. I'm shaking because I'm so nervous, and these dishes are rattling. I go in and guess

Marcia Mae with Alma Kruger and Bonita Granville in a scene from United Artists' *These Three* (1936).

who misses their lines. Paul Muni," she laughed, "and from then on I thought he was terrific. He was very nice to me and I was nice to him. I thought he was okay then because he missed his lines."

Marcia Mae mentioned that she worked on *The Adventures of Tom Sawyer* for six months. "It was wonderful. I was originally signed to play Becky, but when they got Tommy Kelly I was much taller, so that's why I played Mary Sawyer. It was on the backlot of David Selznick. I really felt bad when it was over because it was like a family. Everyone liked each other and we all got along. They even made Tommy's father the policeman at the gate. It was marvelous. The same as Shirley's movies, it was always happy."

She appeared with Shirley Temple in *Heidi*. Marcia Mae recalled, "I remember they had Jean Hersholt padded so he would appear heavier, and made him look like an old man. We were on the back lot of 20th Century filming the scene where he's calling 'Heidi! Heidi!' as he's chasing after the sled that she was in. He collapsed from heat exhaustion. We were all scared to death, because he was not an old man when he did *Heidi*."

Speaking about working with Shirley Temple, she reflected, "She's a wonderful person. I used to love to go into her dressing room because she had all of these dolls. Mrs. Temple would have us come in around four o'clock. She called it tea time. I would get a square piece of chocolate and so would Shirley. Her mother would say, 'Sparkle Marcia Mae' and 'Sparkle Shirley.' She did that in jest. I always laughed. In fact I was going to write a book and call it *Sparkle Marcia Mae*, but I have put that on hold. When Shirley walked she bounced. She was very sweet to work with and so was Mrs. Temple; she was lovely to me. People used to say because I got as much fan mail as Shirley—because I played a crippled girl—that Mrs. Temple wouldn't allow me to be in another movie, and that's not true. She requested me for *The Little Princess*. So all those stories you hear are just stories. Shirley was very close to her parents and loved them dearly.

"I didn't enjoy being mean in *The Little Princess*," Marcia Mae continued. "I was the mean girl that Shirley dumped ashes all over. The ashes were made out of corn flakes and flour. They rehearsed it and rehearsed it without throwing the ashes. They had another set of clothes in case the take didn't go. So, here comes Shirley and she dumps the ashes on me, and out the door she goes, and the director says 'Cut!' Shirley comes right back in the door and looks at me, and goes over to the director and says, 'Can we do this again.' I had said in one review that I wanted to kill her, but that's what I meant as a child, not as an adult. But I really wanted to run. They got it in one take. There's something about Shirley: you show her one time how to do something, she had it. You didn't need to tell her again. She just had a special kind of talent. I didn't enjoy being the mean girl in *The Little Princess*. I kind of felt like I was left out because I had been in *Heidi* and everything was so wonderful, and I didn't feel like I felt on *Heidi*. I didn't enjoy being mean to Shirley, but I was," she laughed.

Concerning her schooling while making movies, Marcia Mae reflected, "I went to school on the set, and at that time I think I was in Bancroft Junior High School. It was difficult. The kids make fun of you that you're an actress and so you develop an attitude of 'I don't care,' when you really do care. You were constantly interrupted with your schooling to go on the set to do the scene. We had to do three hours of school each day, but it wasn't a steady three hours. It may be 15 minutes, it may be 20 minutes, and it was difficult. I don't recommend it. That's my own personal opinion. I don't think it bothered Jane Withers, I don't think it bothered Shirley, but it bothered me. Of course, they were on the lot; they stayed there. They had their own little school room. But for those of us who were featured players, we went back to public school when the movie was over and it made it difficult for me. When I would go back to school I didn't know where they were, I didn't know what they were studying. I wasn't the best student, let's put it that way," she laughed.

Marcia Mae enjoyed working with Deanna Durbin in *Mad About Music* and *First Love*. "She was marvelous. Deanna is my favorite. I think we were more of an age at that time. We were around 14 and 15, and she was fun to be with. I loved to hear her sing. I don't mean that I didn't like anybody else, but she was kind of my favorite."

Marcia Mae starred with Jackie Moran in six films for Monogram Pictures. "We made them in seven days. It was hard. I get such a kick when I hear: 'Well, they went to Paris for this location.' I only went to Newhall or Lancaster," she laughed. "We never went very far. Bette Davis taught me a very valuable lesson when I worked in the movie *The Star*. At Monogram we didn't rehearse with props because it took up too much time. We only used props when we were doing the scene. So now here I am working with Bette Davis at 20th Century–Fox. I played a waitress, and they didn't have the cup and saucer for the scene. Finally the cup and saucer arrive and I'm still not using the props. I'll never forget it. She looked up at me and said, 'Would you mind giving me the cup and saucer?' I wanted to die, because having been in all the A movies I did know the professional thing to do, but I'd been in these Monogram movies and I was getting into a bad habit. So I thanked her afterwards to bring me back to what I knew that I should do."

"Jackie Moran was very nice," she noted. "I don't know what happened to him. I know he got arrested for forging checks and then the judge put him under probation to his mother-in-law. Then he turned around and did it again and he was sent to prison. It's a sad story. I know they interviewed him and he was very bitter about Hollywood. He didn't want to see any of us. Something happened, but I don't know what."

Marcia Mae worked with Robert Taylor in the feature, *The Youngest Profession*. "I played another mean girl. The day Mr. Taylor was to arrive they said we should rehearse the scene beforehand. I was supposed to believe that he was not going to arrive so when we rehearsed I opened the door and there he stood. I couldn't remember my lines as he was the most handsome man I had ever seen. Everyone broke out laughing, even Mr. Taylor."

In reference to horseback riding, she related an incident which happened while making *Yellow Haired Kid*, an episode of the TV series *Wild Bill Hickok*. "It's a funny story. I'm on a horse and the scene starts. They hit the horse to go and I came right off the back. Andy Devine came over and looked down at me and said, 'You really don't know how to ride, do you?' I've never forgotten that," she smiled. "But that's when they hyped the horses up and did things that they should not have done. That's all been changed now, thank God."

In 1950, Marcia Mae worked in *The Daughter of Rosie O'Grady*. "It was the first major movie role for Debbie Reynolds. At that time there was a strike in the motion picture industry, and it was hard to cross the picket line. After that it became hard because everyone was out of work. Nobody was working. I had two children at the time so I went to work for Gregg Bautzer, a very prominent attorney. He was attorney for Howard Hughes, Hearst, Ingrid Bergman. That's when I started doing a lot of television. He was marvelous to me. He'd let me have this steady job and he'd let me go every time I had a part, because he knew it would be only a couple of days. I did a lot of shows, including *The Burns and Allen Show*, *Mr. Ed*, *The Donald O'Connor Show*, and *I Married Joan*. I did a series with Buster Keaton. That's the only series that he talked in and it did not go over. So he sold it to a man and they put it on at midnight. Well, to make a long story short, they moved it up to the Saturday morning show for the children and it became an instant hit. But by then he'd sold us all out including himself, so none of us got anything for it."

After working on the television series *Marcus Welby, M.D.* in 1970, Marcia Mae married Bill Davenport, who wrote for such shows as *Mr. Ed*, *All In The Family*, and *December Bride*. "He started *Gilligan's Island* when I put him in the hospital. He had a problem with pills and booze, so the marriage did not last," she stated. "When I married him, I didn't work for a long time. I didn't want to. I just really wanted to stay home. Bill told me that I shouldn't quit, and now that I look back he was right. But that's what I wanted to do, so I did it.

"Then I came back again in television—*Streets of San Francisco, Temperature Rising*, and *Cannon*. I also did the movie *The Way We Were*. I had a marvelous part: I played Hedda Hopper. Right at the beginning of the movie I say, 'That son of a bitch is dead.' Then I open the paper and it says Roosevelt, and I say, 'Now it's our turn,' and go on and on. But it got different reactions and they cut it out. They were afraid, but I loved it," she laughed.

"Then I played Luke and Laura's landlady for a long time on *General Hospital*. I loved that. I thought at that time 'Oh, I'm making it back,' and Laura quit the show, and that was the end of me." When asked how it was working on the soap, she answered, "It's very hard. It's not like the movies. I mean, I marveled at Genie Francis. When she was working in this particular scene, she was studying lines for the next day. It was hard and I didn't blame her for quitting. She said she hadn't had any life, and she wanted a life. She did get married and has a child. I was upset because I knew that would be the end of me," she laughed.

"I did a part on *Simon & Simon*. After that, you know, it's very hard for old-timers. Everybody thinks it's easy because you're an old-timer. I got to tell you it's very difficult because the young casting people don't know you. They not only don't know you, they don't want to know you. It's hard and I just got tired of fighting it and decided to retire," she chuckled. "So that's what I'm doing."

Since her retirement, Marcia Mae has been kept busy as a member of the Academy of Motion Picture Arts and Sciences in the documentary and foreign film departments. Asked what she enjoys doing in her spare time, she replied, "I have a lot of friends and I do a lot of things. It's just that I'm happy. I know that, thank God. A lot of child actors are not. A lot of them ended it all or have done something terrible."

Asked if there was a favorite film that she had worked in, Marcia Mae replied, "*These Three*. That was my favorite because it was the first big part that I ever had and it was difficult. I thought it was a marvelous movie. I was working with pros: Merle Oberon, Miriam Hopkins, Joel McCrea. I was thrilled and I was scared. It wasn't easy because that was a very dramatic movie. It's a classic now."

Commenting on the life of a child performer in the movies, she said, "It's not a normal life. I don't care what anybody says, it can't be. You're on the set, you're working. It's a make believe world that you're in, and you're treated marvelously. But then the boat sails. It's over. A lot of them don't make it. Child actors, not in my generation, but later on, have committed suicide. It's just very hard to adjust to a normal life. Everybody kept saying that Deanna Durbin would come back from Paris, and I knew she wouldn't. She only flew in when her mother died and flew out that night. She hated Hollywood."

Asked if she had any regrets about being a child actress, Marcia Mae responded, "No. I do think that it caused me some emotional problems. I was dominated by my mother and it was hard to finally break the apron strings. My mother [Freda Jones] had worked in pictures, and she died in the motion picture home. She and I became very close and I was with her when she died, which I'm very grateful for. My mother just loved show business. That was her life. I had two brothers and a sister and they were all in pictures. In fact, my brother Marvin had a big part in a movie called *Wake Island*. At the end he's the one that is saying the Lord's Prayer. But he didn't care for it. Neither did my other brother or sister. I was it. I didn't have any choice," she laughed.

In conclusion, Marcia Mae said, "Well, I must tell you how I feel about it now. I was privileged to do a lot of things that most people are not. I got to meet so many wonderful and interesting people. I'm now a member of the academy and I realize where it took me to."

Mickey Kuhn

Mickey Kuhn was born on September 21, 1932, in Waukegan, Illinois. In 1934, the family moved to Southern California. "On a lark my mother took me to 20th Century-Fox studio where I was cast as a baby in a movie caled *Change of Heart*. I was only 18 months old at the time, so I don't remember that."

Mickey's first recollection of working in a picture was when he was six years old. "In 1938 I did a movie at Warners Bros. called *Juarez* with Paul Muni and I got a hundred dollars a week. Gilbert Roland also appeared in *Juarez*, and I'll tell an interesting little sidelight in regards to that. He and his wife were childless and wanted to adopt a child. He approached my mother in all seriousness to work out an arrangement to adopt me. Of course my mother said, 'No, I'm sorry.'"

From *Juarez*, Mickey went into a movie with Humphrey Bogart, *King of the Underworld*, followed by *S.O.S. Tidal Wave* with Ralph Byrd. "That was the first time I ever rode in an ambulance with the siren going. And one of the policemen was a highway patrolman on the location set who was there on his motorcycle. He took me for my first motorcycle ride. I remember when we went to see it it scared the daylights out of me because I felt this was what was really going to happen. The world was going to come to an end just this way. I was between six and seven at that time.

"I went directly from that movie into *Gone with the Wind*," Mickey continued. "We finished up on *SOS Tidal Wave* and my mother said we had to go to the Selznick Studio. We worked all day and I was very tired, but she said we had to go. I said, 'Okay, we'll go.' We got there and I walked into the casting office and I've never seen so many kids in my life. At seven years old it looked like there were a thousand, but there *were* many; it could have been 40 or 50. I turned to my mother and I started to tear up. I was a tired and cranky kid, and said 'I don't want to stay here.' She said, 'Go give your name; we'll stay five minutes because you're the last one here, and then we will just leave.' I went up and gave my name to the lady in the casting office. I remember this just as clear as if it was yesterday. She said, 'Thank God, you've arrived. We've been waiting for you,' and ushered me into the office. Then she said to the others, 'Thank you all for coming, the part's been cast.' That has stuck with me. Looking back in retrospect it was really quite flattering. I felt sorry for all of these other kids, but I was just a very, very fortunate

Mickey Kuhn in Warner Bros. *Juarez* (1936).

young child." Speaking of some of the stars of the film, Mickey related, "Leslie Howard was very good to work with, very much a professional, worked well with children, at least he did with me. He gave me every benefit of the doubt. Olivia De Havilland was a very lovely lady, always very kind. The part she portrayed was the way she appeared on the set. Clark Gable, a super guy. I had two scenes with him and in both of them he was wonderful. He talked to Cammie King and I like we were human beings. Vivian Leigh, I didn't have much to do with her on *Gone with the Wind*. At the end, Mr. Selznick called my mother and I into his office and said to me, 'Thank you so much, we appreciate your job.' It really made me feel like I was somebody at seven years old. Then he gave me a 16mm movie camera and movie projector. That always stayed with me. Victor Fleming was magnificent. He was one of the best directors I ever worked with. By just a simple little chitchat, at least with me, whatever he needed he got. I didn't have any trouble crying except when you don't want to. It's tough at seven years old, but Victor Fleming got the tears, and what you saw in the scene were actual tears. They just started by chatting with Victor Fleming."

The next film was *I Want a Divorce* with Joan Blondell and Dick Powell. "They played my aunt and uncle in the show. Nice people," Mickey added. "At the end they sent me a gift: a wallet that was engraved, 'To Mickey, best wishes Joan Blondell and Dick Powell.' You don't see that too much today."

Mickey didn't appear in another film until *Roughly Speaking* in 1945 with Rosalind Russell in which he played Robert Hutton's character as a boy. This was followed by *This Love of Ours* with Claude Raines and Mickey's friend, Leon Tyler. "Leon Tyler and I were very good friends when we grew up, in fact he went to high school with a girl I was dating at the time as we got into our teenage years, so Leon and I kind of grew up together. We appeared in another movie together called *That's My Boy* in 1950 with Dean Martin and Jerry Lewis." *A Tree Grows in Brooklyn* in 1945 was Mickey's next film. "I grew up with Ted Donaldson, but to be honest I don't remember what I did in that film. I by no means was a star and never would have been, but I would have been a good journeyman actor, the kind of a person that you would say, 'Gosh, I recognize his face, but what's his name.'"

Mickey's last film, released in 1945, was *Dick Tracy*. "I played Dick Tracy, Jr. in it. I worked with a fellow named Morgan Conway and you wonder what happened to some of these people because I never heard of him again. But he was fun to work with. Arlene Dahl played Tess. I got an autographed picture of her on which she wrote, 'I'll wait till you grow up.' And I often wonder, maybe I'll go out and look her up and see what she's doing now," he laughed. "That was fun." Mickey also acted onstage in Los Angeles. "I've appeared in the old Pasadena Playhouse, and interestingly enough I was cast in a show in Boston in 1945 called *Georgia Boy*. Jack Kirkland was the writer, and the director was Josh Logan. It closed there because there was some racial overtones in it and back in those days it was a case of 'banned in Boston.' Kirkland and his wife invited my mother and I to their home on Fifth Avenue in New York for a week to enjoy the city as their guests because we didn't get to open there on Broadway. I also did a couple of shows in Los Angeles but don't remember the names."

The Searching Wind and *The Strange Love of Martha Ivers* were his next features. *The Searching Wind* starred Robert Young. Mickey stated this film was "just something to do to occupy those awkward years; I was in the early teens. William Dieterle was the director. He directed *Juarez*, so I was reunited with him for that." We asked him whether it was difficult to find work when he got to that age. "Yeah," he responded. "I was kind of like my friend Teddy Infuhr. I didn't really care if I worked or not; if it came along it came along. My mother was more interested in me working than I was. I was interested in school; I was interested in sports. When I was a kid I loved to play baseball. I liked to swim and I liked to horseback ride. I ran track when I went to Hollywood High, but I was never able to participate in any varsity sports at school because of the motion picture aspect. It was interesting except in your teenage years, the way I feel anyway, when I'm just starting in high school and trying to get an identity for myself and make friends and then all of a sudden I'd have to work for a couple of weeks and was gone. And I was never the kind of person to brag about it. I just went to work and they'd say, 'Where were you, what did you do for school?' It was a hard way to grow up."

In *The Strange Love of Martha Ivers*, Mickey played Kirk Douglas as a boy. "I seemed to wind up playing the star as a kid in several of the star's first movies. This was Kirk Douglas's first picture, and I also played Montgomery Clift as a child in his first. I never met Kirk Douglas, but I did have the opportunity of working with Dame Judith Anderson though and she was a lesson in acting. A magnificent lady. To just watch her, I wanted to be able to produce onto the screen what she did. Just like with Jimmy Stewart, Gilbert Roland, John Wayne, and all of those people you learn something from. At that time acting was going to be my career. In fact, it was going to be my career until I got out of the military. I always just wanted to recall things that I have learned and that I had seen in actions and reactions to various sets of circumstances over the years, and they were all great people to work with and be associated with." *Roaring Rangers* with Charles Starrett as the Durango Kid was Mickey's first western. "I was thrilled to be doing it. In fact, Columbia indicated they wanted to put me under contract but fortunately my mother didn't want to. Charles Starrett was great to work with. He would sit and talk with me between takes and give advice or acting counsel. He did everything to enhance my performance as a cowboy."

Mickey received a bad burn on his hand in *High Conquest*. "I carried a flare and fell off a mountain and tumbled to my death. In that particular scene something happened with the flare and it spewed out and landed on my hand and burned it. Not a whole lot, but just enough to put a good scar on it. Working with Gilbert Roland again was a thrill beyond all thrills because I really thought the world of that man. When he died I hadn't realized he had been at the Motion Picture Home. If I had known

I would have certainly gone and seen him because he was always one of my favorites. He was a nice, nice man, and that's hard to come by."

Most of Mickey's pictures were filmed on the studio sets, but there were two that he went on location for. "I went on location for *Red River* for ten weeks in Sedona, Arizona. I also went on location for *Broken Arrow* at Redrock Canyon in Sedona." Mickey also performed his own horse fall and stunts on *Broken Arrow*. "When I got shot with the arrow I did the fall and hurt my back pretty bad, but I went ahead and worked and never turned in any injuries on duty papers. Other than that I was too young and too stupid to know the dangers that were involved. On *High Conquest* I wanted to do one of the falls and was told I couldn't because they hired professionals to do it. That was hard for me to understand. As I got older I still wanted to do them because I thought I was invincible, just as we all did at 16 and 17."

Mickey found his role as a heavy in *Broken Arrow* to be an interesting part. "I never played a bad guy before. And I look at it now and see things that if I had the opportunity to do it again I would do differently. It was fun. It gave me an insight into what it was like to not be liked by people. That was Jeff Chandler's first important role and I tried to talk to him off-camera. He told me, 'Look, you're the bad guy and I don't like you. So don't try to be nice to me.' But it was all to just keep himself in character because he was working more than I was during the day and wanted to keep the character in the continuity of the scene. Yet for me it was a little bit of a shock. I was 17, but when I stopped and thought about it, I'd tell myself, 'Okay, I can understand that. I'd probably do the same thing.' After the movie was over he came up to me and said, 'It's been nice.' He was ever the professional, as was Jimmy Stewart. Jimmy Stewart was just magnificent. Will Geer was a character. I didn't have too much to do with him, but again he was very helpful in the scenes that I appear with him in, particularly in the beginning where we were sitting at the dinner table. He had many years of experience and he was good with young people. A nice, nice man.

"There was another interesting sidelight concerning Jimmy Stewart. I had done *Magic Town* with him and they had already been filming on *Broken Arrow* when I got there. I arrived in the morning and they put me in wardrobe and make-up, and then they put me on a horse and sent me out to the set. As I rode onto the set this fellow rides up to me and he sticks out his hand and says, 'Mick, Jim Stewart. It was *Magic Town* wasn't it?' It's a thrill, a big thrill. It was just like on *Red River* where we watched the rushes, and John Wayne came up to me and said, 'Good job, Mick. Thanks a lot.' Things like that remain with you. I mean, that's

John Wayne! It was a lot of fun. I made a nice acquaintance of John Wayne's boy, Mike Wayne, and everybody on the set was great.

"I never really had any bad experiences," Mickey stated. "Except on *Juarez* with Bette Davis. But everybody else—like in *Red River*: John Wayne, Montgomery Clift, Joanne Dru, John Ireland and Walter Brennan, what a prince—just a lot of fun. We all got a belt buckle with our initials on one side. I still have mine, and if you look at a lot of the John Wayne movies afterwards you will see him wearing one. It's a silver buckle with a gold rope lariat around it, and a D for the Dunson and Red River brand in the center. It's a real treasure. My son has already said that that's his. Howard Hawks was a very demanding director, but I liked that. He wanted something, and he would come up to me (and he realized that I was 14 years old) and say, 'Look, this is what I want to do. Now I know you think of doing it this way, but believe me it is going to look better if you do it my way,' and he'd tell me what he wanted and we never got out of sorts. Had I pursued the business he would have been one of the inspirations."

Mickey appeared in *A Streetcar Named Desire* as the sailor who put Vivian Leigh on the streetcar. "We were shooting down in New Orleans, Louisiana, my first trip away from home by myself. I was 18 years old. We were setting up a shot and I said to one of the crew members, 'You know, 11 years ago I appeared with Lady Olivier in *Gone with the Wind*, and this is just a real thrill for me to be in this movie with her.' About five minutes later everything stopped and Lady Olivier summoned me into her dressing room and we sat there for a good half-hour and just talked. She was very interested in my career: what I was doing and what the future held for me. I have to say, whatever has been said about her, she was nothing but an elegant, elegant lady as far as I was concerned. Nobody could ever say anything bad about her to me because I would defend her with vigor."

Shortly after *A Streetcar Named Desire*, Mickey did another movie called *On the Loose*. "It was just a nothing part. That was the last movie I did before I went into the military. Two days later I went in the navy, and came out in 1955." The first movie Mickey appeared in after his discharge was called *Savage Wilderness*. "I worked with Anne Bancroft, Victor Mature, Robert Preston, and James Whitmore, an excellent actor. Again, a great learning process. Three weeks down in Mexico City and being involved with these people. Every night we'd go out and talk theater, and of course Robert Preston was not only an excellent movie actor but an outstanding theater actor. We talked the profession and it was quite a thrill. Again, had I stayed in the business I would have learned an awful lot.

Mickey with John Wayne and Walter Brennan as they look over their Texas range in *Red River* (United Artists, 1948). Mickey was 14 when he played Matthew Garth as an adult.

"I got married in 1956, kicked around and did a few TV shows. I did a couple of shows on *Matinee Theater* which I enjoyed because in my opinion the theater is the only place that an actor can truly be appreciated. You have a live audience out there and if you do a good job the applause is going to be deafening. If you do a bad job, you'll know it. The audience is very honest with you. I found live television to be close to the same although there is no applause. But you went on and you did it and you'd better be a damn good actor because you only get one shot at it."

Mickey also worked in a couple of episodes of *Alfred Hitchcock Presents* and *G.E. Theater*. "I was kind of stupid in those days," Mickey confided, "because I didn't like television. I was a motion picture and theater actor. At least that is the way I was raised, and I didn't see anything in television; it didn't do anything for me. When I was in the navy they wanted me for the *Robert Cummings Show* that Dwayne Hickman did, but I was in the military. Then I did a very nothing part in a show [a movie] called *Away All Boats* in 1956. I was just coming back, getting my feet wet in the motion picture industry. I was married at that time and messed up in the head, but I can honestly and truthfully say I never went onto drugs, never got into alcohol. The way it was going at that time in the business with the Tab Hunters, Rock Hudsons and Henry Wilsons, well, it was not my cup of tea. I didn't like the things that were being required of young actors at the time to further their careers. So I said that's it, I'm out of here." Mickey went to work for American Airlines from which he retired in 1995 after 30 years as a supervisor of flight attendants. "My wife, Barbara Traci, is the love of my life. We have been married 15 years. I have two children by my first wife and I'm a grandfather from my daughter. We have a good life and we have each other, and my kids like her very much. Now, in the spring and the fall, I guide historical tours in the Boston area. It just keeps me busy. I don't work in the winter and I don't work in the summer. I have a boat and I fish in the summer." Reflecting on his feelings about his career, Mickey said, "In summation, it was a great experience. I learned a lot. I enjoyed being an actor. It was very, very difficult as a child going to school and being raised in that environment. I wouldn't subject either of my children to that. But I enjoyed it; it was a good learning experience for me. To anyone who wants to get into the business I would say do it as a young adult. Getting into it as a child is very, very, *very* difficult. But I learned to get along with people. I had some bad reactions from it. I became very self-absorbed because of the way we were treated in the business. If you're any good you get treated very, very well, and sometimes it's tough to handle that if you don't have any help. Because of it I probably didn't become a mature adult until I was about 40 years old. It got in the way of a normal childhood that was offset by the 'glory and adoration' of people as you went from place to place. You sign this autograph and 'Oh, it's wonderful,' 'It's good to see you,' and such, but in retrospect I could have done without that and probably had a normal childhood and grown into maturity a lot faster."

Gordon Lee

Gordon Lee was born October 25, 1933, in Fort Worth, Texas. "I was adopted as an infant by Roland and Eva Lee, and mother sent a photograph to Roach Studios because I bore a striking resemblance to Spanky. Just by happenstance they were looking for a younger brother for the Spanky character. The story is that somebody brought my picture and tossed it on the casting director's desk, and said, 'Look, I just found this picture of Spanky when he was really young.' The casting director bought it. So that was the in. They contacted my parents and asked, 'Would you have a screen test done there and send it to us?' Well, my mother didn't quite operate that way. She was chief stenographer for Rock Island Railroad, and as such we had free passage. We jumped a train and headed toward Los Angeles."

They arrived in Los Angeles and Gordon was signed to a four-year contract by Hal Roach to play the character of Porky. "That was pretty much the way Roach worked. Tommy Bond, who played Butch, was walking down the street with his aunt or grandmother and this guy came up and said, 'That face is perfect. Mr. Roach is going to love that.' She thought she had a molester on her hands. He said 'No, no', and handed her his card, and he was a talent scout for Roach. So they drove out. Spanky was doing some still photography adds for baby clothes, and Roach saw that. He made those kind of choices. Strangely enough, Butch, Spanky and I were all from Fort Worth/Dallas, Texas, which is a 30-mile area. No contact beforehand at all; different ages and at different times, but that was just the way it hit." Gordon was 19 months old when the family came west to California. "I was two years and one month when my first one, *Little Sinner*, was released," he stated. Asked if he had many reflections on working on the *Little Rascals* films, he said, "I think of the magic of

Gordon Lee as Porky in Hal Roach's *Little Rascals* shorts.

Roach, and of Gordon Douglas and the other people there. The younger kids there had no idea that we were making movies. Spanky told me later that at about seven they figured out that somebody had another agenda going. Dickie Moore said the same thing. But Roach and his people were so good with it, and by catching us that early, we thought that was what everybody did. So I'd go and play with all my friends and with all these wonderful toys that Roach had for the movies, and a group of grownups would show up and they would play with their toys, which happened to be movie cameras and sound equipment and so forth. That's how he got the natural aspects of the kids in the movies. I have all kinds of memories of being on the set and on the studio lots and of going out on location, and the box lunches that they would provide us and that sort of thing. But as far as knowing that we were making movies, I didn't have any idea," Gordon laughed.

Besides playing with his friends and the various toys that Roach had for props, there was also dialogue to be memorized. When asked if he had any difficulty in learning the lines, Gordon replied, "Well, there's two or three answers to that. One, I had a strange sort of speech impediment in my early days. That accounts for the 'Otay Panky, tay Bucwheet'; I couldn't pronounce s's and k's. That was just the way I talked. I was never treated for it, and there was no hint of that in later years. I have copies of some of the scripts, and obviously I did have to memorize some lines. But I would say the proof of how I must have felt about that is that I taught history for 20 years and never asked a question on a test or quiz that you could memorize an answer for," Gordon mused. "It was never that kind of specific information that I asked for. So, I must deep down not have liked it."

During the time Gordon was working in the *Little Rascals* series, another famous comedy team named Laurel and Hardy were also working on the Roach studio lot. "They were just one sound stage down from us. They were sort of like our uncles. Spanky did a picture with them, but I never did that. As far as I was concerned they were just some of the other adults that were wandering around."

Gordon's film credits include 43 of the *Little Rascals* shorts. We asked him if he ever worked in any other films during his four-year stay in Hollywood. "No," he responded. "Spanky did a few outside, and I think Darla may have done one or two. Tommy Bond went on and did a number of features and had quite a career, and, of course, Mickey Gubitosi became Bobby Blake. But, no, I was strictly on the Little Rascals."

Gordon left the series when he was only six years old. He explained why he did so while still that young. "I had a four-year contract. It was up and I had hit a growth spurt at about five. So instead of being the little chubby heir-apparent to Spanky—he stayed little and chubby—I suddenly was the tallest kid in the gang. Then along came Bobby Blake. He looked a lot like me and was quite articulate and came just about up to my shoulder, so my contract went out the window."

At this time the family left Los Angeles and returned to their normal lives in Texas. "My father was a mortician; he had been managing the biggest funeral home in Fort Worth before we went out there. Economically, moving to California probably wasn't a good thing for them," he reflected, "but who knew?" Gordon was asked if he felt sorry that his film work had come to a close. "Yeah, growing up I thought a lot about it," he said. He was also asked if, in attending public school in Texas, did the other kids recognized him as Porky. "Well, I don't know if they recognized me, but quite possibly so. Kids can be cruel about that sort of thing. I put up with a lot of harassing, and then when I was a freshman in high school I was six foot two and I hospitalized a couple of kids for

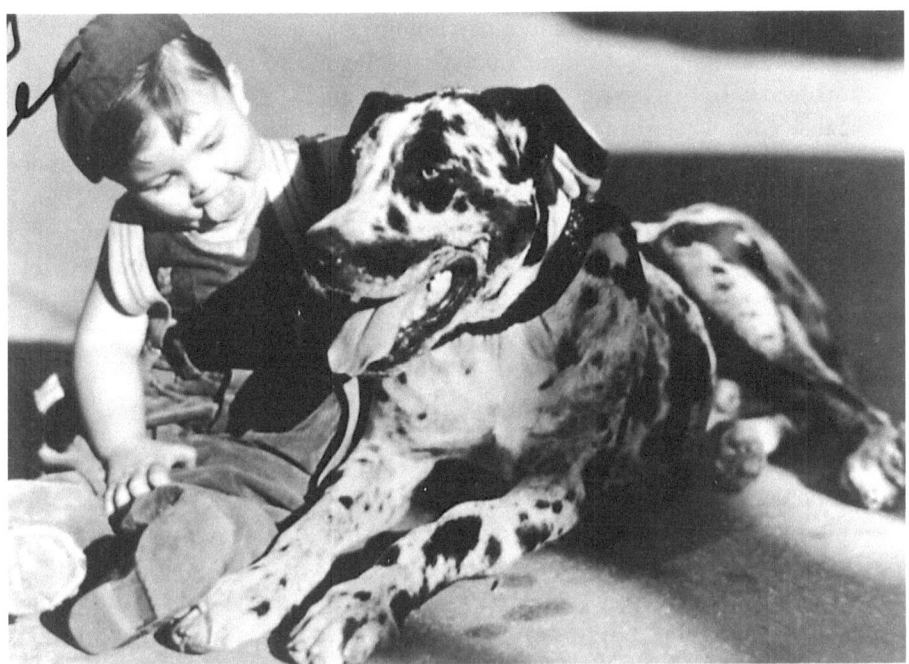

Gordon with a dog that was given as a present to Hal Roach by Italian President Benito Mussolini. "It wasn't used in any of the pictures," Gordon noted. "This is just a publicity still. Roach had photographers that went around all the time catching pictures of the kids for publicity shots. Pete, the dog that was used in the movies, was Roach's animal trainer's dog. Roach had all sorts of animals. He owned Hollywood Downs and had a string of race horses and was deeply involved in horse racing right up to the very end."

giving me trouble about Porky, and then it stopped. No one but my mother called me Porky anymore."

Gordon had another memory of working on the Roach studio that he shared. "We had all kinds of neat toys, and then the ice cream truck would come and we'd all go down and get ice cream. Roach had for definitional purposes what I guess you'd call a go-cart. It was a wooden-framed machine with bicycle wheels on it with little motors, and we'd run around on those. I was always a car freak. In my third or fourth year, I got 47 toy cars for Christmas. I didn't get anything else; didn't want anything. And that has carried on. I've had over 200 cars in my life. I spent a lot of time restoring English and Italian automobiles."

After graduating from college, Gordon began his career as an adult as a teacher. "Actually I started out wanting to be a counseling psychologist for kids. I did a major in psychology, and then found out you have to have a teaching major and a psychology minor and psychology wasn't offered. So then I got off into political science and history and became involved with that, so my undergraduate and graduate degrees are in political science. I taught for nearly 20 years in Texas and Colorado. I ended up in alternative schools, and for the State Department of Education designing and implementing alternative high schools for dropouts. Then I ran programs for a community college in Denver." Gordon also worked in various other capacities while living for over 20 years in Denver. He was a training officer for Colorado Emergency Services and ran a regional training program for the Federal Emergency Management Agency.

Since about 1980, Gordon has enjoyed attending various movie nostalgia shows. He stated: "It's a fascinating thing. We encounter people who talk in terms of fourth-generation watching us within their families, and now with this *Cabin Fever* release on videos, Tommy Bond, who worked as their spokesman, tells me that they sold better than four million sets of ten videos each. Now that's 40 million video tapes out there with three pictures each on them. So there's a lot of it still floating about."

In summing up his career as a child actor, Gordon noted, "I've said before that I think I'm terribly fortunate in that I don't have any real ego involvement in it because it's not something I did, it's someplace where I was. But I was a part of it. I stayed completely separate from it until about 1980, and had my whole other career. That has been my life. When I attend the autograph shows, I'm basically a history teacher who happens to be connected with the history of what we're talking about. So from that standpoint, I'm delighted with it and have a great deal of fun. Spanky, for instance, on the other hand, was completely involved in his aspect of the business, and was rather bitter about it because he tried to work back into it unsuccessfully. It's a little chance for a kid star to go on as an adult; it just doesn't work that way. So my career was in teaching and designing educational programs, and with the emergency services for the state of Colorado, and those are the things that I'm proud of. I had my own thoroughbred and classic automobiles on the side for most of my life, restored MGs, Triumphs, Jaguars and all of that sort of thing for many years, and have had great fun with that. But at the same time, I got back into the nostalgia of the *Little Rascals* and found that I just love it. So it's sort of a sometimes profitable hobby now that I'm retired. I love traveling and love people, so it's a great deal of fun."

Sammy McKim

Sammy McKim was born December 20, 1924, in North Vancouver, British Columbia. "I was only two years of age when we moved to Seattle. My mom's parents lived with us so we were a three-generation family. There were the grandparents, my parents, and the five kids. All five of us children eventually got into pictures."

The family lost their home in Seattle during the depression when both Sammy's father and grandfather lost their jobs, at which time they moved to California. Sammy's father became ill and was advised by the doctors, who believed he had tuberculosis, that it could be harmful if he was in close contact with his children, so he lived away. The family eventually settled in Los Angeles. "My grandfather ran the family and was a good-hearted old gent. He was the spirit behind my brothers and sisters and me getting into films. I was the first one to get in, but this was an accidental thing. A few days after we moved there my grandfather said to me, 'Hey Sammy, I'm going over to see a relative of ours in Beverly Hills.' So I jumped in our little 1927 two-door Chrysler with him and the two of us drove there and knocked on the door. There was no answer. The next door neighbor was outside watering his lawn, and said, 'Are you looking for Harry Bouquet?' My grandfather said, 'Yes. We're relatives from up north and have come to visit him.' The neighbor said, 'Why don't you go see him where he works?' So we went to see him, and it turned out that he was screen test director for MGM at the time."

Sammy sat in Bouquet's secretary's reception room quietly looking at the pictures in a magazine while his grandfather was in the office talking to his relative about the old days in Wales. As he waited there, an associate casting director named Jerry Herdan came in and wanted to see Bou-

Sammy McKim as "Boots" in Republic's 1938 serial, *The Great Adventures of Wild Bill Hickok*.

quet. "As he came in he looked at me. I had a mop of hair and a million and one freckles. I guess I was a bit of a character in appearance. He stopped and said, 'Hi, who are you?' I introduced myself. 'You work in pictures don't you?' he asked. I said, 'No.' But for some reason, you know the cat being thrown out of the window during the depression always lands on its feet, and something told me to say, 'But I'd like to.' He went on into the office and told my grandfather, 'Don't leave yet. I want to write a letter of introduction to the children's portion of Central Casting for extra work for all the studios around town.' And so he did that and gave it to my grandfather. He said for us to go down there and get me registered right away. So we did."

A couple of weeks later, Sammy received his first call on an interview at 20th Century–Fox. "I had to borrow a suit with knickers from a friend and had three or four days work in *This Is the Life*. The scene took place during a Sunday School picnic with a ball game going on. Jane Withers starred in it as a little singing, dancing star on Broadway who had run away from home, and her stepparents were trying to find her. The film was originally named *Meal Ticket* because she figured she was just a meal ticket for her stepparents. I used to collect autographs of the actors, directors, the prop people because it was all kind of exciting to me. Hollywood in 1935 was an exciting place. And here I was part of it, not on a high level, but a foot in the door. I got an autograph from a casting officer who wrote, 'Sammy, one of these days you'll be a meal ticket for your family.' The way it turned out, what my two brothers and two sisters and I earned as extras, bit players and later with parts, put bread on the table and paid the rent. And we didn't mind that a bit. We were brought up during the depression days in a good Christian home and were taught never to envy anybody who had more than we had and be grateful for what you get, and everything went into the family pot whoever was working."

Afterwards there was a picture called *Pepper* with Jane Withers. "Irving S. Cobb and Slim Summerville were character actors in that one. Slim would take his teeth out for certain films like Walter Brennan did. They were nice, and it was nice to work with Jane again. And then I jumped around—I worked at Warner Bros, RKO, Paramount, Columbia, MGM, and back at Fox. I used to go on interviews for bits and wouldn't get two thirds of them, but that lucky one third was great. There would be dozens and dozens of kids and they would line us up and call us out and you'd step forward and smile."

Sammy worked in a bit part in *The Plough and the Stars* in 1936. "I was on the film two or three days at RKO working for John Ford. The stars were Barbara Stanwyck and Preston Foster. Preston Foster took a shine to me. I was an undersized freckle-faced kid and dressed in terrible clothes, one of about ten poor kids in the neighborhood running the streets. He called me over for a publicity shot to be taken with him, which was nice of him to do. He had his pistol, showing me how to sight it." Sammy also worked with Preston Foster in *Annie Oakley*. "Five or six months after the film, my older brother David and I went into the publicity area at RKO studio where they sold stills over the counter. Actors and agents would come in to get pictures, and when I went in to get a few stills, Preston Foster was there. He looked over at me with a grin and I looked at him and nodded and walked on by. He said, 'Hey Sammy, are you stuck up or something to walk past an old friend without saying hello.' I said, 'I didn't think you'd remember me, Mr. Foster.' 'Of course I remember you, Sammy,' he replied. We shook hands and had a little talk. He was a first-class person. He didn't mind treating bit players decently."

Sammy obtained his first job at Republic Studios when he was selected to play Lila Lee's son in the Olson and Johnson comedy, *Country Gentlemen*. "I'd had bit parts in films before, but that was my first real role." After finishing that picture, the casting office was pleased with Sammy's performance and put him in his first western. "I didn't have to go on an interview for that one. It was with the *Three Mesquiteers* in *Hit the Saddle*. They just asked, 'You can ride, can't you?' and my grandfather said, 'Sure, he can ride.' That afternoon he took me out to a riding academy and I rode a pony that had a little spirit. As I was riding around the ring I was instructed, 'Jump over the little bar.' I'd do anything I was told, so I took him at a bit of a gallop and he stopped, and I flew over his head. But you got to get dirty now and then and get back in the saddle. So I was familiar with riding a couple of horses before starting on the picture. But I learned to ride, you might say, as I worked in more westerns. I liked westerns very much, and the more I was in them the more I liked them."

Then they put Sammy in a 12-chapter serial. "That was a big break for me. It was *The Painted Stallion* with Ray Corrigan and Hoot Gibson. I had fifth billing. On *The Painted Stallion* we were in St. George, Utah. They had two units going and they had a standby car that they had rented to drive to one location over three miles away where the other unit was filming all the horseback riding and shooting. They used a lot of genuine cowboys, either from the rodeos or from riding fence in Texas, Oklahoma or the Northwest. These guys would hang out with their boots and hats waiting for a casting call on Melrose Avenue at a drug store near Columbia Studio, hence the term 'drugstore cowboys.' A lot of these people I worked with on the westerns were these cowboys, and I liked being around them.

"I got along well with the adults on the set and tried not to be what they called around town a movie brat. I'm sure you heard about the movie mothers. They'd get in the hair of the assistant directors and had to be dealt with firmly at times. But I behaved myself on the set and knew how to take direction. Never went to acting school, just kind of a natural thing and it worked out. I met people like Yakima Canutt and witnessed him do some of his stunts in the *Three Mesquiteers* and other films. The stunts, just like the fight scenes, were choreographed. I might say that Yakima doubled me once on *The Painted Stallion*. Bill Witney was directing this. It was up at Lake Sherwood and I was supposed to swim a horse along with Ray Corrigan. Well, I had never swum a horse, and this horse wasn't acting too well. Time is money and film is money, so Bill said, 'Yak, slip on a jacket that fits you but looks like Sammy's, pull his hat down over your eyes and get on the horse.' So it was Ray Corrigan, and Yakima pretending to be Sammy McKim, swimming the horse. So it's interesting to say that Yakima Canutt doubled me.

"Kids used to ask me why the arrows in *The Painted Stallion* always whistled. I didn't really know if they added the sound, so I'd just say, 'They tied a whistle to it.' That would satisfy the kids," Sammy smiled.

After *The Painted Stallion*, Sammy was placed under contract at Republic and appeared in 12 features over the following two years. "I have a lot of happy memories with my Republic days. I was under contract there in 1937 and '38. The studio released lobby cards of *The Painted Stallion* with me in third billing because they were going to build me up. Betty Burbridge, one of the writers at Republic, had already written a script for me to star in."

In Sammy's contract at Republic the small print read "If you are not active with any film work at the time, the studio is not liable to pay you for a six week period." "I started at $50 per week," Sammy explained, "and we knew that every six months I'd get $25 a week more, and so on. During one long stretch I had not worked and all of a sudden we found out that I was laid off. We hadn't read all the teeny print in the contract. I couldn't go work anywhere else because I was still under contract, and my brothers and sisters weren't working much at the time. My grandfather used to write articles and send them in freelance to different papers. Sometimes they'd buy them and sometimes they wouldn't. So we were behind in rent."

One of Herbert Yates' key men at Republic told Sammy's grandfather, "We have big plans for Sammy. We are going to star him in his own series, but we want him to stay for the next six months at $50 per week and then he'll be bumped up to $75 for six months, and then a hundred." "It was a five year contract. Gramps could be blunt at times, and he told the guy to go to blazes. Well, the guy didn't like the way my grandfather talked to him, and failed in whoever told him to get the agreement; so they dropped my contract. Within two months I was back there working for $125 a week, but it wasn't every week. My part would be through in a week, but it's funny what people do."

Sammy worked with Gene Autry in *The Old Barn Dance*. "In the movie I trip and fall in the street when there's a bunch of cattle stampeding through town. But Autry gets on Champion and rushes by and picks me up and gets out of the way. Gene did it himself, and so did I. They shot it in such a way to assure the cattle didn't get too close to us."

Sammy mentioned a situation he found himself in while filming *The Painted Stallion* that could have proved fatal. "I was riding out front of the wagon train with Hoot Gibson and Ray Corrigan, going through some beautiful scenery in Utah. It was a local pony they hired for me, belonging to a boy in St. George. Well, I was a different kid in the saddle and the horse knew it. The teams behind us were picking up a little speed when the harness broke on the first one and they began running. I kicked my horse (the horse had been a little sluggish in a few scenes so they gave me one spur to wear on the offside of the camera) and it got into a gallop, but it was a small horse compared to what the adults were riding. I saw the horses of the lead team start on each side of me and I would have been run down if it wasn't for Hoot Gibson, who was a heck of a horseman. He whipped around and pulled the team up and stopped it. So you might say that Hoot Gibson saved my bacon that day.

"Another time I remember was when I lose my footing and fall off

Sammy with Max Terhune's dummy "Elmer," and his German shepherd dog who sniffed out the silk robbers' hideout in a deserted town. From Republic's *Call The Mesquiteers* (1938).

a cliff in *Heart of the Rockies*. I was going around stealing the animals out of my no-good stepfather's traps and bringing them back with hurt paws and legs where the traps had grabbed them. I even had a pet bear I released from one of his traps. A middle-sized one, four or five hundred pounds. But in this scene I'm going after a mountain lion cub over the side of the cliff and I slip and fall out of sight. They had some guys down below holding a net and that was the first time I ever fell into one. I didn't think it was big enough, but it worked. Then they filmed Max Terhune going over the side on a rope, and then Ray Corrigan pulled him and me up with my holding this cat. They shot this on location near Palm Springs in the Tahquitz Mountains. Later they covered that location shot on the stage with process behind showing the terrain. We had a fake rock and ledge that I had fallen down on—still hanging on to this little lion—and Max came down a rope and grabbed hold of me and we were pulled up by Ray. Max's hand slipped on the rope and came down over mine, and with his weight on top of my hand on the rope, and this little mountain lion cub getting wild and scratching me, I went 'owww!' Max felt so badly about that, but he couldn't help it. He was hanging in air as I was getting pulled up on the rope and he knew that my hand was hurting under his grip, but that was kind of an ending to the other scene where I fell into the net."

When World War II came along, Sammy went into the service in April 1943. He was with the American Division on Cebu in the Philippines and at Luzon with a unit called the Alamo Scouts. "We were trained to do reconnaissance work behind Japanese lines. Then they dropped the two atomic bombs and the war was over. I went for occupation duty in Japan where I joined the 11th Airborne Division. I was in the service for 3½ years and went from private to first lieutenant."

When Sammy came home he thought that he would continue as an actor. "I did some picture work, but it wasn't going too good so after a year I went to school full time. I had started drawing ever since I could hold a pencil and I've been drawing ever since. I was always drawing in school. On the set I did sketches of Duncan Renaldo, Pat O'Brien and others, then had them sign them. When I was an extra on *The Frisco Kid*, Jimmy Cagney took a shine to me and introduced himself. The next day I had done a cartoon of him taken from something I saw in the paper and asked for his signature. He signed it to me, and then drew a sketch of himself, and it was a good one. It was between scenes and he asked me to go into his dressing room to keep him company. He said, 'I wanted to be an artist when I was a kid. I wanted to be a political cartoonist on one of the New York papers, but it didn't turn out that way.' He did do a lot of oil paintings after he retired. I'd always wanted to be an artist, so I decided to get some professional training and went to Art Center and took advertising and illustration. My brother David and I got our degrees in September of 1950. I was one of ten that got bachelor degrees from the art department and my brother was the only one in the photo department. The next day I was back in uniform at Ford Ord. I had been recalled."

In the meantime the war in Korea had started. "Looking back at this point in my life now, I'm glad it happened. I didn't have personal combat in World War II, but this second time around I was among the first reservists recalled. They were in a hurry for us because casualties were mounting overseas. I joined K Company of the Eighth Cavalry Regiment of the First Cavalry Division as a platoon leader. It was a rifle company of an infantry outfit; they kept the cavalry name for traditional purposes. I had about four months on line of rather rigorous duty through those hills, and I saw combat both in the attack and the defense. So I was making up for what I had missed at the tag end of World War II."

Sammy won the Distinguished Service Cross during his tour of duty in Korea.

After returning home from Korea, Sammy obtained a role in the World War II film *Thunderbirds*. Also within a month of getting back, he began classes at Chouinard Art Institute. "I took illustration, water color painting, and oil classes. When I got out I began freelancing around town. I started by working for 20th Century-Fox in the publicity department, doing the illustrations for the coming attractions trailers for a few of the early Cinemascope films, the first one being *King of the Khyber Rifles*. I did a lot of exciting stuff like the fight with Tyrone Power and the villain, and Power with the leading lady. I could capture their likeness and do them rather well. I was able to get a nice feel of the brush work, and they looked like the actors. The studio liked that and gave me *Prince Valiant* and *Hell and High Water*. The man who had hired me at 20th liked my work. He told me that all the other illustrators were busy and they could use me on another film coming up and asked if I could start the next Monday. I said I would be there."

Sammy freelanced at Fox for a number of months, and then obtained work for Walt Disney as an illustrator for the park he was developing that became Disneyland. While at Disney, Sammy helped visualize attractions for both Disneyland and Disney World in Florida. "I did the first souvenir map for Disneyland. I updated it when we redid Frontierland, and when we redid Adventureland. The first one I did didn't have the Matterhorn in it nor the monorail." At Disney World, Sammy worked on the Exxon Energy Pavilion and other smaller jobs. "There were about five of us illustrators working on putting continuity together, showing the story on story boards." Sammy began sketching the arcade games outside of the *Pirates of the Caribbean*, but they were set aside when he was called over to the motion picture studio where he worked on *The Gnome-Mobile* with Walter Brennan. "I had over a year's work on that, and then went into the *Great Moments with Mr. Lincoln* show and did all the paintings in the stand-up theater in the preshow before the doors would open and the people would go in, sit down and Lincoln would get up and speak. When I got through with these two assignments I got a call from Walt. He said, 'Remember all those sketches you made for the arcade? We're going to quit talking about it and do it.'" So Sammy spent a lot of time sketching and developing many of these games. When the new Disney World opened in France he made the souvenir map. Sammy worked for Disney for a little over 32 years, and has been retired since 1987.

Sammy has been married for 46 years to his wife Dorothy, and has two sons. "Brian is in feature animation for Disney and his wife Dorothy is director of production, and they have given us two fine grandkids. The little boy turned nine and likes to draw, so he may be like his daddy and granddaddy. Matthew is a project designer at Walt Disney Imagineering, helping plan and design all the theme parks—two artists and one executive, three McKims still on the Disney payroll!" Sammy summed up his feelings of being a child actor by saying, "I enjoyed it, and I enjoyed the people I met. I got a lot of small parts on big pictures with big stars, and I've had a lot of big parts in B-westerns with relatively small stars. I didn't dwell so much on it when I was doing the work at Fox and Disney, so some of my friends at Disney didn't even know I had worked in pictures until a story came out in one of the Disney papers with a reference made to my having been a kid actor. But I enjoyed it very much and met a lot of grand people. And then there were disappointing times like when my contract was dropped at Republic, but looking back at it from this perspective at 76 years of age, I'm glad that everything happened the way it did because if things hadn't who knows what would have happened. Maybe I would have been a miserable Hollywood type. If I had been fortunate enough to be deemed successful maybe I would have gone through four or five marriages and have the same irresponsible attitude that a lot of actors do. But I enjoyed this as a kid, a young man, and later as a young adult. I went on the set to work and if it and the people I worked with were enjoyable, that was another good memory. Just like at Disney, I went to work to work, not to have a good time."

Shirley Mills

Shirley Mills was born April 8, 1926, in Tacoma, Washington. "We moved to Seattle when I was about four and my mother enrolled me in a dancing school that was very popular. The next thing I knew I was one of the soldiers in the parade of the wooden soldiers for *Babes in Toyland*. The thing that was really unusual was that I'd only gone to the dancing school for two weeks. The others had gone months and months, but I had a very good memory and they immediately picked me and put me in front of the line, which was very upsetting to a lot of the mothers there. But I was the only one that could remember the steps and the songs that we had to do. Then I did recitals around Seattle.

"I studied accordion and drums and had a little vaudeville act. I was featured at holiday times like Easter and Christmas and during summer vacation in some of the large theaters in Seattle where they would put on shows with talented young people. So I did quite a few things like that, including narrating children's fashions on my own radio programs in Seattle and Tacoma. At the age of seven I conducted the Seattle Baby Symphony Orchestra. Then also there was the Bert Levy booking agency, and I was the only child that they ever booked in the Northwest. I was in Oregon and Vancouver (both British Columbia and Washington), but always in theaters and always at holiday times. I was never taken out of school. I just loved it. I loved the applause, I loved the spotlights."

Shirley said that the reason her mother had her and her sisters take lessons was that it was "just the normal thing to do so that we would have poise, and also to give us a beginning in music. I don't think there was anything other than that. The only difference was that my two older sisters didn't care much about it and I loved it. I begged to practice and would cry if I couldn't take dancing and singing lessons. I think really it was from my own enthusiasm rather than hers. I came from a very strong Christian home. My parents and my grandparents on both sides were very conservative, and children working in the theatrical field in Tacoma and Seattle did not bring about any great approval from members of our family. But mother said, 'The children love to do it. It's good for them because they're not afraid to get up and speak in front of the public. Someday when they're older and go on to whatever they're going to do, this will serve them very well.' She was absolutely right, because my sisters were successful in what they did, although it wasn't in the theatrical field. So that was how I started."

Shirley Mills from *Child Bride* (1938).

Shirley's father did not enjoy good health and was advised (because the weather was so wet and damp) that he should move to a warmer climate. "That's how we happened to come to southern California. I was 10½ when we moved and I just sort of picked up where I left off. I was one of the Meglin Kiddys at Ethel Meglin's, a very famous talent school for children. First of all, it was just for singing and dancing and what they call personality singing. But after that, from time to time she would produce recitals and would have different people from the studio come in and see the children. I had been in a couple of recitals and would do monologues. This is what I had done in Seattle at the theaters reciting long monologues and interpreting them with all of the gestures. Then Ethel produced some plays. It was at one of these plays in Hollywood that an agent came to see the children and maybe find talent for motion pictures. Her name was Evelyn Byrd, first cousin of Admiral Richard Byrd. I think that was one reason why my parents didn't mind when she said, 'I think maybe I could put your daughter in motion pictures.' They were reluctant at first because they were very conservative, but the fact that she was a lady and had the lovely background that she had, they said, 'If you want to try, we'll see.' So we had pictures taken and she started submitting me."

Shirley auditioned for her first screen role at Ethel Meglin's Studio for a bit in *Little Miss Broadway*. "It was the only time that I sang in a movie. Near the beginning little girls were filmed singing *Auld Lange Syne* from the windows of an orphanage and waving goodbye as Shirley Temple left with her newly adoptive parents."

In 1938, Shirley starred in the movie *Child Bride*, filmed near Placerville, California. "That was a very interesting experience. They were looking for a child to play a role in that movie because at that time in the Ozarks older men were marrying little girls. There was legislation on the board trying to make that practice illegal, stating a child had to be either 18, or if 16 had to have the consent of the parent. It's just a little movie that they put together. They tested quite a few children for it and I was selected. They made it in about five weeks and it was released in schools, auditoriums and churches. The legislation did go through; the law was passed."

The second film Miss Byrd submitted Shirley for was at Universal for Joe Pasternak's production of *The Under-Pup*, which was Gloria Jean's first movie. "They had signed Gloria to replace Deanna Durbin and were looking for a little girl who was aristocratic and who could play a real brat, so the agent took me out to meet the director, Richard Wallace. As we parked the car and walked down to Universal Studio, this gentleman came up to us and looked at me and said, 'I'm looking for a little girl just like you to costar in a movie that I'm making.' My agent, showing herself to be kind of a novice, said, 'Oh, are you Richard Wallace?' and he said, 'No, I'm Joe Pasternak.' I was wearing a hat and gloves; the character was supposed to be a little society girl. He said, 'When you see Richard Wallace you tell him that I think you would be perfect for the role of Cecilia.' I met Richard Wallace and they tested about 16 girls, and I was selected to play that role. So that was my third movie and it was a real thrill."

Talking about her first day on the set, Shirley remembered, "I was amazed by everything. The first scene that we shot was where we're riding on the train going from wealthy homes up to the summer camp. Gloria Jean is with us because we had staged a contest for some underprivileged child living in Brooklyn to write about trees, and we selected her because all she said was, 'I can't write about it. I've never seen a tree.'

"Now I must tell you, I was such a movie fan. We saw movies from the time I was a little girl in Seattle. At a very young age I loved Bette Davis and really wanted to be a dramatic actress. That was my heart's desire, to be another Bette Davis. What was so amazing to me was that on the first day of shooting we were in a train car on the sound stage and I just couldn't get over it because I thought we would get on a real train and go down the tracks. Instead they put us on this car and then rocked it and ran movie footage outside that made it look like we were moving. I remember going home to my father that night, saying, 'Oh Daddy, you can't believe it. We weren't really on a train. Everything was just artificial.' So that was my first impression."

Shirley said it was fun playing a brat. "I loved it because it gave me a chance to really develop the dramatic side, because I did want to be a character actress. It was just wonderful and so thrilling. Joe Pasternak was marvelous. Those were the days when children were very well protected in the industry."

Evelyn Byrd heard that John Ford was going to direct *The Grapes of Wrath* so she took 13-year-old Shirley out on an interview for that. "I didn't play a brat in that one, but I did get my brother in a little bit of trouble from time to time. John Ford was a real gentleman. He was an outstanding person and very quiet.

"Everyday before shooting, John Ford would talk to us about the Joad family and their circumstances. They were called Okies and the states didn't want them and the unions were afraid of them. The thing that he stressed and what carried them through was the fact that they were a family and everything counted on hanging together, being together; the closeness of the family. When you watch *The Grapes of Wrath* you'll notice Darryl and I, in almost every scene we had together, were either holding hands or I had my arm around his shoulder. John Ford had a real heart for the Joad family and stressed that these people were not bums. They were victims of circumstances. All of these people that came out had to leave their homes and what they had worked for all their lives. That was the real tragedy of it all. I'm glad that I was old enough and was a good student in school and read a lot so I was able to appreciate the importance of this movie. It was a fantastic experience."

Another part of the dignity of the Joad family that Ford stressed was that they were clean, wholesome, God-fearing people, unused to living in the conditions they found themselves in. "In every single scene I wore my hair in braids and they were always perfect. Before every scene he would have the hairdresser undo it and carefully rebraid them so that we looked immaculately clean all the time. I thought that was very interesting."

Shirley reflected on some of her fellow cast members from the movie. "Jane Darwell was wonderful to work with. She was really sweet. Jane had never married and she was raising her two nieces, so they were frequently on the set to visit. Jane really did act as if she were our mother. She'd come in to visit with us sometimes while we were going to school. I was fortunately a very good student so I loved all the extra hours where I could just study. Russell Simpson was great. He was like a real papa and he would tell these stories which you wouldn't believe," Shirley laughed. "He'd put Darryl on one knee and me on the other and he'd pass the time of day when we were in-between shots telling us all of these funny stories."

Another cast member was Dorris Bowdon, the wife of Nunnally Johnson, who played Rosasharon. "She was a dear. The whole cast really did become a family. Henry Fonda was a very quiet and reserved person, but the very last day Darryl and I finally worked up our courage and went and knocked on his door to ask for his autograph. He said, 'I knew it. I knew before this was over that you would come knocking on my door.' He was very kind and invited us in. John Carradine was quite a character. He would stretch out in the back seat of his old car and sleep, but he was always at the scene and always knew his lines."

Asked if there were any humorous experiences while making *The Grapes of Wrath*, Shirley reflected, "I can think of one thing right away because it's always my favorite. When we were in the infamous truck going along there was a scene where we pull off the road. When we went to drive it back on the road again it almost tipped over and you can hear all of us scream. Ford said, 'Leave it in! That's wonderful.' That really happened. Then there were a lot of other little things, like when they took the truck out on the road for the long shots they'd put new tires on it, but when they brought it in for the closeups they'd put the old beat-up ones on."

In January 2001, the Alex Film Society had a screening of *The Grapes of Wrath* at the Alex Theater in Glendale, California. Attending the event were Shirley, Darryl Hickman and Dorris Bowdon. They were honored as the only three living actors of the Joad Family. After the movie was shown, Leonard Maltin hosted a panel with the three actors on stage. Shirley mentioned, "The theater was packed, including both balconies. When he completed our panel interview and as we rose to leave every person stood and gave us an ovation that lasted for several minutes. I shall never, never forget that night."

Asked whether the authorities would stop a child actor from taking time off to do films if their grades didn't stay up in school, Shirley answered, "That's a very interesting subject because it was very difficult in public schools. The schools are paid per child per day. So anytime that

Shirley with Henry Fonda and Darryl Hickman as members of the Joad family from John Ford's classic, *The Grapes of Wrath* (20th Century-Fox, 1940).

a child is absent it not only could reflect on the child's education but also against the income of the schools. I was a straight A student so I always came back to school way ahead of the class. In junior high school I never had any problem except in gym and art. They kept giving me incompletes because I wasn't there to do the art and go on field trips, and I wasn't there to partake in sports. Finally at the end of ninth grade I was so upset when everything else was As and then they called them incompletes. I said to my mother, 'It's not fair. I go back and I'm way ahead of the other students in everything else. I don't know what to do.' She told me, 'You need to go to the principal and talk to her about it.' So I did. The principal said, 'Well, that's the only way that we can handle it.' I came home and told my parents, 'I want to go to a private school. I don't want to go back there again.'

"I even had a couple of experiences where they were very insulting to me. In *The Under-Pup* there's a scene at the very beginning at a church where they are looking for some children. During that scene I'm sitting there and I kind of roll my eyes up to heaven when this little girl is talking. When the movie was released, the schoolteacher in my geography class brought me up in front of the class and said that what I had done was an insult, sacrilegious, and shameful. She disgraced me in front of the entire class. I still get upset when I think about it. Here I was a straight A student, I had been voted president, vice president and secretary of my senior class in junior high school. I was that popular with everyone, and then to have her do that. And then right after that I received this last report card and I just knew I needed to do something different. The following September when I started the tenth grade, my mother enrolled me in Hollywood Professional School. I went there for my high school years and really enjoyed it. I went to school in the morning and carried six solids, and in the afternoon I took language lessons, singing, dancing and all the things that I wanted to do, which were the equivalent of all of the sport events that I wasn't doing in junior high school. Certainly I received a much better musical education and related subjects that went along with it. But yes it was very difficult for the schools to accept children that worked in motion pictures."

In *Virginia City,* Shirley was featured in a bit part. "I was starting to go through kind of an in-between age and I had just one scene. It was very dramatic. My father has just been shot by the Indians and died. I pick up a gun and shoot, all the while crying and screaming, and Errol Flynn comes over and takes me in his arms. I was 14, but I looked like I was ten; I've always looked younger than my age. Michael Curtiz was the director and when it was over he complimented me because the crew had applauded when I had finished the scene. He said, 'You were so wonderful. What would you like to be when you grow up?' I said, 'More than anything else I would like to be a dramatic actress like Bette Davis.' Curtiz said, 'Well, you probably have the most potential of any young person I've seen in a long time.' It was a moment I will always remember."

Shirley shared an interesting anecdote. "I found out after I made the movie that in real life my great aunt living in Long Beach was married to the character that Errol Flynn played in the film." During the making of the film Shirley almost killed Flynn's dog. "They took me out on the back lot to get used to shooting. He had a dog that he had with him all the time and it was running around. I had never shot a gun before and just as I pulled the trigger the dog ran in front of me; he yelped and ran off. We thought that I had hit him, but it was just that the shot had frightened him, and I had not hit the dog. I was really relieved."

When Shirley went back to school—she was in the ninth grade at the time—all the girls wanted to know about the movie and what she did.

When she explained to them what the scene was about, they swooned. "Oh, Errol Flynn held you in his arms."

Reflecting on her work in *Five Little Peppers in Trouble*, Shirley said, "I loved Edith Fellows. She is a darling person and had that beautiful voice that they never did enough with. By that time I had made three brat movies and what Mel, my husband, always liked about *Five Little Peppers in Trouble* involved two things that happened to me in that movie. One, I was slapped in the face, and the other I was pushed in the pool. Mel said, 'At last you get something that's coming to you.' He always enjoyed that." Shirley continued working in such pictures as *Young People* and *Miss Annie Rooney* with Shirley Temple—"She was a doll. It was always amazing to me that she was so unspoiled;" *Henry Aldrich Gets Glamour;* and *Betty Co-Ed*—"That was a fun movie to make. I was a brat again in this one.

"What I really loved was light opera and musical comedy because of my prior years of dancing. While I was having my teeth straightened and couldn't test for speaking roles, I became one of the *Jivin' Jacks and Jills*. They needed a boy dancer, so I went out and auditioned with a young man. We jitterbugged and danced, but they didn't select him. They selected me instead. I made five musicals with Donald O'Connor and Peggy Ryan. Then toward the end of two years when I no longer needed braces I tested for *Nine Girls* and *None Shall Escape* and was signed for both of those roles.

"Every film was just a different experience and I have been grateful that I was in movies during the golden age of motion pictures, when everything was at its best and the movies were for the whole family. What went on behind the scenes nobody really knew much about; the major studios protected their stars and we only saw the best of them, and they were stars. They were rare and special, so that when they made an appearance somewhere the audience was in awe of them. I think it's too bad that today everybody's private lives are made so public. It stripped the industry of the real wonder and the glamour of it all. It makes it an entirely different world and I'm just grateful that I was in it at the time that I was."

Asked if it was harder to get parts because she had reached a certain age, Shirley said, "Yes, it really was. When I was 15, I started studying voice seriously. I really did have a good voice and I began with opera and became caught up more in the singing at that point. That was really what was on my mind the last three years that I was in motion pictures. I think the last movie that I made was *The Model and the Marriage Broker*."

When Shirley was 18, she decided to leave the motion-picture industry and went to New York and played Laurie on Broadway in *Oklahoma*.

"Working on stage was the essence of everything. There's nothing like that live audience. From then on I was under contract with MCA and had an extended singing career. I was in Paris for a year and a half at the famous Gaslight Club and under contract singing for royalty from many countries and notable international dignitaries. While in Paris they made me assistant manager, so when they brought me to the Gaslight Club in Beverly Hills I was not only the starring attraction there for three years, but was managing the Paris Room as well. After I left the Gaslight Club, I was very busy with my singing career. I was featured with Robert Goulet; I played Reno, Vegas and Tahoe; I was featured with Frankie Laine. So I was always in the main room. Then one day I thought, 'What am I going to be doing ten years from now? Am I still going to be living out of a suitcase?' When I was at the Gaslight Club, I bought a home and my parents shared it with me. I had a dog and I really liked being in one place. I thought, 'I've done well in business also. Maybe I should go into the business field.'"

Shirley had a resume printed stressing the management that she had done in Paris and Los Angeles. "At that time (1969) there was no woman involved in data processing other than being a keypunch operator or an analyst's assistant. So it went on record that I was the first woman in the United States to sell data processing services. I worked in public relations and marketing. In the first year I tripled their business. I became very successful at it and the challenge was exciting. All of my background in theatrics helped me because I wasn't afraid to get up and give presentations. I wasn't afraid to pick up a telephone and say, 'We haven't met before, but I represent a company that I think has a service that might be very valuable to your company.' Another factor that was easier for me was disappointments. I was used to them because of the times I had tested for movie roles and didn't get them."

Shirley's first advice to parents who would like to have their children in movies is not to let it get in the way of an education. She then said, "But so much depends on the parents. I would need to know where the personal desire ended with the parent and whether the child really wanted to do it. I wanted it so much that I think it was a privilege for me and it was such a desire of my heart. But if it's the parent saying, 'I want them to do it,' then I would say 'no.' If a child really has a desire to do it themselves and approaches the parents and says, 'You know, I really would like to try that,' then I would say, 'Let them give it a try.' But if it's the heart's desire of one parent or the other or both, then I would say, 'No, it's not fair to the child.'"

Of all her films, two stand out as favorites "*Grapes of Wrath* would be number one. It really impacted my life, not only professionally but as a person. It made me think about a lot of things that I wouldn't have thought about for quite a few more years: what people suffer but endure, not only for existence but also for maintaining their own dignity. I learned a lot from working on that movie and the content of the whole story.

"The other one would be *Nine Girls*. I had more fun on it than I could ever begin to tell you. And because I was the youngest I was spoiled rotten. All of the crew and everybody catered to me. It was fun to be spoiled. That was really almost overwhelming to be with all of these glamour girls. Marcia Mae Jones and I were the only two who were not under contract. At a time when Columbia wanted to put me under contract, I was 17 and my parents said, 'No.' They didn't want a studio to own me, they wanted to finish raising me the way they wanted to."

On summing up her career as a child actress, Shirley said, "For my years in the movie industry as a youthful active professional, in these years from 11 to 18, I would say it was a rare opportunity that has benefited me enormously through the course of my entire life. I drew on the experiences of those young years and they prepared me to enjoy achievements in all of the following opportunities that framed my future.

"I feel that if a child could grow up as I did in the environment of parents who loved, protected and guided me then that child, following their parent's wisdom, could pursue a desired dream to be successful in a branch of the media. Success and career contentment can become a reality ... they did for me."

Roger Mobley

Roger Mobley was born January 16, 1949, in Evansville, Indiana. The family later moved to Texas. When Roger was three years old, he and his older brother and sister formed a musical trio. "My brother and sister could play just about every instrument they could pick up. We sang at the churches and brush arbors and all night sings and county fairs."

In 1957 the family moved from Pecos, Texas, to California. "I think some friends of ours had moved to California and wrote back that this was the land flowing with milk and honey, and at that time it was. We continued to sing at school carnivals; you name it, we sang at it." The Mobley trio performed on the *Original Amateur Hour* with Ted Mack. "There used to be an agent named Lola Moore and she contacted us through the Ted Mack show, and expressed interest in signing all of us. We had only been out there a couple of months and my parents at first thought it was some kind of weird scheme. We met with her and she had an interview lined up for me the next day, which was for *Fury*, and I got the part." When Roger went to the interview for the role of Packy Lambert in *Fury*, they liked the way he looked, although he had no acting experience. They asked him, "Can you ride a horse?" and Roger answered, "Yes, I can ride a horse." They separated the children that could ride from those who couldn't because they knew that the show was 75 to 80 percent riding. "They felt they could probably teach an eight year old to act easier than they could teach an eight year old actor how to ride a horse. So out of 250 boys that were there, I was hired. I played Packy for almost three years. When that show was canceled, I went on to make other shows."

Roger reflected on the first day on the series. "First day on the set I didn't know what to think because I had watched the show four or five years before moving to California and now here I was making the show with the people that I had been watching every Saturday morning. I remember coming in from the first night of work: I went to play little league and was playing catcher. I had thrown the mask off too early and got hit in the nose with a bat. It smashed and broke my nose and I had to be taken to the emergency room. I was supposed to be on the set the next morning at six to go to Chatsworth on location, and when we showed up there those people just about had a fit. My eyes were black and my nose and face were swollen, so until the swelling went down and the black and blue went away they had to film behind me. I didn't get one day off. That was quite a memory, and not a very fond one. From then on they nicknamed me 'the trooper,' but I really didn't have a choice. My parents were a little intimidated—those people said 'You're going to be here.' So I was there everyday, sick as a dog. When the swelling went down enough they could shoot from the sides, and then finally they could resume normal filming. If a person knows to watch for it, there's several episodes where you never see Packy's face; it's always from the back."

Roger Mobley from *The Idol*, an episode of *Cheyenne* (Warner Bros., 1962).

It wasn't long after Roger recovered from having his nose broken that he did an episode of *Fury* in which he befriends a wild stallion who is supposed to be a mad killer. "But Packy could do anything he wanted to with this horse. Lane Bradford had been thrown from the horse and was going to kill it with his Winchester and I was trying to keep him from shooting it. In this scene he's supposed to pick me up over his head and throw me and then shoot the horse, but Fury comes in and knocks him over. While we were wrestling, the hammer on that Winchester—the firing pin—locked in the crook of my arm and neither he or I knew it. When he took me over his head and threw me off-camera (there were people there to catch me) about four inches of my arm got left in the hammer of that Winchester. I ended up needing 48 stitches. We drove into Chatsworth to the emergency room and I was stitched up. Instead of them sending me on home, I went back to the set that very same day. Once I got there they tried setting up for the next shot. I mean, you figure a kid just going through a thing like that and then going right back to work. I was sick and nauseous and scared to death, and I ended up passing out a few times on the set. So they sent us home, but I was back the next morning at six o'clock and didn't miss a day. Instead of shooting around me, they shot from one side because my arm was immobile for several weeks."

Fury was owned by Ralph McCutcheon. He had actually five black horses that played the part of Fury. "There was one that he had trained to do the tricks. Actually they weren't really tricks because the horse was intelligent enough and knew what he was doing. McCutcheon would be off-camera and say, 'Beaut,' (the horse's name was Beaut), 'go pull the boy by his shirt, and pull him backwards.' That horse would go grab my shirt-tail or the seat of my pants and pull me backwards," Roger related. "There were four other horses besides Beaut. One was used for long shots; one was used for the stand-in; one was used when there were scenes with long stretches of dialogue in which the horse needed to stand real still, because the main one was pretty hyper, and nobody rode her. When there was just a riding scene they used another. Then they had one that was used especially for the rearing scenes. I believe Beaut took sick and passed away in Hawaii. I'm not sure; that's just hearsay. Three or four years later while I was filming either *The Dakotas* or *The Outlaws* on the Paramount lot, I heard that Beaut was in an episode of *Bonanza*, which was three or four sound stages away from where we were working. When we had a break, I went to that sound stage and I believe that the way the horse reacted she remembered me. We had about a five or ten minute reunion and then I went back to work and that's the last time I saw the horse."

After *Fury* ended, Roger worked for just about every western series that was on television in those days. Some of these included *Gunsmoke*, *Death Valley Days*, *The Virginian*, *Frontier Circus*, *Lawman*, *Destry* and *Wagon Train*. His television work was not limited to the westerns. He appeared also in such comedies as *I'm Dickens, He's Fenster*, and *The Farmer's Daughter*; dramas such as *Dr. Kildare*, *Route 66* and *87th Precinct*; and thrillers like *Night Gallery*. He also had the title role in *Inside Danny*

Baker, a pilot for a series in 1963 that never sold. "Mel Brooks produced two different pilots for that season. My show was filmed in New York City where the newspaper comic strip of Danny Baker had been a big hit. Each episode was to go into one of Danny Baker's fantasies—it had him as a cowboy, a baseball pitcher for the New York Yankees, and other such adventures. The networks picked up the second Mel Brooks series which became a big hit, *The Patty Duke Show*."

Roger was about 12 when he had an interview at Disney. "It was strange because I didn't have an interview for a part in years; it just seemed like I was called for a role. I remember having to interview at Disney's and we thought it was kind of different. But just going to the Disney Studio was exciting. Everything was so family orientated, it was so unlike the other studios. To go into the Disney studio, for me, was like going to Disneyland, with Mickey Mouse and Donald Duck everywhere." Roger interviewed for *For The Love of Willadean* which was being made for *Walt Disney's Wonderful World of Color*. "I got the part, and after that it seemed like Disney's was about the only place I worked," he reflected. "I was under contract with him, but it wasn't exclusive. I was permitted to work other places too, but working for Disney was wonderful. It was the happiest time of my life in Hollywood because that was when Mr. Disney was still alive and the people were just wonderful."

Roger starred as Gallegher in Disney's *Gallegher* on *Walt Disney's Wonderful World of Color*—playing the newsboy who worked for Edmond O'Brien in the East and later for John McIntire out west. They

Roger Mobley starred in *The Boy Who Caught a Crook* (United Artists, 1961).

made 16 episodes, and among those who worked in them were Peter Graves (his old costar from *Fury*), Bruce Dern and Warren Oates. "Oates taught me how to chew tobacco, so my mom didn't think too highly of him for a while, but I thought he was great." Reflecting back on this series, Roger said, "Bruce Dern was pretty strange; he was different. I was 16 so I had to have a welfare worker there because I was a minor. I remember Bruce used to jog to work with sweat pants that were ripped in the seams in the back. He didn't care. His hair was real long before it was fashionable, and he acted the part of a real flaky gunfighter. He was about 30 then and would tell me all these stories, and I just gravitated to him. So the welfare worker finally told me, 'Roger, you're going to have to stop hanging around with him. He's not a very good influence.' But every chance I got I would sneak around and ask him, 'Tell me some more stories.'"

Roger shared an amusing story that happened during his first week of working on *Gallegher*. "The first time I saw Walt Disney I didn't recognize him and walked right past him. He said, 'Hello Gallegher.' I said 'Hello' and kept walking. Then it dawned on me who he was and I stopped and turned around and looked. He stood there looking at me with an expression like 'You're just going to pass me? You know, I could make you or break you.' So I went back to him and said, 'Hello Mr. Disney, how are you doing?' He said, 'I'm doing fine, Roger. I just want you to know that we're real pleased with you. *Gallegher* is exactly like I envisioned it.' Someone had told me, and I repeat this not as fact, but as hearsay, that Mr. Disney said the *Gallegher* episodes was one of his favorites of all the years that they had been making *The Wonderful World of Color*. I like to think that it was true."

Roger's performances were not limited to the TV screen. One of the features he costarred in was *Jack the Giant Killer*. "We worked on a barge off of Catalina Island. I think it was six weeks. I made eight films for Edward Small Productions and those films were like wham, bam, thank you ma'am. Six weeks for Edward Small is an epic, because the other films I made for him were like five days. *Jack the Giant Killer* was a lot of fun. We acted against a black screen in the scenes with the creatures, so you're reacting to something that's not there. To me that wasn't hard because I always had a vivid imagination."

Roger starred in the 1963 film *Dime with a Halo* which was directed by Boris Sagal. The film centered around five poor Mexican kids who take ten cents from a collection plate in a church and bet it on a racehorse. "My fondest memory of that was being madly in love with Barbara Luna. I was about 13 and I fell so madly in love with that woman, it was unbelievable.

I was sick to my stomach, I loved her so much. The movie was filmed at the old Hal Roach Studios which had been abandoned at that time, so we were the only thing going on the lot. I think they had just rented the facilities, and I believe we went out to the racetrack in Pomona instead of going to Tijuana."

Roger said that one of his favorite people that he worked with was Clint Walker. "I made a *Cheyenne* and he was just so nice. We filmed on the back lot, and when they called lunch he would walk on his hands going to the commissary. He tried to teach me how to do it, but I just never got the hang of it. I guess he took a liking to me because the next season they had another part that called for a child, and he said that he personally requested me."

Roger costarred with child actors Bryan Russell and Cindy Cassell in Disney's *Emil and the Detectives* which was filmed in West Berlin. "That was after I graduated from eighth or ninth grade. My mom went with me to Germany. After we were there about a month they gave us expense money and we rented an apartment. A Volkswagen van would pick us up, and after we were through filming they'd bring us back. But we were kind of lost. Neither one of us spoke German, and we had a German landlord. While we were over there, one of my sisters got real sick so my mom came back to California to be with her. I stayed with a German family the 4½ months that I was there that had been approved by the studio. It was a lot of fun when we were filming, but staying with a strange family when you're 14 or 15 years old was pretty unpleasant. But they had kids my age and after they got used to me and I got used to them it was wonderful. Of course that was Disney, and anytime I worked for them it was a good experience. The director was Peter Tewksbury, and he was the most favorite director I had ever worked with. That's probably my favorite film."

After Roger graduated from high school, he made a film for Disney titled *The Treasure of San Bosco Reef*, and was then called by Jack Webb to make his third episode of *Dragnet*. A little later, he was drafted and served with the Green Berets in Vietnam. Roger returned to California in November of 1970 and contacted his agent. "I went on a few interviews. I was married to Sherry, my high school sweetheart, and we went back to Texas to visit my folks. That was Christmas of 1970. In January we were still in Texas." The agent had been calling him, saying, "Hey look, I've got interviews lined up. These people are interested in you. You've been gone three years and we need to let people know you're back in town." Roger told him, "Okay, I'll be back February or March." When February and March came he hadn't gone back. Roger ended up getting a job as a policeman in Beaumont.

"I stayed there until 1978 and I really started missing film work. I called Disney's and talked to Ron Miller." "What do you think the chances are of me getting some work if I moved back out there?" Roger asked. "Chances are good with us," Miller answered. "I don't know about any place else. Have you changed much?" "No, not really," Roger said. "I can't guarantee you anything, but I don't see why you couldn't get a lot of work with us." So Roger quit the police department, sold their home and moved back to California. He walked into Disney's studios and said, "I'm here." They told him, "We really don't have anything right now, unless you don't mind taking a bit part just to get your foot back in the door." Roger replied, "I'll take it." The film was *The Apple Dumpling Gang Rides Again*. "I went to Kanab, Utah, for six weeks, but only had two or three lines. I liked the filming and enjoyed myself immensely up there, but in coming back I went to one interview after another and didn't like it. I was 30 years old and many of the casting directors were like 23 years old. I would bring my resume and my pictures. They would ask me, 'What have you done?'" They would tell Roger that they had never heard of those shows. "I'd say, 'Those were back in the '50s and '60s.' They said, 'This is almost the '80s. What have you been doing the last ten years?' I said, 'Well, I was out of the business. I've been a cop in Texas,' and I couldn't even get a reading. It was just like if I was lost in a time warp. They didn't know me, and I didn't know them, and the ones who knew me were no longer active in the business. The more interviews that I went on, the more I hated it. And I would tell these people, 'If you'd just let me read, I promise you you're going to like it. Just let me read for the part.' 'No, we're looking for people with experience.' I would get so aggravated that I called the agent and said, 'Don't send me on anymore interviews unless you can send me to somebody that at least knows me.' It had changed quite a bit. I stayed out there a year and a half and worked twice, and both those times were for Disney. I could have stuck it out but I guess my pride got in the way. I told my agent, 'Look, I consider myself a veteran in this industry. I've got 12 years, over a hundred episodes plus features, and I'm not going to grovel to somebody that's been in the business less than a year.' He said, 'Roger, if you want back in it bad enough you're going to have to grovel.' I guess I didn't want it bad enough. He told me, 'Let's face it, you're not exactly a household name. You're going to have to start over.' Obviously I wasn't willing to start over. We kind of missed Texas and I missed being a policeman."

In 1979, Roger moved his family back to Texas. "We sold everything we had in Texas to move out to California, and what we had acquired the two times I did work out there we sold. We left Texas and went out there with nothing and we came back to Texas with nothing. I haven't been to Los Angeles since. Sometimes I think that maybe I should have stayed; maybe I didn't give it enough time. Some of my friends did. Kurt Russell stuck it out and he's real successful. Tim Matheson stuck it out and he's got a good thing going now."

In looking back over his whole career, Roger summed up his feelings by saying, "I liked it well enough that if it was still like that today I'd go back to it in a heartbeat, if the opportunity existed. Some people tell me, 'Roger, you gave up your childhood to be in movies,' but I really didn't because I still played little league. I played sports because Disney's was nice enough to not use me during the school year. I was just a regular kid. I had to get extra jobs, throw papers, and pump gas on the weekends like every other kid. Saved up my own money to get a little old Volkswagen, and I'd cruise the Boulevard like everybody else. I didn't miss anything, but I had so much more than those other kids by the experiences that I had. I know of some kids that seemed like they did give up their childhood for an acting career, but like I said, I don't feel that way at all because I *had* a childhood. On top of my childhood, I had the other. I wouldn't trade it for nothing.

"Financially, I didn't get anything out of it. I don't know why. I don't know if it was bad investments on somebody's part, or what. I'm sure I'm not the only one that ended up that way, but it's just something that happened and you just turn it off and go on." Roger mentioned that he had read in the paper of a child actor who did a series that ran about two seasons, and from this actor's earnings and investments he would never have to work a day in his life again. Roger said, "I read something like that and I tend to get bitter. I don't know why it happened like that to me, but it happened and I didn't end up with anything. You can't go back and relive it, and if you harbor on it it's going to make you sick, so you just get over it. I guess the most unpleasant thing is to think what could have been if the money had been handled properly because it probably would have been pretty sizable. But that's what got me through Vietnam. I was thinking: I got three more months left, two more months left. I'm also thinking 'You're going to go back, you'll be 21, you can get that trust fund; you got your wife that you love and you can do anything you want to.' So that kind of kept me going. I got back, the wife was there, but the money wasn't. But I think having the wife and not the money, I got the better deal."

Roger, who is now a grandfather, is currently a minister for a local church in Pineland, Texas.

Larry Olsen

Larry Joe Olsen was born May 16, 1938, in Marshalltown, Iowa. The family moved to Florida when he was two years old, and right after Pearl Harbor moved again to California. It wasn't long before Larry was introduced to the world of motion pictures. "It sounds phony, but I was discovered on the street by Lola Moore, who was the famous agent for children. I was in a bank with my mother. Miss Moore was impressed with my looks and asked mother if she would be interested in my being in pictures. My mom just being a hick from Iowa said 'Yes'. She took my name and address, and that's basically how I started."

Larry's mother enrolled him in a tap dancing class, where he performed before an audience, and when he was about four years old he did the balcony scene in *Romeo and Juliet*. Larry also traveled around the Los Angeles area on USO tours, where he would recite poetry, so by the time he appeared in his first picture "I was kind of used to being in front of people and doing things."

Lola Moore sent Larry almost immediately on an interview, and it wasn't long before he landed his first job. "I was right around five years old. I don't remember the title, but it was a Red Cross film short for the war effort. I had to run past a burning building and as soon as I got past the whole wall collapsed. I later did religious films and shorts, but they weren't commercial. I worked with Jimmy Hunt in some of those."

The first feature film Larry worked in came shortly after the Red Cross short. It was called *Happy Land*, produced by 20th Century–Fox. "We went on location up to Santa Rosa, California. I remember fleeting moments, like the train ride. I worked with a dog and I liked that. There was another child quite a bit older than me named James West playing the same part. I played Rusty as a little boy, and he played him as a subteen.

He was kind of my hero because he was older than I was. That's where I learned 'Good better best, never let it rest till the good is better and the better best.' He used to recite that to me.

"When we did some shots on the back lot I was very impressed with how realistic everything looked. They had candy bars in the drug store where Don Ameche worked, and I asked, 'Can I have one of the candy bars?' In fact, I've always been impressed working on the back lot and seeing the old western sets. They just looked so real. I wanted to play in them."

Speaking about westerns, Larry reflected on working in *Lone Texas Ranger* with Bill Elliott as Red Ryder. "What I

Larry Olsen

remember is that Bobby Blake was Little Beaver, and he was so lucky because he got to carry that knife. That really impressed me."

Larry remained quite busy at this time. "This was during the war and right afterwards. My mom and I went to interviews all over the city from Universal to Metro to Fox, and all by streetcar and bus. We had quite a system down here at that time. We took them all over the city." Larry shared a memory about an incident that happened behind the camera while working in *The Seventh Cross*. "I was just playing around as a kid and went to climb a fence. It wasn't made out of rod iron like it appeared to be. It was made out of plastic. I fell from there and landed right on my back and knocked the wind out of me. They were all upset because I was hurt."

In the 1945 film release, *Sergeant Mike*, Larry worked with a friend of the family, Larry Parks. "He was a very close friend of Lloyd Bridges, and the Bridges lived in the same court we did in the Park LaBrea Apartments. My mom and Dorothy Bridges became very good friends, and my dad went out and helped them put up their first beach home in Malibu.

I used to go with them quite often and spend the night. So I grew up with them as my neighbors, and Larry Parks was a very good friend of theirs. So, after I worked with Larry I'd also see him quite frequently when he was over to the Bridges' house with his wife, Betty Garrett." In his reflections on the film, Larry stated "I loved working with the German shepherd. I always loved working with dogs."

At about this same time, Larry said, "I worked with another German shepherd named Grey Shadow in *My Pal Wolf* with Sharyn Moffett. I was offered one of Grey Shadow's puppies, but since I lived in Park LaBrea I couldn't accept it. That was a fun movie to do. They had the swimming hole built right there on the set, and it was fun to go swimming in it. Also, there was a bunch of kids there so it was enjoyable. I know a lot of child actors said it was a miserable time for them, but I have no bad memories of doing movies at all. Mom was always of the opinion that if at anytime I didn't like it, I would just say so and not do it."

Most actors have their own techniques for bringing out the various emotions that they are called upon to employ. For crying scenes, Larry explained "All mom had to do was talk about *Bambi* and start singing *Love is a song that never ends* ... and I'd just burst out crying. If I hear that song today, I think of my mom and still get teary-eyed."

The movies for which Larry is best remembered are the two Hal Roach comedies, *Curly* and *Who Killed Doc Robbin?* Hal Roach, Jr. was trying to revive the old *Our Gang* situation, and Larry was one of the children called to audition for Curly, the leader of the kids. "It was just an interview, and I was chosen. They had brought out a kid from back east and promised him the role, and then I got it. They kept him out here, but he just had a minor part in it. He was going to be Curly, and I always felt kind of bad about that because he came all the way from back east to do the thing. I was put under contract there for about three years and only did the two films.

"I went to school there. There was Eilene Janssen, Dale Belding, Gerald Perreau, and myself. There was an old schoolroom up at the top in one of the buildings with the old-fashioned desks; I guess the old *Our Gang* had used them. Mrs. Carter was our teacher. That was our regular schooling for three years. Eilene used to throw the best Christmas parties. They were really terrific, and all us kids would come. They had a Spanish-style home in North Hollywood, and we always looked forward to going to her house at Christmastime."

Curly was a remake of one of the old *Little Rascals* films with Jackie Cooper. "It was the story of a classroom getting a new teacher, and the kids all loved the old teacher and didn't want to see her go. So we set up all these tricks to play on the new teacher, like tacks in her chair, a fountain pen that leaks, and so on. But unbeknownst to me, I get a ride to school by a lady in a car and don't know she was to be our new teacher, and I'm telling her all these nasty tricks we're going to do. When she walks into the classroom I just shrink down in my seat, and she turns the tricks all around on us guys. It was a good film. It's actually better than *Who Killed Doc Robbin? Who Killed Doc Robbin?* was a more fun film to do, but the film itself, *Curly*, is better. Frances Dee played the teacher and she was very nice to work with."

Larry shared a story about the filming of a scene from *Curly* that was cut out of the television version. "It was a scene where I'm in a tree talking to my pet frog named Froggie. My sister had just given him a bubble bath and I was trying to soothe him, and as I was doing the scene bubbles were coming out of his mouth. They did that by killing one of the frogs and running a tube up it, then having a guy down below blow bubbles through the tube with his mouth. I'm doing this scene and I'm supposed to be so sympathetic with him, and all I can remember is the blood coming out. *That* was a job of acting."

Larry mentioned that Hal Roach, Jr. did a very foolish thing: "He didn't present the movie by itself in the theaters, but it was called *Hal Roach's Comedy Classics* and we were just half of the thing. The other half was more of a sophisticated adult comedy, and we thought at the time it was kind of silly because one was for kids and one was more or less for adults. But a lot of people have seen it."

A year later Roach produced the second and final film in the series, *Who Killed Doc Robbin?* "I enjoyed the Curly films. The other kids and I got along good together, and they were just fun. Especially *Who Killed Doc Robbin?* with the haunted mansion. Dale Belding and I got the giggles. We were suspended on a thing and supposedly had just fallen down through a trapdoor. So they lifted us up and we had to drop and fall, and we couldn't do the scene because we kept laughing. Every time Dale would say a line I'd start laughing. This happened to adults too. Bernard Carr, the director, was getting so mad at us and we would start to do it serious and all of a sudden crack up. Finally he just called it quits and let us go for about an hour, and then we came back and did the scene. We had a lot of fun doing it. George Zucco wasn't very friendly and was a very sinister looking man. I'd seen him in a lot of movies and he seemed to be that way; at least he impressed me that way," Larry laughed. "Of course we had the chimpanzee working with us in the movie, my dog, and the guy in the gorilla outfit, and that fascinated me. He was teaching me how to walk like a gorilla."

Samuel White, who with his brother Jules had produced the Three Stooges comedies, started Lone Star Productions with the intention of producing a television series. "It was a western series for children like *Wild Bill Hickok*," Larry stated. "It was financed in part from the city of Tucson. We did a pilot called *Rawhide Riley* when I was 13 years old and didn't hear anymore about it for two years. Then all of a sudden Sam called up and said, 'Hey, we think we sold the thing, and we want to go down to Tucson and make six more episodes.' So I went. Richard Arlen was the star of it, and played Rawhide Riley, the foreman of my ranch. My father had been killed, so he was also my guardian. We did the six episodes, but they never did sell. Some guy from Tucson absconded with the money, but Sam always had hopes, even when I was 17 years old, that someday it was going to sell. But it never did. That would have been a great opportunity for me."

Larry had a lot of horse-riding scenes to perform in the series, but at the time of his interview did not have experience in this skill. "It was

Larry and his dog "Rags" on the witness stand from *Who Killed Doc Robbin?* (United Artists release, 1948, produced by Hal Roach, Jr). Wilton Graff as the prosecuting attorney questions Larry about the murder of Doc Robbin (George Zucco).

always commonplace that when you went on an interview if they asked if you could sword-fight, dance or walk on the ceiling, you always said yes. So I went on the interview and they asked if I could ride a horse. I said yes. They said, 'Good, we want to do some tests on you,' and they gave me a date. So mother took me right down to the riding stable in Griffith Park and gave me two days of lessons. And that was it," he chuckled. "So I passed. And I became quite a good rider. They had one scene where Richard Arlen and I are riding together, and all of a sudden we supposedly see something and start galloping. Everyone was impressed because my little horse was jumping over the sagebrush, and so it worked out pretty good. That was in 1952. I was 15. And that was the last thing I did."

Reflecting on one other experience in *Rawhide Riley*, Larry said, "I was supposed to get bucked off a horse. I didn't do the riding in that scene, but when I landed on the ground they wanted me to just roll into the frame. I said, 'I can do better than that. Give me a box.' I loved doing stunts and used to practice in my back yard. I got the box and made a high dive in front of the camera so that I looked like I was coming straight down on my head, and boom! I went into the roll. They were all impressed with that. I did a lot of my own stunt work, but nothing extremely dangerous."

Larry reminisced about several noted directors and stars that he worked with. "Michael Curtiz was a little bit cold, and Sam Woods [*My Pal Wolf*] was just as nice as could be. Walter Lang was the director on *Sitting Pretty*, in which I played the son of Robert Young and Maureen O'Hara. Actually, it was the very first of the Mr. Belvedere series. It was very enjoyable. Bob Young was one of the nicest guys I ever worked with. My mother and I listened to a radio program on the way to work every morning, *Haynes of the Range* with Dick Haynes. He had a silly program and told the corniest jokes, so as soon as I got to the studio I'd tell Bob Young all those jokes. He would be busy trying to learn his script, but he always had time for me. He was just a wonderful guy. Maureen O'Hara was as sweet as could be. They were the only two people I ever worked with that I ever asked for an autograph."

Larry worked with Leslie Caron and Ricky Nelson in *The Story of Three Loves*. "Leslie was just the sweetest girl, just like a young kid herself. She'd go out and play catch with Ricky and I. She was just a very vivacious, very sweet, innocent girl. I have very good memories of that. Ethel Barrymore was in the film, and she was very much Ethel Barrymore," Larry laughed. "It was a good film to do."

Another star that Larry enjoyed working with was Cary Grant in

Room for One More. "Outside of Bob Young, Cary Grant was one of the nicest guys. He was an extremely nice fellow. I had been originally hired to play his son in the movie, but his wife—played by his real wife Betsy Drake—figured she was too young to have a son my age. So they gave me a secondary role of the boyfriend of one of their adopted daughters. Cary gave everybody gifts at the end of the film, and he even apologized to me that I didn't get the role of the son."

We asked Larry if he had a favorite among all the films he made. "I enjoyed doing *Curly* and *Who Killed Doc Robbin?*," he replied. "And I loved doing *Rawhide Riley*, and am just sorry that never panned out. That was fun. We went to Tucson, Arizona to do them at Old Tucson, and riding the horses, that was just like a cup of tea. I loved that."

After his work on *Rawhide Riley*, Larry decided to leave the business. "I just became a regular teenager and didn't want to do it anymore," he related. "Back then there was mandatory military service, and I was going to turn 16 and couldn't wait to get in. In fact, I ended up quitting high school and joining the navy much to my parents' chagrin, but I insisted on it. The navy's policy was that if you joined when you were 17 you were discharged the day before you turned 21. So I went in six days before my 18th birthday, and was regular navy, but only spent three years."

After his discharge from the navy, Larry said "I got a job, got married, had a child and have been working ever since. Of course my marriages haven't been too good. I have three ex-wives. But Jane and I have been together over 20 years now so I think that will last," he smiled. "I started work at Litton as a receiving clerk, and from there went to various companies. I became a planner, a senior planner, production manager at Data Products, and now I'm a senior planner at California Microwave."

If someone asked him for his opinion about using his grandchild in a movie, Larry stated "that he would be enthusiastic about it. "Like I say, I have no bad memories of it at all. There were a few episodes though, like when I did a bunch of Corn Pops commercials. In junior high school the kids called me Corn Pops, but my true friends didn't bother me. There were some kids in the crowd that thought I was stuck up, but they would have thought that no matter what I did. For the most part, though, most of my friends—once they found out—couldn't care less. So I don't regret it."

Larry had a brother Chris and a sister Susan in the business as well. "Chris is eight years younger than me. My sister became the only *real* star in the family. She was Cindy in *The Brady Bunch*. I'm 23 years older than she is. My mother had the distinction of being the longest active movie mother in history, from 1942 till 1974. She belonged to the movie mothers' club."

Larry summed up his feelings about his career as a child performer, saying, "It really didn't amount to much. It could have. There were opportunities that didn't pull through, like the Curlys. They could have gone someplace, but didn't. *Rawhide Riley* could have gone somewhere, but it didn't. So actually, I was never a big success at it. But it was a lot of fun, and educational. It really was. In working around adults as a child you grew up a lot sooner, I think, and became a little more mature and sophisticated. And it was fun."

Gigi Perreau

Gigi Perreau was born February 6, 1941, in Los Angeles, California. "My father was French and my mother is of English ancestry, born in Newport, Rhode Island," Gigi mentioned. "My parents had escaped through Spain at the end of 1940 and were very eager to have number two child, which is me, born in the United States. So I was born in the beginning of 1941 in Los Angeles and grew up there because my mother's mother and sister were here."

Gigi broke into the movie business when she was only two years old, quite by accident. "One of the Warner brothers was an avid tennis player and brought Jacques Brunet here from France. He was one of the four musketeers of tennis, a very fine tennis player, and he was a very dear friend of my father. My mother would occasionally drive him to the Warner Bros. Studio to meet with Mr. Warner and play tennis. There was an agent named Lola Moore, who had really had her eye on my brother; she had seen my mother dropping off this gentleman, and my brother would always be with her. To make a long story short, my mother agreed to let my brother go on an interview at MGM Studios and had nobody to leave me with. So she took me to the studio, sat me down in the little waiting room and said 'Don't move,' and went off with my brother. In those days it was very safe; we were inside the studio and the receptionist was there. Mervyn LeRoy came by and saw this little girl and started talking to me: I have this gift of gab. I started talking very early. So Mr. LeRoy waited till my mother came back and said, 'We have a new young girl we're using named Margaret O'Brien, and we need a younger sister to play Eve Currie as a baby, so would you mind bringing her on an interview tomorrow? We have a lot of girls coming.' My mother thought that would be fun because the picture, *Madame Curie*, would go to France, and since my relatives in France hadn't seen me, wouldn't that be cute?: they could see what I looked like. A home movie on an MGM scale."

Gigi went to the interview the next day and was immediately hired for the part. "Mr. LeRoy was just enchanted evidently. I was a very plain-looking little girl. My mom remembers that all the little girls had rouge on their cheeks and little Shirley Temple curls, and I had kind of a Dutch boy haircut and was just like everybody's little girl. So I did the film, and Mr. LeRoy wanted to put me under contract. Louis B. Mayer said, 'You don't put a two-year-old girl under contract; if she's still in the business when she's five we'll think about it.' So I was under contract with MGM when I was five."

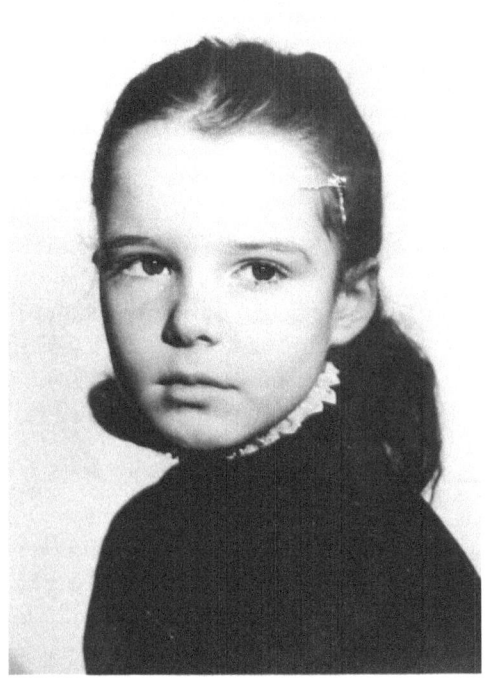

Gigi Perreau

The next film Gigi made for MGM was *Two Girls and A Sailor* with Jimmy Durante. "Eilene Janssen and I played sisters and are still very good friends. From there I worked a lot." Among her credits at this studio were *God Is My Co-Pilot*, *High Barbaree*, and *Green Dolphin Street*. In 1947, Gigi appeared with Katherine Hepburn in *The Song of Love*. "The little girl who was supposed to play my younger sister balked at the whole thing. She didn't want to perform once they hired her and brought her to the set. So, they were racking their brains and said, 'Gosh, do you know another kid we could get?' My mother said, 'I have another one at home.' So they sent her down to the board of education to get her work permit, and within about two hours she was on the set. So that was my sister Janine's beginning. She had fun doing it, but it was never a big love of hers. There were other things that interested her more than acting. She did a few films (*Weekend with Father*, *Red Danube*, *Invaders from Mars*) and enjoyed what she did, but has gone on to other things."

After being under contract to MGM, Gigi went under contract to Samuel Goldwyn Studios where she did *Enchantment* in 1948, which was one of her favorites. She played the character of Little Lark, who was Teresa Wright as a child. "I remember really loving Irving Reis, the director, and I connected very well with the character of the little orphan for some reason, having never been near a real little orphan. It was a very sad role and I had this incredible crying scene. I remember the scene when Little Lark comes into the bedroom and the older adopted sister is very rough with her. She sends Little Lark into her room, and on the mantel is a picture of her parents who had just died. This little six year old looks at the picture and slowly gives into tears and starts to cry. I wasn't told to do this, but with the crying and the loneliness of the room I just sunk on to the floor in a little heap, and the camera pulled back and cut. The minute I finished the scene, I looked up and Irving Reis and every single crew person were in tears. I said with this big grin on my face, 'Why are you crying?' At this moment I realized how much you could affect the emotions of people.

"That was really the beginning of being taken seriously about being an actor," Gigi stated. "You know, it was kind of like everybody thought we were like little puppets. I am one of the few child actors, I think, that really, really enjoyed working. My brother was working periodically, and my sister was working, but I really loved doing it. I had a very solid family; very supportive, wonderful parents. I went to Beverly Hills Catholic School for grammar school, so anytime I wasn't actually filming I was at school with my friends. When I did a movie I had my tutoring on the set, and then went right back to school, so my life was not really that disrupted. I feel I gained a tremendous amount and was able to do a lot of things that other kids never had the opportunity to do—traveling, personal appearance tours, and so on."

In 1949, Gigi appeared in the Samuel Goldwyn production of *Rosanna McCoy*, along with Joan Evans in her film debut. "There was this scene where they come in with some bad news and I'm supposed to burst into tears, and so was Joan Evans. Joan was only about 14 and very inexperienced. We did something like 20 takes, and it didn't work because she couldn't cry. My mother, who was very discreet and a wonderful movie mother, came up to the director and said, 'I think Gigi's out of tears, you've done 20 takes.' So they broke for lunch. I drank lots of water, and in the meantime the director talked to Joan and prepared her, and when we came back from lunch we did the scene. Joan was a lovely girl and is now a principal at a private school in the San Fernando Valley. Crying was just sort of my specialty. When I was at Universal I did four or five films in a row and if I didn't have a crying scene they wrote one in. It works; a little kid crying just grabs you somehow."

When Gigi was about 12 years old, she began working on television in shows like *Ford Theater* and *Four Star Playhouse* as well as some of the live shows such as *Climax* and *Studio One*. "I did a lot of television at that point, and then I was going to high school at Immaculate Heart. I worked really when I wanted to, but was very serious about my education. Then I got married very young, at 19, two years into college and had my first two children, and that really became my main career. I was always busy: for instance, I was the Mother's March chairman for the March of Dimes, and did a lot of PR things for them, but it was time to give back rather than just be working. I think because I really had a lot of success as a kid it was never a burning desire. I have a feeling that some people who really want work when they grow up is because maybe they haven't been fulfilled when they were working younger. This is just something off the top of my head. But I love acting, I love directing—that's what I would really love to be doing. I'm doing it now here in teaching, but to do it in the industry would be wonderful."

When Gigi was a senior at Immaculate Heart High School, she was awarded a special honor. "I have a star on the Hollywood Walk of Fame.

Gigi with Raymond Massey in a scene from RKO's *Roseanna McCoy* (1949).

I was one of the first 50, so I was there at the ground-breaking ceremony with Linda Darnell and Francis X. Bushman.

"After I was a teenager and a little older, I was offered some really tacky films where they were interested in using my name because I had a good reputation in the industry. I mean some really raunchy kind of stuff and I just decided that I would not do anything that my mother and my children or anyone that I knew couldn't see. My father and mother brought me up with a real sense of morality and what's right, and I don't think it's necessary to be a good actor to have to compromise your morals and your judgment at what works, and you can be very effective without doing that.

"Once I got married and my children came along that was my main thrust. I always kind of kept my finger in it, but on a minimal level. In 1997, I did a film called *The Sleepless* that my son-in-law wrote and directed, and my oldest daughter edited, which was great fun. That was the first time in front of a camera in about 20 years. I must say, getting in front of the camera was a great experience and I realized 'Oh, I think I do miss this.'"

Gigi is now teaching drama and directing plays as a school teacher. Asked how she came to find herself in this capacity, she said, "It was just by accident. The principal of a boys high school had seen some work I had been doing for community theater and he asked me if I'd be willing to teach a class. I thought 'Piece of cake, one class. That would be great.' I got hooked. I taught one the first year, then two, and then three. Then I was asked if I would be interested in teaching at Immaculate Heart, so I started teaching here, and I've been here for 14 years. I'm given a lot of freedom as far as choices of plays and so on, so it's fun to be here at my alma mater.

"Basically you are acting every day when you're teaching and directing with the kids. So I feel very blessed. I had a wonderful career and am having a wonderful time teaching. My mother is still alive and healthy and living very close. My two sisters and brother are close. I have four grandsons. So we are very lucky; we have a very wonderful family."

When asked about her experience working in live television, Gigi responded, "Oh, I wish that the young actors today could experience what live TV was. Even the soaps are on tape; it's a very tight schedule and very close to doing live television, but there is *nothing* quite like it, even stage. On stage, although you are still dealing with the audience, if you have an off night it's not really the end of the world. There's always another night. But when you're doing live TV, when it goes out on the air, it went all over the country live. There were no second chances. It was amazing.

You really did have to wing it and, of course, it was fabulous experience. Everything I have learned and everything I am sharing with my students basically is what I've learned by working my whole life. Wonderful directors and producers and actors, and just by osmosis, hopefully, all of that was sort of soaked in. I have really enjoyed my work and can't think of anything else I would have rather done with my life.

"A friend of mine, Paul Petersen, has an organization called *A Minor Consideration*," Gigi continued. "Paul and I are also very active in the Donna Reed festival every summer. Paul has a certain attitude about the industry and feels we are very put upon as child actors, and I'm sure that many of them really were and exploited to a certain degree. But I personally never felt that, so I always say, 'Paul, you should have a balance and mention that there really are some of us, that as far as the industry goes, were really very unscathed.' I had a very happy childhood, so I'm very grateful for it. It's been very good to me."

Responding to the question about what advice she would give a parent considering a career in the movies for their child, Gigi said, "The best advice I could give anyone is if they really feel their child is talented, give them their lessons; the dance lessons and all of that. But encourage them to get their education because that's something you can never take away from anyone. Do school plays, do community theater, do things where you are, wherever it is in the United States, and somehow if it's meant to be it will happen. We go to Denison, Iowa, and see incredibly talented students from the Midwest, and after they perform and win scholarships to universities and colleges a lot of them come to Hollywood. But they got their degrees, they got their background, they got experience. I have some seniors who are adorable. I have one girl that has done something like 12 full-length Broadway-type plays here, because I do the entire show. I try to pick shows that are known and well-written, and give them a really good background in theater. So I would advise anyone to encourage their child and get involved with their school's theater if they have a theater department, and if not, yes—let them do some community theater during the holidays. Every place has a production of Dickens's *A Christmas Carol*, for instance, that they do at Christmastime, so any cute little kid could certainly audition for something like that locally. And take classes and be prepared because when the moment comes you want to be prepared, and they will be if they go about it the right way. I find it very difficult to deal with parents that say, 'We are in Cincinnati, Ohio, and I'm bringing my daughter to Hollywood. We're leaving my husband and other three children.' That's really not a great thing to do to a family. Encourage the child *where* they are and then afterwards let them come here.

"The business is very different now; it's a matter of bucks," Gigi continued. "It was very warm. It was like a family when I was under contract to Universal. For instance, Joe and Josie had a little coffee shop, and I could go from the little schoolhouse and grab some lunch and go back to school, and everybody knew you. And it was wonderful. But now it's such big bucks. We weren't making any kind of money compared to what they are now, so I can understand that it's very enticing and must be very difficult for some parents and their kids to deal with some of the enormous pressures and the desire to make money. It's a different business. I can't imagine some of the pressures that the kids today have that we didn't."

Gigi's brother, Gerald Perreau (who later used the screen name of Peter Miles) was also a prominent child actor, appearing in such films as *Who Killed Doc Robbin?*, *Family Honeymoon* (with Gigi), *Quo Vadis*, and *The Red Pony*, which included the classic scene of him battling the vultures to keep them away from his dead pony. Gigi was asked what he was doing now. "He has gone on to writing and has several published books. He is an art appraiser and connoisseur. He enjoyed his work as a child, but he started high school when he was 12 and I think boys maybe treat guys a little differently when they are in the industry. He was just not comfortable with going in and out of school. He was very serious about his studies, so once he started high school he gave it up himself. Our parents never pressured us; we did what we wanted. After high school and college he was conned back and we did a TV series together called *The Betty Hutton Show*. That was the only time he worked in the industry as an adult."

In summing up, Gigi stated, "It's been very, very good to me and I enjoyed every minute of it. I think as a result I have been able to have a certain effect, maybe be a role model. I still get an amazing number of fan letters. I don't know when people are seeing what, maybe on the late late show, but they say, 'You touched my life as a child.' That part is very gratifying."

Jon Provost

Jon Provost was born March 12, 1950, in Los Angeles, California. When Jon was three years old an article appeared in the *Los Angeles Times* which said that Warner Bros. was looking for a two-to-three-year-old blond boy to be in the movie *So Big* with Jane Wyman and Sterling Hayden. "When my mom saw that, the light bulb went off in her head, 'Maybe I could meet Jane Wyman if I took Jon on this interview.' My dad said, 'You're wasting your time; you won't meet her. But if you want to do it, go ahead, take the chance.' So we went to the audition and there were over 200 little boys there." At the audition Jon and his mom were asked again and again to stay, while other kids were being dismissed and left. "They called me back into the room to meet somebody else and basically I did what I was told. If they said, 'Go and sit on that lady's lap and call her mommy,' I did it. Towards the end of the day my mom was approached by a woman who at that time was the number one child agent in L.A. She said, 'Excuse me. My name is Lola Moore. Your son, I think, will be getting this job. Do you have an agent?' and my mom said, 'We have a real estate agent.' Lola said, 'No, you don't understand.' 'We have an insurance agent.' 'No, you don't understand. You need a theatrical agent.' To make a long story short, I ended up getting the job."

From that point, Jon worked in such films as *Country Girl* with Bing Crosby and Grace Kelly, and *Back from Eternity* with Rod Steiger and Robert Ryan. Reflecting on *Back from Eternity*, Jon said, "Anita Ekberg, who was the big sex symbol of the time, really kind of befriended me on the set, so I would always be sitting on her lap or she would be holding me. In the movie, it was the same thing because she was the stewardess on the plane and I was the only child and she had to help me out. After about a week of this, I remember a couple of the crew saying, 'Hey Jon,

Jon Provost and Lassie from the CBS television series, *Lassie*.

we'll give you five bucks to trade places with you.' I didn't know what they were talking about until later," Jon laughed. "It was just a fun movie because there were headhunters and an airplane crash in the jungle. Being a little kid, those kind of things are really exciting."

Jon had done six movies and some early television prior to the television series *Lassie* from 1957 to 1964. "I was under contract with RKO and one of the last films that they did was called *Escapade in Japan*. Prior to leaving for Japan my mom and I had to get 13 shots to go there. We spent 3½ months there filming. My hair was really blond when I was young and my mother had gorgeous blonde hair, and wherever we went the people acted as though they never had seen anybody like that before. It was an unusual thing for them, but everybody was just so nice, so gracious and so hospitable. You would think being so close to the war that it might be different. I really liked it over there and it was a lot of fun. That's one of the perks of being in the business, you get to travel a lot."

At the time *Escapade in Japan* was being made, a replacement for Tommy Rettig in the television series of *Lassie* was being sought because he had outgrown the part. The wife of the producer of *Escapade in Japan* and the wife of the producer of *Lassie* were having lunch one day and the conversation came up about a replacement in the series. The film producer's wife said, "It sounds like the boy you're looking for is in Japan right now making this movie," and invited her to watch the dailies. Afterwards, the woman said, "When he gets back, we've got to see him."

"I came back, went on an interview with the producer, the writer and director, and they all said 'Yes, you are perfect for the part for Timmy.' But they didn't know how I would react with Lassie and how Lassie would interact with me, because you can't fake that. So I basically had to get Lassie's approval. I went and lived with Lassie and Rudd Weatherwax on his ranch for a week to see how we got along together and bonded, and the rest is history.

"Here's a little bit of trivia. In *So Big*, I played a character that grew up on screen. I was the youngest of the character. One of the older 'me's' was Tommy Rettig, and there was a dog in the movie, not a collie, but its trainer was Rudd Weatherwax. Who would know that so many years later I would be replacing Tommy and working with Lassie?"

In the seven years on the series, Jon worked with three different Lassies. "The first dog I worked with was the son of Pal who was the original Lassie and was the one who worked with Tommy. His nickname was the Old Man. All Lassies had nicknames. I only worked with him for one season because he was very old. Then his son took over and I worked with him for a couple of years. We had an incident on the set where June, Lassie and I were at the end of a long dolly shot. The camera was on the dolly—and those things weighed a ton because the operator and his assistant were sitting on it along with the man that controlled it—so we were at the end of this long runway and as they were coming in the guy in control of the dolly tripped and lost control of it. It rolled and knocked over a couple of lamps. It didn't hit us but it spooked the dog. Whenever we would have a scene that in anyway resembled that kind of an experience, he couldn't work. He'd start shaking, and once something like that happened chances were you weren't going to get the dog out of that mode. So his son Baby took over.

"I worked with Baby for about four years. The dog was so incredibly smart it was spooky. I used to spend a lot of weekends at Rudd's ranch. I never knew either one of my grandfathers; they were both dead. Rudd kind of became my surrogate grandfather. He had a small lake which was about a quarter of a mile or so from the house. We were sitting down there one day. I was fishing and he was reading the newspaper and had run out of cigarettes. Rudd said, 'Lassie, go up to the house and get me a pack of cigarettes.' Amazingly, about three or four minutes later here comes Lassie down the hill with a pack of cigarettes in his mouth. Now he knew where to go in the house to get them, to open the drawer or whatever he had to do, but that's how smart this dog was. We would be filming a scene and of course the adults and the actors made more mistakes than Lassie did. Normally when the director wanted that scene as the print, Lassie would know even before the director would say 'print it.' He would just take off and go lay down on his bed, whereas the other dogs I worked with would just sit there until Rudd Weatherwax said, 'Okay. Good. Now go back and rest until the next shot.' Baby knew. He was just so smart. I loved that dog. I liked them all, but he was my favorite."

Asked what were some things he enjoyed doing in his time away from the set, Jon answered, "We worked nine months out of the year, five days a week, basically ten hours a day. When we were on hiatus we'd do a lot of publicity. Every year we would travel around the country promoting the show, and it was basically me and Lassie. When we were filming I'd go to work before my dad left and I'd come home after him, so there wasn't a whole lot of time, but I always enjoyed swimming and bike riding. I was never really allowed to play football or baseball or something like that for fear that I might get hurt. I mean you basically had to get permission to do just about anything because they ran the show. I think I did as much as I could just being a regular kid."

Asked if there was a reason why he, June Lockhart and Hugh Reilly left the show, he said, "I had a seven-year contract plus a three-year option that was our option. Of course the studio could drop you any year. But we did the seven years and were always in the top ten. I was 14. I was going through puberty and started looking at the girls, so my parents said, 'It's up to you. You could say no if you don't want to continue for three more years.' I said, 'I don't want to be Timmy until I'm 17 or 18 years old.' So my parents said, 'Okay, then we'll just not sign the contract.'"

Jack Wrather, the owner of the series, and his wife Bonita Granville, who was the executive producer, started making offers to get Jon to stay. "At that time Jack Wrather owned Chris Craft boats," Jon explained. "He said, 'You want a yacht? We'll give you a boat,' if I stayed on the show. They offered more money and more offtime, but that's not what was important to me. What was important was for me to grow. So I was the one who actually brought about the demise of the Martin family, and [in the show] we moved to Australia. We couldn't take Lassie because there was a six months' quarantine, so we had to say, 'Sorry Lassie, you can't come.' I gave Lassie to Cully Wilson who was the old guy on the show that drove a Model T Ford truck and delivered the coal. He was played by Andy Clyde. Then he had a stroke or something and then the forest ranger got her."

Asked if he could recall any situations that might have been dangerous during his career as a child actor, Jon remarked, "When I started, like any kid, I wanted to do it all, but they wouldn't let me do some of the stunts. I had a stand-in who was a midget named Nils Nelson, a great guy. He would do some of the stunts for me or they would have other kids come in. Stan Livingston of *My Three Sons* was a double for me one time. But I always wanted to do my own stunts, so they started letting me do a little bit more and a little bit more. The only thing on *Lassie* that we filmed in color was a five-parter shown on five consecutive Sundays that was later released as a movie called *Lassie's Great Adventure*. In that, Lassie and I are up in the wilderness and we're stuck because the balloon that we were in had crashed. We built a raft because I knew that if we went downstream eventually we'd find people. So Lassie and I went down

Jon as Timmy Martin and Billy Hughes as Billy Joe Yochim enjoy a cup of hot chocolate on a winter day in an episode of *Lassie* titled *Yochim's Christmas* (CBS-TV, 1959. A Jack Wrather Production).

this river and the raft broke up and we got separated. We couldn't rehearse it and they did whatever they could to make things as safe as possible. We went down, the raft broke up and Lassie and I went into the water. This was in the fall and the Sonora River was freezing. I got sucked under and a rock underneath the water hit me right in my chest and knocked the air out of me. I came up and screamed 'Help! Help!' Bonita Granville, Jack Wrather, along with a lot of people, were there watching, and the director says, 'Oh, he's great. Look at this. He's just doing great.' Well, I wasn't. I was really in trouble. They had a safety line going across the river that I was supposed to grab, but I missed it. Rudd Weatherwax had two men in wet suits jump in and pull Lassie out. Then Rudd said, 'Jon's not kidding,' so he had his guys jump in and pull me out too, and save me. If you ever see that show it's not a great acting job; it was real!

"Another time we did an episode where we were working with a chimpanzee," Jon continued. "He was an older chimp and they get real cranky. At the end of the second day of the shoot as I was leaving, the chimp was sitting on a chair. I said, 'Okay, see you tomorrow,' and rubbed his head. He grabbed my hand, stuck my thumb into his mouth and proceeded to chew it off. I screamed and the chimp jumped off the chair and started running with me behind him. His trainer started yelling and screaming 'Let go!' but the chimp wouldn't. His trainer was right out of one of these old movies. He had the riding pants and the high boots, a hat, and a gun that had blanks in it like you would see in a circus. Well, the chimp wouldn't let go. The trainer pulled out his gun and fired it, bam! bam! bam! which startled the chimp and it let go of me. Then they rushed me to the nurse at the commissary, who said, 'I can't do this.' So they rushed me to the emergency hospital. We had a few things like that happen, but I think those two were the worst."

After his seven years on *Lassie*, Jon worked in three more movies, along with other television shows. "I did *Mr. Ed* in which I had a small reoccurring role. One of the movies I did was *This Property Is Condemned* with Natalie Wood and Robert Redford. We filmed it in Mississippi. It was fun, though I remember a very strange incident that occurred. One morning when the crew got up and was getting ready to start shooting, it was discovered that someone had come along during the evening and put a flyer on all the vehicles which warned us not to come to a certain area. It said, 'You guys stay away. We don't want you people coming here.' It turned out that there was some kind of Klan rally going on and they didn't want any outsiders coming around."

The second movie was the 1970 release *The Secret of the Sacred Forest* which was filmed in the Philippines. "It was a B film which played as a second run at drive-ins. I spent a couple of months there in the Philippines. I was 18. It was really neat with the jungles and all that. What I really remember, though, was that there was no middle class. You were either rich or you had nothing. That sticks with you. I really liked the people in the Philippines. They were so nice and friendly.

"The last thing I did was a Disney movie called *The Computer Wore Tennis Shoes* with Kurt Russell. Then I graduated from high school and my father said, 'All of my kids go to college.' I was kind of bumming around down in southern California and going to college there, but my girlfriend from high school was going to college up in Santa Rosa at Sonoma State. So I came up, became a resident and went to Santa Rosa Junior College for one semester and then transferred to Sonoma State.

"I majored in psychology and minored in special ed. I student-taught for one year to see if I wanted to get my credentials. I really enjoyed it, but I got too involved with the kids and it was emotionally draining to me. I ended up getting a real-estate license and sold real estate for 12 years; then I got out of that in 1993. Now I work for a title escrow company. I've stayed with the business because I knew everybody in real estate and wanted to stay somewhere in the field, so it's worked out great."

We asked Jon if, after the *Lassie* series, he found that work was harder to get. "Not really. I wasn't really typecast because I was changing. I wasn't that little boy anymore. My voice had changed, I was shaving, I wasn't the same kid. At that time I was thinking that I would like to be behind the camera either writing or directing, but it was time to go to college and there is no way you can do both. I was also approaching 19 and we're talking about the end of the sixties. I had the war thing hanging over my head, and they wanted me very badly. They needed 'tunnel rats' which I would have been great for—I was little. So I had to deal with that. Those times were different, real different. The music and the drug scene, especially in L.A., was really getting heavy. I decided I had to get out of there. If I didn't, who knows what would have happened? So because of that and my girlfriend having moved, I made that break. It was time for me to leave southern California. I was looking around and seeing some of my contemporaries falling off the edge and so for me, okay, I was out of there. I wanted to be me—Jon—not Timmy. When I came up here I had some anonymity. I was a hippie like everybody and I had a great head of hair," he laughed. "A ponytail halfway down my back. Some people would say, 'Gosh, you look like ... Were you...?' 'Yeah, people say that all the time.' I'd skirt it until I finally became more comfortable. There was a time I didn't want anybody to know who I was. I didn't want them to know that

I was Timmy from *Lassie*. I wanted to blend in. I just wanted to be a normal kid. But you get by all of that and then you just grow up. As time passed I realized it's a great legacy to have. Even today people recognize me, or if my name comes up that does it too. It's acceptable now. My kids get teased at school, even now. My daughter just started high school and she says, 'I walk home from school and kids bark at me.' What are you going to do? Nobody's ever approached me and said they hated *Lassie*."

Jon worked in *The New Lassie* series in 1990 and 1991. As a matter of fact, he wrote an episode in the 1990 season titled *A Rabbit's Tale*. "It was about testing rabbits for cosmetics and that kind of thing. I won a Genesis award for the best episode in a family series from the Ark Trust. They look at shows and specials that have to do with animal rights and that kind of thing. That was really neat. "I had a recurring role every fourth or fifth episode. I'd go down to Los Angeles for a week and then I'd be home for three or four weeks, and then go down for a week. It was great and I had a lot of fun. The first day back on the set, once I was in costume and make-up, it was like déjà vu, like going home. I mean everything smelled the same, sounded the same. The only difference was that the cameras were smaller, quieter, more maneuverable, and the lights were smaller and brighter. But it was the same thing. That was a really neat feeling, and I think that's because once it's in your blood, once you've done it, it's always there. I grew up on a sound stage. I learned the craft through osmosis, just doing it day after day after day.

Some of the hobbies that Jon enjoys are swimming, motorcycle riding, and skeet shooting. "My son and I like to go out and do that kind of stuff. We also like to go hiking and target shooting. Every summer we go camping for about a week. I do Hollywood collectible shows, autograph shows. I enjoy meeting the fans. I've kept in touch with June over the years and we still make appearances together. I take my kids and they go around and find Lassie memorabilia for me. When you're doing the show, you don't think about saving things because it's in your face all the time.

"In 1988, I got a letter from the Smithsonian. They were doing an exhibition on television in America in the American History Museum, and they wanted to know if I had anything to donate. I had pictures, but didn't have much else, so I called my mom. She said, 'I have your whole outfit.' She sent it and I opened this box. It hadn't been opened in 20, 30 years, and it was real heavy déjà vu. I pulled out my little check shirt, my blue jeans and my tennis shoes. They invited us back for the debut of the exhibit, and my parents and I were able to go. What an honor that is. In the exhibit they had a little mannequin of me wearing my costume. Sitting next to it was Archie Bunker's chair and on the other side was the

Fonz's leather jacket. That was really cool. And a few years ago I received another great honor. I got my star on the Hollywood Walk of Fame. Those kind of things are great," Jon stated. "One big thing that I'm very involved in is Canine Companions for Independence. We supply dogs to people who have every kind of disability except blindness because they have their own organization. I've been involved with them for more than 12 years and I'm on the local board. We supply dogs to people all over the world, but mainly in the United States. The dogs are taught more than 90 commands. They allow physically challenged people to get back out there and participate in life. I donate my time to different events. It's a great organization."

We asked Jon whether, if someone from Los Angeles called and said they had a part for him, he would do it. "Yeah, if it was a good part and was something I could relate to. I have a secret desire to play a bad guy. I hope I get to do that one day. It's in my blood and it's really fun. I couldn't go down to L.A. full time, though. My kids are here and they are what's really important."

Summarizing his feelings on his career as a child actor, Jon said, "It was hard work. There were days when I didn't want to go, but there are days when my kids don't want to go to school. It was really all I knew until I turned 18 and moved out. It's like if you never tasted chocolate ice cream you have nothing to compare it to. I think if I had a chance to do it over again, I would, but it's a crazy business. The Screen Actors Guild has the highest unemployment rate of any union in the world. That part's tough. I think I was in the right place at the right time or I had the right look that they were seeking. I was really lucky as far as that goes. People have asked if my kids wanted to act, would I let them. If they wanted to I would support them, but it would be tough. If my kids wanted to pursue it I know what to look out for because I've been there. My son and I went on one audition for an Ivory Soap commercial years ago when he was about five or six. They wanted to do a father and son. They called me and said, 'We know you have a son. You do our commercial and his college is paid for.' Halfway there my son said he didn't want to do it. That was it. I turned around and drove home.

"I had a completely different kind of childhood than other kids. Whenever I meet a child star or a child celebrity from my era, we have this immediate bond. It's like we belong to a special club, and that's a great feeling."

Gene Reynolds

Gene Reynolds was born April 4, 1923, in Cleveland, Ohio, and grew up in the Highland Park area of Detroit, Michigan. "I lived in Detroit the first ten years of my life, and started acting when I was very little. I was a very energetic child and my mother mistook that for talent. She thought I was an actor from the beginning, so I was in a little acting group that used to meet Friday afternoons. We used to do scenes and plays in churches and clubs. I worked in school plays, and then began doing commercials in Detroit and acting in radio and doing amateur plays. My father had been a businessman and, like everybody else in the '30s, he was suffering. He was from the west originally, so we moved to California, and then I started working as an extra in films."

The first film that Gene worked in was the Laurel and Hardy classic *Babes in Toyland* at the Hal Roach Studio. "I was an extra, one of the kids running around in toyland. We were in a whole bunch of scenes running through the film. The boogie men would come and grab me and I would scream and holler. I was the kid whose mouth was wider open than anybody's. I had a lot of enthusiasm, a lot of energy."

This was followed by extra work in *Our Gang* comedies. "I did a lot of extra work for a while, and then began to get called on interviews for bit parts. They used to interview 200 kids for a two-line part. It was very unfair, but they'd bring out every kid in town and walk along the line looking them over. The kids would light up like a light as the people walked by and then the light would dim as they walked away."

Gene went to the Pasadena Playhouse and started acting in plays there. "I got the part of Prince Arthur in *Prince John* after reading for it about five times. It's a beautiful role for a child, about the best part for a kid in Shakespeare. From that, an agent named George Ullman came backstage and signed me up and began getting me interviews. I started getting some bits, and then some better parts."

Gene played a number of the stars as a child. He was Tyrone Power as a boy in *In Old Chicago*; Ricardo Cortez as a child in *The Californians*; in *The Flying Irishman*, Gene played Wrongway Corrigan as a boy. He was Bob Taylor as a kid in *The Crowd Roars*; Don Ameche as a lad in *Sins of Man*; and in *Madame X* he played John Beal as a boy. "At any rate, I finally got a wonderful opportunity. I tested and got the part in *Of Human Hearts* in 1938, an MGM film in which I played Jimmy Stewart as a boy. A very nice movie, and from that I got a contract at MGM, and went all through high school there. I worked in *Boys Town*, *Bad Little Angel*, *Captains Courageous* and *The Mortal Storm*. They loaned me to Samuel Goldwyn for *They Shall Have Music*, and to Warner Bros. for *Santa Fe Trail*. At any rate, I made quite a few films as a kid," he concluded.

Gene Reynolds

Gene was acting in the film *Tuttles of Tahiti* when the war broke out and he went into the service. "I went into the Naval Reserve Officers Training Corps, got a commission and went aboard the *DMS 14*, the destroyer mine sweeper 14, an old World War I four-stacked destroyer which had been converted to minesweeping. I picked the ship up in the Marshal Islands and served a couple of years on the *Zane* during the war. Herman Wouk was the senior watch officer, and he would get up every morning very early and would write. He wrote *The Caine Mutiny*, a lot of which was based on characters on the *Zane*."

After the *Zane*, Gene went aboard a ship called the *Powell* in the Mediterranean, which he said was much better duty. "I served on that for six months until I finally had enough points to be mustered out. I went back to UCLA, got a degree and began acting in Los Angeles. I studied at the Actors Lab Theatre and did some radio, but Hollywood was hit very badly after the war with frozen funds and the separation between theaters and the production units, what they called the divorcement. So I went to Europe and stayed there for about a year and a half, just knocking around. Then I went to New York and worked in live television for a year or two, and then came back to Los Angeles and acted for a while."

Reflecting on his work in live television, Gene said, "They had a great excitement, and you were always dealing with a lot of wonderful actors. On *Danger*, I worked with Sidney Lumet and he was terrific. But it was very scary because it was live. The directors would give everybody a big hysterical pep talk before you went on, and everybody went on like they were just kicked in the shins. It had a wonderful vitality, probably a synthetic vitality, but what was great about it was that it was like being in a Broadway show. The next day people would say I saw it and loved it, or I saw it and hated it. You had this immediate reaction, whereas when you worked in film you had forgotten what you had done by the time somebody would say 'Hey, I saw you on something you did,' because of the time lapse."

Besides working in such television shows as *The Lone Ranger* and *Annie Oakley*, Gene appeared in motion pictures such as *The Country Girl*, *Down Three Dark Streets* and *Bridges at Toko-Ri*. But the day came when he decided to leave the acting profession. "I woke up one morning and was very depressed. My career wasn't going anyplace and I was just at a spot in my life where I had to do something. I felt that I would be happier if I went to work every day—and I was. So I decided to get out of acting and try to go for a job behind the camera. One reason was I was kind of depressed psychologically, but the other reason—and maybe it's just coincidence—about a month before I started really seriously searching for any kind of a job behind the camera, I was in a TV show called *The Whirlybirds*. I was in a helicopter with the pilot, and there was a guy dressed in a gorilla suit who was supposed to latch on to the helicopter and then let go. He weighed (with the suit) about 300 pounds, and the helicopters are very delicate. They can't carry great weights, and the damn thing began to crash. He was only about five or six feet off the ground, but as the helicopter gunned, the guy—instead of letting go—grabbed hold, which is a natural reaction, because it started to speed up. So he held on rather than letting go and we went right over the cameras. There were a bunch of people sitting quite casually in director chairs, and as this gorilla came flying through the air at them they all went over backwards like dominos. We carried him for about a hundred yards and he finally let go and landed on a car. He laid there for about a minute, but finally got up and said, 'Oh, I'm okay.' That was one.

"Another time I was up at Bay Meadows in a show called *The Lineup* and they had me playing a jockey," Gene continued. "I was supposed to ride a quarter horse into the scene, stop and get off and talk. So I said to the unit production manager, 'Where is the double?' 'Double,' he answered, 'hell, you don't need any double. You just walk up and stop.' Well, as soon as they put me on the horse the damn horse took off. A quarter horse, they run a quarter of a mile. So he ran lickety-split a quarter of a mile. I leaned forward and my feet were deep in the stirrups, my boots were all the way in. Then he turned around and came running back a quarter of a mile. Thank God, when he finally got back and turned toward the stables he slowed up and stopped. But had I fallen off that horse I would have been dead, because I could not get my damn feet out of the stirrups.

"In the same month I was in a show at Connie Stevens Productions about ministers playing a guy that's supposed to get killed when a stove blows up. They had a stunt man ready to do the scene when the actual thing blew up. First, they just wanted a puff of smoke. Everybody was very nervous and they were trying to shoot fast. They got to this moment where I'm supposed to light the stove and have the little puff of smoke come out, and then they're supposed to clear away and get the stunt man in there and blow the thing. So they turned to this special effects man, who was this old nervous guy, and they said to him, 'Now we just want a little puff of smoke.' But they didn't say no explosion. He thought they wanted an explosion accompanied by a little puff of smoke. He shrugged and said, 'Yeah, there will be some smoke.' Well, the stove blew and the heavy lid, that must have weighed about 60 pounds, flew right over my head. If it had hit me it would have killed me. Fortunately, I was scrunched down. It went right over my head; the explosion threw me against the wall—pow! So I thought maybe God was trying to tell me something."

So Gene left acting, but not the picture business. "It took about six months to get the job, but I became a casting director. I knew a lot of actors and I knew what they could do. I cast a show called *Matinee Theatre*, an hour-long live daily anthology. Every day it was a different show, so it was a marvelous experience for a casting director. When that show went off, I went to Universal and cast the first year of *Peter Gunn*." Gene then became casting director for *Bonanza*, and while in this position was asked to act in a pilot. "Jackie Cooper and Dom McGuire were making a show called *Hennesy*, so I took a day or two off and acted in the pilot. Then when they got the show on the air they asked me to direct, so I started directing on that show. I directed a great many half-hour comedies: *Andy Griffith, My Three Sons, Pete and Gladys, Leave It to Beaver,* and *F-Troop.*" Gene also directed drama series like *Alfred Hitchcock, Peter Gunn,* and *Wanted: Dead or Alive.*

"I got the opportunity to produce and direct a pilot at Fox called *The Ghost and Mrs. Muir.* I had done a show at Fox, so they knew my work and gave me a shot at producing and directing this pilot, which came out great. The show got on the air and they wanted me to produce it, but I still had my eye on directing, so I asked to remain a director. I probably should have produced *The Ghost and Mrs. Muir,* but any rate Fox asked me to develop a show. I had this idea of an African-American high school teacher in an integrated school, and I got Jim Brooks to write the pilot. He and I went to Los Angeles High School and did our research. We spent a week there talking with the teachers and got a bunch of stories and came back to the studio and whipped up the pilot for *Room 222.* I produced that for two years and then was asked off it by ABC. They didn't think it was funny enough, but we were getting the Writers Guild Award every year. It was a good show and I was very serious about it. It dealt with revolution: there was a black revolution, a youth revolution going on in the country, and there was a revolution in education. It dealt with a lot of interesting issues, but they wanted only fun and games so they asked me off the show."

It was at this time that 20th Century–Fox asked Gene to produce and direct the pilot of *M*A*S*H.* Again, he spent many hours interviewing MASH doctors and nurses for research on the series. Gene served as producer on the show for five years. "Then I had some money problems with Fox. I had a percentage of the show that they beat me out of—a very unorthodox, very dishonest manipulation. At any rate, they worked me over, so I got sore at Fox. I was offered a pilot at MTM, a new show involved with print journalism starring Ed Asner as Lou Grant. I produced that for five years."

After *Lou Grant,* Gene produced a couple of two-hour movies for television and then did a few shorter-lived TV series. "Then I did some freelance television as a director (such as *Touched by an Angel* in 1994). Now I am semiretired." Gene also served two terms as president of the Directors Guild of America. "I follow my avocations. I'm in a book club, I direct scenes in an acting class, I'm trying to get some two-hour movies on the air, I play golf, I have a son that's in UCLA, and my wife and I travel. So that's where I am today."

In as much as Gene worked a full range of jobs in the movie industry, he was asked if any particular one was a favorite. "I think that they all have their moments. When I've had a great part as an actor, I enjoyed that enormously. Directing is very satisfying because you have great control. You influence the material and the whole project strongly. When it's right, it's very gratifying. You can be extremely creative and helpful to all facets, and you are responsible for the product. But I enjoyed producing. In television the producer is strong because he has influence over the story lines, the statement of the show and the theme of the show; what the show is saying week after week after week. So you are able to express yourself in terms of your idea and your point of view and your taste. And then, of course, casting I enjoyed also because it can be extremely creative. So they all have their moments. But I think that directing—because you're in the trenches, you're right on the set, you're right with the people—is hard to beat."

Of all his film roles, Gene chose *Of Human Hearts*, *They Shall Have Music*, and *Boys Town* as his favorites. He was asked for his reflections on these three films.

"I had a wonderful experience on *Of Human Hearts*. I worked with a wonderful director, Clarence Brown, and he was encouraging to me. It was a lovely part, and it was a part that Brown actually tried to get one of the Mauch twins to play. I had tested and tested well, but the studio wanted to get a name. At any rate, they called me the night before and said, 'You've got the part. We're picking you up in the morning, and we're going to go to Lake Arrowhead.' It was a wonderful experience. That shows you how these careers are so fluky. Had whatever project one of the Mauch twins had been on wrapped and he was available, it would have changed my whole life, because that job got me a contract at Metro, and Metro got me *Boys Town* and all the other stuff."

They Shall Have Music: "They have a violin competition in Indianapolis every four years, and this last year the theme was Heifetz. They flew me back and ran the film. I spoke before the screening. It was the first time in all those years that I had seen the film. I was only about 14 or 15 when I made it, so it was a very nice experience. I think the director could have helped me play with greater variety. But a lot of my work I thought was good and it was a sweet little film. It was filmed at Goldwyn Studios, and I only lived a block and a half away. I walked across Poinsettia Playgrounds to Goldwyn Studios, and walked home every night. It was the only time I ever did that, walking to work in this business. The kids in the Meremblum Children's Orchestra were wonderful, and I made good friends there. *They Shall Have Music* was a great experience for me, a wonderful acting part, and a nice little film."

Gene reflected on *Boys Town*. "Again, I had a very good director in

Beulah Bondi and Gene in a scene from Metro-Goldwyn-Mayer's *Of Human Hearts* (1938).

Norman Taurog, and a good part. I had a great experience going back to Boys Town and working in it. It's one of those parts that was really very easy for me, felt right for me, and worked out very well. And working with Tracy, he was very kind to me and very reassuring. And I was friends with Bobs Watson, and used him several times on *Lou Grant*. He was a very good actor."

Most child performers during this era of Hollywood filmmaking were called on at some time in their career in a scene to cry. For some, this came easily, but not for Gene. He went on location to Modesto, California, on a movie called *In Old Chicago* with Bobs and Billy Watson, in which they played the O'Leary children. "When I got into Modesto at the hotel, I went up to see the Watson brothers. The father had the two boys sitting on the bed and he was going over their lines in the script with them. He would look at one boy and say, 'Okay' and the kid's face would crumple up and he would cry; then he'd look at the other one and say 'Well,' and the other kid would break up and cry, and I thought 'Holy smoke.' When we did the scene of Mr. O'Leary dying these two kids were crying like crazy, and I had real feeling, but I didn't cry. I was close to it, but they had this technique where the tears would come flying. So I realized that if I was going to stay in the business in those days, I had to learn to cry. That was one of the damn necessities at the time because they had all these scenes in which boys were losing their mothers or their dog. So I would practice. I would walk home from Bancroft Junior High — I lived about 12 blocks away — and as I walked along I would try to get myself to cry. I thought about all kinds of things and worked myself up. I got to the point where before I got home I would be crying. Then I would do it again and this time instead of taking me 12 blocks it would take me ten, and then eight, then six, and then four and finally I got to where within a block or so I could cry. And that was how I developed that. It was very much a sense memory thing. I found different things that meant something to me and I would just touch on them. Finally, it became like a button where you just begin to play around in your thoughts associating something to which you are very sensitive, and God knows what it is, it's different for all people. Those were the things that would get me to the point of crying."

Asked if he felt he was cheated out of his childhood in any way, he answered, "You lose enormously in terms of the normal events that occur to kids. The business of growing up and learning socialization, the interplay, learning how to make friends, learning to hold on to friends and so forth. Having been away from high school for three years, I missed all that. I think it's a great loss. At my school there was only four or five kids in the classroom, sometimes only three. It would break up at noon and I would go off, and of course you give up an awful lot when you're working, and I was working a good deal. So a lot of the normal pleasures of growing up I missed."

We wanted to know what Gene's response would be if a parent came to him and asked him what his opinion was on an acting career for their child. "No, I would not recommend it. But at the same time, my kid is interested in the business. He's grown up here and he's seen all the stuff going down. He's at UCLA now and wants to get into film school. He's in an acting class, and a writing class off-campus, but because he's interested I will help him all I can. I'd never say I don't want you to go into that business. But he hasn't been deprived of any of his high school experience or anything. It was different with me; I was never clamoring to be an actor. He was interested in acting. But I think it's not a normal life for a child and it's always the parents who are hot to get the kid either for the money or the prestige of having him be on the silver screen or television. It's fulfilling the ambition of the parents and not the child."

"I enjoyed school," Gene continued. "I was not a spectacular student, but I was a very conscientious one. If I had stayed in a regular school with competent teachers, and a variety of teachers all of whom were expert in their particular disciplines, I think I would have been a much better student and probably a better worker today. But you go to studio school where you don't have competition, you don't have other kids and you don't have really outstanding experts in their field; your education is blighted. So I've been a student all my life."

In summing up his feelings about his career thus far in the motion-picture industry, and about actors in general, Gene said, "Well, I think I have been very lucky and very fortunate. I think about my experience on *M*A*S*H,* and working with Alan Alda; it was just an enormous privilege because he is such a decent man. He's very talented, but also very professional and considerate. I worked with some wonderful people, and I've worked with some people who were not so wonderful, but I have been fortunate because I've been active. I've directed hundreds of television shows, I have acted in a great number of films, and I produced three or four hundred television shows, so I had a lot of work. In our business you have the opportunity to meet people who are not only talented, but also very giving and generous, exceptionally evolved people. It's a blessing in that way. Although people complain about actors, actors are generally extremely generous. They give of their time and energy and talent. There is a generosity there, and very sweet."

Bryan Russell

Bryan Russell was born December 3, 1952, in Los Angeles, California. "For the first five or six years of my life I lived at Hermosa Beach and Hollywood, right around the corner from KTTV and KTLA studios where they filmed *Lassie*. They didn't have good parking facilities so the people from the studios would park on the street in front of our apartment. One day I was out front playing, and someone affiliated with the *Lassie* series thought I was a kid that had potential and went up to my grandmother and asked, 'Would you be interested in bringing this boy over to talk to us?' When my mom came home my grandmother told her about it and she said, 'Sure, let's go see what happens.' So they took me over to the studio and met with them, and I did an episode of *Lassie*."

Bryan's first role consisted of walking past the camera carrying cotton candy in a scene that took place at a county fair. "My direction was to just look at the cotton candy and not at the camera. The cotton candy was made of something like angel hair, that spun glass they used to use for decorating Christmas trees. One of my other directions was, 'Whatever you do, don't take a bite out of this.' Jon Provost was Timmy in the series and his mother was just wonderfully open and receiving to my mom and made the experience very comfortable. So that was how it all started. I was five years old."

Bryan's mother was a concert pianist, and his dad an opera singer. "So they knew people on the periphery of the industry. One of their friends was Glenn Shaw, a theatrical agent. They called him and said, 'You want to represent Bryan? Maybe this could go somewhere.' That's when I started going out on interviews and that's how it all began."

Bryan's numerous television credits include many of the western shows made during the 1959 through 1961 seasons. Some of those he

Bryan Russell

worked on were *Death Valley Days*, *Law of the Plainsman* and *Tales of Wells Fargo*. He reflected on working with Steve McQueen in *Wanted: Dead or Alive*, in which Bryan played a little boy who ran away from home. "It was one of the earlier western TV shows that I did. We were doing a location shoot not far out of Hollywood in the mountains where they used to do westerns. There was a caterer set up to do lunch and I was in my little trailer with a welfare worker doing school. When lunch hour was over we went to do a scene and nobody could find Steve. They got on the blowhorn and said, 'Steve, come on, we're ready to do the shoot.' Nobody knew where the heck he was. Everybody's looking around and finally somebody said, 'Last time I saw him he was headed over that hill on his motorcycle.' After lunch he had gone off on his scooter and was out in the mountains somewhere doodling around. He had either got a flat tire or ran out of gas, and was stranded out in the middle of nowhere. So they went out and found him. A half-hour later they came back and we did the shot. He was just like a big kid and was a lot of fun to work with."

One thing Bryan enjoyed doing away from work was horseback riding. "I think most of the kids that grew up in that era in the industry were horse fanciers. At that time in the San Fernando Valley there must have been a half-dozen riding stables. That was something kids and their families did together. If you had a birthday party, you'd take six or eight kids and all go riding for an hour. That's something that I really enjoyed, and as a youngster I used to ride all the time with my sister and my father. That's what we did on the weekends. A lot of that experience was from having been in TV shows where you were comfortable around horses and on saddleback. On these shows, if you weren't riding you were at least sitting on the back of a horse or you were around them."

Troubleshooters was a television show Bryan did that was a nonwestern. Keenan Wynn and Bob Mathias drove around on heavy equipment and rescued people with their bulldozers and caterpillars. "I was a kid that fell down in a ditch in one of the episodes and it collapsed. That was a miserable experience. I spent the entire shoot in a hole covered with dirt. All the dirt, except for an occasional rock, was false dirt. It was like popcorn weight; super light. All the same, for 30 minutes of filming I was in the hole."

Bryan with Steve McQueen in "One Mother Too Many" (1960), an episode of *Wanted: Dead or Alive* (CBS-Television).

Bryan's feature film credits include *The Wonderful World of the Brothers Grimm.* and *How the West Was Won.* "I always thought it was kind of a neat thing that I got to do both of those big cinerama productions." Bryan reflected on *The Wonderful World of the Brothers Grimm*, in which he played the son of Laurence Harvey, "That was a fun and real interesting film to do, but a short shoot because I didn't have much of a part in it. There was talk of taking us to Europe to do just one train station scene in that film but it never materialized. Instead, they wound up building an incredible set and doing it stateside. It was one of the final episodes when the brothers come into a train station at the end of the movie and there's a zillion kids. Laurence Harvey was wonderful and a lot of fun to work with. He was a character, just a high energy guy. Tammy Marihugh played my little sister. She was a doll. At the premiere of *The Wonderful World of the Brothers Grimm*, I was all tuxedoed up, and Barbara Eden—who must have been in her early or mid twenties at that time—was just a goddess. There's a picture in the newspaper of her bending over and giving me a kiss on the cheek and I've got this ear-to-ear grin."

Bryan and Kim Charney played the sons of Karl Malden and Agnes Moorehead in *How the West Was Won*. Their memorable scene takes place aboard a raft being swept along in the rapids of a raging river. "I didn't actually do the stunt work. What we did was a process in those days where they had a projection on a screen behind us and we were in an enormous tank with the wave-making machinery on a sound stage at MGM. We were on a life-size raft, doing it all—with the scenery taken when they actually did the stunt work. There were adults dressed up as kids for the stunt work. I believe Billy Curtis was one of them. The work on the sound stage replicating that raft going over the rapids was in itself a pretty harrowing experience. It's kind of easy to act in a situation like that because a lot of times the conditions are so believable, so realistic, that you can really throw yourself into that make-believe pretty easy. That was quite an experience.

"Actually, stunt men on *How the West Was Won* taught me how to swim. We were staying at Holiday Inn and there was a swimming pool. I was holding on to the edge of the pool and these stunt guys were saying, 'What? You're eight or nine and you can't swim? Come here.' One guy was out in the water and another pulled my life vest off and set me up on the diving board and said, 'We can do this.' These are stunt guys, so if they say, 'We can do this,' you believe them. He said, 'Kind of lean over,' and then he pushed me off the diving board. The other guy in the water let me float up and taught me how to swim. So I learned at Paducah, Kentucky, at the Holiday Inn. A great experience.

"As a matter of fact, I broke my tooth in that swimming pool," Bryan laughed. "Seems that something was always happening to the kids on location. We took a little steamboat to the location on the Missouri River where we were doing our shoot. At the end of the day as we were going back to our hotel everybody was laying around drinking coffee. I was walking across the deck of the boat and kind of lost my balance and put my hands on the blazing hot steam exhaust chamber and really blistered them badly. They had to take me to the emergency hospital. So in the scene at the grave site after the raft goes over the rapids and we're burying our parents my hands are all bandaged up."

Henry Hathaway directed the sequence of *How the West Was Won* that Bryan worked in. "He was a character and would just scream and yell," Bryan smiled. "Getting ready to do a shoot everybody had to get way back because this camera filmed everything at such a wide angle instead of just the normal shot. One time while we were doing a scene Bernard Smith, who was the producer of the film, walked up quietly to the set and into the scene. Hathaway gave him all kinds of grief, up one side and down the next before he realized who it was. So that was kind of comical. Henry Hathaway was profane. He could curse a blue streak. And of course with myself and the fellow who played my older brother on the set he needed to watch his language. He was really good about catching himself from what I remember, but as it turned out Debbie Reynolds had an ongoing bet with the crew that she could keep him from cursing and every time he would cuss she'd lose money. Debbie was just wonderful to work with."

Commenting on his work in *Bye Bye Birdie*, Bryan smiled. "Talk about being stricken. That was Ann-Margret's first big debut performance. One of the things I used to do after we did a shoot with the people that were really good to me and who I actually had this family experience with was to get them to sign pictures for me. Kind of a memorabilia scrapbook thing. The picture was a full-profile shot of her in tights, and she signed it in pink marks-a-lot so it looks like she signed it with lipstick. I remember the entire time I was on the set with her—I must have been about nine years old—it was just jaw dropping. She's my older sister in it and was just an incredibly voluptuous teenage girl and so full of energy. That's one of the memories about the business: how warm and genuinely caring the older people were for the youngsters on the set. That was a great cast: Paul Lynde, Janet Leigh, Dick Van Dyke, Bobby Rydell, and Ann-Margret. Bobby was great. I used to sit and watch them do their scenes and it was really neat. You felt like you had a family experience, and that's what made it difficult when the movies were over. There was this void, like you're leaving your family. It was always a sad thing. I think that's maybe how the picture collecting started. My mother felt that if I had a little something to take with me as a memory it would kind of make that separation thing a little less painful. You spend a week on a television show, but in a feature you can spend three months with a group of people and it really is family, and then when it's done it's sad, it's good-byes. What is really a kick is to have the opportunity to work with the people again, which is something I got to do with Karl Malden. We worked in *The Adventures of Bullwhip Griffin* together after having worked in *How the West Was Won*.

"*Bye Bye Birdie* was wonderful," Bryan continued. "That was a musical, so there was this incredible energy. I remember doing one of the shoots at Hollywood High School. There was all of these kids in this dance number. It was all choreographed and the camera was up on booms. It was a great experience and the talent was incredible." Bryan also sang in the picture. "That was under the tutelage of Johnny Green, one of the great musical people in the business. We did the studio stuff and then did the lip-synching when we actually did the film. What was really neat was being in the music studio on the headphones and behind the scenes of the recording when the group sang. I cut a record, too, when I was a kid. A rock and roll version of 'Supercalifragilisticexpialidocious.' It was a pretty funny song. I'm always singing, much to the amusement of the fellows I work with now. *Bye Bye Birdie* was a trip, specifically I guess because of it being a musical and so different from the other things I had done."

Bryan was signed under an exclusive two-year contract with Walt Disney Studios after being cast as Emil in *Emil and the Detectives*. "I would have to say that the experience of the traveling, getting to meet Walt Disney and working in that production was probably the highlight of my career. We shot it in Berlin at a time when it was a very volatile environment. We saw the atrocities of the Berlin Wall and the guards at the divided city. It was a cultural experience to see all of that going on. As a matter of fact, we were in Berlin when President Kennedy was assassinated and that city was in mourning. It was an incredible experience for me to see. For one thing, being out of the United States when the President was shot, and second, to see how that city grieved. There were pictures of him in every shop, candles burning in every window. It was a phenomenally emotional experience. We had the opportunity to do some traveling and actually meet some family in France and spend some time with them. After the film, we traveled to Rome, Paris, and London. It was just an experience that gave me perspective I carry with me to this day—what goes on in the world other than your own little secluded area coming from Hollywood, California. That was one of the great things about my experience in the industry was the traveling we got to do. Not just to Europe, but I did a baseball film in Florida called *Safe at Home*."

Safe at Home featured baseball legends Roger Maris and Mickey Mantle. "That was another highlight of my career. We went to Fort Lauderdale, Florida, to the spring training camp facility where I spent two weeks rubbing shoulders with the Yankees, and that was the year after Roger Maris had hit 61 home runs. That was a great experience. It was a little black-and-white low-budget film that was very well-received. After filming the movie, Mickey Mantle autographed and gave me his baseball glove."

Bryan later appeared in a number of episodes of Disney's *Gallegher* with his *Emil* costar, Roger Mobley. "That was a very successful series. It was a lot of fun to go back and do a little guest spot on Roger's show and be the shoeshine kid." Bryan, however, explained that his contract at Disney had its pros and cons. "Right after coming back from Germany from doing *Emil, The Sound of Music* was casting. I went out on an interview and was selected for one of the Von Trapp children, but there was a conflict. The Disney studio actually gave the production company a stop date; it had to be done by a certain date which was just unreachable. So I missed the opportunity to go back to Europe. It was really disillusioning. To do a four-part *Wonderful World of Disney* television show called *Kilroy* instead was kind of neither here nor there."

As a child actor attending the public school system, Bryan noticed that he was treated differently than nonmovie kids. "The first memories I have of almost special treatment was in fourth grade in the public school I was going to. I was infatuated with my teacher and she was infatuated with me. I think that I might have gotten a little bit of special treatment because I was in the motion-picture business. I was one of the better students academically and she wanted to pass me ahead a grade. About that time I started becoming aware that I was getting treated a little differently by the other kids, and it ranged from one extreme to the other—from adulation to resentment. Several girls wanted to hang out with me because I was in the business. There were even times when I came home from work with make-up on; I wouldn't take it off until after I got home. So here's a kid coming home with make-up on. I guess he would get a little bit of extra attention or extra looks from the various kids in the neighborhood, and at that time the kids I was living with in the neighborhood were the kids I was going to school with, too. But like I said, the treatment I got, ranged from special or privileged treatment to almost resentment. I guess some people would see this and not appreciate it. I hate to use the word jealous or envious, but it happened. Most of the people that I really identified with were the other kid actors like Jon Provost and Jay North.

"As I got older it became a little more difficult for me to have what I consider to be a normal relationship," Bryan continued. "It was almost like 'Are we friends because I'm an actor?' So it was not until I actually got into high school and kind of left my theatrical identity behind me that I really started feeling confident about my friendships because there was really not much reference there to my previous career. It was not something that I brought up; so consequently it wasn't a focal point."

Bryan explained why he left the motion-picture business. "I worked pretty steadily from the time I was five until I was 13. At 13 I did a film for Walt Disney called *The Adventures of Bullwhip Griffin* with Roddy

McDowall. It was the last feature film I did. I went from that into Notre Dame Catholic High School and had a pretty conservative teenage life outside of the limelight. There were times I thought about maybe pursuing an acting career. I hooked up with Pat Holms who used to work with the Glenn Shaw agency. She talked about the commitment needed for an acting career. I went out on a couple of interviews and it just wasn't a fulfilling experience. As a matter of fact, if anything it was a little on the negative side."

After high school, Bryan went to junior college in the San Fernando Valley and took some basic classes. "I decided that what I really enjoyed doing at the time was building things. I joined the carpenters' apprenticeship program and became a union carpenter and really enjoyed it. It was always one of my dreams to build my own home, so we did." Away from his carpentry career, Bryan is very active in his kids' sports programs. "Being pretty much involved in their activities is how I recreate these days. My wife Cathryn and I met at my high school graduation party, so we go back a long way."

Looking over his child actor career, Bryan expressed his feelings by saying, "I really feel privileged to have had the experience of meeting the people I did and being involved in the industry. I know there's a lot of talk about the downside of child acting. I think I was just very blessed to have had a mother who was very intuitive as to the basic rights and wrongs. I look back on the experiences that I had, the relationships that I was able to make during the filming of the shows, and the traveling. But overall I would say it was invaluable in terms of the development of the person that I am. Ask me what I like to do and what some of my hobbies are, hey, I love cinema. The advent of video is great. My kids love movies, we all do. That's something I don't think will ever change. Some people just don't like sitting around watching movies, but I do. But my acting career was a real positive experience and helped shape me, my values, and the way I interact and deal with people."

Jeanne Russell

Jeanne Russell was born in Pasco, Washington. "My father was in the service and we moved to Hollywood in 1952. He was a singer and was trained as a classical tenor. My mother is a concert pianist and accompanist. Our childhood was very vaudevillian. They taught me to sing an aria phonetically and before I could do anything else my grandmother was stretching me. She had me hold on to a door post and she'd stretch my leg over my head, and stretch my arches for point. My father was singing with a woman named Althea Shaw, and her husband was Glenn Shaw, an agent. We always had singers and theatrical types over at the house and my brother and I were like a little performing team, routinely singing for our parents' friends. One day Althea said, 'Glenn has opened up a children's department; why don't we put the kids in it and see what happens.'"

Jeanne said that a lot of things happened simultaneously, and that was so often how people broke into the industry. "There is a lot of magic and mysticism in this. It doesn't just have to do with talent. We lived on a street called Fernwood that ran parallel in back of two major studios, KTTV and KTLA, which was where they were shooting *Lassie*. One day there was a knock on our door. It was the secretary from the *Lassie* production, and she said, 'One of our production people spotted your son and we need a small child on the *Lassie* set for some pickup shots. Are you interested in letting your little boy do it?' They knocked on the right door. Literally. And invited us in. That's how we started."

Jeanne and her brother Bryan worked as extras on *Lassie* and hung out with Jon Provost. "He and his mom used to come over to the house for lunch. My grandmother was into health foods and was making her own carrot juice and culturing her own yogurt, so she would give them

Jeanne Russell, *Dennis the Menace* (1959–63, CBS Television).

health lunches. That was about the same time Glenn Shaw came into the picture. So we were invited in. It's almost a mystic karmic thing of who gets chosen, and that's why it's such a clique. Once you've worked as a child you are a member of a society of a tribe that is unmistakable."

Jeanne went on interviews for about six months straight, sometimes as many as two a day, but was not successful in obtaining work. "They were casting little blonde girls with blue eyes, and I had red hair and freckles. Finally, they started casting for *Dennis the Menace* and Bryan went on the interview for Dennis. They said, 'You're a little young,' and he said, 'But I have a sister who's older.' My mother had such smarts that she would put one of my photographs in his pictures and vice versa. So here's my little brother pitching me," she laughed. "And the director said, 'Let's see her.' So I went through the interview process. They held extensive interviews in Los Angeles and New York and then came back here and narrowed it down to Rickie Sorensen's sister, Leilani, and me. When they first brought me in to see Jay North and the director, Jay said, 'I like Jeanne.' The last test was to see if they could make me look like the character of Margaret. They put us on a sound stage and did my hair and then had Jay and I play a scene with direction, and I got it."

Jeanne enjoyed her work on *Dennis the Menace*. "It was a very happy set. Our directors worked very well with kids. William Russell was our first director; halfway through, Charlie Barton took over. Charlie was just a fabulous physical comedy director. It was just like a family."

Jeanne appeared in about a quarter of the episodes so remained enrolled in public school. "I sort of fluctuated between the two worlds of regular school and set school. It helped me a lot because I was pathologically shy and was very timid in school and wouldn't ask questions, so I was not doing so great. My studio tutor would give me individual attention and, in my case, it pulled me up by the bootstraps. Which is why we [she and Paul Petersen of Minor Consideration and the Screen Actors Guild] fought recently to keep the credentials of the studio teacher as high as they are. They were watering down the field shall we say. The state had licensed underqualified studio teachers and when we found out about it we spent all summer one year in hearings with the Governor's office, private meetings with his chief policymaker, along with producers. We fought very hard to have the regulation upheld and so they are giving the teachers two years to come up to spec. Now for the first time they are demanding a training session for studio teachers before they are given credentials."

In school Jeanne noticed a difference in how she was treated after obtaining the role of Margaret. "When you're on television you are the closest thing to royalty in this country. Everyone knows who you are. It is part of the turf of working. You're treated differently."

When away from the movie set and school, Jeanne's two hobbies were horses and ballet. "My parents took me riding at every opportunity. That was a real passion, which I guess is not unusual for little girls. And I excelled at ballet." When asked if she was able to incorporate these two loves into her work, Jeanne replied, "There were a couple of episodes in *Dennis the Menace* where I was called on to dance. One was pretty comical. I had to do a hula. I was in a grass skirt and a little bikini bra. My mother, who had been raised by her parents to be a performer, had done a Hawaiian routine in her years and so we had the dance choreographed when we came in and showed it to the director and he nearly fell over."

Jeanne was also cast for a two-day shoot on a *Mr. Ed* episode to play a little girl riding a horse in the park; the horse was scripted to run away with her and Mr. Ed was to come to the rescue. "I was so excited about that. But wouldn't you know it, I got a call to do a *Dennis the Menace* for one day and it conflicted, so I didn't get to do it. I was so disappointed."

Behind the scenes on the series there was a lot of camaraderie. "The crew was a lot of fun. There was one character on the set who would come in and slip a nail in your shoe, not to hurt you, and he'd get away with it every time. You'd be walking and say, 'What's that in my shoe?' When it happened to you you felt like you'd been initiated. I never knew who did that. Gale Gordon and Joseph Kearns had very different personalities, but they were both very nice, very professional, and worked well with kids. Jay North was very sweet, very sensitive. If he messed up a take he would apologize to everyone, the actors, the director and the crew. He was a great kid."

Jeanne shared a humorous anecdote that happened during an episode titled *Man of the House*. "Mrs. Mitchell was sick in bed, so Dennis called me to come over and help him clean up the house. This was quite a switch because I was usually the one chasing him. We were one of the first to use that sight gag of having a washing machine run over with soap suds. It took us a day to shoot that sequence. The floor was slippery; one time Jay fell and got completely submerged under the soap suds and we were laughing hysterically. But every time we goofed they had to dry us both off because we were up to our knees in soap. Then they would have to swab the floor and do the whole thing again. That was pretty funny."

When *Dennis the Menace* came to a close, Jeanne did numerous television spots. "During hiatus and afterwards I did things like *Day in Court*. I also did *The Birds* for Alfred Hitchcock in the schoolhouse sequence. That was shot while I was actively participating in *Dennis the Menace*. I had a one-on-one interview with Alfred Hitchcock at his office at Universal. I walked in and he was sitting behind his desk. He had artists' renditions of what he thought the scenes were going to look like; kids with their eyes gouged out, and like that. I looked around the room and said, 'Oh great, I love horror films.' I had never done one. When I got home Althea Shaw called and said, 'Jeanne's got the job. You leave for Bodega Bay on Monday and pick up a script when you get up there.'"

When Jeanne and her mother arrived at Bodega Bay, they realized that Hitchcock had hired a group of experienced Hollywood kids as well as a group of local extras, and none had speaking parts. "Once we were on the set, Hitchcock wouldn't speak to us. 'Hello Mr. Hitchcock,' and he would just look straight ahead. Finally, whoever happened to be standing next to him at the time, would respond. Some of the mothers and agents were pretty furious about that because you just don't take an extra job after you've done principal roles. But we were there and figured, 'Why not. Let's do it.'"

Jeanne stated it was an amazing experience. "I had a mechanical bird strapped to my back and when we started down the hill, I pulled a switch. The first time it actually drew a little blood from my scalp so they had to wrap the beak with something. They used those mechanical birds and also took some footage of real birds, and then did some treadmill work back at Universal." When the children were running down the hill a huge camera truck followed closely behind with Hitchcock sitting atop it. The teacher was concerned that it was following a little too closely. "One kid could fall because—the hill was gravelly—and roll down and take out a few more kids. So they stopped production for a little while until the teacher was satisfied that they could control the truck. She then made

Jeanne as Margaret with Jay North as Dennis from the CBS television series *Dennis the Menace* (1959–63).

them get pink tights for all the girls so in case they fell they wouldn't get scratched up."

Jeanne's mother was a big help to her. "She was our coach. She was a huge fan of Jane Withers and patterned my character of Margaret after her. It was like handing down the little spunky girl role from generation to generation. Margaret was the character you love to hate. My husband says that when I used to come on-screen he'd run out of the room."

Referring to her relationship with her actor brother, Jeanne said, "It helped tremendously that we were both working because there was no sibling rivalry. In fact, Bryan and I were more like little comrades in the same army. It really gave us a common ground because from my observation it can be quite traumatic when you've got one kid that works a lot and maybe one or two at home that don't. It can split a family in two, so we functioned as a unit in this sense. Bryan and I even performed together. We did a *Dinah Shore Chevy Show* where they used Hollywood kids. We dressed up as tramps and performed a musical number called *Midnight Choo Choo*. And we did a commercial together once."

Like most child actors, Jeanne was unable to make the transition to adult roles. "I had my last job when I was 16. The work sort of dwindles, particularly in those days. They weren't worried about realistic adolescent casting so once you hit 14 you were in no man's land because they would hire an 18 year old to play down. There were very few jobs available at that age span unless you were a star like Natalie Wood. So there wasn't a real opportunity for a smooth transition. I think there is more opportunity now, but it's still very difficult for a child actor to transition. One of the reasons, I believe, is because a child actor who has worked a lot has had a sheltered life just by definition of how much time they spent interviewing, training, working, and they are not getting the street experience that a normal kid would. So you have a normal kid who has a certain degree of maturity development in ways that a child actor a lot of times doesn't and is therefore more interesting to watch as a young adult actor. While the child actor's got all of his tremendous professional expertise there is not an awful lot of life experience there necessarily. So you are competing with a whole new crop of people who have expertise in other fields."

Jeanne missed the work tremendously. "It's kind of hard to ask an adolescent to redirect their life when they have been trained every waking minute of the day to do a certain thing. It's like being kicked out of your country or the analogy that I use is that your tribe wanders off and leaves you sitting in the desert. I don't want to sound negative but it's just the reality of it. But if that's the price you pay, I'd pay it again in a hot second because the industry gives so much. However, there is a trick to handling that time in your life. The trick is that if your parents saved for you some of the money you made, it's very helpful. When I was 18 and I hadn't been working for a few years and was really unhappy, really at a loss, my mother handed me a savings account book and said, 'Honey, your career may be over but look what show business did for you.' That made a tremendous difference because that was like a severance package. I have to say that's fair. I redirected my energy, and that's the trick.

"I tell people when I do orientations at SAG that you have to have an exit strategy, you've got to be prepared to leave the business as much as you prefer to work in it. You've got to have outside interests. The trick is to take everything you learn from show business, the training and professional ethic, and parlay it into something else because if you really look at it, hardly anyone's career lasts a lifetime in that business. You just have to say, 'Wasn't I lucky that I was one of the chosen.' I'm a card-carrying member of the tribe. Forever. My work is there and I was part of classic television."

Jeanne didn't know what she really wanted to do for a long time, but because of the work ethic instilled in her, she knew that she should be progressing some way. "So I went to junior college and then decided on chiropractic as a career. That made a big difference. I knew I needed a sizable career to take the place of my show business because that was the way I was raised. So it turns out it was good. By 25 I was in chiropractic school and at 28 I was out and had my own practice."

Jeanne has dedicated much of her time in laboring to bring about fairer practices for children working in the motion-picture industry. "One of my patients knew someone who had come to town to shoot a bunch of *Where Are They Now* spots for Bobby Rivers. He said to me, 'Why don't you do this? They got Jay North; why don't I give her your number?' I said, 'Sure.' I hadn't seen Jay in about 20 years and we connected like it was yesterday. Paul Petersen and a couple of other people were also on that shoot. That started it. People kept asking us the same questions. We talked about it and I became a pretty good extemporaneous speaker on the situation. I did the *Geraldo Show*, *Sally Jesse Raphael*, *Montel Williams*, *Suzanne Somers*, and others."

One example of the conditions Jeanne and Paul Petersen were attempting to change was that working in the business did not constitute an excused absence from school. "You have a tutor and do your work and go back to school. But a lot of teachers were harassing child actors, giving them fails and marking them unexcused. When I met Shirley Mills, she said, 'You mean that has not been fixed yet.' So just as the genial conversation started to flow, you realized that there was some work to be done and it was totally compelling. I dove into this to the detriment of my chiropractic business. It is all volunteer work, but it's been a tremendous growth experience, plus I feel I've given back something and I've utilized some unique knowledge that I have."

Jeanne has chaired the Young Performers Committee at the Screen Actors Guild for a number of years. "The committee was already in existence. Paul and I joined the committee and directed the agenda towards some overdue reform." As such, she has participated in contract negotiations and legislative hearings and chairs the guild's orientation meetings for new minor members and their parents. "The committee has been instrumental in getting some children's issues into the contract for the first time." At one time the committee was interested in revising the antiquated Coogan Law, but the time wasn't right. "They didn't have the former child actors in the committee at the time and the parents outscreamed them. The parents didn't want their control taken away so the committee backed off. It took a group like Paul and me and our committee members such as Johnny Whitaker, Mary McDonough and Mimi Gibson to change that. We were glad to go on television and talk about this. Our committee has spent the last six years educating the guild and it's a constant turnover on the board of directors, but Richard Masur [president of the Screen Actors Guild] was tremendously intelligent, tremendously articulate and a great leader. He's been very helpful. Because of our tireless efforts, the needed changes in closing some of the loopholes in the Coogan Law to bring about better protection for the child performer was finally passed by the State of California and the education code now has provisions for working to be an excused absence from public schools."

One of the very first things that the Young Performers Committee initiated at SAG was a special orientation for child actors. Adults had an orientation, but children under a certain age were not invited to attend. "The parents were invited, but the kids weren't. I said, 'This is happening to the kids. I was a sponge when I was eight years old. If I had gone to a meeting at my acting guild when I was eight I would remember.' So we have been doing the orientations once a month for over six years and not just for new members but for people who have been out there for awhile. I've got to say I'm a little disappointed in the attendance. A parent will bend over backwards to get their kid to an interview, but it's only the real good parents who show up [at the orientations]. I figure if we are helping one kid it's the right thing to do. We basically just talk about the experience in general and give them the labor and teacher issues they may face. We used to do a formal transition section but I found out it's like a parent saving a child from making their own mistakes. We were getting a lot of blank stares about transition because when you're working you feel like you'll be doing it forever. When you are working it's such a clique, you can't fathom that you could possibly ever be out of it. So we just sort of weave transition issues in and out of what we do now. We figure they've heard it once and they know where to call if they want to talk to someone about it."

Jeanne's mother, as well as the mothers of Jay North and Jon Provost, thought their children were being set for life and would be in this industry forever. "Speaking for my mom, I know that she was really surprised when it took the downturn. In fact, my brother's last film was with Roddy McDowall, who spent a lot of time on the set talking to my mother about his transition years. That put the concept in her mind for the first time and she was able to make some very good decisions because of that. He was always very generous with every child performer he met. Happily, I was able to have a discussion with Roddy four years ago and tell him the impact that he made and thank him, and say that I was inspired by what he did and that it is one of the reasons why I'm doing what I'm doing with the guild. People should not confuse activism with negativity, because it is like when a stewardess stands up in an airplane and tells you how to put on your safety belt, shows you where the emergency exits are, and points out the oxygen. She is not trying to make you get off that plane and say, 'I'm not flying.' No, she's giving you the tools you would need to handle any scenario that might come up, and that's the spirit that I've been working on." We wanted to know what Jeanne's response would be if a mother asked for her advice about putting her child in pictures. "If the child really wants to do that and if he is lucky enough to work in the business it can be an experience of a lifetime. I would not discourage anyone from having the same kind of experience that I did. It's wonderful to be one of the chosen. But I would also sit down and tell that parent that there are 50 kids a month joining Screen Actors Guild in Los Angeles alone right now, and for every 50 that join there are a couple of hundred out there beating the boards and trying to get in. Of those 50 that join, a lot of them do one or two jobs and still have to ante up the eleven hundred dollars to join the guild and are gone in a year or two. They shouldn't use any money to pursue this career that they are not willing to take and play in Vegas. No parent should mortgage their home to put a child into a management scam where you get a lot of pictures made because it's such a crap shoot. There are no guarantees. You still hear things like my story, where the industry knocks on your door, but the most important message is there are no guarantees and don't do anything with sacred money. Talent and desire, unfortunately, is not all that it takes. It's got that magical mystic element that comes into play and I don't have an explanation for that. So that's the picture. You've got to weigh if you are sacrificing your financial well-being."

Jeanne explained that there are psychological things at play as well.

"If you take a child's experience—five years in a child's life is so much vaster than five years in an adult's life. I think adults in the business think, 'Oh, this is just a kid. The kid's going to get over this. This will go away and the kid will get into something else.' But what is happening is that they are putting a dye pellet in this child and everything in his world is being colored by the adults and the industry that they're in. When I read *An Interview with a Vampire* where these guys make a little six year old into a vampire, I thought, 'Oh God, this is like being a child actor.' It's like, where you're made, a large part of you stays there for life. It absolutely influences every fiber of the child's life. The danger is that you are modeling a world on a very transitory business at best. In our time, maybe there were 40 kids in Hollywood who did all the work. Now there's 50 kids a month joining SAG. I think there's more opportunity for a kid to work today, but they're always interested in the new and it's more disposable now."

Jeanne explained that the parents are the most important factor influencing how the child actor functions when his or her career is over. "My mother did the best she could and I would still have suggestions on how she could have done it better. So many times a parent will tell me, 'I put my kids in because it looked like you guys were having so much fun.' Well, yeah, but that's not necessarily a reason to do it, because there is a tremendous price, ... a tremendous trade-off. The older I get I just think it's some sort of a mystic tribe."

Jeanne reflected further on her years as a child actor. "I'm tremendously proud and tremendously grateful that I have been able to work. It's a real privilege when you're in and are welcomed to the club, but you just have to be prepared to land on your feet one way or the other, for the simple fact is that the majority of child actors do not continue on as actors even if they want to."

Mickey Sholdar

Mickey Sholdar was born in March 1949 in Indianapolis, Indiana. "My family moved out here [southern California] when I was about four years old. My dad was a salesman and worked with a man who was a part-time agent. I had gone to work with him one day when I was ten years old, and the guy saw me and said, 'Gee, you look like you'd be good for commercials or something. Would you like to try that out?' So I thought, 'Sure, that would be great.' My dad thought it would be a good idea too, so we had some pictures taken. I went out on an interview and got the first job that I tried out for."

Mickey's first job was an unsold pilot for a series in 1959 with Jack Carson and John Dehner titled *How's Business*. "The character's name happened to be Mickey and I got the part. I went on the set and was able to memorize the lines and it just felt kind of natural. Jack Carson was a salesman in the show who had an idea for a toy that he wanted to market that he called a 'Nothing Box.' It was like a little cigar box with springs and it would kind of dance around. He had a son played by a kid named Flip Mark who had a bunch of friends, and I was one of them. And that's how I got started."

After the pilot, Mickey worked in a number of commercials and television shows. "I'd go on interviews and they'd ask me, 'What have you done?' I knew you had to have experience and at the time I was just starting out, so I would make up things and say that I was on *Playhouse 90* and different commercials and just started getting parts. I got quite a few roles for about three or four years before I got the part in the series that I did, *The Farmer's Daughter*, and that worked out great. That ran for three years and we did over a hundred episodes."

When Mickey auditioned for the part of Steve Morley in *The Farmer's*

Mickey Sholdar

Daughter, he remembers there being a number of other kids there. "I interviewed two or three times all together for the part before they called and said that I got it. I remember celebrating with my family and thinking that that was great, and it turned into a terrific job."

In filming the pilot for *The Farmer's Daughter* they went to Washington, D.C. "We had gone there to shoot it because the premise of the show was that my father was a congressman. I remember when we weren't shooting we had a limo driver who took us all over. We went to the Washington Monument, the Jefferson Memorial, the Bureau of Engraving and Printing, and all the other places of interest. It was a real fun time.

"When we did the pilot for *The Farmer's Daughter*, part of what we were doing was out on the street. I think Jay North, who did *Dennis the Menace*, had been in Washington, D.C., prior to that, and there were a lot of people who were asking me if I was him. People didn't know who I was before the series. I had done a lot of acting but nothing that was real prominent."

Reflecting on his work in this series, Mickey said, "It was wonderful. Inger Stevens and Bill Windom were both really great people and fun to work with. When we did the pilot for the series I was 13, and when we finished it I was just turning 17. So I did a lot of growing up with them and everybody treated me very well. I was really pleased with it and it was a lot of fun. They used to send me out on personal appearances and people would recognize me and ask for my autograph. There were a couple of times when I went out and sang. They wanted to try to promote me as a singer. One of the episodes that we did had me starting up a singing group. It was with Davy Jones just after he did the pilot for *The Monkees*. We did some singing and they started to get a little contract together, but I never really did any recordings."

Mickey, who had worked on a number of television western shows, learned to ride a horse for his work in those. "As a matter of fact, the first western I had to ride in was on a *Wagon Train*. They asked me if I could ride and I said, 'Of course,' and I had never been on a horse before. I got the job and the next day my folks took me out and I had a couple of lessons on how to ride. It came fairly natural. I remember there was a *Gunsmoke* that I did where we had to shoot a scene several times, because getting on the horse was the hard part. I had to lead it out of the corral and then get on it, but the stirrup was so high and I was so small I had a hard time mounting it." Asked if he enjoyed doing the westerns, Mickey answered, "Oh yeah. It was a lot of fun getting all dressed up. Often they'd be shot out on location in the mountains and I enjoyed that. I went to Santa Fe, New Mexico where I did a show called *Empire*. The riding and playing Cowboys and Indians and getting paid for it was great," Mickey laughed.

"One of the *Wagon Trains* I did was an episode called *Charlie Wooster—Outlaw*. The character actors in it were L.Q. Jones and Morgan Woodward. There was a scene where I had been killed and was laying either in the barn or in the stable and a fly landed on my face. I remember concentrating so hard not to flinch and move and swat it away, and it was crawling all over the place. I made it through the scene without jumping or twitching or anything like that," he laughed. We asked him if he

Mickey played Steve Morley, son of the congressman played by William Windom, in ABC's television series *The Farmer's Daughter* (1963–66). Inger Stevens played Katy Holstrum, the governess of Windom's two children.

had to hold his breath for the entire scene. "No. I was breathing very shallow. One of the things that I learned in the singing lessons I had taken was to breathe from my diaphragm, so I could breathe without my chest rising up and down.

"I did one of the last episodes of *Wagon Train* that Ward Bond was in before he died. I remember having a lot of fun doing the westerns. The *Wagon Train* was the first western that I did where they filmed it on a sound stage. They had it all dressed up: the painting backdrop, the cactus and covered wagons. It was the first time that I had been on a set that was decorated in that manner. Everything else that I had done on the set was either a house or a building somewhere. I remember that as being fun and interesting when I first did that.

"There were only two or three people out of everyone I worked with that didn't impress me as being friendly. I did an episode of *Bonanza*. Michael Landon, Lorne Greene and Dan Blocker were really nice, but Pernell Roberts wasn't real friendly. I think there was an incident, not anything major, between him and my mother which caused some friction. It was not a friendly kind of situation. I did a movie with William Bendix called *Boys' Night Out*. I remember something happened so that my impression of him wasn't a friendly one. But other than that I think everybody that I worked with were fine. It was just a great time and I don't have any real bad memories at all."

Asked if anything dangerous ever happened while he was working, Mickey said, "Something happened in a TV movie that I did when I was about 18 called *Shadow on the Land*. It was a military situation and Jackie Cooper was in it. There were some stunts being done and I had been rigged up with squibs where I was supposed to get shot by a machine gun. I got tangled up in a flag as I fell. A stunt man was supposed to do something after I fell, but because I got tangled up in the ropes that held the flag up he didn't quite clear me when he jumped and I was injured very slightly. There were a couple of shows, however, where I saw other people get injured doing stunts."

One of Mickey's schoolmates was another child actor named Billy Hughes. "He lived a couple of blocks away and we knew each other as friends and as actors. His father and uncle were both stunt men so he kind of grew up with that in his family. I was always interested in athletics and enjoyed gymnastics and tumbling. I'd go to his house and he'd come to my house, and we did little practice fake fights throwing punches and doing those kinds of things. There was one time when Billy and I were practicing and he threw a punch. I went one way and he went the other way and he actually hit me and chipped my tooth, though I didn't get mad about it. The chip is still there today, but I wasn't really injured. I remember playing with Billy and liking him and being friends."

Mickey played Norman Vincent Peale as a teenager in *One Man's Way*. Reflecting on that film he reminisced, "It was after we had done the pilot for *The Farmer's Daughter*. William Windom, who played the father in *The Farmer's Daughter*, played Norman Peale's father in *One Man's Way*. Rory O'Brien, who played the little brother on *The Farmer's Daughter*, played the little brother of Norman Vincent Peale also. That brings to memory a little stunt fight that I had to do with one of the other kids in the film. The scene took place at church. Norman Vincent Peale was upset about somebody calling him a preacher's boy and they got into a little fist fight and I tussle with him. So there was a little bit of a stunt involved there and that was kind of fun."

Two motion pictures that Mickey appeared in were *The Facts of Life* with Bob Hope and Lucille Ball ("I played Bob Hope's son"), and *Boys' Night Out* with James Garner and Kim Novak. "James Garner had a convertible Jaguar XK-E and he took me for a ride on a mountain road where he was speeding along and going kind of fast; it was exciting and fun. In *Boys' Night Out*, Howard Morris and Patti Page played a couple and I was their son. In that movie there was a scene where we were playing baseball. I was a terrible pitcher and we were losing the game. It started to rain, which meant the game would be canceled, so I was supposed to be all excited. At the time I was doing gymnastics, so I asked the director if he wanted me to do a back flip or a flip flop, being excited that the rain was going to cancel out the game. He said, 'Sure,' so I threw that in and did a flip flop."

Mickey remembers there being different styles in which the directors worked with the kids. "Some were very friendly and open and worked very easily with kids, while others didn't seem to get along with children. I remember one of the episodes of *The Farmer's Daughter* in which there were a number of kids. Mel Ferrer directed it. I don't remember specific things, but I remember not feeling real comfortable with him. Most everybody else that I worked with treated me professionally and were great. I always felt like I was a professional as a kid. I always knew my lines. I was there on time and did everything that they asked me to do. My folks were great; they stayed out of the way. I think maybe that had something to do with the fact that I worked a lot. Besides, it just seemed to come kind of naturally. I practiced and learned my lines with my mom and dad or sometimes with my brother or sister. They helped me a lot. Mostly my mom would be on the set with me, although occasionally my dad would go."

In 1962 Mickey went to St. Louis for a guest spot, along with Harry Guardino and Mike Kellin, for an episode of *Route 66* with George Maharis and Martin Milner. "I was there for about nine days and my dad went with me. Even though I was only 13 years old, they let me drive the Corvette a block or two down the street. That was a lot of fun to be able to do that. I played Harry Guardino's son and it was a very good role, one of the larger roles I had. That was real interesting."

Asked if any role he played stood out as a particular favorite, Mickey replied, "I think my favorite role in what probably showcased my acting ability best was an hour episode I did called *To Catch a Butterfly* on *The Alfred Hitchcock Hour*. That was with Edward Asner, Bradford Dillman and Diana Hyland. I played a real disturbed kid who killed the next door neighbor's dog and tried to kill the next door neighbor and my father, and set fire to the house. It was kind of the male counterpart to the girl in *The Bad Seed*."

Reflecting on that show, Mickey mentioned, "I interviewed with Alfred Hitchcock for the part, but he didn't direct it. The director, David Lowell Rich, submitted my name—I guess it was to the Academy—because he thought that the job that I did was worthy of an Emmy nomination. It never got that far. I was never nominated, but the fact that he had thought I had done that good of a job was terrific. I did get a lot of recognition from that show, but again, the character was really kind of spooky, a real troubled kid. After it aired there were actually a couple of kids
that I had played with and were friends of, whose parents said, 'Maybe you ought to not play with this kid. He's a little strange,'" Mickey chuckled.

Besides his film work, Mickey also appeared in the stage production of *A Thousand Clowns* with Peter Breck at a small theater in the round on Melrose Boulevard. "That was an experience because it was my only professional thing on stage. There was one time during a blackout for a scene change that Peter Breck had gone to put a couple of props onstage and he reached into a box and cut his hand on something made of glass. He went ahead and did the scene and realized that he was bleeding, so he put his hand in his pocket. I looked at him and saw that his white pants was getting all red from the blood. The people in the audience started noticing it. We kept on and finished the scene; then he went in and got a bandage and finished the show."

We asked Mickey if, as he got older, he found that the number of his acting jobs began to decline. "When I was 17, there weren't a lot of jobs because people were waiting to hire a kid actor until he turned 18 when he could work full hours. So there was just a short period where it was a little slow and then it started picking up again. I did six or seven episodes of *Dragnet* and a couple of other TV shows."

Speaking of working with Jack Webb on *Dragnet*, Mickey said, "Jack Webb had a method of getting that show done. Everybody's lines were on the teleprompter. He was doing half-hour shows in two days. A lot of the half-hour shows were being done in three days and some were taking five days, but he would just zip zip zip right through. I enjoyed working with him. He was nice and he gave me quite a bit of work. He was different than he was on-screen. On-screen he always came off as very robotic to me. He was very professional and knew what he wanted and got it done."

In 1970, Mickey became very involved in golf. "My dad had introduced me to it when I was about 12. I fell in love with the game immediately. I knew from the first bucket of balls that I wanted to be a golf pro. In 1970, I had an opportunity to just do nothing but practice golf and had gotten to a point where I could play fairly well." We asked him if he walked away from the movies to play professional golf. "Yes, absolutely. I had gotten so involved in golf that I spent 2½ years where I was was literally practicing from seven in the morning until ten at night. I turned pro and started teaching and playing for about 12 years. I won 23 tournaments as a golf pro, traveled all over Asia and South America and Mexico playing different tours and tournaments. That's how I made my living from 1970 to 1983.

"I played well and there was enough money to kind of keep me out there but not enough to put away," Mickey noted, "so I got into the mortgage business. I became a manager for Great American Bank and spent about another eight or nine years doing that. Then I got a little tired of it and heard about another golf tour. I had turned 40 and there was a golf tour for guys over 40, so I started playing again. That was in 1990. In 1992, I was the leading money winner on the tour but that still wasn't enough to put me over the edge. I could play, I could be competitive, but I was never as good as the guys who made the big money. So I played again for about another three years and then went back into the mortgage business, which is what I'm doing now."

Mickey mentioned that in 1975 he was offered a job that he enjoyed very much. "They were doing a TV movie about Babe Zaharias, who was an Olympic athlete and became one of the best women golfers of her time." The producer, one of Mickey's golf students, asked him if he would teach the actress playing the role some golf lessons. Mickey agreed. "She was very tall; we were like eyeball to eyeball. I had about three months with her, and during the process I said, 'She's going to be able to do closeup shots, but some of the things that the script calls for her to do she won't be able to; the specific kinds of shots and the trick things. We're about the same size. You could put me in a wig and a dress and I'll double her, because I'm going to teach her the same style of swing that I have.' So I arranged for that as another part of the contract, and I doubled her. In the story, she goes to a golf pro because she had never played before and she was taking lessons. So another part of the contract was for me to play the golf pro in the movie. At the time I was married and had an infant daughter. My wife was one of the extras in the show and she was carrying our little daughter. Buzz Kulik, the director, also carried my daughter around, and they put a closeup of her in the show. So it was great."

Looking back over his career as a child actor, Mickey said, "It was a terrific time of my life. If somebody walked up to me today and asked, 'Hey, how would you like to be in a TV show?' I'd do it in a minute. Looking back at it I realize how competitive it is and how much involved you have to be in that. I like the idea of getting a steady paycheck, of being able to know pretty much what's going to happen next week—if I'm going to work or not going to work. I look back at it and think what a wonderful time that was in my life. It was an experience that I just loved. I think maybe once or twice I might have had negative feelings when I wanted to go play football with my friends or something like that and my mother would say, 'You've got to be careful. You don't want to break an arm.' I'd say, 'Oh, I just want to be one of the guys.' But other than maybe a little minor incident here or there, it was just great. I loved every bit of it.

"I'll look at an episode of something that I did when I was 12 or 13 years old and think, 'I know that's me; I know I did that,' but it's like another person. It's like I don't even remember doing the scenes or the job itself, but there I am. It's just so long ago and some of those memories are completely faded; other things are real vivid. I'll look at some of those shows and say, 'Hey, I was a pretty good little kid actor,' and with other shows I'll say, 'I'm not so sure I like that.' But most of the time I thought I did a good job. I could cry on cue and scream and yell and do all those things. Just everything about acting seemed to come to me. I didn't take any lessons, but I started working right away and got all kinds of different roles. Some parts that weren't really much of a challenge—you were just a kid and so you played a kid. Other parts were very much of a challenge where you really had to do some dramatic emotional type scenes. But it just seemed to come, so I guess I was kind of lucky."

Frankie Thomas

Frankie Thomas, son of Frank and Mona Thomas, was born April 9, 1921, in Manhattan, New York City. "My father and mother were both actors on the New York stage." Outside of being carried onstage as a child anytime they needed a baby, Frankie's first professional job was by chance. "I was going to the professional children's school in New York. This was for kids who worked in the business, where the arrangements were that child performers could get away and do matinees. Mostly it was only four hours a day in school, but they had a lot of homework and a lot of correspondence work for kids that went on tour. One day mother picked me up after school on her way to a casting call for a play called *Carrie Nation*. The director, Blanche Yurka, said to mother, 'Mona, you are much too young for any part in this play.' Then she indicated towards me, standing in the doorway, and continued: 'but I can use the boy.' So I got my first job on Broadway by being at the right place at the right time, a happy combination which has served as the turning point in the careers of many performers. I was about nine and played a newsboy. The play did not make theatrical history but the cast was interesting. It was Jimmy Stewart's first Broadway appearance. Likewise Myron McCormick. Josh Logan, later famous as the foremost producer-director in the theater, was the stage manager. I drove him crazy. He was always trying to find me when I was running around the theater," he smiled.

In those days there were a number of parts for children on the stage, and Frankie went from *Carrie Nation* to *Little 'Ol Boy*, which was a story of a reform school for juvenile delinquents. "It made a star out of a young actor named Burgess Meredith, who scored a tremendous hit in it. The play did not have a lengthy run, but I received my first review from Robert Benchley, who was reviewing plays at that time. He wrote 'Possum is

Frankie Thomas

played by youthful Frankie Thomas, watch him.' It was my first notice. Next I did a play called *Thunder on the Left*, and all three of these plays were flops. Then came the turning point. I was cast in the title role in *Wednesday's Child* and everything changed."

The role of Bobby Phillips was the longest part ever written for a youthful performer, and it still is. "The part was so good that it was difficult to miss, a fact that I learned when I took my final curtain call on opening night and the audience stood up and cheered," Frankie reflected. *Wednesday's Child* was selected as one of the ten best plays of the year, though one critic disagreed and wrote: "If there is a play at the Longacre Theatre, Frankie Thomas is it."

Frankie's parents told him that there were three things about the business that he should know: always know your lines; always listen to the director and be at rehearsals early; and don't read your own notices. "I was lauded as 'The Wonder Boy of Broadway' but all that did not mean as much as the inscription in the Samuel French edition of the play by the author, Leopold Atlas: 'To Frankie, the one, the only Bobby Phillips.' No other performer ever played the part. RKO bought the picture rights. I came out to Hollywood in 1934 and recreated the role in the film and it was selected as one of the ten best pictures of the year." There is an interesting sidebar to this story. At that time, the parents of child performers were looked upon somewhat askance. Called stage-door mothers, they were regarded as a considerable nuisance. Part of the original contract between Frankie Thomas and RKO stipulated that Frankie's parents could not appear on the set. "Dad took exception to that," Frankie explained. "So that clause was deleted and RKO was just delighted, because they suddenly found that instead of having a couple of stage-door parents they had a couple of professionals. They gave mother the part she created in the original show, a small part of the nurse, and they wrote in a part for dad just so he would be in the picture."

The role of Bobby made Frankie a star, and from then on it was Broadway to Hollywood and the reverse. "The following year I did *The First Legion* on the stage. It was a big hit too, and had a marvelous cast: Bert Lytell, Whitford Kane, and John Litel, who I later played with in the Nancy Drew pictures." Frankie then returned to Hollywood to film *Dog of Flanders* at RKO. "For six weeks I was wearing wooden shoes, and that got a little bit bothersome. They don't wear too well, you know. I remember we were shooting the picture and all of a sudden they called a halt to the production and my mother and I were whisked off the set into a waiting limousine and driven to Culver City. I did not know what was going on at the time, but I knew shortly thereafter. We were ushered into this large room at MGM, and there was Louis B. Mayer, Irving Thalberg, Eddie Mannix, the top brass of Metro. Mayer looked at me and said, 'Oh no, he looks too strong.' Thalberg, who had seen me in New York and was always recommending me for jobs, said 'No, I saw him play a crippled boy in a wheelchair in *The First Legion*.' Mayer said, 'No, no. Women have got to feel sorry for him. He looks too strong.' So we were taken back to RKO and started shooting *Dog of Flanders* again. Can you imagine; they stopped production just because Louis B. Mayer wanted to see me. He was a power in the land. Well, that was on a Wednesday, and on Friday the Hollywood Reporter came out with 'Metro signs Australian [sic] boy actor Freddie Bartholomew to play David Copperfield.' And Mayer was right. I wouldn't have been as good as he was in that part because he looked emaciated and thin, and women wanted to mother him. It was a whale of a part and I wish I could have gotten it, but I don't think I could have done it as well as he did."

At the close of filming on *Dog of Flanders*, Frankie's name went up in lights for the Broadway production of *Remember the Day* at the National Theatre. "I had the extreme pleasure of appearing with my father. The producer, Philip Dunning, went to dad saying: 'The part of Frankie's father is not all that much, but would you do it just to be with him?' Dad, bless his heart, said 'Sure.' Sam Briskin, president of RKO, attended the opening night naturally. I had just starred in two pictures for his studio. To this day I don't know what Mr. Briskin thought of my performance but he signed my dad to a seven-year contract at RKO."

The Thomas family moved their headquarters to Hollywood, and

Frankie's father appeared in over 200 films. "I lagged far behind, doing around 30," Frankie recalled. "The following year my name was up in lights again at the Henry Miller Theatre as the lead in *Seen but Not Heard*. I was proud of that one, and it was a hit. A young girl about my age named Anne Baxter made her Broadway debut in it."

After *Seen but Not Heard* and up to the war, Frankie was so busy in films that he could not return to his home town. There was *Boy's Town*, *One Foot in Heaven*, *Always in My Hearrt*, the *Nancy Drew* series with Bonita Granville, a serial titled *Tim Tyler's Luck*, and *The Major and the Minor*. Frankie talked about some of the experiences working in these films.

Reflecting on *Boy's Town*: "Mickey Rooney and I got along great. That was a marvelous picture. We were on it for 22 weeks, and went on location to *Boy's Town* in Omaha, Nebraska. I remember when we arrived, the whole town of Omaha was at the railroad station. We drove back with a police escort and there wasn't anybody in town. You could have shot a gun anywhere and not hit anybody, they were all down at the station."

Frankie was a contender for the part of Andy Hardy, but he confided, "I don't think I could have done that as well as Mickey did. Mickey played farce, broad farce, and that's what made it a hit, and that's what put it over, and he was better at that than I was. Andy Hardy was so popular that every other studio was looking for something like it. Bryan Foy, who was head of B productions of Warners, asked his daughter what she would like for Christmas, and she said she would like a complete set of the *Nancy Drew* books. He sent out one of his gofers who came back and said, 'I can't get it; they're all sold out.' 'Well if they're that popular we will buy them,' Foy said, and so they did. They began looking for a way of putting this on the screen as a series to compete with *Andy Hardy*, but couldn't come up with a script. They had about three writers working on it, and finally they gave it to a young fellow they just signed at a small salary. His previous claim to fame was writing a radio show about a boy and a girl in their early or mid-teens and that's what he knew how to write. So his version of *Nancy Drew* didn't come out as it was in the book with Nancy and two girlfriends; it came out with Nancy and a character he located in the books that presumably was Nancy's boyfriend, Ned Nickerson. Nobody was called Ned in those days, so they changed it to Ted and we did the first show, *Nancy Drew, Detective*. Warners always had their people up front on the cast of characters because those were the people they were pushing, their contract people, and my name was listed fourth, but it really was the male lead in the show. When they previewed it we got to a scene very early on where Nancy and Ted are outside of Nancy's house, and they see this dark figure at the window trying to get in. Nancy grabs a wrench and says, 'Here's what we'll do. You tackle him and I'll hit him.' Ted, who was on the football team, says, 'All right, all set to go, but hit *him*.' That was a big laugh and from that moment on the audience was laughing and they thought it was a lot of fun.

"For a B picture, the Drew series was very popular," Frankie explained. "We did *Nancy Drew, Detective*, *Nancy Drew, Reporter*, *Nancy Drew and the Hidden Staircase*, and *Nancy Drew, Trouble Shooter*. Warners signed me to a contract after the first Drew, and at Warners you never stopped working. They always found something for you to do. So we'd finish a *Nancy Drew* and they'd put the two of us, Bonita Granville and myself, into another picture right away as a team. Now there really wasn't a part for Bonnie in *Angels Wash Their Faces*, so they wrote one in because they always wanted us together as a team."

Reminiscing on working with the *Dead End Kids* cast in *Angels Wash Their Faces* and *Dress Parade*, Frankie replied, "I'd known them in New York. I was running at the National in *Remember the Day*, and they were running at the Belasco in *Dead End*. Billy Halop was not a *Dead End* Kid. The rest of them, Bobby Jordan, Huntz Hall, and Leo Gorcey, I don't think had been professionals. But Billy Halop had played a very successful radio show called *Robby Benson and Sonny Jim*. Leo played the real tough guy, but was really a very bright fellow. I didn't have any trouble with them. They tried to live up to the *Dead End* reputation of being crazy, and I remember one of them had an argument with the director and floored him with a punch. But they were pleasant enough to work with."

Prior to going under contract with Warner Bros., Frankie starred in a Universal Pictures serial. *Tim Tyler's Luck* was based on a very popular comic strip of the same name; and its producer, Henry MacRae, made a policy of doing serials based on comic strips. MacRae's prior serial, *Flash Gordon*, spawned two sequels. Frankie had several recollections that he shared concerning *Tim Tyler's Luck*. "When I was up for the job, my agent brought over a copy of *Wednesday's Child* and MacRae looked at it and said, 'Well, of course Tim Tyler is much older, but what the hell, he can act,' and he signed me. He had never met me. The picture was a lot of fun. We worked at Universal in a jungle set which they had on the back lot, and it was elaborate. They had cliffs that ran up three or four stories, all papier-mâché. There was a girl who came every day when she had a chance to watch us shoot: Deanna Durbin. She was crazy about the jungle atmosphere."

Frankie discussed one problem he had while working on the serial. "I worked with a chimpanzee throughout the picture named JuJu. He was a pet of Tim Tyler, and we're always walking together. The chimp is small but his arms are very long. I didn't come on the show till the third day of shooting. On the first two days they were filming a lot of stuff on a wharf and didn't need me, but they had one scene when JuJu was in a cage, where he's mad and shaking the bars. To make him mad, they took his trainer, who was a woman, and had my double—who was in my costume—struggle with her. This made the chimp mad. And he thought I was the guy through the rest of the picture that had been struggling with his trainer, so he didn't like me. We would go walking down the jungle path, and the first thing he'd do was get his teeth around my wrist. Well, we were on to that, and fortunately I wore a long sleeved costume, so I played it with ace bandages all the way up both arms. Finally, after four or five weeks, the monkey got the idea that he wasn't getting anywhere with my wrist, so he went for the throat and got his hands around my neck. He was torn off, but as they were tearing him off he scratched with his nails and laid the back of my neck open pretty good. Thank heaven we had a prop man who knew what he was doing. He took one look and grabbed the first thing he could find, which happened to be absorbine

Frankie as Tim Tyler and Frances Robinson as Lora Lacy face innumerable dangers in Universal's 1937 serial, *Tim Tyler's Luck.*

junior, and poured it all down that open wound. I'm telling you, that was like fire! Thank God he did it, because the next day my neck was swollen up halfway. It was in the back so it didn't show, but they had to lance it because the chimp was so dirty, and infection had set in. If he hadn't have used that absorbine junior, I don't know what would have happened."

Some child actors have a difficult time making the transition from younger children to teen and on to adolescent roles. Frankie was asked about his experience regarding this time of his life. "When I was under contract to Warners, I was 15 or 16. Fortunately, I just kept working. In other words, past mid-teenage, then the *Drews*, and then sort of matriculated into films like *The Major and the Minor*, with Ginger Rogers and Ray Milland. We finished *Major and the Minor* just before the war."

Reflecting on this, his last motion picture, Frankie said, "If I had it all to do over again, I'd have done it for free. Ginger was so wonderful to work with, so considerate. She didn't have to be — she had just won the Academy Award. She and Ray Milland were two of the nicest people it has ever been my pleasure to know.

"My father was a great sailor, and I sailed with him a lot. We had a boat here, and another one in New York. Frankie volunteered for the navy before the war broke out, because "I could box the compass and knew dead reckoning and Morse, so I got into officers' training. I walked practically off the set of *The Major and the Minor* and went into the war."

After five years in the service, Frankie returned to Broadway since his parents were there in a hit show, *Chicken Every Sunday*. "Things were not all that good after the war. There were a lot of fellows who didn't like to see us come back because they, for one reason or whatever, hadn't been in the war and they had been doing all the work and had a cushy go at it. There wasn't a way of making any money except radio, so I went into that and it was very good to me. I did at least fifteen hundred shows before dramatic radio fell prey to TV.

"At first, all TV came out of New York and was live. Tape hadn't come into being and teleprompters hadn't been invented. In pretape years, actors with stage and film experience were in demand and I did all the shows of that period: *Studio One*, *Philco*, et cetera, and in 1949 was cast in the first five a week TV soap, *Women to Remember*, which only ran 26 weeks but was of assistance later." *Tom Corbett, Space Cadet* came into being in 1950. "Like all other production units, Rockhill Radio — owners of the show — were worried about their actors being able to remember lines. Producers mostly knew radio performers, many of whom had no experience with memory work. My previous stage experience plus the fact that I had done the five a week TV series influenced my being cast in the title role.

"*Corbett* was a little bit like *Wednesday's Child*," Frankie said. "It was an instant success. From our first show it was all upbeat. By the second week the disk jockies were picking up our space lingo: 'Go blow your jets,' 'Don't fuse your tubes,' and the byword of the show, 'Spaceman's luck.' *Tom* was as close to being an instant hit as you can get. In no time, the secondary rights machinery ground into action. We added two half-hour radio shows a week and took on an extra Saturday half-hour on NBC, while our three a week ran on ABC. I don't know of any other show that ran on two networks at the same time. On weekends I was flying all over the country making personal appearances for the secondary rights. At the first of these in Philadelphia, there were 10,000 children plus parents in a line that stretched out through the store. We had more people in Boston and Detroit. Before we were through, there were over 160 items bearing the name of Tom Corbett." Jan Merlin and Al Markim were featured as Tom's space cadets in the series and Ed Bryce played Captain Strong.

When Tom Corbett and the Polaris crew took their last flight into the unknown and the series went off the air after a five-year run, Frankie retired from acting. "I decided to call it a day. I had experienced the best of the stage, motion pictures, radio and television during the best of times."

While acting in the *Corbett* series, Frankie also wrote some of the episodes. After the series, he wrote a radio show called *Theatre Five*, which comprised five half-hour stories a week. "I wrote shows for NBC TV's *True Story*, and then branched out into writing ten *Sherlock Holmes* novels published in this country, England, Germany, Israel and Russia. I had always been fascinated by Sherlock Holmes; Doyle had created a great character." Frankie mentioned that his interests today are with bridge. For about 25 years he was one of the leading bridge teachers in the country. "I became president of the American Bridge Teachers Association, editor and publisher of *The Quarterly* bridge magazine and associate editor of *Popular Bridge* magazine. That became quite a business, but I never looked at it as a business because to me it was fun. I still do it."

As for his school experience, Frankie said, "I always had somebody on the set, but let's say they didn't get in the way of production. It worked out fine. I was going to the best school in the world; I was learning the business which became my life work, so what could be better."

When asked how he would like to sum up his feelings about his career as an actor, Frankie said, "One thing I would like to underscore. There have been youthful performers who have bemoaned the fact that they were cheated out of their childhood, that their early association with the adult world ruined their chances in later life. None of that is true in my case. I loved every bit of my childhood. I was able to meet and listen to so many wonderful and talented actors, especially the supporting performers, well-named the bricks and mortar of those great plays and pictures of days gone by. To me that was the drama of the world. I met all these people through my parents and heard all these marvelous stories, people like Sidney Blackmer, Otto Kruger, Lloyd Corrigan, Minor Watson, Moroni Olsen and so many more. These fellows had been through the mill; they had done all those things and, you know, the most fascinating stories are the ones that never find the printed page. I loved it; and it couldn't have been better."

Leon Tyler

Leon Tyler was born Connie Leo Sperl in 1932 in St. Louis, Missouri. "My father was a grocery store manager for Kroeger Groceries. Those were rough times as my dad was making $33 a week. There were two fellows who had a daily morning radio show on KNOX called *Jimmy and Dick, the Novelty Boys*. They would come in and buy from him, and were very friendly. They would come to my folks' house, bring their guitar and accordion, and play, and I would get up and jig around and do a little schtick. They asked, 'Can we use him?' My parents were wonderful people. I was 2½ years old, and they didn't think a thing in the world about me going to nightclubs where Jimmy and Dick used me in their act. I vaguely remember knock-down, drag-out brawls and bloody bodies. It was just chaos. But we'd go from nightclub to nightclub and put on a little show. They would put me in a big box, wrap it up and then raffle me off. The box would open and I jumped out and worked up a little schtick, and they'd throw coins. This was right after the Depression. I'd pick up the coins and bite them to see if they were good and throw them in my cowboy hat. I became Connie the Little Cowboy. We'd make maybe a hundred bucks a night."

Jimmy and Dick then took Leon on their radio show, and from there they recommended that he take some lessons. "So I did. I took dancing lessons and all the garbage stuff that you do, and came out to California for a visit." Leon had relatives there, and somebody requested that he should go into a show at the Masquers Club. At that time the Masquers Club had people like George E. Jessell and Eddie Cantor in it. "So I did a show there and a fellow by the name of Charles Rodgers from Paramount Studios saw me. We were just going to be in California for a couple of weeks, but he had me come over and I was put under contract to

Paramount. Rodgers was doing a film on the life of Gus Edwards, a vaudevillian who did shows with kids. He had George E. Jessell, Eddie Cantor, Fanny Brice, Gypsy Rose Lee, and a lot of kids in the cast. It was totally a kid show, and Bing Crosby played Gus Edwards. So I did the movie, *The Starmaker*. We did a song called *An Apple for the Teacher*. "Darryl Hickman was in that one too. The last time I worked with him was with Ronald Reagan in *Prisoner of War*. We were both young soldiers in a concentration camp. Anyway, when I went under contract at Paramount they thought Sperl was too German, and said Leo's too strange so let's make it Leon. They asked my mother what her maiden name was, and she answered Tyler. So I became Leon Tyler."

Leon Tyler

Leon's early days in California were rough. He told of an early experience there. "This is kind of weird, but we had an unusual thing happen. We got out to California and, like I said, things were tough. When I say tough, I mean when I went under contract my mother and I stayed out here. We didn't have any money so we stayed with a couple that had a little theater. There used to be a lot of little theaters around. They were like a training ground. You do the shows there and call the talent scouts. Every studio had talent scouts, and they'd come out to see the show and bring you back and start grooming you to go into movies. This couple used mom like a maid, and we slept in a dog kennel at their place. My folks were very unsophisticated, so this couple were going to give me drama lessons, and got 20 percent of what I made. Then when I was about six or seven they decided—this was kind of dramatic—that my mom wasn't competent to raise me and take care of me, so they were trying to take me away. So they were kind of interesting times, but the problem didn't last too long and it worked out fine. My mom's a half-breed Indian, so she would have brought the tomahawk out real fast," Leon laughed.

Leon remained under contract to Paramount for about two years, and then started working at other studios. "I went into the *Jones Family* series starring Spring Byington, and from there I went into the *Dr. Christian* series with Jean Hersholt. MGM had taken over the *Our Gang* series and they became the *Little Rascals*, so I worked in a lot of those. I played a character called Four Eyes, and actually did the Froggie part for a while when he was off. They did a voice-over because I didn't have the voice. Then I just continued on working right on through as a kid growing up."

While Leon was working on the MGM lot in the *Little Rascals*, he heard they were looking for an actor to play Boy in the Tarzan movies. "To me Tarzan was God. When he got on that elephant there was no doubt about it, he *was* God. Well, I wanted to do Boy so bad, but I had white hair that was always in my face and I was so skinny. They wouldn't even consider me for the part. I was crushed, but as I look back on it now, it was really funny. When I was working on the *Little Rascals* comedies I would sneak over to the Tarzan set. They had a big lake on the back lot and had an artificial mountain built there. I think the last big thing they did on that lake was *Showboat*. It's now condominiums and the lake is probably gone. I remember getting over there one time and no one knew where I was. I climbed up this artificial mountain and went into a cave. Well, the cave had a stuffed leopard or lion in there. I didn't know what it was, but I *knew* it was alive, and I knew Tarzan wasn't there to save me. I fell all the way down the mountain and was bloody all over. Well, I yelled for mommy and went back to the *Little Rascals* set, but I didn't get sympathy because the production closed for a couple of days till I was well enough to go back to work again. I was just a mess. I did get a spanking," Leon laughed. "It's not that mom was mean. Not at all. I had absolutely wonderful parents, but we needed the money. I mean the money was real important for us to live on."

Reflecting on his work in the *Little Rascals* shorts, Leon said, "When I first started we worked six days a week. We had to be schooled three hours a day, have one hour of free time, and we could work three hours. It didn't quite happen that way. We worked long, long hours. We didn't really socialize that much with the kids because we'd go and come and there were always a bunch of new people on the sets. I remember more than anything that they tried new directors on the *Our Gang* comedies to see how good they would do and how they could get the kids to do things. I did a couple of movies with Alfalfa Switzer afterwards. He was very different. He could cause some problems on the set," Leon laughed. "I remember one time where he was gambling with some of the crew and almost wiped them out and he was under age, about 14 or 15 years old.

"I also did the first movie that Roddy McDowall did here in the states called *On the Sunnyside*. Roddy had just recently come over from England to do his first big movie, *How Green Was My Valley*. This film was the prep to see how good he was going to be because he might have not been the right person for it. He was having some difficulties with becoming Americanized in regards to what we all did. We'd play games and he was just kind of lost. I felt sorry for him. He was very, very nice, and I remember in school he was ahead of us. His schooling was much superior to what we had. Over the years I'd occasionally see him, and, of course, everybody loved him."

Leon was featured with Anna Bella in *Bomber's Moon*. "I had the white hair, so I was often a mean little ornery cuss German kid," he smiled. Another film Leon worked in was *The Sullivans*. When asked if he had any reflections on working in that one, Leon replied, "I don't remember doing that one. I did so many of them. Our only stipulation was that I never did an extra part, extra being nonspeaking. I always had a speaking role, but I didn't care what it was. Pay the money and I'll do it. When I was a kid I just didn't care. I had no interest in the business at that time, and I look back on it now and say, 'Gosh, what a blessing it was.' I don't think I disliked it, but I wasn't emphatically in love with the idea of not being able to do all the other things that kids my age did. I had to have long hair. If somebody wanted to cut it for a role they could cut it, but stupid little things like that. I couldn't get sunburned. I remember doing *Son of Lassie* up at Jackson Lake and the Tetons in Wyoming. They were so concerned because I would blister easily. I would blister all day long and they would have to bleach me out at nighttime so I could go back the next day and get blistered all over again. I worked with Terry Moore, Patty Prest—she played my sister—and a little boy named Billy Severn. We hid out the dog in the picture. I do remember it concerned the Germans. My last name is actually Sperl and my grandfather was very appalled at being a German because it was at the time of all the horrors going on, so you couldn't be German. I do remember that there were some fellows working in the movie that were German and they were just lovely people, but in that era they were Germans and you just weren't too friendly with them.

"Lassie was absolutely lovely to work with. It was the first Lassie, and of course he was really a male dog. Rudd Weatherwax was the trainer. It was just a dog Weatherwax had found somewhere. I think he got it from the pound. But Lassie was just incredible. He offered me Lassie's pup but we didn't have a place to keep it."

Leon kept very busy in the business and just went from one film to another. "I can remember that when I was doing the *Jones Family* they had a standby car for me because I was shooting two movies at the same time. They picked me up from one set and drove me over to the other, back and forth. Half a day here and half a day there. Strange times."

Leon worked with Bill Elliott and Bobby Blake in the Red Ryder western, *Great Stagecoach Robbery*. Leon, reflecting on working with these two actors, said "I was so impressed with Wild Bill Elliott that I got an autographed picture of him. I also did another one with Bobby Blake. There used to be a series of shorts that were done at MGM called *Pete Smith Specials*. We played brothers in it and it was really funny because I'm very blond and he's very Italian. They had to dye my hair black so we would look like brothers."

Leon spoke of some of the other stars he worked with throughout his career. "The big ones I remember working with, some of the ones you say, 'Wow.' People like Marilyn Monroe and Elvis. It was fascinating working with Jimmy Cagney because I just always thought he was an idol, and I saw how nervous he was. He was so insecure and nervous before a scene that he would wipe his hands, but then he would go into the scene and was perfectly wonderful. The prettiest woman I ever worked with was Merle Oberon. She'd walk on the set and was so breathtakingly beautiful that everybody, no matter who it was, would just stop and watch her walk. I have a photograph that she autographed to me. She was just absolutely gorgeous and sweet. I worked with her in *This Love of Ours*. Claude Raines was also in it. He was very reserved, and very nice. I must admit that all the people I worked with over the years have been very sweet."

Leon appeared in a Warner Bros. short, *Magical Movieland*, featuring Mel Torme, Wanda Hendrix and Robert Arthur. "Mel was under contract at Warners and they were going to make him a singing sensation. His singing voice was incredible, but his looks didn't have the charisma for it. This was before Wanda married Audie Murphy. She was an absolutely beautiful girl." Wanda and Mel played greeters at the studio who led a group of people around the various places on the lot. "Of course I was the obnoxious fan," Leon added.

Mickey was another film Leon appeared in. It starred Skip Homeier, Lois Butler, Rose Hobart, and Bill Goodwin. "Rose was my mother in *Mickey*. I went out to the motion-picture home in 1997 and saw her name there. We had a nice visit and she was still just lovely. In *Mickey* I was a haughty, snippy little kid, but usually I played the goofballs and the nerds. They were fun, but it was also fun to be mean."

Leon worked in the Columbia feature, *Mr. Soft Touch*, with Glenn Ford. "The four of us—Stanley Clements, Marion Welton, Gene Collins and myself—were in the movie, and Harry Cohn at Columbia liked us.

Leon is flanked by Wanda Hendrix and Mel Torme in the Warner Bros. 1945 short, *Magical Movielamd*.

Afterwards we did a movie called *The Tenth Avenue Gang*. It was going to be like the Bowery Boys, but one of the guys had some real problems so they dropped the whole thing."

Leon and Debbie Reynolds worked together on the USO shows. "We went to Korea and did it for the Northeast Air Command during the war. And I went to Italy. I would never have done that, so those shows were good to me that way." Leon later became very active in musical comedies. Toward the end of his career, he began doing Broadway types of shows, some nightclub work with Beverly Wills, the daughter of Joan Davis, and a lot of early television shows. He played a boyfriend on the *Stu Erwin Show* and two or three different characters on *I Married Joan*. "And gee whiz, I just went from one show to another. *Father Knows Best*; a regular on the old *Ray Milland Show*; Red Skelton used to always love to have me on. I did his first movie, *Whistling in the Dark*. I was in it a whole five or six minutes. I picked up a video of it the other day and it's really strange when you see yourself and you don't remember doing it. But Red Skelton was absolutely wonderful. He was funny. I was really fortunate to have worked with him. When I was doing his television show, he liked having me because I'd break up. It was done live, and he always did two shows. He did a warm-up show and had all the audience there, and after that was over with he worked out any bugs and you'd go ahead and do the full-blown show live. I remember one show when he did Clem Kadiddlehopper, and I got laughing so hard I just couldn't get my lines out. I said, 'I apologize. I won't do that.' And he said 'I want you to do that. If you don't do it you're fired.'"

Leon was in the first television show that Michael Landon appeared in. They played high school students on *The Loretta Young Show*. "I was this nerdy little guy who completely flips out and becomes a psycho. I pull a knife and go after Landon. It was really interesting because that was the era where method acting was the big thing. I remember going home at night really wiped out because we were very much into it. I'm surprised Michael still had a throat because I had a knife right there," Leon laughed. "So I did do a lot of television and continued on, and finally toward the end I got over to Disney and did the Flubber pictures—*Absent Minded Professor* and *Son of Flubber*—and then did one with Annette [Funicello] and Tommy Kirk called *The Monkey's Uncle*, and that's the last one I did.

"Actually, I had started working outside of the business when I got a call from Disney. I said, 'Sorry, I can't do it.' They sent me the script and they had the character's name Leon—they wrote it for me! So how could I turn it down? I was working for an oil company and I said to them, 'I've got to get off to do this film. Walt Disney wrote a movie and put my name in it. That's my character. I can't let anybody else do it. I've *got* to do it.' I was actually going to quit to do the movie. But they were just gracious. They said to go ahead and do it and to take as much time as I wanted. I loved Disney. I had done *So Dear to My Heart*, and some voice-overs on *Bambi*, so I knew him for a thousand years."

Leon does not have a particular favorite role among his numerous credits, but can quickly point out the worst film that he appeared in. "It was called *The Ghost of Dragstrip Hollow* for Roger Corman and American International. I did four or five there and finally this one came up. I've seen bad films, but I've never seen anything like this. It was absolutely asinine, but it sold and Corman is now highly respected in the business. There were some really strange ones that we did over there, but that one was the worst," Leon laughed. We wanted to know if Leon felt that his career interfered at all in his being a regular kid. "Of course," he answered. "But you have to look at which is better, which is worse. I think possibly *the* one thing is that I've never grown up. I'm a 66-year-old kid and I don't know if that's bad. It's okay I think. I get really excited about stupid things. I do stupid things just because I never had the opportunity to do them growing up. There was a long time where I wasn't thinking as an adult; I was always a child in my rationale and perspective. But going into the business world, after a while you better shape up or you're not there anymore," Leon laughed. "You know what I said? I've always wanted to have a life where I was married, had 2½ kids, a dog and a cat, play bridge every Friday night, every Saturday play golf, go to church on Sunday morning, drink a martini when I come home from work, and I'd be bored to tears. That would last about two months and I would scream. I envy those kinds of lives, but...." he trailed off.

We asked him whether, as a child actor, he was treated any differently by the director than the adult actors. "They didn't dare because they had the teachers there," Leon replied. "I've seen them try and I've seen the teacher go up and say, 'All right, if you do that one more time we're leaving.' And they would. As a child, I've never had a director go after me, but I've seen them go after others and make the kids cry. You're talking about a little baby, and that's not right. Unfortunately, many times the parents didn't know what to do. They were lost so they would just let it happen. I worked with John Ford just before he did the trilogy of films with John Wayne, but can't remember the name of the film. Isn't it awful not to remember what you did? But we were so young and didn't care, but when I got older it put me through college, so it was absolutely wonderful."

In summing up his feelings about his acting career, Leon stated, "I had tremendous opportunities that I would have never had and I met people I would have never met. Jimmy Dean, Natalie Wood and I did a television show on *G.E. Theater* and that kicked off *Rebel Without a Cause*. So I worked with these kind of people. I've really had some wonderful experiences. Also, I think, because I grew up in an era where there were very artistic people working in the business, and you, as a child, almost had to know how to handle them as much as them handling you because some could be very mean. Some, like Michael Curtiz, were just artistically different. If they were *with* you it made it so much easier for you as a kid, and a kid knows. You manipulate a little bit with those people, which, as a result, has helped me all of my life. I just don't know a stranger, I'm very easy with people, and it just seems like everything works well. I have to attribute it to that early schooling. Actually, it was a schooling. As far as the actor part itself, I always kind of laughed at myself and thought I was pretty bad, but that's not true. I've seen some things that I'm really impressed with, like the other day when I saw that film with Red Skelton. I thought, 'That's good.' *Son of Lassie* and *Just for You* with Jane Wyman and Bing Crosby were on television the other night, and I thought 'I remember that. That's interesting. Not bad.'"

Beverly Washburn

Beverly Washburn was born in Hollywood, California on Thanksgiving Day, November 25, 1943. She got her start in the business at the age of three. "I modeled children's clothes, and also had an agent who sent me around on film auditions, but I never got anything because I didn't have any credits. My older sister Audrey was an acrobat and did benefit shows at various veteran hospitals and I sort of tagged along and sang. When I was six, I was with my sister at the Long Beach hospital, and met Jock Mahoney. He asked my mother if I had an agent, and when she said yes, he said that I should be working."

About six months later, Beverly's agent sent her on a film audition to Columbia studios. "While my mother and I were in the waiting room, she read the script which said 'There sits little Welda Kowalski with her big brown eyes and long brown hair.' Well, I am blonde and blue eyed. Mother turned to me and said, 'Honey, you won't get this part because you're not what they're looking for, but just go in and read to the best of your knowledge.' Just then Jock Mahoney, who was under contract to Columbia, happened to walk through the lobby. He saw us and asked my mother what I was there for and she told him. He then went in the office and told the producer I had done this and that, and I hadn't done a thing. They gave me the part on his say so. That was my first part."

In the picture, Beverly played a little girl who contracts smallpox from Evelyn Keyes. "It's called *The Killer That Stalked New York* because everybody that she comes in contact with dies from catching smallpox. We are in a waiting room where I'm talking to her. She has a really neat broach on her coat and I tell her that it's pretty; she gives it to me and I give her a hug and thank her, and that's how I contract smallpox. In the next scene I'm in the hospital bed with an oxygen tent, and then I die. So I died in my first film.

"After I had that one speaking role, it was a lot easier to go on from there. After that I did *Here Comes the Groom* with Bing Crosby, and then *The Greatest Show on Earth* with Jimmy Stewart." Reflecting on her work with Cecil B. DeMille, Beverly said, "He was great. I was seven years old at the time and it was not until years later that I realized I had worked with Cecil B. DeMille, but when you're that little he is just a person. You don't have the concept of fame, but he was very nice to me and so was Jimmy Stewart. Then I did *Shane*." During the making of *Shane* in Jackson Hole, Wyoming, Beverly became very ill. "I contracted some really bad flu. They thought I had polio so they took me to emergency. Instead of sending me back to Los Angeles, they kept me in the hospital there for a week. I didn't have a big part—I was one of the Lewis children. I already had the contract so they waited for me rather than replacing me, which was really nice. I remember we went up to the ski lift one day and Alan Ladd got up to the top and was too scared to go back down. They had to send a helicopter for him. That was so funny because after that everyone teased him unmercifully because he was supposed to be the rough and tough guy." Beverly next worked with Dinah Shore and Alan Young in a picture called *Aaron Slick from Pumpkin Crick* which was followed by *The Juggler* with Kirk Douglas at Columbia. "Part of that was filmed in Jerusalem, but I didn't get to go on location. They filmed my part right on the stage at Columbia. Then I started getting into television."

Beverly Washburn

Beverly worked with Jack Benny on both television and radio. "I did a couple of the *Jack Benny Radio Show*s and they were great. In fact he became my lifelong hero and mentor. I worked with Jack throughout my whole life in the business and we became best friends. I toured with him in 1971 in a comedy skit that played Lake Tahoe, Las Vegas, all over the

Beverly was featured with Kirk Douglas in the Columbia drama, *The Juggler* (1953).

East Coast, and on *The Hollywood Palace*. It was a wonderful experience. He was a very giving, generous man. He gave me many gifts throughout my lifetime: a Saint Christopher with 'To Beverly, with love, Jack Benny' on it, a string of pearls, and when I had my appendix out, he sent me flowers at the hospital. He was just really wonderful."

Conditions arose in the family which resulted in Beverly becoming the major source of income. "My mother was a homemaker and never did work," she explained. "Then when my dad's health began to fail, I basically was the breadwinner. I worked so much growing up. But that's a whole other story because in the end I had nothing left of all the money I made."

Beverly worked with Clayton Moore and Jay Silverheels in the feature film *The Lone Ranger*. "That was really fun. In fact, when Clayton Moore was getting on Silver to ride off into the sunset, his pants split open, but he didn't know it. The director decided to let the film roll as a gag. So he was riding out with his bare butt hanging out. Of course when they finally said, 'Cut,' everybody was laughing really hard. He was embarrassed, but he was a sport about it. We filmed the location scenes in Kanab,

Utah, like when the Indians kidnap me. The sets were filmed at the Warner Bros. lot and at Iversons Ranch."

Beverly also had enjoyable memories of her work on Walt Disney's *Old Yeller*. "It was wonderful. It was during the days of *The Mickey Mouse Club*, so I felt very fortunate that I was selected. After all, they could have used any one of the Mouseketeers because they were all good actresses. I had to read for the part, and I got it. They had a big red trailer on the lot that all the kids had school in, so I had school with all the Mouseketeers and have remained friends with some of them throughout the years. Tommy Kirk and I hit it off real well. We went steady for about an hour I think," she laughed. "He gave me this really romantic ring. It was like a skull and crossbones. I think I was 12 and he was 13. We have remained friends, as I have with Kevin Corcoran. Kevin got out of the business and likes being on the other side of the camera. Tommy had some bad things happen to him over the years, but now he's back on his feet and has his own carpet cleaning business."

Beverly met Walt Disney at the auditions for her part but didn't get to know him very well. "He pretty much stayed away from the set. *Old Yeller* was filmed on the Disney Ranch in Lake Sherwood and on the Disney lot. The dog was fabulous. His name was Spike. They got him out of the dog pound for four dollars and trained him."

Beverly performed in many television shows, and one of her favorite people she worked with was Loretta Young. They remained close up to the time of Young's death in 2000. "One Christmas she sent me a beautiful dove made out of stained glass that you hook on to a window as a symbol of love and devotion, and also a little angel book. She was really sweet. I did about five or six of her anthology shows where I usually had the lead. Years later when I was 19 she did the *New Loretta Young Show* and asked me if I would play one of her daughters."

Beverly played Kit Wilson in the situation comedy series, *Professional Father*. "I did that when I was 11. It was with Steve Dunne and Barbara Billingsley, who went on after that to become June Cleaver on *Leave It to Beaver*. I worked on that show too. I had a mad crush on Tony Dow, so it was like a dream come true for me to work on that show. And it was wonderful to see Barbara again. Tony's directing now. He directed a couple of episodes of *Babylon Five*. He said it was too hard for him to make the transition in acting because no matter what else he would do, people always associated him with Wally Cleaver."

Beverly's television credits also include the science fiction and horror shows *Thriller*, *One Step Beyond* and *Star Trek*. "All of those were fun for me. I had worked for John Newland when he directed two of the

Loretta Young Show episodes that I had done. So when *One Step Beyond* came about I didn't have to read for it. When I went to the audition he just said, 'You got the part.' *Thriller* was great because that was Boris Karloff. He wasn't in the episode, but he was the host. He was on the set because the platform for that show had him introduce each guest, and the camera would pan around to each person, so I got to meet him."

Speaking of *Star Trek*, Beverly stated, "When I did *Star Trek* I had no idea at the time it would go on to be such a world-renowned program. It's amazing to me because the show was only on for three seasons. My episode, *The Deadly Years*, was the second season, and the series wasn't all that popular then. I just had a small part. I get a virus and start to age, and then we all age and I die from it. Old age. I was in make-up for 4½ hours every day. They had to make a plaster cast of my face and then from that they made a rubber mask. While the cast was drying I had to breathe from a straw because everything was closed around my face. That was kind of tricky, but it was fun. This was one of my best things because I had no idea that 32 years later I would be going around on tours for *Star Trek*. I never was much of a science fiction fan, so it was amazing."

Beverly enjoyed every part she did. "It was something I really looked forward to and I had a photographic memory when I was little. I was blessed with the ability to just look at the script and know my lines, which came in handy when I had to do a show called *Matinee Theater*. It was on every day at noon on NBC, and in those days it was live. It was scary because you didn't get that second chance. One of the episodes I did, I played this very precocious little girl. I had the lead in it so I had tons of dialogue, but on top of that in every scene I would start to recite poetry, so not only did I have to memorize all my lines but I had to learn all of this poetry. I probably couldn't do that now, but back then it was easy for me because I could visualize it as I was saying it."

The TV westerns of the 1950s took advantage of Beverly's talents. He appeared in such shows as *Fury, Wagon Train, Zane Grey Theater* and *The Texan*. "I did about three episodes of *Wagon Train*. My favorite one was *The Tobias Jones Story* with Lou Costello. It was the only dramatic role that he ever did, and he was great. He had a hard time memorizing his lines because when he did Abbott and Costello he pretty much had free rein, he could ad-lib and do whatever he wanted. Ward Bond was the star of the show, and every time Lou would go up on his lines instead of stopping he would look right into the camera and say, 'How are you Ward?' It was so funny. And Ward Bond, I really loved him. He was very gruff but he was very nice, and he liked me. He gave me an autographed picture that I have on my wall. It says, 'To Beverly, the finest little actress.'

So that was really a treasure for me. But he had a very foul mouth, not meaning to, but was just one of those people where it just kind of rolled off his tongue. They had a school teacher on the set from the Los Angeles Board of Education. These teachers were called welfare workers because they were there for your welfare, to make sure everything was okay. One day she threatened to pull me from the set if Ward used one more cuss word because she felt it was inappropriate for a child's ears. She had that much power—if she wanted to pull me from the set she could have. So they had to talk to Ward, and after that he watched his mouth around me."

The first time that Beverly had to ride a horse was for an episode of *Fury*. "I don't think I rode very well. I never took lessons, but if you were a minor usually what they would do—even in *The Lone Ranger* when I'm riding the pony which I could have done—because of insurance purposes, they would have a double for me, and she was a midget because I was a child. They wouldn't allow me to do it even though I wanted to."

Beverly's preference appeared to be dramatic roles. "I seem to do more of the dramas and it seemed like I was always crying. When I was about 12 I worked at MGM in a show called *The Best of Post*, in an episode called *Martha*. I was Martha and Jackie Coogan was my father. It was a really wonderful role. The mother died and I'm left in charge of the family, but I'm just a little girl. I can't remember the whole gist of it, but I loved working with Jackie Coogan. That was a favorite. And then on *The Bell Telephone Hour* I did a show called *The Man with a Beard*. It called for a lot of screaming and crying. In it my father grows a beard and all the townspeople are up in arms because of it. They beat me up, cover me in filth and cut off part of my hair, and I come in screaming. How they did this with my hair was interesting because I had very long blonde hair. They parted it in the middle and then took one side and braided it and pinned it down flat against my head. From the make-up room they took Van Heflin's toupee and pinned it on because his hair color was the same as mine. So on one side of my head is this toupee, making it appear as though my hair was about an inch long on that side. It was pretty funny that I was wearing Van Heflin's toupee."

After that role the producer told Beverly, "I have another part that I've never been able to find anybody to do, but now I'm going to bring it off the shelf and let you do it." That's when Beverly made another of her favorites, *The Key*, with Kevin McCarthy. "I played a deaf-dumb mute. It was the true story of a girl named Laura Bridgeman who later became one of the teachers of Helen Keller. It was a difficult part because my eyes were supposed to have been burned out by a fever, so I wore a blindfold.

Usually if you can't emote with your voice you can emote with your eyes because you can use your eyes to express yourself, but I couldn't do that. I couldn't speak and I couldn't show any emotion so it was kind of a challenging role, but I really loved doing it."

Beverly recalled a potentially dangerous situation when she was working in an episode of *Fury*. "A scene called for me to be on a mountain on which I slip and fall down the side, and of course Fury comes to the rescue. They throw a rope down to me and tie the other end around Fury's neck and he backs up and pulls me up. They had a double for me who was dressed in the same wardrobe, but when she got on top of the fake cliff and saw that they were going to have her jump about 30 feet into a firemen's net and film her doing the fall, she looked down and refused to do it. The director came to me and asked if I would do it. It became a big deal because the welfare worker said I didn't have to do it and was going to report them. But the director said, 'It will be fun and you'll really like it. You'll be saving the day if you do it because if you don't, it's going to hold up production since we don't have a double for you.' I really was petrified, but I didn't want them to know because I felt like I would be letting them down. The welfare worker said, 'No. You're not doing it.' I said, 'I don't want to let them down; maybe it'll be fun,' but I was really scared. She said, 'I'll leave it up to you.' My mother asked me and I said, 'I'll do it.' When I went up there it looked like a million miles down. I was petrified. The director said, 'Take you're time. I'm going to roll the camera. When you're ready, just jump.' I came so close to saying, 'No, I can't do it,' but the longer they waited the worse it got because I thought, 'Oh my goodness, if I back out now they'll really be upset.' I was just petrified, but I did it. Looking back, I don't know why I did because it was dangerous. That was the only time I remember anything like that."

In 1964, Beverly appeared in *Spider Baby* with Lon Chaney, Jr. "The reason why I decided to do that movie was because I wanted the opportunity to work with him," Beverly explained. "It was a really low-budget film and now it has been rereleased after 30 years and has become a cult classic. It's very big in Europe. It was great because Lon Chaney was just a sweet, gentle soul and I loved him."

Beverly had a difficult time in the transition years between child actress and adult actress. "I never really quit the business, but my roles gradually got less and less and it was hard to make the transition. Then I got married, but I was too young. I was in my twenties and never should have gotten married. We got divorced and I decided to just go away. My sister was living in Spain at the time so I went there and lived for seven months. Then I came back and did a little bit of acting, but nothing to speak of. The parts were fewer and farther between. I never had any other skills besides acting because that's all I had done all my life, so I just took odd jobs doing things I really didn't like. I didn't think I would ever work again in the business, and then one day while shopping I ran into Marvin Paige who was the casting director from *General Hospital*. I hadn't seen him in many years. He had cast me in a lot of things as a child. He asked me what I was doing and I said I was on my way to work. He said, 'Great. What show.' 'Oh no,' I said, 'not that kind of work. I'm going to work as a receptionist.' 'You've got to be kidding,' he replied. 'How would you like to work on *General Hospital?* There's no role right now, but I can get you on as one of the nurses at the hub.' So he kept me busy on that. I worked at least once a week for four years.

"Then I met the man who was to become my husband. He was working for Hilton Hotels and got transferred to Dallas so I had to leave *General Hospital*. About four years ago, my husband got transferred to Las Vegas, and during this time I started doing commercials. I've done 50 since I've been here. It's different than the L.A. market, though; they are local commercials so you don't get any residuals, but these commercials have been a good thing. Then I got hooked up with this promoter from *Star Trek* and last year did 12 shows. And I'm a massage therapist and have a clientele for that. So that is what I'm doing now."

Beverly spoke of the time before she left Hollywood when the offers for work came to and end and her feelings of rejection. "That always happens, and that's part of being in the business because there is a lot of it. I've had some parents ask if I thought they should put their child in the business and the only advice I can give them is to make sure it is what the child wants to do and not what the parents want them to do, because there is nothing sadder than a child who's pushed into it because the parents want it. But if the child does want it, if that's their dream, they have to at least try it because all of a sudden one day you're going to be 40 and look back and think, 'What if?' You have to follow your dreams and follow your heart and if it's something you really want just go for it, but you have to be prepared for the rejection because there's a lot of it. Sometimes you take it real personally, but it's not anything you did. It has nothing to do with how you read for the part; they may not think you looked right or wanted your hair color to be different. It's real easy to feel rejected. As a child I was really lucky because I went from one job to the next pretty much."

When Beverly was not working as a child, she enjoyed her dolls. "That was my hobby when I was a little girl. In fact, Bing Crosby gave me one when I worked on *Here Comes the Groom* and got me started on that. I got very upset if anyone called them dolls because to me they were my babies. They all had names. When I went on location I wanted to take them all with me, but my mother said I could only take two. I couldn't take them all because there would be no room in the suitcase. So I put all their names in a hat and drew two names because I didn't want to hurt their feelings. So as a child, I must say my main pastime was playing with my dolls." As for today when she is not at work, Beverly said, "I like going to movies. I like reading, doing crafts. I enjoy cooking, and when the weather is nice I like playing tennis. My pet charities are all animal charities. I have three dogs, two cats and fish."

In summarizing her feelings regarding her career as a child on celluloid, Beverly said, "Looking back, my mother always wanted me to be a star, but she never pushed me. It was left up to me. I never really achieved stardom, but I have some of the most wonderful memories and I wouldn't trade them for anything in the world. When I look back and think of the people that I worked with, like Loretta Young, Jack Benny, Bing Crosby, George Stevens, Cecil B. DeMille, George Reeves, Kirk Douglas and on and on, I feel very blessed. I think I had a pretty normal childhood because I went to public school in between shows and my parents kept me grounded. I wish a few things could have been different, like the way my money was spent. I made quite a bit of money as a child because I worked constantly, and when I came of age I had nothing. Everybody looks back over their lives and there is always things you would change, but then everything kind of leads to other things. I guess if you changed them you wouldn't be led into certain circumstances, so I feel I had a good childhood and a nice career. I wish I had had a better direction in it, maybe an agent or manager who could have geared me a little bit better. I didn't make great choices and it was harder in the end to get parts. But I like being in Vegas; it's kind of like the story about being a big fish in a small pond. In Los Angeles it was very difficult for me to get roles. People that remember me are people who are in their fifties and sixties, and nowadays all the casting people are like 12, and they don't know me from Adam. So it has been really fun for me here in Vegas. I don't know what the future is going to hold, but for now I think I am just going to stay here and see what happens. It's a great place to live."

Bobs Watson

Bobs Watson was born November 16, 1930, in Glendale, California. "I'm the youngest of nine children," Bobs said. "All my brothers and sisters and my father had appeared in motion pictures before I came along. Collectively our whole family has done over a thousand motion pictures. We were all born at home on Berkeley Avenue about six hundred feet from the offices of Mack Sennett. "Hollywood did not start out where it is now known as Hollywood today. It started on Glendale Boulevard between where Alvarado and Glendale Boulevard come together. The studios were all up and down on either side of the road, so whenever they needed a kid for a movie they would come over and ask my dad if he had a kid at home about so big. So one of us would wind up being in the film playing that particular part. There were no unions then, there were no agents per se and you pretty well dealt with the people who were involved. It was a great upbringing for me. We were known as the First Family of Hollywood. That's what they called us because we had been around since the very beginning and when they made movies they could always count on the Watson kids. We grew up in an atmosphere of God and Christ. That was our mainstream. That's what kept us together as a family and which pretty well still keeps us together. That was the one ace in the hole for any kid actor, and without that Hollywood is going to ruin them. So if you talk to kids that had the rug pulled out underneath them, that's a general story. They are children that are used up. When the cuteness is gone they throw them on the heap with all the other kids. It happens to every kid actor that there is. If anyone would come to me and ask me, 'I have a child that's talented. What should I do?' I'd say 'Don't do it. Keep them out of it; it's going to ruin him.' At one point there were seven major studios who wanted me under contract. That was after I had done *Boys Town*

Bobs Watson

and *On Borrowed Time*. I made about six major films in one year and I was a free-lance actor. MGM wanted me under contract so bad that they could taste it. My dad didn't know what to do. He had nine kids and he wanted to treat them all fairly, so one day he went over to see Spencer Tracy who was on the lot and asked him what he should do. He said 'I respect you as a man, I respect you as an actor and I would really appreciate any input that you can give me as to what I should do with Bobs.' Tracy said, 'You really want to know, Mr. Watson? Don't do it. Do not put him under contract. The studio will own him and they will ruin him. He's a sweet little boy. He's a good little actor. Don't put him under contract because they'll just walk all over him and you will lose your son. It's as simple as that.' So my dad turned down a really big seven-year contract. I continued to do films until the early forties. Then World War II started and I began to grow up. I wasn't the tiny cute boy that I was and they stopped making kid films for the most part and turned to war movies and the like. I was at an awkward age anyway, so I was like any other kid thrown on the heap.

"I received fan mail from every country that showed motion pictures throughout the world. My job on Saturdays was to sit down and answer every letter that I got. I personally autographed every picture I sent out. My dad said that if they thought enough of you to write, you should do that. Times have changed. Many people are really not much interested in having something personal from you; they want it as a collector's item;

they want to be able to sell it. A lot of that commercialism I find is disheartening.

"So, being a kid actor is not all that it's cracked up to be. When I first saw Macaulay Culkin in *Home Alone,* all my brother Delmar and I could do was to shake our heads and say what is that kid going to be like in another ten years. It's all come to pass. His mother and father used him and fought over the money, and this happens to kids all the time. You talk to any of them. Jay North—that poor kid must have gone through hell from what I have heard. It's tragic to hear the pain that young fellow has gone through. I really feel badly about that. I was lucky because I had a father who believed in God. I look back on my dad and he was an outstanding man. He was one in a million. He and my mother raised nine children, never went on welfare during the depression; he always got out and worked and made money to put food on the table. There wasn't much of it, but what was there was nourishing. There were 11 people at every meal and he always found a way somehow to put food on the table.

"I never knew what it was to be home on Christmas Eve because our whole family would go out caroling. We'd go to the Children's French Hospital downtown Los Angeles and put on a whole show for them. My mother would make clothing so we'd all be dressed the same. We'd go to some of the older people of our church that had been pretty well forgotten, and they always looked forward to us coming around and singing to them. Sometimes my folks would have something to give to sustain them. That's how I was raised. So when I worked in films, I was blessed with an awareness of people's feelings. My dad and my mother were both wonderful people."

In Bobs' first film, he was carried on as a baby. "I was six months old," he noted. "They would need people from time to time, and I had so many brothers and sisters that they could always depend upon us to do what the director wanted and get it in the first take."

Bobs reflected on his role in the 1938 film *In Old Chicago.* "My brother Bill, Gene Reynolds and I played the O'Leary boys as children. Our father, who was played by J. Anthony Hughes, was a nice guy and had a wonderful Irish brogue. We went to Modesto to film the prairie scenes where we were in a wagon on our way to Chicago. In the story a train goes by and the kids say, 'Let's race the train, Dad.' So he says, 'Okay. I think I will.' He starts the horses running and we're racing the train. The whistle is blowing and the wagon hits a ditch and the tongue pulls loose from the wagon and drags our father to death. Just before he dies we all come running up to him and we were all supposed to cry. Well, they didn't know what they were going to get with me because I just opened up a faucet. I was sobbing my head off. It came very easily to me. From that I got an interview to have a screen test for *Boys Town*, and then from there it just took off."

Talking about *Boys Town*, Bobs said, "Spencer Tracy was great. The thing I remember most about him were his eyes. In one of the first scenes I come in and ask for candy and they establish that I get it. In the next scene when I came in for candy he gives me some and asks 'Have you brushed your teeth?' I hadn't brushed my teeth and I lie about it and say, 'I lost my toothbrush.' 'Lost it? Well, we're going to have to do something about this,' and he makes a big thing about it which plays on my guilt. So I start to put the candy back. Just before we shot the scene, Norman Taurog, the director, said, 'Bobby, now when you're putting the candy back don't look at it. Reach in your pocket, take it out and look Uncle Spencer right in the eyes.' And I'll never forget those eyes. I remember the scene, not from the camera's point of view but from mine. He was just a marvelous guy. I liked most of the people I worked with. I tried not to be a fresh little brat and my dad always tried to keep me a nice kid, always call people mister, never by their first names. The closest I came to using first names was my reference to Tracy and Taurog as Uncle Spencer and Uncle Norman. Those were wonderful days."

Bobs went on to say, "When Spencer Tracy won the Academy Award for playing the part of Father Flannigan in *Boys Town*, the night that he received the Oscar he sent it to Father Flannigan. It is in Boys Town right now in their Hall of History. Also the night that he received it he sent me a telegram saying, 'Thank you Bobby dear. Half of this statue belongs to you. Love, Uncle Spencer.'"

Asked if he had any reflections on working with Lionel Barrymore, Bobs replied, "He was a remarkable man. The first time I worked with him was in *Calling Dr. Kildare*. I played a cripple in it. I'm in a lot of pain; both legs have been crippled, and he tries to get me to walk. He puts braces on my legs. I remember my first scene with him. Whenever I met someone I was very shy. My dad always told me never to be a smart aleck, so I always kind of hung back. I would never just go up and say, 'Hello, my name is Bobs Watson.' I would be introduced. I met him and was awestruck. I had seen him in motion pictures many times, admired his work even as a child, but we rehearsed this scene and then when it came time for the take Mr. Barrymore became Dr. Gillespie and I became that little boy. I would usually get it in the first take. I knew my lines. I knew everybody's lines. I had rehearsed it with my dad so I knew the kind of relationship I wanted to have with this man. Maybe a little fearful, a little shy, whatever it was. The scene where I'm supposed to walk after the roller skates was very powerful and done in the first take. At that time if a kid could do something like that he was one of a kind. I would always look over at my dad after a take and he would nod if it was good. Sometimes we would want to take the scene over, but the director was satisfied and we had to move on. But that was the check and balance of working.

"Barrymore was a very unusual man. I never knew my grandfather, so he was sort of like a grandpa to me. Especially in *On Borrowed Time*. We had a number of scenes together which were pretty heavy duty. When you're working in a film, especially with big stars, they'll shoot a master shot and then they will come in for a two shot and then go to closeups. Very often they will shoot the star first for the closeups and get them done while it's still fresh in their minds, then they go to the other people. And very often the star that you would be working with will go off to the dressing room and the script girl would come in and give you his lines, which really doesn't give you a chance to play off the real character. But Barrymore, crippled up as he was with arthritis at the time, would squeeze his way in beside the camera and give me his dialogue. I didn't think too much about it at the time, but when you look back on things like that and then start working with other people and see how they don't treat you well or they don't aid you in doing your part, then you began to realize how well you had it working with people like Barrymore and Tracy.

"When I played the part of Pud, a child whose grandfather was going to die in *On Borrowed Time*, my dad said to me, 'How would you feel if I was going to go away and you'd never see me again?' Just based upon that, I would learn my dialogue and go out and cry, and they were sincere, real tears. It was no acting.

"Every once in a while a movie that I did would be showing in some theater and

Bobs as "Pud" and Lionel Barrymore as "Gramps" in the film *On Borrowed Time* (MGM, 1939).

maybe the family would all get together and go out and see it. I'd sit there and wait and see if it was like I thought it was. I was astounded by what I was able to do and very proud of my work. It was because of my home life. I was not aware that we were poor. We had one another and that was all that mattered. From my own personal experiences at home and the love that I received there from my folks, I think that was why I was able to do what I did. My dad literally directed me in the films that I did. We'd go to the studio and the director would always say the blocking is going to be this way and I want you to do this and that, but primarily my interpretation of what I did was because of my dad. He always went to the film set with me. That was it: if he wasn't there, I didn't work."

When asked if it was easy to bring on the tears, Bobs answered, "Oh yeah. You just tell me what you wanted. In the scene in *Men of Boys Town* where my dog is killed and we're going to bury it, Norman Taurog, who directed, said, 'All right Bobby, this is the scene where I want you to cry.' I said to Uncle Norman, as he wanted me to refer to him, 'Do you want halfway down tears or all the way down tears?' A friend who was an extra said that he was astounded because I could control my crying that much. I could either hold it back or really let it go. Every once in a while we'd have to shoot a scene over because I was crying so hard that they couldn't understand what I was saying. But that's what I was able to do and that was the thing I did as a child."

Bobs worked with Errol Flynn in *Dodge City*. "Flynn was a likable guy. I mean you couldn't help but like him. He was a scoundrel," Bobs laughed, "but he was very alive, very fine. He was a movie star. Some of the scenes I had with him were not the close scenes which I had with Tracy, Barrymore, and Mickey Rooney, but he appreciated my work and we were friends. I didn't have the opportunity to get to know him as well as I would have liked to, but he was quite a guy."

Bobs worked in the film *Wyoming* with Wallace Beery. Reflecting on that, Bobs said, "I liked him. We did not hit it off at first. He played Mr. Big, but there was something—I don't know what I did, maybe it was the Pee Wee in me—and we grew very close and he was just a wonderful guy. He wanted to redo *The Champ* and do it with me, but time and whatever did not allow that to happen. He was for the most part a mean son-of-a-gun and a terrible ad-libber, just the worst," Bobs laughed. "But he was sure nice to me."

When asked if he was ever in a dangerous situation while filming, Bobs replied, "I guess you might say that being dragged to death by horses in *Dodge City* was potentially dangerous. I always did my own stunts though. We were in the wagon coming along when a gunfight breaks out.

There were wires on the horses so they wouldn't get away. There were doubles for Olivia de Havilland and me in the wagon until they came in for a closeup. I got my hands around the reins and I'm pulling them, and the camera was down shooting up, and I'm jerked out of the wagon. I was afraid at first. The wagon was way up high and I was little. Some guy was going to catch me and that worried me. When I heard that it was my dad, no problem; then it was fun. They jerked me out of the wagon and my dad caught me. Then they cut to a long shot and the horses break loose and pull a dummy out. But then they wanted to get a closeup of me being dragged, and so they did. I put on some body padding and went to work. So I did my own stunt work."

Talking about the problems facing kid actors, Bobs related, "I kept my head screwed on as much as possible. I still have a lot of scars from working in films. Being a child actor does take its toll. There is no getting away from it; you do have scars, and I'm still carrying the pain of a lot of them that I don't know about. Just in the past eight or nine years I've become more aware of who I really am and equally aware of a lot of the little red wagons that I've been dragging around behind me with all kinds of scars in them. I was so well known I couldn't go anywhere. I don't blame people if they identify you and want your autograph. But when you go somewhere you can't do anything. I went downtown one day with my mother and stopped at a hot dog stand where you could get a hot dog and a root beer for a dime. Someone recognized me and there must have been a hundred people around there. No privacy. There was a municipal swimming pool in Griffith Park where I used to go when I was a kid. I was in the water playing and was asked if I was Bobs Watson. I thought, 'Oh my gosh, I don't want this to happen here,' so I said, 'No, I'm not.' And they kept pushing it. Pretty soon it got so bad that I had to get out of the pool. As I started to walk around to go in and change, some kid had a tennis ball soaking wet and threw it. It hit me on the head like a rock. Those kind of things take a toll.

"Those kind of things also take its toll when suddenly you're at a certain age and you're not the cute little boy you used to be and suddenly you're not working. And you think, 'What happened to the world I used to live in?' It's gone. The worst thing that a child would say is, 'I've done something wrong. I am not acceptable. I'm not what people want anymore.' You get a complex about it. I had to live with that type of thing. You think it's just you. Dick Moore wrote a book titled *Twinkle Twinkle Little Star* on the result of what happens. That book should be like a bible to all kid actors. I'm not trying to say that I had a terrible life, because I haven't. I've had a wonderful life. I'm just saying that there is a price to be paid for being a child actor if it's nothing more than 'Hey, I was really something. Now I'm nothing.' What do you do with that?

"When you're not wanted anymore, what resources are you going to use to feel good about yourself? There were things I needed to do. I obtained a college education, I worked for my brothers in the photo business, and I was called to the ministry. I literally had a calling. I went to Claremont School of Theology, which was 40 days in the wilderness for me. It was a very liberal college and I was always more conservative, but I needed to go there in order to find out how liberal people thought. That challenged me in what I believe and I can now find myself standing toe to toe with some of these people. "While I was going to seminary I felt very insecure and like I didn't belong there. I was wondering why God called me to the ministry, which He did. It was a calling as if God was asking me, 'Isn't there something more in life than just being in motion pictures?' I had a television series at the time called *Hot Off the Wires* with Jim Backus. It was a syndicated show made by California National Productions—a subsidiary of NBC—in conjunction with MGM. At the time of the series, I lived in a home that Charlie Chaplin built on Poinsettia Place. It was built on the order of French Normandy. I was single, had a '56 Thunderbird and a television series. I had the world by the tail. I worked 45 or 60 of the television shows including *Bonanza* and *The Virginian*. Nobody ever mentions that. They only talk about when I was a kid, but I was one of the ones that made the bridge. I went into films and I was doing well. They were sending me scripts, and that was when I was called to the ministry. I gave up a lot to go into it. I didn't do sour grapes as if I had nothing else to do. I was on my way and I gave it up. I'm happy I did it. I have no regrets whatsoever. I have used my talents in radio, television, stage and motion pictures in my ministry, and my faith in God is what kept me going.

"I have scars within me which not everybody knows about—they're my own personal scars. I've learned to deal with some of them and I'm able to better put them into perspective now. That was because I had a good family that taught me about God and Christ. I'm not a holier-than-thou; I don't beat people over the head with the Bible and say you've got to do it my way. When I talk to people I say, 'You've got to do it your way. You make your own decisions. If you have questions you want to ask, come ask them. I'll give you some alternatives, but I'll never tell anybody what to do. I've never preached at anybody or at any group. I have never deliberately tried to hurt anybody from my pulpit. I have always preached what I felt was in my heart to preach on that Sunday morning. I've had a very honest ministry. For 33 years I was a minister. I retired July of 1997.

I've had 33 years as an actor. Evenly divided. Now I'm retired. I have prostate cancer and probably a year of quality life. I know where I've been, where I am, where I'm going, and I'm going to die and it's not going to be pleasant. It's going to be very difficult. But I have my relationship with God so I know it's going to be okay. We all have to go sometime; nobody gets out of this world alive," he laughed. "I believe that our families go on and we'll all be together again and will know each other, and we're going to find out some startling things when we get there."

Asked if, when he was a kid in school, he was treated any differently by his schoolmates because of being in films, Bobs stated, "You can't help but be. I mean, I was a movie star. I was known all over the world. I suppose there had to be some jealousy along that line when one student has great renown. I don't say any of this egotistically; it's just the way that it was. Heck, when I was a kid I thought everybody had nine kids in their families and that everybody was poor, and that everybody worked in motion pictures. I didn't give it much thought.

"But many of the other kids were a little standoffish. They didn't know quite how to speak to me. There were others that were friends and I always tried to be friendly. When I stopped making films I was about at that time in life when you're starting to grow up. I became very self-conscious and had a very low self-esteem. I was short and fat, so that didn't help it any. I thought no girl would ever want to date me or be my girlfriend. I had that attitude until I went into college. I carried that stigma with me, but you would never know it. I wore my masks very carefully. I knew how to act, I knew how to cover, and so I covered mainly with fun and with activities. I was the extrovert. If anything was going on, I was right in the middle of it and I made friends. I was a cheerleader in high school and was in every play that they did. But there was something else: I was a member of the Watson family and the last one to go through all the schools where my brothers and sisters had gone. I wanted to close up the reputation of the Watson family in good style. So I tried to be a good guy all the way through.

"In city college I got my AA degree in radio broadcasting production, and in L.A. State College I got my degree in drama and language arts. I had a B+ average in all the college work I did."

After his graduation, Bobs was drafted into the military. "Literally by the grace of God I got into instruction services and I did what I did best: I entertained. I must have done over 600 shows while I was in the military for civilian and military personnel around Fort Ord. I was loaned to a theater in Monterey where I did four plays, totaling a hundred performances. And I made 15 training films."

Asked if, after getting out of the military, it was easy for him to make the transition back into film acting, Bobs responded, "No, it was difficult. I had been very successful in the military doing plays so it wasn't like I was starting back to acting. But it was difficult in that the whole business had changed. It was re-establishing myself because everyone would say, 'Bobby Watson. I remember you when you were just a little guy.' I kept wanting to say, 'Look at me now. I can still act. Give me a job,' and it finally worked. So I started back. I proved myself. But it was not easy getting back into it. I had to pay my dues all over again with small parts and whatever, but always pretty good parts.

"I worked with my brothers in their photo business while I was trying to find parts, and that kept a roof over my head and food on the table while I was doing this," Bobs reminisced. "And then, like I said, I worked most of the shows of the late fifties and early sixties and had a television series with Jim Backus which I was just delighted with. I signed a contract with them for eight out of every 13 shows. They saw that I was talented. I could do my own stunts. I was a good actor and would get it in one take. I was a professional person. Once they found out all these things that I could do, out of the 39 shows that we did I was in 37 of them. The reason I wasn't in the other two was because they had already bought scripts that did not include my character of Sidney Watson. Toward the end, they were writing scripts for me. I was 30 years old and playing a teenager. I had a high voice, a moon face, was all thumbs, all left feet and a lot of energy, which is basically me. California National Productions made ten pilots that year and our show was the only one which sold. So after 39 episodes, California National Productions went out of business so that NBC could take it as a write-off. Otherwise we would have continued for at least two or three more seasons."

In *Grand Theft Auto*, Bobs was listed in the credits as Reverend Bobs Watson. "That film was directed by Ron Howard. I married Ron and Cheryl at Magnolia Park Church in Burbank. When he and his dad wrote the script of *Grand Theft Auto*, the only one that they wanted for the part of the minister was me. So I did it. Ron asked, 'How do you want your credits?' I said, 'I would like it to be Reverend Bobs Watson.' That's the only time I ever used that."

After retirement, Bobs appeared in a number of stage productions in southern California such as *Light Up the Sky*, *The Hobbit*, and *Of Mice and Men* in which he played the role of Candy.

Asked if he had a favorite film in which he worked, Bobs answered, "I will be the most remembered as Pee Wee, but my favorite film that I did was *On Borrowed Time*. I was eight years old when we made it and I felt in that film I was able to contribute myself. I was at that point in my life where I was able to contribute more of my own perception of Pud as well as what my dad had taught me and what Harold Bucquet, the director, wanted from me. So I would say that is my favorite film. It was the largest part that I had. It was a wonderful part, a wonderful script and had a wonderful director. Everybody in it was perfectly cast and I'm just so pleased to have been a part of a film like that. It's kind of a cult classic. It deals with death, and death is not a favorite subject for a lot of people, but the way in which death is dealt with in the film shows that it's not such a frightening and terrible thing and that families do go on together in the hereafter. Sir Cedric Hardwicke (who played death) was a very nice man and a real gentleman. I really liked him. To see how death was depicted really registers back here for me."

Looking over his acting career, Bobs summed up his feelings, stating, "I was blessed. People wonder why they're born. I don't know specifically why I was born, but I knew that I was in the business that I really enjoyed and loved. When I see some of the old films that my brothers and I were in I say, 'Hey, I'm a part of that era. I'm a part of the golden age of Hollywood which will never come again. It was a great time. Looking back over my life I would say I have fought the good fight, I have finished the course, I have kept the faith. The motion picture business has helped to formulate who I am. I had a good life."

In 1998, Bobs and his brothers and sisters were honored at Cinecon with a lifetime achievement award for their work in motion pictures. Bobs passed away at his home in Laguna Beach, California, on June 26, 1999.

Delmar Watson

Delmar Watson was born July 1, 1926, at his home in Los Angeles. Coy Watson Sr., his father, came to Los Angeles at the turn of the century and owned a couple of horses. "The studios wanted to rent them and when they found out he could ride they hired him to ride them. They paid him two dollars a day for the horse and two-fifty for him to ride. That was pretty good money in 1911. Then he became a property man, a special effects man, a casting director, and an assistant director. He was also a stunt man when he was riding the horses, so he was a real pioneer in the motion-picture industry."

Delmar had eight brothers and sisters who all worked in the movies, and seeing as how they lived next door to Mack Sennett's studio, they were asked on a regular basis to do bits in studio productions. "We were all sizes and sexes, so if they were in a hurry and needed a kid or some lady crossing the street with a baby carriage for the Keystone Cops to run over, they would come down and grab one of us. That's how we got started."

Delmar worked in his first movie when he was six months old. "My dad told me that by the time I was seven years old I had worked in 77 pictures. By the time I quit, I had worked in over 300. My brothers Bobs and Bill liked the business, but I didn't really care for it that much. I'm more of a realist," he laughed. "So that's how I got into the business It was kind of like breathing. We never thought too much about it; that's just what we did. It wasn't until they started all this nostalgia stuff about 20 years ago that I really began to realize what an impact my dad and our family had being pioneers in the business.

"My dad was the *first* Hollywood mother because we lived where Hollywood started. We were the first family of Hollywood, if you want

Delmar Watson in *Heidi* (20th Century–Fox, 1937).

to call it that. He was not a typical Hollywood mother because he knew the business. The directors knew that they could work with him in order to cut a lot of corners, because when you were working in pictures, during the school year you had to go to school three hours a day on the set. They would see to it that we had the three hours, but one day we happened to be working a lot and didn't get in our full hours. My dad told them we would make it up—the next day we would go to school four hours. So my dad knew how to work with them because he wasn't a typical Hollywood mother, but he *was* the first Hollywood mother."

Delmar's favorite film that he was involved with was the Frank Capra classic, *Mr. Smith Goes to Washington*. "That was by far the best picture that I was in. My brothers and I played the governor's sons who, around the dinner table, talk him into sending Jimmy Stewart to Washington. I'm the one that presented Jimmy with the briefcase. Of all the directors that I have worked with, Frank Capra was—as far as I was concerned—the best. This was primarily because he started out as a film editor and then became a director. He knew exactly what he was doing, and knew exactly how he could edit the film. He didn't tire out his actors and was just a good director."

While working with Capra, Delmar witnessed something that he had never seen done before. "Normally you had to know your lines, and when you went on the set, they would light it and get it ready. Then the director would go through the scene on the set, telling you what to do. But Frank Capra did something different. When we did the big scene around the table where there was a lot of really quick dialogue, and a raising of temperatures as far as the dialogue went, he sat us down at one of those long ten-foot tables. He sat down at one end of the table and we would run our lines. The last thing I'm supposed to say is, 'When are you going to stand up like a man and tell Taylor to go to h…?' I'm about to say hell, but get cut off because you couldn't say hell in those days. So we rehearsed the scene sitting around that table instead of on the set. Capra would say, 'No Delmar, don't get excited there. It's when you get to the part where you almost say hell. That's when I want your voice level to go up; that's when I want you to be mad.' So before we went on the set we knew what he wanted, and when you got on the set you had already established the timing. He said to me, 'You just go ahead like you're going to say hell and Guy Kibbee will come in before you say it.' That's the thing I remember about Capra. He was a very patient man and knew what he wanted. There were a lot of good directors that I worked with, but he was the best. Like I said, that was the very best picture that I did. In fact, it was recently voted one of the top 100 films. *Heidi* didn't make the list at all," he laughed.

Delmar reflected on working opposite Shirley Temple in *Heidi* in which he played Goat Peter. "The thing that makes it interesting to me is that I knew Shirley before she was anybody. We worked together in a movie called *To the Last Man* with Randolph Scott, and played brother and sister. We were just two little kids working in the movie. If she caught a cold, I caught a cold; I'd be sitting on my dad's lap and she'd come over and push me off and climb up; that's how close we were. Four or five years later, when we made *Heidi*, she was the box-office queen of Hollywood and it was an altogether different story by then. When they wanted her for a scene—they had a stand-in for her so she wouldn't get sunburned—she would be escorted from her trailer with bodyguards because of the Lindbergh kidnapping. She'd come down and we would do the scene, and they would take her back up to her trailer. Well, we used to have a lot of fun, but now it was like ... I don't know how to explain it. I would like to sit down and talk with her now about her childhood and ask if she felt she got cheated one way or another. But the thing I like about Shirley is that she says, 'That was then and this is now. I did that then and now I'm doing this.' She doesn't live in the past. She's just a very level-headed, nice gal.

"This had nothing to do with Shirley, and I'm not sure if it had anything to do with her mother," Delmar continued, "but her mother was the ultimate Hollywood mother. Shirley made a picture with Jane Withers, and Jane was absolutely wonderful, and practically stole the movie by being the mean little kid. So, after that, they were very cognizant of that fact, and although I was no competition (I was a little boy and she was a little girl) in the movie *Heidi*—if you ever read the book, it's primarily Heidi and Goat Peter—when it came to making the movie, it was primarily Heidi and Grandfather. There were all kinds of scenes in the movie which would really have made it more of a child's movie. For example, we were out in a field and I teach her how to blow the goat's horn, and she teaches me my ABC's. Then there's this whole sequence where she falls over a cliff, but they cut all this out of the movie. The movie in its original form, she gets butted by my goat. Shirley Temple never gets butted by a goat unless whoever's goat it was gets butted later on in the movie. In the television version of the movie, they cut out the sequence where I get butted, and they cut all the stuff with us out in the field playing with the goat. There is one sequence where she gets kidnapped by her aunt and taken into the town. She hears the fishmonger go by tooting his horn. Right out of the clear blue sky, she says, 'Oh, there's Peter and his goats.' And the audience thinks, 'What is she talking about?' because there was nothing that led up to that, because it was cut out. You never see the original version anymore. It's still an interesting movie and was probably her best-produced movie, as far as stages and costuming, and had a little more thought put into it than most of her pictures."

Delmar reflected on his and his brothers' work in the business. "Coy was in the silent movies. I was born just about the time that sound was coming in. When I look at the kids now in television, I think, I had it good. I had brothers who kept me in line. All of us had our time, our 15 minutes in the sun, or whatever you want to call it. The whole family worked in more than a thousand motion pictures. So, by the time each one of us did our thing, it wasn't a big deal to us. We didn't get spoiled because we had too many other brothers that would knock our ears off. Bobs made it bigger than any of us. He came along at the right time when there were a lot of good parts for little kids. The money we made all went into the family kitty, and there was no jealousy as far as I know. That was just the way it was. I'd work in a picture one week, Harry would work the next, then Billy and Bobs."

Delmar expressed his feelings about children working in movies, saying, "As far as a kid working in pictures is concerned, it is a necessary evil. If I had my way, there would be no kids working in pictures, at least not

Delmar as Peter the Goat Boy with Shirley Temple as Heidi in *Heidi* (20th Century–Fox, 1937).

the way it is today. You can go right down the line with all these kids. They have either hung themselves, gotten shot or taken dope. All the bad things that happened to the kids in my generation and today are mostly because their families are complete disasters. Look at Macaulay Culkin. What do you do when you're seven or eight years old and you've had all these accolades? You've had all these people patting you on the head telling you how wonderful you are, and then you reach puberty. Kids get pimples, are immature, and suddenly nobody wants them anymore. It's hard enough for an adult to cope with this, but a little kid says, 'What did I do wrong? I tried to please my mother and father, I tried to please the director, the photographers, the make-up man, I tried to please all these people. What do I do? Now they don't want me anymore.' How do you cope with that as a little kid? It's sad. If I had a little kid, which I don't, and he even looked like he was going to tap dance, I'd kick him clear across the room. But not because I had it bad. I didn't. My dad had all of our heads screwed on right. None of us have ever been arrested, none of us have ever done anything like that.

"Bobs stayed in the business; I became a photographer; different ones did different things," Delmar continued. "It was an interesting background for what I'm doing now: I can talk to people; I can set up pictures; I know how they want pictures taken and how to cheat your looks. These are all things I learned from being a child actor."

Baseball and football were the two things Delmar enjoyed during his free time away from school and movie sets. "I'd rather have been out playing baseball than going out on stupid movies and wearing funny clothes. When I was about ten years old, I wanted a pair of football shoes, but they didn't make them for kids. So my dad went out and bought a pair of high-top shoes. He left the heels on them and made leather cleats, and I had my football shoes. My dad was my hero, he and Lou Gehrig. There's not too many heroes today. When I grew up, we had heroes: Lou Gehrig, Admiral Byrd, Wrongway Corrigan, Lindbergh. You show me a hero now that isn't some kind of a jerk. There's one guy I like. I'm not a big basketball fan but Michael Jordan seems to be a decent guy. Mark McGwire seems to be a good role model too. I remember my dad saying there are not too many people you can tell your son to emulate. It goes right back to the fact that family values have been lost. I am whatever I am because of my dad, my mom and my family. I figure I won the lottery when I was born. I was born in the United States, I was born in Los Angeles, and I was born into a family that loved me. You can't ask for more than that."

Delmar mentioned that, of all the actors he worked with, his fondest memories are of Pat O'Brien. "He was a very nice person. He told funny stories and was good to us kids. We were making a movie called *The Great O'Malley* with Humphrey Bogart, Ann Sheridan, and a little girl named Sybil Jason. I played her boyfriend. There were a lot of kids in the picture, and it was really hot on the back lot of Warner Bros. Every day (and he didn't want anybody to know this), Pat O'Brien would have 80 gallons of iced lemonade delivered for the kids, which was paid for out of his own pocket. He wasn't my favorite actor—Spencer Tracy I think would be, for all-around abilities—but Pat O'Brien was a good actor and was very generous and thoughtful. Wally Beery was a big s.o.b. My brother Harry and I played his sons in a movie called *Old Hutch*. The only time he would talk with us was when we had lines together. To me he was not a very nice person. But most of these old actors, you could do anything with them. When I was a little kid growing up, I worked with a lot of them. I could name about five or six of them that, later on, were still around when I was working on the newspaper shooting pictures of them. They were decent people. I'd go to shoot these young punk kids that made it overnight, and they didn't have time for me. But the old-timers were always there, were always good. If you told them to 'Cheat your look,' they knew what you were talking about. They knew the value of publicity, they knew the value of having their pictures taken and used, and the value of spelling their names correctly."

Asked for any reflections on working on *Old Hutch*, Delmar said, "Scotty Beckett was in it. He was a nice little kid and we grew up with him, but he later had problems and died of an overdose. And there were the two twins, Caroline Anne and Julia Ellen Perkins, and the dog. When we were on location, and we were outside, it was always a lot more fun. We had box lunches, and that was fun. We went down to the pier at the beach for a motorboat ride one time, but we didn't have much time to do other things. It was always pretty much cut and dried when we were working in pictures. We had our lines to memorize, and when we'd get on the set, we'd do our thing and hopefully do it in one take."

Delmar's favorite location shoot was the week spent at Lake Arrowhead on *Heidi*. "That was nice because it was in the summer. We could swim on the beach by the lake and we played up in the trees. I remember it was when Jim Braddock beat Max Baer for the boxing title in '37. I listened to it on a radio up there. There were a lot of pleasurable times.

"The bad thing about working in pictures was that you could never have any after-school activities. You would get out of school at three o'clock and you always had to come right home because you might have to go out on an interview. You never knew when the studio was going to call. They knew you were in school, so they would set interviews for four or four-thirty in the afternoon. Therefore, you couldn't have after-school baseball or football. But we had a big lot so we could play with each other, and enough kids would come from the neighborhood to play football down on what we called Watson's Lot. That was fun. We'd be playing football down at the lot and an airplane or dirigible would fly over. Everything would stop while we watched it fly over. It was a completely different time. If you had a dog you didn't have to chain it up; you could run all over the hills. You could do things without being afraid of some pervert molesting you. The only rule was, when the sun went down, we'd better be home. We would sit down at the table for dinner every night and there were 11 of us. We'd always eat together, and that was when families talked. How can you talk when you're sitting in front of a television with a TV dinner? Every night we would talk about family things that were going on. If one of us worked in a picture, we would be asked how we did that day. So we would talk about what we did on the movie, talk about family values and, before every meal, we would say the blessing. But we had to be home by a certain time. If we weren't home, my dad would get a switch!"

We asked him if being a child actor cheated him out of a childhood. "No, except like I said, coming home after school. But it taught me a lot. I know people most people never got to see or talk to. And luckily, like I say, it was my family. But I have no regrets of working, I don't think any of my brothers do either. Some liked it better than others. My brother Harry didn't like it much, and I thought, 'Who cares.'"

Delmar's acting career ended when he went into the service during World War II where he served as a photographer in the Coast Guard. "When I was 12 years old I started shooting pictures, and when I was in high school I was shooting them for my school paper and our yearbook. During the last two years of high school, I was the school photographer. I graduated from high school on June 28th and enlisted on July 28th and was on my way to boot camp when I was just turned 18. I was stationed in Brooklyn for six or eight months. Then the war ended in Europe and they shipped me back here to the west coast where I spent the next year and a half taking pictures. So, when I got out of the service, I loved photography. I went on to become a newspaper man and worked ten years on a metropolitan newspaper as a photographer."

The studios were trying to give a break to guys coming out of the service who had worked as kids in pictures. They would call and try to give them a part. "My dad had gone up to Oregon with Bobs, and I was here by myself. The studio called and wanted me to go out on an interview. I didn't want to, but I had a couple of brothers who were still interested in working in pictures. I figured I didn't want the word to get around Hollywood that the Watsons weren't working in pictures anymore, so I went out on the dumb interview and got the part," he laughed. "It was the last movie I made. It's funny because I had worked with Alfalfa in the *Our Gang* comedies—the one was called *Pigskin Palooka* where he steals my football uniform to make pictures for Darla. In it I was the captain of the football team. When I got out of the service, they were making a picture called *The Gashouse Kids* with Alfalfa, and I went out and worked one day. I got there at seven in the morning and was there until about eight that night because they didn't know when they were going to shoot my sequence. I was making $40 a month in the service and I got a check in the mail for one day's work $480. I thought, 'This is great money, but not enough for me to want to go back into that.' The business was changed, and the casting directors were trying to pat you on the butt, or were winking at you. Everything had changed and I wasn't a kid anymore. Like I say, I'm a realist. My brother Bobs and I talked about the business all the time. He loved *E.T.* and *Star Wars*, but that's phony to me. I love to go to a movie if it's a good one. I love watching the old movies and I probably love documentaries better. Hollywood, to me, is fantasyland. It's Tinseltown. It's not really what I want to do no matter how much money is offered. I enjoy doing what I'm doing: being a photographer, and editing and publishing books."

Delmar's latest work on a movie was as a technical adviser on a picture called *Public Eye*. "Joe Pesci played a news photographer. I showed him how to, and how not to, hold a camera."

In 1998, Delmar was invited to give a talk on a cruise ship in Venezuela about news photography in regards to public relations. "I also went to Lamar, Colorado, to give a talk on 'When America Had Heroes.'" Delmar also has given talks about how TV and movies are not businesses for kids to become involved in. "Unless the parents keep the kids heads screwed on, which is almost impossible, there is no way that a kid is going to come out normal. What do you do for an encore? This Culkin kid made six million dollars for one movie. What does he do next? He can't pump gas. Somebody needs to look out for his interests and invest his money, and see that he's got his head screwed on right, which he doesn't, because he has no parents who do that. What's going to happen to all these kids? I see them on TV and can't stand to look at them. I think, you poor little bastards. You think you've got it made now, but what's going to happen to you later?"

Asked if he had any meaningful memories of working on the *Our Gang* shorts, Delmar responded, "I only worked in a couple of them. The

Our Gang comedies had about six or seven characters: Spanky, Alfalfa, Butch, Darla, Buckwheat and the dog. The rest of the kids just stood around and said, 'Oh boy,' 'You bet,' and that was about all they did. So when it came time to pay in money, they paid those kids absolutely nothing. I'm very mad about that. Spanky was very discouraged. Eighty years later the producers are still making money and these kids made nothing. About 20 years ago I was invited to a reunion of the *Our Gang* kids with Butch, Spanky, Buckwheat and a couple of the others. There were a lot of people there, and they were signing autographs. Then they had a big dinner where they had different of the old kids get up and talk about what they had done and what they were doing now. I got up and told the crowd that I only did a couple of the *Our Gang*s because they didn't pay any money. About two months later, Buckwheat died in some crummy little place down in Watts with no money. And those bastards are still selling those shows for millions of dollars. The kids made nothing. I look back now and feel sorry for the children who worked in all those comedies and put in all that effort. Poor Spanky. He died very bitter. They finally put his star on Hollywood Boulevard after he was dead. Hollywood has a way of honoring you after you are dead. A friend is trying to get the Watson family a star there, but I'm not sure I want it. They have Snow White and Lassie there," he laughed. The Watson family finally did receive their star on the Hollywood Walk of Fame in April 1999. "Brother Bobs died of cancer two months later," Delmar added. "I'm just glad he lived long enough to receive the star. He earned it."

Delmar summed up his feelings about his career as a child working in the movies, by saying, "I have no regrets. It made it easy for me to do what I later did as a newspaper photographer, because I wasn't in awe of a lot of people. I've shot pictures of I don't know how many presidents, kings and queens. When I was in the service, I was a seaman or whatever, and I was told to photograph the admirals. 'Sir,' I said, 'can you move in? Can you move here?' I'm telling the admirals what to do," he laughed. "And I don't think, if I hadn't had the experience as a child working around the stars, I could have done that.

"It's funny, because when I was a little kid I was in the Boy Scouts and loved that, and then I went into the service in World War II and came out as a photographer. I worked on the afternoon paper for the *Los Angeles Times* for ten years. I was a news photographer for 20 years. I've won two Freedom Foundation awards. I've spoken at the Pentagon. I've edited and published five books, and the only thing anybody really remembers of me is that I played Goat Peter in *Heidi*. It's funny the way people's minds work."

Johnny Whitaker

Johnny Whitaker was born December 13, 1959, in Pacoima, California, and made his first appearance on television when he was six months old. "A neighbor of my mom's was Rick Spalla who was an assistant director or stage manager for a live television show. Its format was something like, guess what we are doing. My mother, and her best friend, along with one other woman from our little cul-de-sac, had babies who were about the same age. The camera was on these mothers' faces while they were feeding us. A panel had to guess what these three women were doing. They had closeups of them and then pulled back and showed three little babies, and I was one of them. That was the first thing that I did."

When Johnny was three years old, his mother was in charge of a primary program at their Sunday church service. "*I'm a Child of God* was the new song that came out that year in the church. My mother didn't get a chance to teach the kids in the primary the song, so she taught it to my sisters and one other little girl, and myself. My sisters would sing the chorus in harmony and the other girl would sing the verses. I was sitting and practicing with my sisters so they could get three-part harmony, and so I was the only other child in the group that knew it. The little girl got the chicken pox so I had to pitch hit for her and came in and sang. I did the first verse, then my sisters sang the chorus. I forgot the words to the second verse and started making up my own words because I was not going to be embarrassed in front of all these people. My sisters were looking over at me and saying 'That's not the right words,' and I was looking at them giving them the eye, 'Hey, go on. Don't worry, just sing it.' Then on the third verse I finally got the second verse out. Anyway, there was a member in the congregation who had had her son in a couple of commercials and had an agent. She told my mom, 'Your kid has the ability to not get too flustered under a bit of pressure. I think he would do good in show business. Why don't you just take him by my son's agent?'"

Johnny and his mother went to meet the agent who was the mother of Ken Osmond, Eddie Haskell in *Leave It To Beaver*. "She loved me and became my first agent. The minute I walked in she said, 'I have an audition at three o'clock. Can you be there?' So my mom and I got to the audition and I got the job. It was for Chevrolet Okay Used Cars. After working for Mrs. Osmond for three or four months she became very ill and had to quit the business. She sent me to Mary Grady, who at the time—

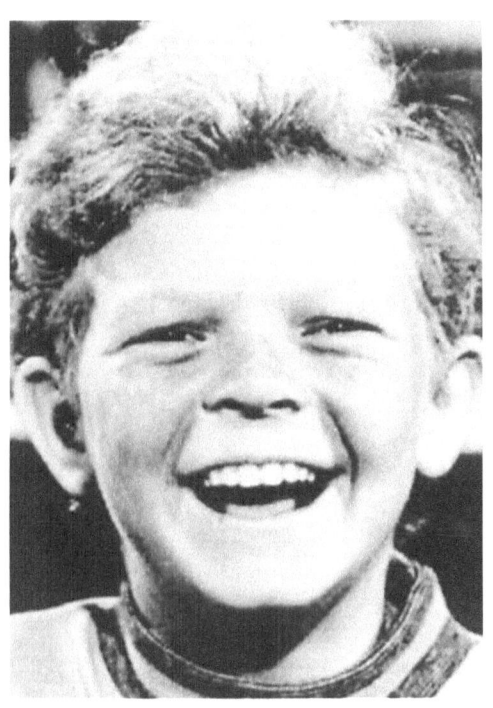

Johnny Whitaker

and up until just a few years ago—was one of the most prolific child agents in town. She became my agent and that's when everything started."

Johnny did a lot of commercials. "One was a Mattel Toy commercial with Pamelyn Ferdin. It's where I pull the string and a toy lion talks. Then I did *Baby Makes Three* with Joan Blondell and Richard Crenna. I was the original Scotty Baldwin on *General Hospital*." Discussing the difference between regular and soap opera TV, Johnny said in reference to the latter, "The big difference was that we read the script on Tuesday and then on Wednesday, Thursday and Friday we filmed. We didn't stop—it was all done live on tape."

From *General Hospital*, Johnny obtained a part in the feature, *The Russians Are Coming! The Russians Are Coming*! "That's where I met Brian Keith. Brian suggested to my agent that I get seen for a role in *Family Affair*. Originally it was scripted for a 16 year old girl, a ten year old boy, and a six year old girl. So my agent had suggested that I come in at the behest of Brian Keith and thought maybe I could be a kid next door. I was the only six year old boy who got to screen-test, all the others were ten years old. I screen-tested with Pamelyn Ferdin and when they looked at it and saw Anissa Jones and I they said, 'Let's change it to twins.' Although Anissa was almost two years older than I, she was small for her age and we continued to play twins up until about the second to last season. I had grown almost a head taller than her, so they decided they would stop calling us twins and see if people would forget we were, and I became an older brother."

We asked him whether it was basically because of Brian Keith that he got the role of Jody in *Family Affair*. "Yeah, but I think it was because Anissa and I looked so much alike and Brian had producerial rights to some extent that they suggested that I be the kid. So, I would say that Brian Keith's support didn't hurt in the least."

In his earlier work, he was listed in the credits as Johnnie Whitaker. When asked if that spelling or the later spelling of his name as Johnny Whitaker was correct, he replied, "There is a story behind that, but it is definitely with a *y*. When I was about eight—two years after *Family Affair* started—we were filming at CBS Studio Center in Studio City. There's a Du Par's Restaurant up the street from where the studio is and so we would go there quite often for lunch. One day when a waitress served us I looked at her name and it was spelt Johnnie. I said, 'Girls spell their name with an "ie"; I don't want my name spelt like that anymore.' They thought the ie was cute, but from then on I had it changed to 'y.'"

In reflecting on working in the series, Johnny stated, "I remember it was just good times. *Family Affair*, along with *To Rome with Love* and *My Three Sons* with Don Fedderson Productions, had a very strange shooting schedule. Most shows do 1½ to two shows a week and start from the beginning of a show and go to the end—maybe they will mix a couple of different scenes from the two episodes of a specific area and then take it to the cutting room and split it up. But on *Family Affair* Brian Keith would only be working for three months and we would be working for nine months. So during the three months that Brian was there we would do all of his scenes from all the episodes. It was a continuity director's nightmare because she and the wardrobe people had to know exactly what we were wearing when, and we had to have triples of all the clothing that we wore because it was impossible to make sure that the kids wouldn't dirty one. Also, just in case I had grown from one scene to the next, because we may have started scene one in January with Brian Keith and scene two without Brian may have been filmed in August. So it was very difficult, but we just knew our lines in each scene and tried to get into it without knowing what was going on. That is the most interesting thing I remember from *Family Affair*—that weird schedule. It was not unnatural for me to wake up at six in the morning, get my bath or shower, eat breakfast, get in the car by seven and be to the set by eight to work and go to school until five, get back in the car and go home—that was normal for me. That is not a normal childhood, but for me it was."

In April 1971, the cast of *Family Affair* learned that it was going to be canceled. "It didn't really matter to me. I enjoyed it and had a lot of fun, but then I realized that I wasn't going to continue seeing John Gaudioso—the first assistant director—and the people who had become family that I'd been working with for five years. Anissa and I were together in Nashville, Tennessee, doing a publicity tour when we found out that the show was canceled. The big thing that we were upset about was that we had just made a decision to have a Don Fedderson Productions newsletter and we were going to be the editors of it. We were really pissed because we wouldn't be able to have our newsletter. That's why we were mad."

Family Affair made Johnny a top child star in Hollywood and he continued working in features and as a guest star in various television shows. "I became a household face because *Family Affair* was in the top ten for the five years that it ran, until the last season we stayed in the top 20. I had been working on *Family Affair* for five years, and then while I was on hiatus I was doing guest roles on *Gunsmoke*, *Lancer*, *Bonanza*, *Bewitched*, and just about anything my agent could get me work on. I was never not working; either doing the clothing line or guest-starring, I was working almost 365 days a year. After *Family Affair* some people thought, 'Oh, he's Jody.' But my agent told them, 'Look at all these other things he did while he was doing *Family Affair*.' Vincent McEveety hired me for *The Biscuit Eater* which was a Disney film and suggested to his brother after working with me that I do this other film with Jodie Foster called *Napoleon and Samantha*. So Jodie and I did that together. It was her first feature film. Disney was a great company, but because I didn't do *Charlie and the Angel* and did *Tom Sawyer* instead, they were upset, and I haven't worked for them since," he laughed.

Tom Sawyer was produced by Arthur P. Jacobs, who also did *Planet of the Apes*, for United Artists. "That was one of the best summers of my life," Johnny noted. "I got to be the star, I got to be *the* kid, and it was just tons of fun. I think any kid would love to be Tom Sawyer. My whole family came out to Missouri that summer. It was filmed on the Missouri River in a little city called Arrow Rock."

Discussing the songs in *Tom Sawyer*, Johnny said, "Actually they wanted Donny Osmond to be the voice of Tom Sawyer singing, but they had all of the songs prerecorded already with a group of kids just for a scratch track and so we just lip-synched to that. I need to give my thanks for having my voice in the film to Arthur P. Jacobs' wife who was on the set when we went back to do the sweetening of the track. The first song we did was one called *If'n I Was God*. It is a real touching song where Tom just feels like he's a nobody. He had just got slapped by Aunt Polly and is leaving the house to go to the Island with Huckleberry Finn to get away from Injun' Joe. It is a very sweet song. We had John Williams and the entire orchestra playing and I was singing. There was no lip-synching at this time because a lot of the songs that were more pensive weren't done with anybody's mouth moving. You just saw the action taking place. The song was in the background as the memories or thoughts of the character who was singing. So I was just walking down the street and as I sang it I just got a lump in my throat. It was just brilliant acting on my part by the way," Johnny laughed. "When we finished doing that there wasn't a dry eye with any of the orchestra—everybody that was there were just bawling their eyes out. The producer's wife said, 'Arthur, if anybody but Johnny sings any of his songs, you're not getting any.' So I got to sing all of the songs except for *Freebootin'* because one of the kids had a contract stating that he was to sing at least one of the songs, with his credit. So except for that I did all of my own singing."

Johnny mentioned several of his costars in *Tom Sawyer*. "Jeff East and I had a great time. I hadn't seen Jeff since then until about two years ago when the Gay and Lesbian Film Festival for West Hollywood had *Tom Sawyer* as its family feature and invited Jeff and I to come. It was fun. We got to see the film on a big screen. Anyway, I saw Jeff and his three sons and it was great. I've seen him a couple of other times at autograph shows. Warren Oates was really a great man. He was lots of fun. He didn't spend lots of time with the kids, but when we were on the set he was pleasant and nice to work with. Dub Taylor was the one I remember most. He was a great character actor in all those westerns. In *Tom Sawyer* he was the lawyer for Muff Potter as well as the coffin builder. He was just crazy, but it was fun. I remember him specifically."

Johnny enjoyed the western shows that he appeared in. "I loved to ride horses. I come from a Utah family that were all farmers so I learned how to ride a horse from cousins and friends. My mother grew up in Laketown, Utah, and we went up there when I was ten or 11 for a family reunion and a cousin let me ride his horse. At that point, I learned the importance of knowing where the barn is. I was racing my cousin back to the barn on the horse and going down this little street. All of a sudden the horse was no longer under me. It had gone to the right and I was going straight because I didn't know where the barn was. I flew right into a telephone pole going 15 to 20 miles an hour while the horse made the turn and went into the barn," Johnny laughed.

"Actually my eighth birthday was spent on the set of *Bonanza*, and Dan Blocker bought me a ten-gallon hat, new boots, chaps, and a cowboy vest for my birthday. They had a great big celebration for me. It seems that all the production stopped for five or ten minutes for me to blow out the candles on a big beautiful cake and open up presents from Dan Blocker. I had only been on the set for a week. He was a real sweet guy."

Johnny also guest-starred in a two-part episode of *Gunsmoke* called *Waste*, filmed in Kanab, Utah. "It was fun to get to travel a little bit," he said. "My grandparents were living in Arizona at the time—they were snowbirds—and when we were filming they were on their way back up to Salt Lake. It so happened that they were driving through Kanab when I was crossing the street and said, 'Grandma! Grandpa!' They didn't know that I was there and we didn't know they were moving, so that was kind of strange. My grandpa slammed on his brakes and said, 'What are you doing here?' I said, 'I'm working. Come on into our hotel.' So they stayed with us that night. There was nobody that my grandfather admired more than James Arness, and he got to meet him and take his picture with him the next day. It was just like the greatest day of my grandfather's life. Ellen Burstyn played my mother."

Reflecting on James Arness and Jeremy Slate (who played the heavy in the episode), Johnny said, "James Arness I remember being very tall. When I was sitting on the back of the horse I was still only up to about his shoulder. He was a real sweet man. I remember Jeremy as being a really nice bad guy off the set. In my whole career I don't remember ever having anything negative or having any negative people around me. Most everything was really pretty positive.

"I also did a movie of the week for Steven Spielberg before he became Steven Spielberg, called *Something Evil*, which was right after he had done *Duel*. That was pretty interesting, and to find out later on that he is one of the biggest names in Hollywood and won't ever return any of my phone calls," Johnny laughed.

Johnny mentioned a dangerous situation that he experienced on one of his pictures. "When I was at Billy Barty's funeral I saw Felix Silla who was a little person that was my stand-in and stunt man on *The Russians Are Coming! The Russians Are Coming*! John Phillip Law was the Russian who came to rescue this little kid who was hanging from a church steeple by his belt buckle 150 feet up in the air. Felix did all of the long shots. They put a red wig on his head and dressed him in my clothes and in a long shot you couldn't tell. But for some of the shots we had to actually be there, so they built a scaffolding seven stories high right off of a church steeple. My mother was watching, and John Phillip Law grabbed and unhooked me—and at that point we are actually seven stories up. John threw me over his shoulder, but his hand slipped and I started to fall and then he grabbed me. It's half a second or so, but we're seven stories up and you can hear my mother's bloodcurdling scream above all the rest in the movie, and they kept it in," Johnny laughed.

Johnny recounted a scene he and Jodie Foster did with a lion in Disney's *Napoleon and Samantha*. "Jodie Foster talked about having been mauled by the lion in the film when we were on a precipice. It wasn't too far up, but we were on a very thin mountain trail and at one point she slipped. Well, the lion grabbed her with its paw—he was using his other three paws to maintain his position—and picked her up and put her in his mouth, to hold her. She thought she was being mauled. She had two puncture wounds and in some people's opinion the lion was trying to hurt her, but in my opinion he didn't have anyplace else to hold her and was trying to help her."

When asked if he had a favorite film or part, Johnny responded, "I would definitely say *Tom Sawyer* was one of my favorites. *Sigmund and the Sea Monsters* was tons of fun, and I'm still good friends with Rick Taylor today from *Sigmund*. I enjoyed everything that I have done. Some I would say is better work than others, but I'm not ashamed of any of it and think that some of my latest work is some of my best. Although I wasn't the star or anything of note, I think I'm a better actor today than I was 30 years ago. About three years ago, I did an episode of *Beyond Belief* on Fox where I was a redneck deer hunter. It was lots of fun and I was able to be a little bit crazy on that. Then I did one where I was a policeman that cracked down on some crack dealers. It was a special for PBS. That one was really good work."

Johnny also enjoyed performing onstage before a live audience. "I did a Jay Livingston musical when I was about nine or ten that was called *The Odyssey of Runyon Jones*. It was done at a theater in the round in the San Fernando Valley. In the play I lose my dog and go somewhere between heaven and hell. It's kind of like *Little Princess*—he's in outer space and meets with Mother Nature and all these outer space people. All I remember is that they kept my microphone on during the intermission. The last thing before the break that Mother Nature said was 'When nature calls, we listen.' Then it's blackout and we go to intermission. So during intermission I went to take a pee or a poop and when I came back out I got an applause," he laughed.

"I produced a play called *Funny Valentine* in Los Angeles, and then when I was in Provo, Utah, I did quite a bit of work with Castle Pro-

An oceanside vacation turns into a secret adventure for two brothers, Johnny (Johnny Whitaker, foreground) and Scotty (Scott Kolden), when they discover a friendly sea monster, Sigmund (Billy Barty), on the beach and help him escape his mean sea monster family. *Sigmund and the Sea Monsters,* a live-action children's drama, was shown on NBC television and premiered in 1973.

ductions at the Castle Theater. I did *Butterflies Are Free* and a few others that I really liked doing."

When he wasn't working under contract, Johnny attended public school. "My teachers loved me because they had seen me on TV and thought, 'I got little Jody and he's a sweet boy,' and the kids thought I was thinking that I was better than them. I don't remember having thought that I was any better or acted like that, but some people said I did. Others said I was a pretty normal kid. So it all depends on if it was somebody that was jealous or not."

Johnny never had any trouble getting work because he had a good agent and a good track record. "I was basically at the top of my form in 1976," Johnny stated. "I was on the cover of *Teen Beat Magazine* with Donny Osmond and on *Heartthrob for America*, and I was doing *The Johnny Whitaker Show*. It was a stage variety show that my brother, sisters, and I took throughout the country for the bicentennial. That's when I found out that Anissa Jones had passed of a drug overdose and I told Mary, my agent, 'Hey, maybe it's time for me to take a second look at what I'm doing.' I had been basically working continuously since I was three till I was 16, with very little breaks. So I asked Mary, 'Don't go after parts. If something comes up let me know about it, but let's not seek after anything.' So I did another series pilot called *Mulligan's Stew* and a couple of other things. Then I finished high school and went on to college at Brigham Young University.

"I graduated from BYU in 1986 and stayed in Provo with my then wife and had a restaurant at Provo Town Square. That was doing fairly well but we needed some more support and didn't have any more money so I went back to Los Angeles to work. Well, it had been eight to ten years since I had really been Johnny Whitaker and Hollywood is very unforgiving. If you don't keep up who you are for your fans or for Hollywood, they say, 'bye-bye.' In the meantime my wife decided she didn't love me and wanted a divorce. So we got a divorce a year after that and I moved back to Los Angeles. I had the opportunity of doing some acting, but nothing as great as I had as a youngster. I worked as a computer consultant [and] training and support person for various companies. Then I worked for CBS for two years as a help desk computer specialist, and three years ago I started working with my sister as an agent-manager for children. Then with the commercial strike last year, I left the agency business. I think the secret to longevity in the picture business is being able to recreate yourself every five years or so, and that's what I'm working on currently with the *Dr. Zod and Johnny Show*. This is a radio talk show currently on the Internet with me and my psychiatrist, Dr. Ron Zodkevitch. We got the first pilot show done in May of 2000.

We asked Johnny if he felt that his life as a child actor had interfered with a normal childhood. "Definitely. But we talked about the Mayflower in school. I *saw* the Mayflower. Other kids see it in books. We talked about the Presidents of the United States and Congress—I went to Washington, DC, and got a tour by senators and Congress people. When we read *Tom Sawyer*—I *was* Tom Sawyer. Yes, I did not have a normal childhood and I'm paying for that today. I'm 41 years old, I've been divorced and have certain other emotional problems that I've got to deal with myself, but I don't blame the film or television industry. I take it upon myself as my own choices and responsibility. Maybe I haven't dealt with everything as best as I could, but I work with my psychiatrist Dr. Zod and others and maybe before I leave this world I'll be normal. So, yeah, there are a lot of problems, and to a certain extent I wouldn't suggest an acting career to all kids. There were some kids that had parents who were just awful and terrible, and having their kids doing it for the wrong reason. And the wrong reason is to make money. The right reason is because your child has some talent and you want to share them with the world. That's a good reason, but just to make money, meet movie stars and be in television that's not the reason you become an actor. You do it because you have a love to entertain and to perform. But it's a very, very cutthroat business. There are a lot of evil, mean people that are out for their own personal gain and it doesn't bother them who they hurt on their way up or down or all around. But then there's a lot of really nice people who believe that it's a good medium for teaching, and I have had the benefit of working with a lot of people who do it because they love the work and to entertain. It all depends on who you're working with and who you're working for."

When asked to sum up his experience as a child actor, he said, "I had a rather prolific career as a child actor, having the time of my life and enjoying every minute of it."

Jane Withers

Jane Withers was born April 12, 1926, in Atlanta, Georgia. "From the time my mother was 15 years old, she wanted to have one child, a little girl, and thought it would be fascinating to have a child that might be in show business. From the minute I was born, she started playing music and records for me, and then she taught me how to sing."

When Jane was two years old, she was on the stage in Atlanta at the Fox Theater, from which she won first prize at an amateur contest which, in turn, gave her a chance to go on *Aunt Sally's Kiddie Revue*, a Saturday morning program for children on radio station WGST. "That's how it started. I got so much fan mail that the radio station said they had been looking for a little girl to have her own show 'and we think that you're it.' They dubbed me *Dixie's Dainty Dewdrop*. I was three and had to carry the whole radio show. I would sing and dance. One of the things that made me so different from all the other children talentwise was that I could do impersonations. I did all the different stars of the late '20s and early '30s: Mae West, W.C. Fields, ZaSu Pitts, Fanny Brice, and many more. I became known all over the South, and when I had gone as far as I could go as *Dixie's Dainty Dewdrop*, everybody said, 'You must take her to Hollywood. She's just got to be in the movies.'

"It was a big step for us to make the decision for me to go to Hollywood. Daddy said that he couldn't possibly go because he had a job and had to support his family, so he said, 'Why don't I send you two girls out to Hollywood and see how it goes for about six months and then if something happens, wonderful. If not, then you come on back to Georgia.'"

When Jane and her mother arrived in Hollywood on March 10, 1932, they couldn't get inside a studio gate. "It was almost impossible because I was just one of thousands of kids who had come to Hollywood to try and get into the movies. So mother said, 'Let's try radio again because that's your forte.' It was rather popular in those days to have kiddie revues on Saturday morning programs where different kids would entertain. There was a program on KFWB called the *Marco Juvenile Revue* sponsored by Marco Dog Food. I was the little mischievous girl that was always interrupting everybody's singing or dancing, just full of mischief and getting into trouble. That was my part on that particular program. Of course I sang and tap danced and did impersonations, and again got lots of fan mail. Again everybody said, 'Why don't you put her in the movies?'"

Jane Withers

Mrs. Grundy, one of Jane's neighbors who lived in the same apartment building, was taking her child one day on an interview for a film titled *Handle with Care*. Mrs. Grundy asked Jane's mother, "Why don't you ride out with us in our car. Jane has never been inside of a studio gate and I think it would be wonderful for her to get an idea of what interviews are like and how they choose children to be in films." They accepted the woman's cordial invitation. "All of the children were gathered in kind of a clump and the director asked them different questions. I was standing by the car so the assistant director came up to me and asked, 'What are you doing over here, little girl? The interview is over there.' I said, 'Sir, I was not invited to the interview. I came with our friends.' He said, 'Well, the director saw you and asked for you to join the others.' The director was David Butler, and lo and behold, he chose me to be in that film. You never see the children's faces in the film, only their backs because all of the attention was on Boots Mallory and James Dunn who were performing puppets in a puppet show. When the film was released, my daddy spent every lunch hour going to the theater in Atlanta trying to see me. The only way he recognized me was because I was the only kid that had a Dutchboy bob. I had straight bangs in front and longer hair in the back cut straight across. I never had curls in my life. I was very different looking than most of the other little girls because they were always in fluffy dresses and party dresses, and I've always been a plain Jane with very tailored clothes. Anyway, that's how I got into the movies: David Butler saw me standing there and asked me to come over."

During the filming of the picture, Mr. Butler was very interested in Jane. He said, "You're different than any other kid that I've ever seen in Hollywood. You've got a special quality and someday you are going to be a famous little star." Jane told him that she did impersonations. "So in between the scenes he would have me entertain the crew doing impersonations of the different movie stars. He couldn't have been nicer. He was the first to give any kind of recognition other than the radio show that I was already doing."

It was also at KFWB that Jane began doing voice-overs for the *Silly Symphonies* cartoons. "They needed a child one day and came running in and said, 'Where's that little girl with the straight cut Dutchboy bob? She does all kinds of impersonations. We need to talk to her.' I was in the other room rehearsing, so they came in and asked, 'Do you think you could imitate a dog, a bird, or a cat?' 'Sure. I could probably imitate all of them.' So they took me in another room and stood me up on a chair by the microphone and that's how I started doing voice-overs. I did voice-overs for the whole *Willie Wopper* series. I was Willie Wopper, his sister, his mother and father, grandmother and grandfather, the dog and the cat," she laughed.

Jane would also do extra work in films. "The mothers used to pitch in together and buy a newspaper that gave all the cattle calls for the kids that were needed for different parts so the mothers would know where to take them. Finally one day when I was rehearsing for the *Marco Juvenile Revue*, the paper said that they were looking for a little girl to play opposite Shirley Temple in *Bright Eyes*. I was in the middle of a dance step and stopped dead in my tracks. I said, 'Whoopee! I think it's finally my turn.' Every interview I ever went on I was the only one with a tailored dress, with straight bangs and straight haircut, and no curls and no frills. My mother would get so discouraged, and I would say, 'Mommy, you know we have put this in God's hands and that if I'm supposed to do it He will lead me to the way that we're supposed to go. That's what you've always told me and I believe that with all my heart. When the time comes and they're looking for not a pretty little girl, then it will be my turn because I do have some kind of a personality and I have something to share in the way of talent. Don't give up. I'm not about to because I think this is fun and I love what I am doing. So we'll just keep putting it into prayer and know that my day will come.' So when I heard this I said, 'Mommy, get me to that studio as quickly as you can.'"

When they arrived for the interview, there were many kids waiting in line to see the director. Jane, who had been very patient ever since she arrived in Hollywood from Atlanta, asked the assistant director, "Can you kindly tell me who's directing this film?" "David Butler," was the answer. "Oh, dear Gussie," Jane exclaimed. "He gave me my first chance here in Hollywood. He was so gracious and I know that he would remember me. Is there any way I could just talk to him?" "He's a very busy man," he replied. "I'm very aware of that and I certainly wouldn't dream of disturbing him," Jane said. "But he is looking for a little girl to play opposite Shirley Temple, and boy! if anybody is an opposite of Shirley Temple it's me." The phone rang about that time and somebody said to the assistant director, "It's Mr. Butler on the phone." Jane then explained what happened next. "I have never done this before in my life, not since or before then, but I followed him to the telephone. Something just seemed to be pushing me in that direction. When he got on the phone he said, 'I really don't see any children here that I feel are right for the role.' I said, 'Oh sir, excuse me please. Could you just tell Mr. Butler it's the little Southern girl that he gave a job to on *Handle with Care*.' The man said, 'Go away; please don't bother me. I've got to talk to Mr. Butler.' When he returned to his conversation on the telephone, Mr. Butler said, 'Get that little girl. I've been looking all over this town for her. Ask if her name is Jane.' He said, 'Hey kid, is your name Jane?' I said, 'You betcha.' He said, 'Oh my goodness, Mr. Butler really does remember you and he wants me to bring you to his office right away.' Mom and I were very thrilled and excited, and I was scared to death that I wouldn't get this role because we had waited so long. I walked through the door and he said, 'Janie, I know you can imitate just about anything. Do you think you could imitate a machine gun?'" Jane thought a minute and then did her imitation. Butler said, "That will do just fine." "Does that mean I've got the role?" Jane asked. "No, honey. I thought of you the minute I read the script and I pray that you can get this role because I think you're absolutely perfect for it, but Janie, it's not entirely my decision. I'll call you and your mom by four o'clock this afternoon." When the phone rang, Mr. Butler said, "Jane has the role. She starts tomorrow morning." "He was a lovely gentleman," Jane reflected. "And I was so grateful that he had remembered me from the first job he gave me. Right after *Bright Eyes*, I signed my first seven-year contract with Fox."

In speaking about her character in the movie, and her memories of Shirley Temple, Jane said, "I thought she was wonderful. I was such a fan of hers and I've always felt so tacky that I had to be so mean to her in the movie. It was an incredible role and so opposite than anything I've ever been. I was very grateful for the opportunity, but I said, 'Oh Mama, everybody's just going to hate me because I'm so mean to Shirley, and I don't like being mean to her or anybody else.' Well, the film was enormously successful, and because I was so mean and so dreadful to her and was such an opposite, that's what got me my contract. But when I signed my contract I said, 'Please, I don't ever want to be a mean little girl again. I can't begin to tell you how awful it feels to be that way. That's just not my nature.' Most of the times my characters got into mischief, all kinds of mischief, and a lot of times by the end of the movie they didn't have me getting punished for some of the things that I did. I was very adamant about having to be punished. If I was to do something wrong in the film, I would not do it unless I got punished by the end of the movie. I said, 'I have become a role model and set a lot of examples for children that watch my films and they go home and emulate everything that I do. I would feel very badly and it would be on my conscience if I didn't get punished by the end of the movie.' They'd say, 'Oh Jane, it's only a movie.' I'd say, 'No, I don't think you understand. It's not just a movie to the kids watching it. So I've really got to be very careful what I do and how I do it because other children might do it and not have a happy ending. We have got to make sure that I get punished for any mischief I get into or do things I'm not supposed to do, otherwise I'm sorry gentlemen, I just plain flat won't do it.'"

Although they worked together throughout the filming of *Bright Eyes*, Jane and Shirley never spent any time together away from the camera. "I was an only child but Mama always said they would make sure I had lots of friends and playmates, and they never picked my friends for me like Shirley's was picked for her. I was never allowed to play with her when we were working together. When we did *Bright Eyes*, we couldn't even talk unless we were speaking in a scene together. The minute the scene was over, she went her way and I went to the teacher on the set. We never played together or got to know each other at all, which always upset me because I was just busting my buttons to get to know her. We had so many things in common with our work, and what fun it would have been if we could only have been friends and shared all these things and friendship too.

"When I was 15 years old they had the opening of the Hollywood Palladium. We both often went to premieres or events, but they would always be very careful to seat us very far apart. We were never together and could never even talk in any way. We could wave to one another, but that would be it." Jane made up her mind about becoming better acquainted with Shirley and prayed about it for a long time, and then they were both at the opening of the Palladium. "She was on the other side of the room. It was jam-packed with people and the photographers were going bananas getting pictures of everybody. I was surrounded by lots of people but kept watching across the room. I called my bodyguard—I had bodyguards around the clock. I called them Uncle Jack and Uncle Bob. Uncle Jack was an ex-Texas Ranger and was six-foot-five without his boots and Stetson hat. We had it all worked out in crowds that when the kids would all be mobbing me he would get my two wrists and swing me up over his head onto his shoulders so the kids couldn't get to me. I said, 'Uncle Jack, please will you do something for me. Shirley Temple's sitting across the room. Would you take this note to her for me. Please. It means a great deal to me.' He said, 'When Bob gets back I'll take your note for you.' So when my other bodyguard came back he took the note to Shirley. In the note I wrote, 'Please meet me in the ladies' room (if you can, if you can't you know I'll understand). I always wanted to talk to you and this may be our only chance. So if you can, please meet me in the ladies' room in about ten or 15 minutes. I'll be watching to see if you leave and then I'll follow you.' I was trying so hard to see through the crowd to see if she read the note, but I couldn't because so many people were crowding around getting autographs. The next time I looked she was gone. I thought, 'Oh dear Gussie, I pray to God she didn't leave but she went to the ladies' room.' So I hightailed it to the ladies' room. I said, 'Where are you, Shirley?' and she said, 'I'm here in the back.' We sat down—I don't know how long we were in there, but it was a long time—and had the best visit you could ever imagine. We laughed and said we both felt the same way: we both wanted to share thoughts and get to know each other better. Later on, after she married John Agar, we went on double dates several times and had the best time in the world. So we did get to become friends and get to know each other."

Jane was able to handpick her own crew during her contract at Fox. "I did maybe two films and then by the end of those films I had the names of the different people that I had handpicked to be on the rest of my films, and they were with me. They were known as the 'Withers Family.' People all over the lot knew that I was the only person that had that in my contract. I said, 'The money doesn't mean a hill of beans to me but the people do. They mean everything in the world to me.' So that was in my contract." At the end of shooting on every movie, Jane would cry and her colleagues would say, "Janie, we're going to see you again in three weeks." She would reply, "I know, but I'll miss you so much in those three weeks." "I loved all those people," she explained. "All the main ones have gone on with God, but I was so lucky to have them in the years that they lived. I still keep up with their children and grandchildren."

Jane reflected upon the 1940 feature *Shooting High* with Gene Autry, sharing an interesting story of how that film came to be. "That was a dream come true for me. That was my idea. I'd always wanted to make a film with Gene Autry, so I went to the head of my studio who was then Joseph Schenck and said, "I know you're busy so I will come right to the point. I want to make a film with Gene Autry." "Oh Janie," he exclaimed, "that would be box-office dynamite!" "Well, I feel the same way," Jane continued, "because his fans are the same kind of folks that like my movies. They're homespun and made for the whole family, they have good morals and happy endings and that's what we're both all about. It would just mean so much to me, Mr. Schenck, if we could work that out." "Well," he cautioned, "I can tell you right now that there is no way we would let Republic borrow you, and knowing our industry they would never let us borrow Gene Autry." "How do you know?" Jane replied. "You've never asked." Mr. Schenck simply answered, "I just know."

"I wouldn't take no for an answer," Jane remarked. "I pondered over that and put it into prayer and said, 'God, I really want to make a film with Gene Autry. There's got to be a way.' Finally I thought, I've never asked the man who's the head of Republic Studios; maybe he might have an idea. So I picked up the phone and called Republic and talked to Mr. Yates. 'I have a favor to ask of you, Mr. Yates. I would like to talk to you and it will probably take 20 to 30 minutes of your time.' He asked, 'When can you come? My doors are open any time to you.' Jane went to Republic Studios and walked in to see Herbert J. Yates. "Mr. Yates," Jane said. "I want to make a film with Gene Autry." He responded with "Wow! That's box-office dynamite!" "That's what Joseph Schenck told me," Jane said, "but he was very discouraging. He said you wouldn't let Gene Autry come to Fox and they wouldn't let me come to Republic. But you know something? There's got to be a way to work this out because I think it's good for all concerned. How do you feel about it?" "Janie," Mr. Yates replied, "I think it's a fabulous idea." Jane said, "Well, I've been doing a lot of careful thinking about this and have put it into prayers as always and this is the idea I came up with. Gene Autry is big at the box office and I'm number six at the box office, so that's good business. Since Gene is a big name, then why couldn't 20th Century–Fox loan two or three of their stars or featured players to you in exchange for Gene Autry for one movie with me and we could make it at 20th Century–Fox." "Janie, how old are you?" Mr. Yates asked. "I'm 14, sir." Mr. Yates said, "You've got a real good business head on your shoulders."

"To make a long story short," Jane explained, "he called Mr. Schenck and said, 'Guess who's in my office?' and Mr. Yates said, 'Your little star, Jane Withers.' 'Oh,' he said. 'She wants to make a picture.' Mr. Yates said, 'Yes, with Gene Autry. And I think it's a dynamite idea, don't you?' 'Of course I do,' Mr. Schenck said. 'But how can we work it out?' 'I think she's already worked it out for us,' Mr. Yates replied. They borrowed one semi-star and two other big feature players for Republic, and Gene Autry came to Fox Studio. That was the first time he had ever been away from his own studio. And we gave him the red carpet and tried to make him feel loved and welcomed. *Shooting High* was always one of my favorite movies too because of him. We had such a good time and became really good friends and remained so until the day he passed. But that was a very special moment to me to think that I actually could work something like that out. It just meant the world to me and was one of the biggest box-office successes of that year."

Of the many pictures that Jane has worked in, several stand out in her mind as favorites. "*Bright Eyes*, of course, because of what did it for me. My first starring film, *Ginger*, was one of the biggest thrills in my life. I loved the story. I loved the little girl I played in it. I think the biggest thrill in my life was when it was playing at Grauman's Chinese Theater. They had a big sign all the way across Hollywood Boulevard that read, 'You'll love *Ginger*.' And then they had my name up in lights, which was so many prayers answered for Mama and Daddy and myself. I've just had the best time. I really have. I love what I do. I love it because it involves so many different people in all walks of life, which I love. I have truly, deeply, sincerely appreciated the opportunities that I had because of my work. Being in front of the public, I have never been a stranger anywhere in the world. *The North Star* which was about the Russian people, was my heaviest dramatic role in my teenage years. Samuel Goldwyn borrowed me for that film. I usually made five movies a year, but it took a year and a half to make. I loved the opportunity and I loved the people with whom I worked. It was an extraordinary cast and a wonderful experience. *The North Star* was one of the highlights in my life." Jane mentioned that "my very favorite leading men were Rand Brooks, Jackie Cooper, Jimmy Lydon, Jackie Searl, and Gig Young."

About her parents, Walter and Ruth Withers, Jane said, "I was always included on everything. My father taught me bookkeeping from the time I was seven years old and how to handle my own affairs. He taught me things that an awful lot of other children never have their parents teach them because my life was so very different. Yet they tried to make it as easygoing and as flowing as it possibly could be under the circumstances because of the pressures and life you have as a child star. And that's exactly the way it is. You have responsibilities as a child star that even a lot of adults can't handle. They were very conscientious about that; they never did anything that concerned my life or my career unless we discussed it as a family together. 'How do you feel about it?' 'What do you think about this?' 'Is there something you really want to do?' 'You don't ever have to do any of these things, and anytime you don't like what you're doing we will leave. We want that understood right now.' I cannot say enough fine things about my parents. I had just incredible parents. We always had a blessing before every meal and I still do. I don't think I ever had a cracker without saying thank you. My son and I call each other every morning and read the daily word which is a thought for the day. God has been a very important part of my upbringing and a part of my life. Honestly, if I hadn't had the faith that I was taught and believed in from such a very early age I often wondered how different my life would be."

Jane spoke of some activities that she enjoyed when she was away from the camera. Besides her doll collection, which started when she was *Dixie's Danty Dewdrop* and has grown into one of the largest doll collections in the world, Jane mentioned that "I was a girl scout and that meant a lot to me. It was very difficult for me to go to where the meetings were in Westwood, so we just had all the girl scout meetings in my house, which all the kids just loved. We did all of our regular girl scout things and then they would stay later so they could swim and play badminton. Again, it meant a great deal to me to be a girl scout." Again on the subject of badminton, Jane stated, "We had our badminton court. Every Wednesday night was badminton night and we had a lot of people: Tommy Kelly, Jackie Hughes and Freddie Bartholomew. Freddie was a top-notch player, an incredible sportsman and swimmer. He was like the brother I never had. Freddie and Lon McAllister are my two brotherlike favorites. All of the kids I knew were just wonderful real people. I still keep up with Marcia Mae Jones, Jeannie Porter, Ann Blyth, Joan Leslie, and Betty Lynn. We've all been friends for over 50 years. Once a month we get together and have lunch. We don't let anything ever interfere with that. We share thoughts, bring new pictures of our kids, our dogs, our grandchildren, our great grandchildren, and it's really joyful.

"I have always dedicated my life to the Lord's work and doing things for other people ever since I was a very small child. We always had six busloads of orphan children come to our home after Sunday school and church in Atlanta, Georgia, and we continued the same thing out here after we bought our home on Sunset Boulevard. And all the kids that I grew up with and did extra work with would all come to my home on Sunday afternoon, along with their families, and we'd have a big barbecue, with square dancing and later on jitterbugging. We just had a really wonderful time."

Jane left the business in 1947 shortly after completing work in *Danger Street*. We asked her why she left. "Because I wanted to. I felt that leaving the business was the only way I could really concentrate on my husband and be the proper kind of wife for him and, prayerfully, a very good mother for my children because I always said I wanted five children. (I have five of the grandest kids in the world. They are my best friends as well as my children.) It was very important to me. I like things right or not at all, giving a 150 percent to what you're doing. I told Mom and Dad when I was about 15, 'I pray I can continue to work until I'm 21.' I worked up until nine days before I got married, never stopping, and loved every smidgen of it and wouldn't have had it any other way. But when I stopped, I really stopped."

Jane and her husband were divorced in 1954. Returning to California, she was invited to a dinner honoring director George Stevens. "All my life I've wanted to work with George Stevens and as a result of becoming acquainted at that dinner party he selected me for the choice role of Vashti

Jane Withers. In the left-hand corner Jane appears as Josephine the Lady Plumber from the longest-running commercial in television history and directly above as the title character in *Paddy O'Day*. Sketch by Bob Harman. (20th Century-Fox, 1935)

in *Giant* and that was one of the biggest thrills in my life. That was also one of my favorite films."

Meeting George Stevens in January 1955 was not the only important event which transpired that year. "I really never dreamed I would ever get married again. I was so terrified. I didn't even date. But then God sent me Kenneth Errair who became my husband eight months later at the conclusion of my role in *Giant*. Kenny was one of the original *The Four Freshmen*, one of the most famous vocal groups in the world in the '50s, and was the real love of my life." Kenneth decided to leave the vocal group so he could live at home and begin a new career as a realtor and land developer.

Jane again came out of retirement in 1961 to make an appearance in the film *The Right Approach* because she was specifically requested for the cameo part by David Butler, the same director who had given her her break in *Bright Eyes*. "He retired for a long time and then came back to Fox to make one movie. I wasn't working at the time—I didn't want to work after I married, but he called me and said, 'You've always been my lucky charm. Would you do me the honor of doing a cameo role. It's a very small part and I almost hate to ask you.' I said, 'Mr. Butler, if I have to walk through carrying a spear, I'd be glad to do it for you no matter what it is.' So I did that film for him."

In 1963, when Kenneth decided to broaden his field to include tax consultation and law, which would require a long period of study, Jane felt it necessary to go back to work. "I prayed, asking God's guidance in helping me find an expression for my talents which would permit me to take care of my family properly as my first concern." Her prayer was answered when she was chosen over 102 other actresses who had tested before her for Josephine the Lady Plumber. The commercial ran for 16 years featuring Josephine in various situations cleaning the dirty sinks with Comet cleanser. "I had the longest-running commercial in the history of television," Jane commented. In addition, Jane also worked in the feature *Captain Newman, M.D.*, as well as television shows such as *The Munsters*, and *Alfred Hitchcock Presents*. "It was just like I'd never left."

According to Jane, she and Kenneth had a wonderful 13½ years of marriage. "We would certainly be together today except he was killed in a private plane crash in 1968. We had a wonderful life together." Regarding the movies of today, Jane stated, "I don't do them now at all because most of the stories I think are appalling. I can't stand the language, I can't stand the violence, the unkindness in the stories. I love happy things. I would love to do more films, but it would have to be something that's geared for family entertainment and there's so little that is geared for families. I've been doing voices for Disney. I just finished the second movie of *Hunchback of Notre Dame*. I was Laverne the Gargoyle. I loved doing this."

Jane concluded by summing up her feelings about her career as a child actor. "Well, I could only say, who could ask for anything more? I've had a ball. A gloriously wonderful intriguing life. I loved it. I always will. I'm very grateful that I still can work whenever I want to and I think that's a glorious thing. I have appreciated the opportunities it's given me. I have had the thrill of having and raising five wonderful children and five grandchildren (so far) and one precious great grandson. There are *so* many things I want to do and see. I want to see as much of this fabulous world we live in that I possibly can—and as always, I've put it into prayer and with God's help, *as always*, I *believe* I will."

Filmographies

Lee Aaker

1952 The Atomic City; Desperate Search; The Greatest Show on Earth; No Room for the Groom; O'Henry's Full House; High Noon; Something to Live For.
1953 Arena; Hondo; Jeopardy; Take Me to Town.
1954 Destry; Ricochet Romance; The Raid.
1963 Bye Bye Birdie.

Phillip Alford

1962 To Kill a Mockingbird.
1965 Shenandoah.
1970 The Intruders.

Baby Peggy

1921 Her Circus Man; On with the Show; The Kid's Pal; Playmates; On Account; Pals; Third Class Male; Golfing; Brownie's Little Venus; Sea Shore Shapes; A Week Off; A Muddy Bride; Brownie's Baby Doll; Teddy's Goat; Get-Rich-Quick Peggy; Chums.
1922 Penrod; Fool's First; The Straphanger; Circus Clowns; Little Miss Mischief; Peggy, Behave!; The Little Rascal; Tips.
1923 Hollywood; The Darling of New York; Peg o' the Movies; Sweetie; The Kid Reporter; Taking Orders; Carmen, Jr.; Nobody's Darling; Little Miss Hollywood; Miles of Smiles; Hansel and Gretel.
1924 The Law Forbids; Captain January; The Family Secret; Helen's Babies; Such Is Life; Peg o' the Mounted; Our Pet; The Flower Girl; Stepping Some; Poor Kid; Jack and the Beanstalk.
1925 Little Red Riding Hood.

1926   April Fool.
1932   Off His Base; Hollywood on Parade.
1934   Eight Girls in a Boat.
1935   Ah! Wilderness.
1936   Girls' Dormitory.

Mary Badham

1962   To Kill a Mockingbird.
1966   This Property Is Condemned; Let's Kill Uncle.

Sonny Bupp

1936   Hearts in Bondage; Rosebowl; San Francisco; Star for a Night; What Became of the Children.
1937   Love Is in the Air; My Dear Miss Aldrich; Cash and Carry; Lost Horizon; Michael O'Halloran; Missing Witness; Murder Goes to College; We Who Are About to Die.
1938   Angels with Dirty Faces; Swing Your Lady; Hollywood Hotel; Men in Fright; Penrod's Double Trouble; The Storm; Valley of the Giants.
1939   On Borrowed Time; Boy Trouble; No Place to Go; Renegade Trail; When Tomorrow Comes; Feathered Pests; Fixer Dugan; Risky Business; Sudden Money.
1940   Half a Sinner; Parole Fixer; Queen of the Mob; Three Faces West; Diamond Frontier; Emergency Squad; Flight Angels; Little Orvie; Slightly Tempted.
1941   The Devil and Daniel Webster; Father's Son; She Couldn't Say No; Citizen Kane; Badmen in Missouri; Code of the Outlaw; International Squadron; One Foot in Heaven; Sergeant York; West of the Cimarron; Wings of the Eagle; Woman Wise.
1942   The Loves of Edgar Allan Poe; Syncopation; Tennessee Johnson.
1943   Eyes of the Underworld.

Michael Chapin

1944   The Sullivans.
1945   The Corn Is Green.
1946   Song of the South (voice only); Song of Arizona; It's a Wonderful Life; Night Editor.
1947   Heaven Only Knows; Backlash. 1948: Under California Stars; The Boy with Green Hair; Night Wind; Call Northside 777.
1949   Strange Bargain.
1950   Summer Stock.
1951   Buckaroo Sheriff of Texas; The Dakota Kid; Wells Fargo Gunmaster; Arizona Manhunt.

1952 Wild Horse Ambush; Wagons West; Springfield Rifle.
1954 Pride of the Bluegrass.
1955 Night of the Hunter.

Ted Donaldson

1944 Once Upon a Time; Mr. Winkle Goes to War.
1945 Adventures of Rusty; A Guy, a Gal and a Pal; A Tree Grows in Brooklyn.
1946 My Pal; Personality Kid; The Return of Rusty.
1947 For the Love of Rusty; The Red Stallion; The Son of Rusty.
1948 The Decision of Christopher Blake; My Dog Rusty; Rusty Leads the Way.
1949 The Green Promise; Rusty Saves a Life; Rusty's Birthday.
1952 Phone Call from a Stranger.
1954 Flight Nurse.

George Ernest

1930 The Medicine Man.
1931 Star Witness; Fly My Kite; Shiver My Timbers; A Connecticut Yankee.
1932 The Deadline; Destry Rides Again; Fireman Save My Child; Handle With Care; Love Is a Racket.
1933 Looking Forward; Speed Demon.
1934 The Human Side.
1935 Dinky; The Glass Key; Little Men; Mystery of Edwin Drood; Racing Luck; Straight from the Heart.
1936 Back to Nature; Educating Father; Man Hunt; Reunion; Song of the Saddle; Too Many Parents; Trail of the Lonesome Pine; Every Saturday Night.
1937 Borrowing Trouble; Hot Water; Lady Behave; Let's Get Married; Motor Madness; Off to the Races; The Plainsman; Wife, Doctor and Nurse.
1938 Down on the Farm; Love on a Budget; Paradise for Three; Safety in Numbers; Sweethearts; A Trip to Paris.
1939 Boy Friend; Everbody's Baby; The Jones Family in Hollywood; Quick Millions; Too Busy to Work; 20,000 Men a Year.
1940 Four Sons; Golden Gloves; Meet the Missus; On Their Own; Young as You Feel.
1941 Mountain Moonlight; Petticoat Politics; Remember the Day.
1942 Starlight on the Sage.

Richard Eyer

1953 It Happens Every Thursday.
1954 Ma and Pa Kettle at Home.
1955 The Desperate Hours; Sincerely Yours.
1956 Canyon River; Come Next Spring; Friendly Persuasion; The Kettles in the Ozarks; Slander.

1957 Bailout at 48,000; The Invisible Boy.
1958 Fort Dobbs; Johnny Rocco; The Seventh Voyage of Sinbad.
1960 Hell to Eternity.

Edith Fellows

1927 Movie Nights.
1930 Shivering Shakespeare.
1931 Cimarron.
1932 Law and Lawless; Rider of Death Valley; Birthday Blues.
1933 The Devil's Brother; Mush and Milk.
1934 His Greatest Gamble; Mrs. Wiggs of the Cabbage Patch.
1935 Dinky; Jane Eyre; One Way Ticket; She Married Her Boss; Keeper of the Bees.
1936 And So They Were Married; Tugboat Princess; Pennies From Heaven.
1937 Life Begins with Love.
1938 City Streets; The Little Adventuress; Little Miss Roughneck.
1939 Five Little Peppers and How They Grew; Pride of the Blue Grass.
1940 Five Little Peppers at Home; Five Little Peppers in Trouble; Her First Romance (*aka* The Right Man); Music in My Heart; Nobody's Children; Out West with the Peppers.
1941 Her First Beau.
1942 Girls' Town; Criminal Investigator; Heart of the Rio Grande; Stardust on the Sage.
1964 Lilith.
1985 The Hills Have Eyes, Part 2.

Billy Gray

1943 Man of Courage.
1945 The Strange Affair of Uncle Harry.
1946 To Each His Own; Cluny Brown; Specter of the Rose.
1947 The Gangster; Curly.
1948 The Bride Goes Wild; Fighting Father Dunne; Parlor, Bedroom and Wrath.
1949 Bad Men of Tombstone; The Talented Tramps; Lust For Gold; Abandoned; Abbott and Costello Meet the Killer; Father Was a Fullback.
1950 Father Is a Bachelor; The Good Humor Man; In a Lonely Place; Three Little Words; Singing Guns; Sierra Passage; Mister 880; The Killer That Stalked New York; Between Midnight and Dawn.
1951 On Moonlight Bay; Gene Autry and the Mounties; The Guy Who Came Back; The Day the Earth Stood Still; Jim Thorpe—All American.
1952 Talk About a Stranger; Return of Gilbert and Sullivan.
1953 All I Desire; The Girl Next Door; By the Light of the Silvery Moon.
1954 Doggie in the Bedroom; The Outlaw Stallion; Superman and the Jungle Devil; Hurricane at Pilgrims Hill.
1955 The Seven Little Foys.
1956 The Scarlet Hour.

1959 Some Like It Hot.
1961 The Explosive Generation.
1962 Two for the Seesaw.
1963 Metempsycho.
1966 The Navy vs the Night Monsters.
1971 Dusty and Sweets McGee; The Last Movie; Werewolves on Wheels.
1974 Citizen Soldier.
1977 Father Knows Best Christmas Reunion.
1979 Love and Bullets.
1980 Pork Lips Now.

Gary Gray

1941 A Woman's Face; Sun Valley Serenade.
1943 Two Tickets to London; It's a Great Life; Heaven Can Wait; Alaska Highway; Where Are Your Children?
1944 Beautiful but Broke; White Cliffs of Dover; Address Unknown; Once Upon a Time; Gaslight; Meet Me in St. Louis; And to Think I Saw It on Mulberry Street; I'll Be Seeing You.
1945 I Am an American; It Happened in Springfield; Adventures of Rusty; Men in Her Diary.
1946 The Wonderful Ears of Johnny McGoggin; Slightly Scandalous; To Each His Own; Rendezvous 24; Little Mr. Jim; Three Wise Fools; Three Little Girls in Blue; My Brother Talks to Horses.
1947 High Conquest; Backlash; Dark Delusion; Living in a Big Way; Too Many Winners; Swing the Western Way; The Millerson Case.
1948 Whispering Smith; Return of the Badmen; Rachel and the Stranger; The Best Man Wins; Fighting Back; Gun Smugglers; Night Wind.
1949 I Found a Dog; Henry the Rainmaker; Streets of San Francisco; Leave It to Henry; The Girl From Jones Beach; The Great Lover; Masked Raiders; It's Your Health; Dog of the Wild.
1950 Father Is a Bachelor; Father Makes Good; Pal's Return; The Jimmy Fund for Boston's Children's Hospital; The Next Voice You Hear; Two Weeks with Love; Father's Wild Game; Pal, Canine Detective; Pal, Fugitive Dog.
1951 The Painted Hills; Father Takes the Air; Pal's Gallant Journey; The Metro Goldwyn Mayer Story.
1952 Rodeo.
1955 The First Hundred Days.
1956 Emergency Hospital; Teenage Rebel.
1958 Wild Heritage; The Party Crashers.
1962 Terror at Black Falls.

Jimmy Hawkins

1943 The Seventh Cross; Marriage Is a Private Affair.
1946 It's a Wonderful Life.

352 Filmographies

1947 Sea of Grass.
1948 Moonrise.
1949 Caught; Holiday Affair; That Forsyte Woman; Connecticut Yankee in King Arthur's Court; Challenge of Lassie; The Red Menace; Down to the Sea in Ships.
1950 Never a Dull Moment; Love That Brute; Winchester 73; Shadow on the Wall.
1951 Jim Thorpe—All American; Here Comes the Groom; Strictly Dishonorable; The Blue Veil; The Groom Wore Spurs.
1952 The Greatest Show on Earth.
1953 The Woman They Almost Lynched; Mr. Scoutmaster; Savage Frontier; El Paso Stampede.
1954 Destry; Private Hell 36; Yankee Pasha.
1955 Count Three and Pray; Not as a Stranger.
1962 Zotz.
1965 Girl Happy.
1966 Spinout.

Billy Hughes

1961 Ole' Rex; Posse from Hell.
1962 Stakeout.
1963 My Six Loves.
1975 Smoke in the Wind.

Jimmy Hunt

1946 My Brother Talks to Horses.
1947 High Barbaree; Song of Love; The Beginning of the End; Living in a Big Way; Daybreak.
1948 Family Honeymoon; Fuller Brush Man; The Mating of Millie; Pitfall; The Sainted Sisters; Sorry, Wrong Number.
1949 Rusty's Birthday; Special Agent; Top O' the Morning; The Romantic Age.
1950 The Capture; Cheaper by the Dozen; Louisa; Rock Island Trail; Saddle Tramp; Shadow on the Wall.
1951 Her First Romance; Katie Did It; The Mating Season; Weekend with Father; The Blue Veil.
1952 Belles on Their Toes.
1953 The All-American; The Lone Hand; She Couldn't Say No; Here Come The Girls; The Invaders from Mars.
1986 Invaders from Mars.

Teddy Infuhr

1942 Tuttles of Tahiti; Ghost of Frankenstein; Pardon My Sarong.
1943 Amazing Mrs. Holiday; She's for Me; North Star; Madame Curie; Hers

to Hold; Gildersleeve on Broadway; The Iron Major; The Heavenly Body; Flesh and Fantasy; Where Are Your Children?
1944 Sherlock Holmes and the Spider Woman; The Unwritten Code; Heavenly Days; San Diego I Love You; Bowery to Broadway; Kitchen Cynic; Army Wives.
1945 Dangerous Partners; A Tree Grows in Brooklyn; That Night with You; Spellbound; The Clock; That's the Spirit; Hold That Blonde; Mama Loves Papa.
1946 Little Miss Big; Till the End of Time; The Best Years of Our Lives; The Virginian; Sentimental Journey; Return of Rusty; Gay Blades; Song of Arizona; Affairs of Geraldine; Sister Kenny; Three Wise Fools; My Brother Talks to Horses; Faithful in My Fashion; The Strange Woman; Because of Him; The Unknown.
1947 Desperate; Driftwood; The Egg and I; For the Love of Rusty; Her Husband's Affairs; Son of Rusty; The Bishop's Wife.
1948 Phantom Valley; Campus Honeymoon; My Dog Rusty; Rusty Leads the Way; The Bride Goes West; The Velvet Touch.
1949 Boy with the Green Hair; Fighting Fools; Ma and Pa Kettle; Madame Bovary; Rusty's Birthday; The Sun Comes Up; They Live by Night; West of El Dorado; Brimstone.
1950 Blonde's Hero; Summer Stock; Grounds for Marriage; California Passage; The Traveling Saleswoman; Ma and Pa Kettle Go to Town; The Killer That Stalked New York.
1951 Gene Autry and the Mounties; Valley of Fire; David and Bathsheba; Too Young to Kiss; Hills of Utah; Cause for Alarm; Ma and Pa Kettle Go to the Fair; Talk About a Stranger; Scaramouche.
1953 Mr. Scoutmaster.
1954 Men of the Fighting Lady.
1955 Blackboard Jungle.

Tommy Ivo

1945 Earl Carroll's Vanities.
1946 Song of Arizona.
1947 Stepchild; Carnival in Costa Rica.
1948 I Remember Mama; Trail to Laredo; Song of Idaho; Secret Service Investigator; Prejudice; Moonrise; Fighting Back; The Babe Ruth Story.
1949 Take One False Step; Smoky Mountain Melody; Outcasts of the Trail; Laramie; Horsemen of the Sierras; Feudin' Rhythm.
1950 Kill the Umpire; The Lost Volcano; Father Is a Bachelor; Operation Haylift; The Killer That Stalked New York; Trail of the Rustlers.
1951 Snake River Desperadoes; The Lemon Drop Kid; Whirlwind; Al Jennings of Oklahoma; Hills of Utah.
1952 The Rough, Tough, West; Plymouth Adventure; Treasure of Lost Canyon; The Yellow Haired Kid; Belles on Their Toes.
1955 You're Never Too Young; Blackboard Jungle.
1957 Dragstrip Girl.
1958 Life Begins at 17; The Beast of Budapest.

1959 Ghost of Dragstrip Hollow.
1961 The Cat Burglar.
1979 American Nitro.
1983 Heart Like a Wheel.

Eilene Janssen

1940 Sandy Gets Her Man.
1944 Where Are Your Children?; Two Girls and a Sailor; Since You Went Away; Till We Meet Again; The Seventh Cross.
1945 It Happened in Springfield.
1946 Renegades; The Green Years; Rendezvous 24.
1947 Song of Love; The Millerson Case; Driftwood; Curly.
1948 Who Killed Doc Robbin?; The Bride Goes West; Borrowed Trouble; On Our Merry Way.
1949 The Boy with Green Hair.
1951 Arizona Manhunt; The Dakota Kid; Buckaroo Sheriff of Texas.
1952 Wild Horse Ambush; Sally and Saint Anne.
1954 About Mrs. Leslie.
1956 The Search for Bridey Murphy.
1957 Beginning of the End.
1958 Escape from Red Rock; The Space Children.
1963 The Black Zoo.
1968 Panic in the City.

Claude Jarman, Jr.

1946 The Yearling.
1947 High Barbaree.
1949 Intruder in the Dust; Roughshod; The Sun Comes Up.
1950 The Outriders; Rio Grande.
1951 Inside Straight.
1952 Hangman's Knot.
1953 Fair Wind to Java.
1956 The Great Locomotive Chase.
1978 Centennial.

Marcia Mae Jones

1925 Mannequin.
1926 Kid Millions.
1927 Smile Brother Smile.
1930 Bride of the Regiment; King of Jazz.
1931 Street Scene; The Champ; Night Nurse.
1932 Birthday Blues.
1933 Mush and Milk.
1934 Imitation of Life; The Girl from Missouri.

Filmographies 355

1935 Gentle Julia; The Good Fairy.
1936 Strike Me Pink; The Garden of Allah; These Three.
1937 Heidi; Two Wise Maids; The Life of Emile Zola; Mountain Justice; Lady Behave.
1938 The Adventures of Tom Sawyer; Barefoot Boy; Mad About Music.
1939 First Love; The Little Princess; Meet Dr. Christian.
1940 Dr. Kildare's Strange Case; Anne of Windy Poplars; Haunted House; Tomboy; The Old Swimming Hole.
1941 The Gang's All Here; Let's Go Collegiate; Nice Girl?
1942 Secrets of a Co-Ed.
1943 Nobody's Darling; The Youngest Profession; Top Man.
1944 Lady in the Death House; Nine Girls.
1945 Snafu.
1948 Street Corner; Arson, Inc.
1949 Trouble Preferred; Tucson; Caught.
1950 The Daughter of Rosie O'Grady; Hi-Jacked.
1951 Chicago Calling.
1952 The Yellow Haired Kid; The Star.
1968 Live a Little, Love a Little.
1969 Gypsy Moths.
1973 The Way They Were.
1974 The Spectre of Edgar Allan Poe.

Mickey Kuhn

1935 Change of Heart.
1937 A Doctor's Diary.
1939 Juarez; King of the Underworld; S.O.S. Tidal Wave; Gone with the Wind; When Tomorrow Comes.
1940 I Want a Divorce.
1945 Roughly Speaking; This Love of Ours; A Tree Grows in Brooklyn; Dick Tracy.
1946 The Searching Wind; The Strange Love of Martha Ivers; Roaring Rangers.
1947 High Conquest; Magic Town.
1948 Red River.
1949 Scene of the Crime.
1950 Broken Arrow; That's My Boy.
1951 A Streetcar Named Desire; On the Loose.
1955 Savage Wilderness (*aka* The Last Frontier).
1956 Away All Boats.

Gordon Lee

1935 Little Sinner; Our Gang Follies of 1936.
1936 Divot Diggers; The Pinch Singer; Second Childhood; Bored of Education; Two Too Young; Pay as You Exit; Spooky Hooky; General Spanky.

1937 Reunion in Rhythm; Glove Taps; Hearts Are Thumps; Rushin' Ballet; Roamin' Holiday; Night n' Gales; Fishy Tales; Framing Youth; The Pigskin Palooka; Mail and Female; Our Gang Follies of 1938.
1938 Canned Fishing; Bear Facts; Three Men in a Tub; Came the Brawn; Feed Em and Weep; The Awful Tooth; Hide and Shriek; The Little Ranger; Party Fever; Aladdin's Lantern; Men in Fright; Football Romeo; Practical Jokers.
1939 Alfalfa's Aunt; Tiny Troubles; Duel Personalities; Clown Princes; Cousin Wilbur; Joy Scouts; Dog Daze; Auto Antics.

Sammy McKim

1935 This Is the Life; Annie Oakley; Frisco Kid; Ceiling Zero.
1936 Pepper; The Plough and the Stars; Country Gentlemen; Free Rent; San Francisco.
1937 Maytime; Hit the Saddle; Gunsmoke Ranch; The Painted Stallion; Bury the Hatchet; Heart of the Rockies; It Happened in Hollywood; Trigger Trio; Mama Runs Wild; The Game That Kills.
1938 Red River Range; Reformatory; Call the Mesquiteers; Great Adventures of Wild Bill Hickok; The Old Barn Dance; The Lone Ranger.
1939 Man of Conquest; The Night Riders; The New Frontier; Western Caravans; Rovin' Tumbleweeds; Flying G-Men; Dick Tracy's G-Men.
1940 Hi-Yo Silver; Texas Terrors; Little Men; Rocky Mountain Ranger; Laddie.
1941 Public Enemies; Pacific Blackout; Father's Son.
1943 We've Never Been Licked.
1947 The Hucksters.
1948 I, Jane Doe.
1949 Flamingo Road; You're My Everything.
1950 Tillers of the Soil; Lonely Heart Bandits; Destination Big House.
1952 Above and Beyond; Thunderbirds.

Shirley Mills

1938 Little Miss Broadway; Child Bride.
1939 The Under-Pup.
1940 The Grapes of Wrath; Diamond Frontier; Virginia City; Five Little Peppers in Trouble; Young People.
1942 Henry Aldrich Gets Glamour; Miss Annie Rooney.
1943 True to Life; Reveille with Beverly; Mr. Big; Top Man; Shadow of a Doubt.
1944 Nine Girls; None Shall Escape.
1945 Patrick the Great.
1946 That Brennan Girl; Betty Co-Ed.
1948 An Old-Fashioned Girl.
1950 It's a Small World.
1951 Fighting Coast Guard; The Model and the Marriage Broker.

Filmographies

Roger Mobley

1960 A Dog's Best Friend.
1961 The Boy Who Caught a Crook; The Comancheros; The Silent Call.
1962 Jack the Giant Killer.
1963 Dime with a Halo; Saint Mike (aka The Runway).
1964 Emil and the Detectives.
1979 The Apple Dumpling Gang Rides Again.
1980 The Kids Who Know Too Much.

Larry Olsen

1943 Red Cross Short; Happy Land; The Chance of a Lifetime.
1944 None Shall Escape; The Seventh Cross; Address Unknown; Casanova Brown.
1945 My Pal Wolf; Lone Texas Ranger; Sergeant Mike; Divorce.
1947 Curly (*aka* Hal Roach's Comedy Classics).
1948 Who Killed Doc Robbin?; Isn't It Romantic; Sitting Pretty.
1950 Winchester 73.
1952 Room for One More.
1953 The Story of Three Loves.
1954 Brigadoon.

Gigi Perreau

1943 Madame Curie.
1944 Two Girls and a Sailor; Dark Waters; Mr. Skeffington; The Master Race.
1945 Yolanda and the Thief; God Is My Co-Pilot; Voice of the Whistler.
1946 Alias Mr. Twilight.
1947 Green Dolphin Street; High Barbaree; The Song of Love.
1948 The Sainted Sisters; Enchanted; Family Honeymoon.
1949 My Foolish Heart; Roseanna McCoy; Song of Surrender.
1950 For Heaven's Sake; Never a Dull Moment; Shadow on the Wall.
1951 The Lady Pays Off; Reunion in Reno; Weekend with Father.
1952 Bonzo Goes to College; Has Anybody Seen My Gal.
1954 Attila.
1956 Dance with Me, Henry; The Man in the Gray Flannel Suit; There's Always Tomorrow.
1958 The Cool and the Crazy; Wild Heritage.
1959 Girls' Town.
1961 Look at Any Window; Tammy, Tell Me True.
1967 Hell on Wheels; Journey to the Center of Time.
1978 High Seas Hijack.
1997 The Sleepless.

Jon Provost

1953 So Big.
1954 Country Girl.

1956 Back from Eternity.
1957 All Mine to Give; Escapade in Japan.
1963 Lassie's Great Adventure.
1966 This Property Is Condemned.
1970 Secret of the Sacred Forest; The Computer Wore Tennis Shoes.

Gene Reynolds

1934 Babes in Toyland.
1935 Teachers Beau; Washee Ironee; Son of Man.
1936 Thank You, Jeeves.
1937 Captains Courageous; Thunder Trail; The Californians; Madame X.
1938 Boys Town; The Crowd Roars; In Old Chicago; Love Finds Andy Hardy; Of Human Hearts.
1939 Bad Little Angel; The Flying Irishman; The Spirit of Culver; They Shall Have Music.
1940 Edison, The Man; Gallant Sons; The Mortal Storm; Santa Fe Trail; The Blue Bird.
1941 Andy Hardy's Pet Secretary; The Penalty; Adventures in Washington.
1942 Eagle Squadron; Tuttles of Tahiti; Junior G-Men of the Air.
1948 Jungle Patrol.
1949 The Big Cat; Slattery's Hurricane.
1953 99 River Street.
1954 The Country Girl; Down Three Dark Streets; Bridges of Toko-Ri; Prisoner of War.
1955 Diane.

Bryan Russell

1961 Babes in Toyland.
1962 Safe at Home; The Wonderful World of the Brothers Grimm.
1963 How the West Was Won; Bye Bye Birdie; A Ticklish Affair.
1964 Emil and the Detectives.
1967 The Adventures of Bullwhip Griffin.

Jeanne Russell

1963 The Birds.

Mickey Sholdar

1960 Facts of Life.
1962 Boy's Night Out.
1964 One Man's Way.

1968 Shadow on the Land.
1970 The Intruders.
1975 Babe.

Frankie Thomas

1934 Wednesday's Child.
1935 Dog of Flanders.
1937 Tim Tyler's Luck.
1938 Boys Town; Little Tough Guys in Society; Nancy Drew, Detective.
1939 Angels Wash Their Faces; Code of the Streets; Nancy Drew and the Hidden Staircase; Nancy Drew, Reporter; Dead End Kids on Dress Parade; Nancy Drew, Trouble Shooter.
1940 Invisible Stripes.
1941 Flying Cadets; One Foot in Heaven.
1942 Always in My Heart; The Major and the Minor.

Leon Tyler

1939 The Star Maker; You Can't Cheat an Honest Man.
1940 Honeymoon Deferred.
1941 Helping Hands; Come Back, Miss Pipps; They Meet Again; Melody for Three; Whistling in the Dark.
1942 Surprised Parties; On the Sunny Side; The Loves of Edgar Allan Poe; Bambi [voice].
1943 I Dood It; Bomber's Moon; The Moon Is Down.
1944 The Great Mike; Maisie Goes to Reno; The Sullivans.
1945 This Love of Ours; Son of Lassie; Great Stagecoach Robbery; Magical Movieland.
1948 Mickey.
1949 Dear Wife; Mr. Soft Touch; So Dear to My Heart.
1950 The Happy Years; Military Academy with the Tenth Avenue Gang.
1951 That's My Baby.
1952 Carrie; Just For You; Has Anybody Seen My Gal.
1953 Sweethearts on Parade.
1954 Prisoner of War.
1955 Lay That Rifle Down.
1956 Accused of Murder; These Wilder Years.
1957 Dragstrip Girl; Spring Reunion; Jeanne Eagels; The Sad Sack; Shake, Rattle and Rock.
1958 King Creole; Submarine Seahawk; Outcasts of the City; Juvenile Jungle.
1959 Ghost of Dragstrip Hollow.
1961 The Absent Minded Professor.
1963 Son of Flubber; My Six Loves.
1966 The Monkey's Uncle.

Beverly Washburn

- *1950* The Killer That Stalked New York.
- *1951* Here Comes the Groom; Superman and the Mole Men.
- *1952* Aaron Slick from Pumpkin Crick; The Greatest Show on Earth.
- *1953* The Juggler; Shane.
- *1955* The Lone Ranger.
- *1957* Old Yeller.
- *1958* Summer Love.
- *1968* Spider Baby.
- *1969* Pit Stop.
- *1973* When the Line Goes Through.
- *1994* Children of the Dark.

Bobs Watson

- *1932* Life Begins.
- *1936* Pay as You Exit; Showboat.
- *1937* Our Gang Follies of 1938; Maytime.
- *1938* Go Chase Yourself; In Old Chicago; Kentucky; Boys Town; Young Dr. Kildare.
- *1939* Blackmail; Dodge City; On Borrowed Time; The Story of Alexander Graham Bell; Calling Dr. Kildare.
- *1940* Dr. Kildare's Crisis; Dreaming Out Loud; Wyoming.
- *1941* Hit the Road; Men of Boys Town; Scattergood Pulls the Strings.
- *1943* Hi Buddy.
- *1956* The Bold and the Brave.
- *1962* Saintly Sinners; What Ever Happened to Baby Jane?
- *1967* First to Fight.
- *1977* Grand Theft Auto.

Delmar Watson

- *1930* The Lone Star Ranger; Outside the Law.
- *1931* Compromise.
- *1932* Wild Girl.
- *1933* The Fourth Horseman; The Right to Romance; To the Last Man.
- *1934* The Painted Veil; Fugitive Lovers; Chained; In the Big House; Shrimps for a Day.
- *1935* Annie Oakley; Silk Hat Kid; Our Gang Follies of 1936.
- *1936* We're Only Human; Old Hutch; Silly Billies; The Pinch Singer; One Live Ghost; The Country Doctor.
- *1937* Maytime; The Great O'Malley; It Happened in Hollywood; Outlaws of the Prairie; The Pigskin Palooka; Tovarich; Heidi.
- *1938* Clipped Wings; Change of Heart; Hunted Men; Kentucky; Breaking the Ice.

Filmographies

1939 Mr. Smith Goes to Washington; When Tomorrow Comes; You Can't Cheat an Honest Man; Adventures of Huckleberry Finn; Young Mr. Lincoln; Here I Am a Stranger.
1940 Legion of the Lawless; My Little Chickadee.
1941 Among the Living.
1946 The Gas House Kids.

Johnny Whitaker

1966 The Russians Are Coming! The Russians Are Coming!
1969 The Littlest Angel.
1972 Snowball Express; The Biscuit Eater; Napoleon and Samantha; Mystery in Dracula's Castle; Something Evil.
1973 Tom Sawyer.
1977 Mulligan's Stew.
1979 Magic Pony.

Jane Withers

1932 Handle with Care.
1933 Zoo in Budapest.
1934 Imitation of Life; Bright Eyes; It's a Gift.
1935 The Farmer Takes a Wife; Ginger; Paddy O'Day; This is the Life.
1936 Can This Be Dixie; Gentle Julia; Little Miss Nobody; Pepper.
1937 Checkers; Angel's Holiday; 45 Fathers; The Holy Terror; Wild and Woolly.
1938 Always in Trouble; Arizona Wildcat; Keep Smiling; Rascals.
1939 Boy Friend; Chicken Wagon Family; Pack Up Your Troubles.
1940 Girl from Avenue A; High School; Shooting High; Youth Will be Served.
1941 Golden Hoofs; Her First Beau; Small Town Deb; A Very Young Lady.
1942 The Mad Martindales; Young America.
1943 Johnny Doughboy; The North Star.
1944 Faces in the Fog; My Best Gal.
1946 Affairs of Geraldine.
1947 Danger Street.
1956 Giant.
1957 The Heart Is a Rebel.
1961 The Right Approach.
1963 Captain Newman, M.D.
1975 All Together Now.
2001 Hunchback of Notre Dame II [voice].

Index

Aaker, Dee 5
Aaker, Lee 5–12
Aaron Slick from Pumpkin Crick 295
Abbott and Costello 139, 298
Abbott and Costello Meet the Killer 94
Abe Lincoln in Illinois 43
About Mrs. Leslie 159
The Absent-Minded Professor 292
Adventures of Bullwhip Griffin 255, 257
Adventures of Jim Bowie 111
Adventures of Ozzie and Harriet 117, 136, 159
Adventures of Rin Tin Tin 6, 8, 10–12
Adventures of Superman 98, 99
Adventures of Tom Sawyer 173
Agar, John 339
Ah, Wilderness! 27
Alda, Alan 250
Alford, Carol 19
Alford, Eugenia 15
Alford, Phillip 13–19, 31
Alfred Hitchcock Hour 274
Alfred Hitchcock Presents 98, 184, 246, 344
The All American 134
All in the Family 175
Allyson, June 154
Always in My Heart 280
Ameche, Don 219, 243
Ames, Leon 96, 154
Anderson, Judith 181
Andrews, Julie 17
The Andy Griffith Show 246
Andy Hardy 117, 118, 280

Angels Wash Their Faces 281
Ann-Margret 255
Annie Laurie 61
Annie Oakley 114, 116, 117, 120, 193, 244
Appalachian Autumn 17
The Apple Dumpling Gang Rides Again 216
An Apple for the Teacher 287
Arena 9
Arizona Manhunt 156
Arlen, Richard 222, 223
Arness, James 125, 328
The Art Linkletter Show 156
Arthur, Robert 290
Astaire, Fred 70
Asner, Ed 246, 274
Atlas, Leopold 278
Atomic City 6
Auld Lange Syne 202
Aunt Sally's Kiddie Revue 334
Auntie Mame 55
Autry, Gene 72, 88–90, 140, 116, 159, 195, 340, 341
Away All Boats 184
Ayres, Gordon 27, 28

Babes in Toyland 200, 242
Baby (Dog) 235, 236
Baby Makes Three 325
Baby Peggy 1, 2, 20–29
Baby Sandy 153
Babylon Five 297
Back from Eternity 233
Backus, Jim 310, 312

363

Index

Bad Little Angel 243
The Bad Seed 274
Badham, John 31
Badham, Mary 13–16, 30–37
Baer, Max 320
Ball, Lucille 273
Bambi 220, 292
Bancroft, Anne 183
Barkley, Lillian 86
Barnes, Frank 10, 108
Barrat, Robert 171
Barrymore, Ethel 223
Barrymore, John 72
Barrymore, Lionel 72, 306–308
Bartholomew, Freddie 63, 279, 342
Barton, Charles 88, 260
Barty, Billy 329, 331
Bautzer, Gregg 175
Baxter, Anne 280
Beal, John 243
Beatty, Warren 65
Beaut (Horse) 212
Beckett, Scotty 4, 320
Beebe, Ford 147
Beery, Wallace 308, 320
Belding, Dale 220
Bell, James 158
The Bell Telephone Hour 299
Bella, Anna 289
Belles on Their Toes 132, 134
Benchley, Robert 277
Bendix, William 272
Benjy 5, 6
Benny, Jack 103, 295, 296, 302
Bergman, Ingrid 175
Bernstein, Elmer 37
The Best of Post 299
Betty Co-Ed 207
The Betty Hutton Show 232
The Beverly Hillbillies 158
Bewitched 327
Beyond Belief 330
Billingsley, Barbara 297
Bird on a Wire 31
The Birds 262
The Biscuit Eater 327
Bishop, Julie 88
Blackmer, Sidney 285
Blake, Bobby 188, 219, 290
Blaustein, Julian 95
Blocker, Dan 272, 329

Blondell, Joan 61, 180, 325
The Blue Danube 88
Blythe, Ann 342
Boatright, Bodie 13
The Bob Hope Show 49
Bogart, Humphry 76, 178, 320
Bomber's Moon 289
Bonanza 212, 245, 272, 310, 327, 329
Bond, Tommy 186, 188, 190
Bond, Ward 125, 272, 298, 299
Bondi, Beulah 115, 248
Booth, Shirley 160
Borrowed Trouble 159
Borzage, Frank 154
Bosworth, Hobart 25, 87
Bouquet, Harry 191
Bowdon, Doris 204
The Bowery Boys 291
The Boy Who Caught a Crook 213
The Boy with Green Hair 154
Boyd, William 40, 41
Boyer, Charles 170
Boys' Night Out 272, 273
Boy's Town 243, 247, 280, 303, 306
Braddock, Jim 320
Bradford, Lane 211
The Brady Bunch 224
Bray, Bob 80
Breck, Peter 274
Brennan, Walter 183, 184, 193, 198
Brice, Fanny 287, 334
Bridges, Dorothy 219
Bridges, Jim 99
Bridges, Lloyd 15, 219
The Bridges at Toko-Ri 244
Bright Eyes 336, 338, 341, 344
Briskin, Fred 279
Bristle Face 15, 17
Broken Arrow 182
Brooks, Doyle 10
Brooks, Jim 246
Brooks, Mel 213
Brooks, Rand 10, 341
Brown, Barbara 110
Brown, Clarence 161–164, 247
Brown, James 10, 12
Brownie (Dog) 20, 21
Brunet, Jacques 226
Bryce, Ed 284
Buckaroo Sheriff of Texas 156, 158
Bucquet, Harold 313

Bupp, Ann 38
Bupp, June 38
Bupp, Moyer *see* Bupp, Sonny
Bupp, Paul 38
Bupp, Sonny 38–46
Bupp, Tommy 38–43, 45
Burbridge, Betty 194
Burnette, Smiley 146
The Burns and Allen Show 175
Burstyn, Ellen 328
Bushman, Francis X. 230
Butler, David 335–337, 344
Butler, Lois 290
Butterflies Are Free 332
By the Light of the Silvery Moon 94
Bye Bye Birdie 11, 255, 256
Byington, Spring 69, 288
Byrd, Evelyn 201–203
Byrd, Ralph 178
Byrd, Admiral Richard 201, 319

Cagney, James 197, 290
Cagney, Jeanne 42
The Caine Mutiny 243
The Californians 243
Call of the Mesquiteers 196
Calling Dr. Kildare 306
Cameron, Rod 52
The Candyed House 98
Cannon 176
Canutt, Yakima 194
Cantor, Eddie 286, 287
Canyon River 80
Capra, Frank 113, 316
Captain January 21, 25
Captain Newman, M.D. 344
Captains Courageous 243
Cardi, Pat 36
Carey, Harry, Jr. 165
Carey, Phil 97
Carillo, Leo 87, 140
Carmen Jr. 22
Caro nome 87
Caron, Leslie 223
Carr, Bernard 221
Carradine, John 204
Carrie Nation 277
Carson, Jack 42, 269
Carter, Mrs. 220
Cary, Bob 28, 29
Cary, Diana Serra *see* Baby Peggy

Cash and Carry 40
Cassell, Cindy 215
Castle, William 34, 36
Catlett, Walter 110
Caulfield, Joan 64
CBS Playhouse 17
Centennial 167
The Challenge to Lassie 114
Chambers, Stan 156
The Champ 169, 308
Champion (Horse) 88, 90, 195
Champion, Gower 126
Chandler, Jeff 182
Chaney, Lon, Jr. 300
Change of Heart 178
Chaplin, Charlie 310
Chicken Every Sunday 283
Child Bride 201, 202
Chapin, Billy 54
Chapin, Lauren 12, 55, 97
Chapin, Michael 47–56, 156–158
Charlie and the Angels 327
Charney, Kim 254
Chase, Charlie 84
Cheaper by the Dozen 132
Cheyenne 98, 211, 215
The Children's Hour 170
China Syndrome 99
A Christmas Carol 38, 231
Cimarron 87
The Cisco Kid 140
Citizen Kane 42
Clampitt, Bob 5
Clements, Stanley 290
Clift, Montgomery 181, 183
Climax 229
Clyde, Andy 237
Cobb, Irving 193
Cobb, Joe 85
Coffin, Tris 52
Cohn, Harry 58, 290
Colbert, Claudette 87, 132
Coleman, Gary 2, 116
Collins, Gene 290
Combat 82
Come Blow Your Horn 99
The Computer Wore Tennis Shoes 239
Conan Doyle, Arthur 284
Confessions of a Nazi Spy 41
Conflict 41
Connors, Chuck 124

Conway, Morgan 180
Coogan, Jackie 1, 2, 21, 22, 29, 44, 220, 299
Coogan, Mrs. 22
Coogan Law 44, 266
Coomes, Carol 115
Cooper, Gary 6, 70, 71, 76, 85
Cooper, Jackie 71, 85, 169, 245, 272, 341
Corcoran, Kevin 297
Corman, Roger 292
The Corn Is Green 49
Corrigan, Lloyd 285
Corrigan, Ray 194–196
Corrigan, Wrongway 243, 319
Cortez, Ricardo 243
Costello, Dolores 169
Costello, Lou 94, 139, 298
Country Gentlemen 193
The Country Girl 233, 244
Crain, Jeanne 133
Crawford, Joan 103
Crawford, Johnny 124
Crenna, Richard 325
Cronyn, Hume 113
Crosby, Bing 134, 233, 287, 293, 295, 301, 302
Crotke, Mrs. 33, 34, 36
The Crowd Roars 243
Cruze, James 169
Culkin, Macaulay 2, 305, 319, 322
Curly 156, 220, 221, 224
Curtis, Billy 11, 81, 109, 254
Curtis, Tony 7, 134
Curtiz, Michael 171, 206, 223, 293
Custer 100

Dahl, Arlene 180
The Dakota Kid 156
The Dakotas 212
Danger 244
Danger Street 343
Daniels, Bebe 154
The Danny Thomas Show 158
Darnell, Linda 230
Darwell, Jane 40, 204
The Daughter of Rosie O'Grady 175
Davenport, Bill 175, 176
David and Bathsheba 140
Davis, Bette 49, 174, 203, 183
Davis, Gail 116, 117

Davis, Joan 291
Davis, Joel 139
Davis, Nancy 108, 109
Day, Doris 94, 96
Day in Court 262
The Day the Earth Stood Still 94, 95
Dead End 281
Dead End Kids 281
The Deadline 72
Dean, James 293
Death Valley Days 212, 252
DeCamp, Rosemary 96
December Bride 158, 175
The Decision of Christopher Blake 62
Dee, Frances 221
De Haven, Gloria 154
De Havilland, Olivia 179, 309
Dehner, John 269
Dekker, Albert 54
Dell, Myrna 164, 165
DeMille, Cecil B. 295, 302
Dennis the Menace 126, 260–263, 270
The Deputy 98
Dern, Bruce 214
The Desperate Hours 76, 77
Desperate Search 6
Destry 7, 212
Destry Rides Again 72
The Detectives 126
The Devil's Brother 84
Devine, Andy 175
Diamond Head 118
Dick Tracy 180
Dickens, Charles 231
Dieterle, William 181
Dietrich, Marlene 170
Dillman, Bradford 274
Dime with a Halo 214
The Dinah Shore Show 264
Dinehart, Alan III 107
Dinky 71
Disney, Walt 16, 17, 166, 213, 214, 198, 256, 257, 292, 297
Divorce Court 126
Dix, Richard 87
Dixie's Dainty Dewdrop 334, 342
Dobkin, Lawrence 124
Dr. Christian 49, 288
Dr. Kildare 36, 212
The Dr. Zod and Johnny Show 332
Dodge City 308

A Dog of Flanders 279
Donahue, Elinor 97
The Donald O'Connor Show 175
Donaldson, Jo 57
Donaldson, Ted 57–66, 180
The Donna Reed Show 117, 118, 120
Donnell, Jeff 165
Donnelly, Ruth 70
Doran, Ann 109
Douglas, Gordon 187
Douglas, Kirk 181, 295, 296, 302
Douglas, Melvyn 87
Douglas, Michael 167
Dow, Tony 297
Down Three Dark Streets 244
Dracula 90
Dragnet 50, 215, 275
Drake, Betsy 224
Dreams Deferred 91
Dress Parade 281
Driscoll, Bobby 4, 48, 54, 65, 102, 105, 151, 164
Dru, Joanne 183
Duel 329
Duke, Patty 33
Duncan, Lee 8, 10
Dunlap, Scott 79
Dunn, James 61, 335
Dunne, Steve 297
Dunning, Philip 279
Durante, Jimmy 154, 227
Durbin, Deanna 26, 174, 202, 281
Dusty and Sweets McGee 100, 101
Dymtryck, Edward 88

E.T. 322
Earl Carroll's Vanities 143, 144, 151
East, Jeff 328
Eckberg, Anita 233
Eden, Barbara 254
The Egg and I 140
87th Precinct 126, 212
Elliott, Bill 219, 290
Emergency Squad 39
Emil and the Detectives 215, 256, 257
Empire 271
Enchantment 227
Enter Laughing 99
Ernest, George 67–75
Errair, Kenneth 344
Escapade in Japan 234, 235

Escape from Freedom 38
Evans, Dale 51, 158
Evans, Joan 228
Evans, Wilbur 88
Evel Knieval 119
Every Sunday Night 68
Excursion 39, 40
Eyer, Bob 80
Eyer, Richard 76–82

F Troop 246
Fabares, Shelley 117, 118, 120
The Facts of Life 273
Fair Wind to Java 165, 166
Family Affair 325–327
The Family Honeymoon 132, 133, 232
Family Theater 49
Fantastic Studios 5
The Farmer's Daughter 212, 269–271, 273
Father Is a Bachelor 105
Father Knows Best 55, 64, 97–99, 101, 102, 136, 158, 291
Father Makes Good 110
Father Was President 54
Fellows, Edith 83–93, 207
Fellows, Elizabeth Lamb 83
Ferdin, Pamelyn 328
Ferrer, Mel 273
Fiddler, Jimmy 51
Field, Sally 119, 120
Fields, W.C. 40, 85, 86, 334
Fillmore 167
Fireside Theatre 111
The First Legion 279
First Love 174
Five Card Stud 128
Five Little Peppers 88
Five Little Peppers in Trouble 207
Flame (Dog) 8, 61, 62, 108, 134, 139
Flannigan, Father 306
Flash Gordon 281
Fleming, Victor 179, 180
The Flower Girl 21
The Flying Irishman 243
Flynn, Errol 206, 207, 308
Fonda, Henry 167, 204, 205
For the Love of Rusty 61, 62
For the Love of Willadean 213
Foran, Dick 72
Ford, Glenn 290

Ford, Harrison 18
Ford, John 165, 193, 203–205, 293
Ford, Paul 18
Ford Theater 8, 229
Fort Dobbs 80
Foster, Jodi 4, 120, 327, 330
Foster, Norman 105
Foster, Preston 193
The Four Freshmen 344
Four Star Playhouse 229
Foy, Brian 280
Fra Diavolo 84
Francis, Genie 176
Frankenstein 90
Freebootin' 328
Friendly Persuasion 77, 78, 81
The Frisco Kid 197
Front Row Center 159
Frontier Circus 212
Four Sons 71, 73
The Fuller Brush Man 134
Funicello, Annette 292
Funny Valentines 330
Furness, Betty 87
Fury 210–212, 214, 298–300

G.E. Theater 184, 293
Gable, Clark 155, 168, 169, 179
The Gale Storm Show 158
Gallegher 213, 214, 256
The Garden of Allah 170
Garland, Judy 69, 86
Garner, James 273
Garner, Peggy Ann 60, 61
Garrett, Betty 220
The Gashouse Kids 322
Gaudioso, John 327
Gaynor, Mitzi 110, 111
Geer, Will 182
Gehrig, Lou 319
Geiger, Maynard 29
The Gene Autry Show 98, 140
General Hospital 126, 176, 301, 325
Georgia Boy 180
The Geraldo Show 265
The Ghost and Mrs. Muir 246
The Ghost of Dragstrip Hollow 292
Giant 344
Gibson, Hoot 194, 195
Gibson, Mimi 265
Gift, Donn 163, 164

Gilligan's Island 175
The Girl from Jones Beach 109
Girl Happy 118, 120
Gish, Lillian 54
The Gnome-Mobile 198
God Is My Co-Pilot 227
Gone with the Wind 178, 183
Goode, Ingrid 111
Goodwin, Bill 290
Gorcey, Leo 281
Gordon, Gale 261
Goulding, Alf 22
Goulet, Robert 208
Gracian, Father 28
Grady, Mary 325, 332
Graff, Wilton 222
Grahame, Gloria 164
Grand Theft Auto 312
Granger, Farley 141
Grant, Cary 58–60, 63, 66, 223, 224
Grant, Katherine 80
Grant, Lance 59
Granville, Bonita 170–172, 236, 238, 280, 281
The Grapes of Wrath 203–205, 208
Grauman, Sid 67
Graves, Peter 214
Gray, Arlene 110
Gray, Beatrice 94
Gray, Billy 94–102, 116, 158
Gray, Gary 103–112, 134
Gray, Jean 109, 111
The Great Adventures of Wild Bill Hickok 192
The Great Locomotive Chase 166
Great Moments with Mr. Lincoln 198
The Great O'Malley 320
The Great Stagecoach Robbery 290
The Greatest Show on Earth 295
Green, Johnny 256
Green, Nigel 36
Green Dolphin Street 227
The Green Years 154
Greene, Lorne 272
Gregory, Paul 54
Grey Shadow (Dog) 220
Grimes, Karolyn 115
Grundy, Mrs. 335
Guardino, Harry 274
Gubitosi, Mickey *see* Blake, Bobby
The Guiding Light 110

Index

Gun Smugglers 106, 107
Gunsmoke 84, 125, 212, 271, 327, 328

Hagen, Jean 9
Hal Roach's Comedy Classics 221
Hall, Alexander 59
Hall, Huntz 281
Halop, Billy 281
Hamer, Rusty 4
Hamilburg, Mitchell J. 104, 116
Hamilton, Neil 87
Handle with Care 335, 337
Hangman's Knot 165
Hansen, Mel 207
Happy Land 218
Hardwicke, Sir Cedric 313
Harlow, Jean 170
Hart, Neal 20
Harvey, Laurence 253
Hathaway, Henry 254, 255
Hawkins, Jimmy 113–120
Hawkins, Tim 113
Hawks, Howard 11, 183
Hawn, Goldie 31
Hayden, Russell 111
Hayden, Sterling 233
Hayes, George "Gabby" 105, 110, 134
Haynes, Dick 223
Haynes on the Range 223
Hayworth, Rita 167
Hearst, William R. 175
Heart of the Rio Grande 88
Heart of the Rockies 196
Heartthrob of America 332
Heflin, Van 135, 136, 299
Heidi 173, 174, 315–318, 320, 323
Helen's Babies 21
Hell and High Water 198
Hellman, Lillian 170
Hendrix, Wanda 290, 291
Hennesey 245
Henry Aldrich Gets Glamour 207
Henry IV 64
Hepburn, Katherine 227
Her First Romance 88
Herdan, Jerry 191
Here Come the Girls 134
Here Comes the Groom 295, 302
Hersholt, Jean 173, 288
Herzbaum, Hilda 124
Herzbaum, Walter 124

Hey, Hey, USA 43
Hey You (Dog) 9
Hickman, Darryl 63, 203–205, 287
Hickman, Dwayne 184
High Barbaree 130, 164, 227
High Conquest 181, 182
High Noon 6
Hinkle, Robert 121
His Greatest Gamble 87
Hit the Saddle 193
The Hit Parade 91
Hitchcock, Alfred 139, 262, 274
Hjorth, Ernst 67
Hobart, Rose 290
The Hobbit 312
Holden, Scott 137
Holden, William 105
The Hollywood Palace 296
Hollywood Posse 28
Hollywood's Children 28
Holms, Pat 258
Holt, Tim 106
Home Alone 305
Homeier, Skip 290
Hondo 7, 10
Hood, Darla 90, 188, 322
Hooker, Joe 10
Hope, Bob 134, 273
Hopkins, Miriam 176
Horn, Mrs. 69
Hot off the Wires 310
Houseman, John 33
Hovious, John 107
How Green Was My Valley 289
How the West Was Won 253–255
Howard, Cheryl 312
Howard, Leslie 179
Howard, Moe 40
Howard, Ron 312
Howe, James Wong 71
How's Business 269
Hoxie, Jack 90
Hudkins, Ace 157
Hudson, Rock 185
Hughes, Aida 128, 129
Hughes, Bill 121, 123
Hughes, Billy 121–129, 237, 272, 273
Hughes, Bill III 128
Hughes, Chris 127
Hughes, Howard 175
Hughes, J. Anthony 305

Hughes, Jackie 342
Hughes, Robert M. 121
Hughes, Whitey 121, 123, 127
The Human Comedy 161
The Hunchback of Notre Dame 345
Hunt, Jimmy 104, 105, 130–137, 218
Hunt, Roswitha 137
Hunter, Tab 185
Hutchinson, Josephine 171
Hutton, Robert 180
Hyland, Diana 274

I Married Joan 175, 291
I Remember Mama 145–147
I Spy
I Want a Divorce 180
Ichabod and Me 117
If'n I Was God 328
I'm a Child of God 324
I'm Dickens, He's Fenster 212
In Old Chicago 243, 249, 305
Infuhr, Teddy 138–142, 181
Inge, William 64, 65
Inside Danny Baker 212, 213
Inside Straight 165
An Interview with a Vampire 268
Intruder in the Dust 163, 165, 166
The Intruders 18
Invaders from Mars 131, 135, 137, 227
The Invisible Boy 79
Ireland, John 183
It's a Wonderful Life 113, 115, 117, 119
It's a Wonderful Life 50th Anniversary Scrapbook 113, 114
It's Your Health 111
Ivo, Don 143, 144
Ivo, Tommy 111, 143–152

J.R. (Dog) 8–10
The Jack Benny Radio Show 295
Jack the Giant Killer 214
Jacobs, Arthur P. 327, 328
Jagger, Dean 124
Janie 90
Janssen, David 126
Janssen, Eilene 51, 52, 153–160, 220, 227
Janssen, Henry 153
Jarman, Claude, Jr. 161–168
Jarman, Natalie 167
Jason, Sybil 320

Jean, Gloria 202
Jenkins, Jackie Butch 63, 130
Jennie Kissed Me 159
Jeopardy 10
Jessell, George 24, 286, 287
Jimenez, Jose 98
Jimmy and Dick, the Novelty Boys 286
Jivin' Jacks and Jills 207
Johnny Rocco 80
The Johnny Whitaker Show 332
Johnson, Albert 166
Johnson, Ben 165
Johnson, Nunnally 204
Johnson, Van 130, 164
Jolson, Al 24, 38
Jones, Anissa 4, 326, 327, 332
Jones, Buck 22, 90
Jones, Davy 270
Jones, Freda 177
Jones, L.Q. 271
Jones, Marcia Mae 169–177, 209, 342
Jones, Marvin 177
Jordan, Bobby 281
Jordan, Michael 319
Juarez 178, 179, 181, 183
The Juggler 295, 296
JuJu (Chimp) 281, 282
Just for You 293

Kane, Whitford 279
Karloff, Boris 90, 144, 145, 298
Karnes, Roscoe 70
Kazan, Elia 60, 61
Kearns, Joseph 261
Keaton, Buster 175
Keeper of the Bees 87
Keith, Brian 15, 17, 325, 326
Kellin, Mike 274
Kelly, Grace 233
Kelly, Paul 109
Kelly, Tommy 173, 342
Kelton, Pert 87
Kennedy, Arthur 17
Kennedy, Edgar 85
Kennedy, President John 256
Keyes, Evelyn 294
The Keystone Kops 113, 314
Kibbee, Guy 316
The Kid Reporter 22
Kilbride, Percy 140
The Killer That Stalked New York 294

Kilroy 257
King, Cammie 179
The King and I 13
King of Jazz 169
King of the Khyber Rifles 198
King of the Underworld 178
Kirk, Tommy 292, 297
Kirkland, Jack 180
Kolden, Scott 331
Kruger, Alma 172
Kruger, Otto 285
Kuhn, Mickey 178–185
Kulik, Buzz 50, 276

LaCava, Gregory 87
Ladd, Alan 88, 103, 295
Laine, Frankie 208
Lancer 327
Landau, Martin 119
Lander, David 92
Lander, Kathy 92
Landon, Michael 159, 272, 292
Lane, Nathan 119
Lang, Walter 223
Lansberg, Klaus 50
Laramie 126
Larson, Jack 98
Lassie 7, 11, 80, 114, 125, 234, 235, 237–240, 251, 259
Lassie (Dog) 7, 78, 108, 109, 125, 165, 234–238, 289, 323
Lassie's Great Adventure 237
The Last Movie 100
Laughton, Charles 54
Laurel and Hardy 22, 40, 84, 188, 242
Laverne and Shirley 92
Law, John Phillip 329, 330
Law and Lawless 90
Law and Mr. Jones 126
Law of the Plainsman 252
Lawman 212
Leave It to Beaver 126, 246, 297, 325
Lee, Billy 89
Lee, Eva 186
Lee, Gordon 186–190
Lee, Gypsy Rose 287
Lee, Harper 14
Lee, Lila 193
Lee, Roland 186
Leigh, Janet 255
Leigh, Vivian 179, 183

Leonard, Bert 8, 11, 12
LeRoy, Mervyn 226, 227
Leslie, Joan 342
Lesser, Sol 21, 23, 25, 26
Let's Kill Uncle 34
Levin, Henry 115, 116
Levinson, Barry 168
Levy, Bert 200
Lewis, Jerry 180
The Life of Emile Zola 171
The Life of Riley 158
Life with Father 57, 66, 158
The Light in Your Life 155
Light Up the Sky 312
Lindbergh, Charles 317, 319
The Lineup 245
Litel, John 279
The Little Adventuress 88
Little Brown Jug 109
Little Miss Broadway 202
Little Miss Roughneck 87
Little Miss Thoroughbred 88
Little 'Ol Boy 277
Little Orvie 44,
The Little Princess 173, 174, 330
The Little Rascals 186–188, 190, 220, 288
Little Sinner 186
Living in a Big Way 130
Livingston, Jay 330
Livingston, Stan 237
Lockhart, June 235, 236, 240
Logan, Josh 180, 277
The Lone Hand 131, 132, 134, 135
The Lone Ranger 106, 244, 296, 299
Lone Texas Ranger 219
Look Homeward Angel 99
Looking Forward 72
Lord, Marjorie 135
Lord, Pauline 85
The Loretta Young Show 292, 298
A Loss of Roses 64
The Lost Volcano 147
Lou Grant 246, 248
Louisa 134
Love Boat 19
Love Is on the Air 39
Love Is the Song That Never Ends 220
Love Leads the Way 119
The Loving Family 135
Lowell, Linda 6

Loy, Myrna 133
Lumet, Sidney 248
Luna, Barbara 214
Lux Radio Theatre 132
Lux Video Theatre 50
Lydon, Jimmy 341
Lynde, Paul 255
Lynn, Betty 342
Lyon, Ben 154
Lyon, Richard 154
Lytell, Bert 279

Ma and Pa Kettle 140
McAllister, Lon 342
MacArthur, Byron 87
MacArthur, Jane 87
McCarthy, Joe 88
McCarthy, Kevin 299
McClure, M'Liss 110
McCormick, Myron 277
McCoy, Tim 5, 42,
McCrea, Joel 131, 134, 176
McCutcheon, Ralph 212
MacDonald, George 110
MacDonald, J. Farrell 103
MacDonald, Jeanette 165
McDonough, Mary 265
McDowall, Roddy 2, 4, 29, 92, 130, 155, 258, 267, 288
McEveety, Vincent 327
McFarland, Spanky 43, 85, 186–188, 190, 323
McGovern, Johnny 49
McGowan, Bob 71, 85
McGuire, Dom 245
McGuire, Dorothy 60, 61
McGuire, Mark 319
McIntire, John 125, 213
Mack, Ted 210
McKim, Brian 198
McKim, David 193, 197
McKim, Dorothy 198
McKim, Matthew 199
McKim, Sammy 191–199
McLaglen, Victor 165
MacMurray, Fred 132, 165
McQueen, Steve 252, 253
MacRae, Gordon 94
MacRae, Henry 281
M*A*S*H 246, 250
Mad About Music 174

Madame Curie 226
Madame X 243
Magic Town 182
The Magical Movieland 290, 291
Maharis, George 274
Mahoney, Jock 146, 294
Main, Marjorie 140
The Major and the Minor 280, 283
Malden, Karl 254, 255
Mallory, Boots 335
Malone, Ted 57
Maltin, Leonard 100, 101, 204
Mamakos, Peter 111
Mannequin 169
Mannix, Eddie 279
Mantle, Mickey 256
March, Fredric 76
Marco Juvenile Revue 335, 336
Marcus Welby, MD 175
Margie 145, 150, 152
Marihugh, Tammy 253
Marinka 91
Maris, Roger 256
Mark, Flip 269
Markim, Al 284
Marlowe, Hugh 96
Martin, Dean 180
Martin, Lock 96
Marvin, Lee 165
Mary Poppins 17
Masked Raiders 106
Massey, Raymond 229
Masur, Richard 265
Mather, Aubrey 61
Matheson, Tim 217
Mathias, Bob 253
Matinee Theatre 64, 99, 184, 245, 298
Matthews, Kerwin 80
Mature, Victor 38, 183
Mauch Twins 247
Mayer, Louis B. 168, 227, 279
Mayo, Archie 71, 73
Mayo, Virginia 109
Meal Ticket 192
Meglin, Ethel 201, 202
Megna, John 14, 31
Men in Fright 44
Men of Boys Town 308
Meredith, Burgess 64, 277
Merlin, Jan 284
Michaeljohn, Bill 74

Mickey 290
The Mickey Mouse Club 297
Midnight Choo Choo 264
Miles, Peter *see* Perreau, Gerald
Milland, Ray 283
Miller, Ron 216
Miller, Sidney 71
Mills, Shirley 200–209, 265
Milner, Martin 274
Mimieux, Yvette 118
The Miracle Worker 33
Miss Annie Rooney 207
Mr. Doc's Examination 124
Mr. Ed 158, 175, 238, 261
Mr. Scoutmaster 115, 116
Mr. Smith Goes to Washington 316
Mr. Soft Touch 290
Mitchell, Thomas 115
Mitchum, Robert 105
Mix, Tom 20
Mobley, Roger 210–217, 256, 257
Mobley, Sherry 215
The Model and the Marriage Broker 207
Moffett, Sharyn 220
The Monkees 270
The Monkey's Uncle 292
Monroe, Marilyn 290
The Montel Williams Show 265
Montgomery, George 80
Montgomery, Jack 20
Montgomery, Peggy Jean *see* Baby Peggy
Moonrise 114
Moore, Clayton 106, 296
Moore, Dickie 187, 309
Moore, Lola 104, 210, 218, 226, 233
Moore, Terry 289
Moorehead, Agnes 254
Moran, Jackie 4, 174, 175
Morgan, Dennis 40
Morgan, Harry 116
Morris, Howard 273
Morris, William 15
The Mortal Storm 243
Mountain Justice 171
Movie and Video Guide 101
Movie Night 84
Mrs. Wiggs and the Cabbage Patch 85
Mulligan, Robert 15, 30, 32
Mulligan's Stew 332
Muni, Paul 171, 173, 178

The Munsters 344
Murphy, Audie 6, 7, 290
Murray, Don 18
Mussolini, Benito 189
My Brother Talks to Horses 130
My Client Curly 58
My Favorite Husband 64
My Friend Irma 76
My Pal Wolf 220
My Six Loves 126
My Three Sons 158, 237, 246, 326
Mystery of Edwin Drood 68

Nancy Drew and the Hidden Treasure 281
Nancy Drew, Detective 280, 281
Nancy Drew, Reporter 281
Nancy Drew, Trouble Shooter 281
Napoleon and Samantha 327, 330
National Velvet 161
Naughty Marietta 90
The Navy vs the Night Monsters 100
Nazarro, Ray 146
Neal, Patricia 96, 135
Negri, Pola 22, 24
Nelson, Barry 64
Nelson, David 159
Nelson, Nils 237
Nelson, Ozzie 159
Nelson, Ricky 159, 223
The New Lassie 240
The New Loretta Young Show 297
Newland, John 297
Newman, Paul 64
The Next Voice You Hear 108
Nicholson, Jack 167
The Night Gallery 212
Night Nurse 169
The Night of the Hunter 54
Night Wind 108
Nine Girls 207, 209
No Place to Go 39–41
No Room for the Groom 7
Nobody's Children 89
Nokes, George 110
Nolan, Lloyd 165
None Shall Escape 207
North, Jay 257, 260–263, 265, 267, 270, 305
The North Star 341
Novak, Kim 273

Nugent, Judy 115
Nunn, Larry 4

O. Henry's Full House 11
Oates, Warren 214, 328
Oberon, Merle 176, 290
O'Brian, Hugh 158
O'Brien, Edmond 18, 213
O'Brien, Margaret 44, 50, 54, 103, 154, 226
O'Brien, Pat 197, 319
O'Brien, Rory 273
O'Connor, Donald 47, 158, 159, 207
O'Donnell, Cathy 141
The Odyssey of Runyon Jones 330
Of Human Hearts 243, 247, 248
Of Mice and Men 312
Oh Mistress Mine 99
O'Hara, Maureen 223
O'Keefe, Dennis 143
Oklahoma 207
The Old Barn Dance 195
Old Hutch 320
Old Yeller 297
Ole' Rex 121
Olmstead, Norman 132
Olsen, Chris 224
Olsen, Jane 224
Olsen, Larry 156, 218–225
Olsen, Moroni 285
Olsen, Susan 224
Olson and Johnson 193
Olynick, Julian 39
On Borrowed Time 144, 304, 307, 312
On Moonlight Bay 94, 96
On the Loose 183
On the Sunnyside 289
On Their Own 68
Once Upon a Time 58–60, 63
One Foot in Heaven 280
One Man's Family 49
One Man's Way 273
One Step Beyond 297, 298
The Original Amateur Hour 210
Osmond, Donny 327, 332
Osmond, Ken 325
Osmond, Mrs. 325
Our Gang 22, 40, 44, 71, 85, 156, 220, 242, 288, 322
The Outlaw Stallion 97

The Outlaws 212
The Outriders 165

Paar, Jack 98
Paddy o' Day 343
Page, Patti 273
Paige, Marvin 301
The Painted Hills 109, 110, 112
The Painted Stallion 194, 195
Pakula, Alan 13, 30, 32
Pal (Dog) 235
Palmer, Max 135
Pardon My Sarong 139
Parks, Larry 219, 220
Parole Fixer 42
Pasternak, Joe 202, 203
Patrick, Dorothy 97
The Patty Duke Show 213
Peabody, Eddie 108
Peck, Gregory 15, 17, 30–32, 33, 35, 37, 58, 139, 163, 167
Peg o' the Movies 24
Pemberton, Brock 90
Pepper 193
Pepper, Cynthia 150
Perkins, Caroline Anne 320
Perkins, Julia Ellen 320
Perreau, Gerald 132, 133, 156, 220, 232
Perreau, Gigi 132, 158, 226–232
Perreau, Janine 227
Perry Mason 158
Pesci, Joe 322
Pete (Dog) 189
Pete and Gladys 246
Pete Smith Specials 290
Peter Gunn 98, 245, 246
Peters, Brock 31
Peters, House, Jr. 52, 53, 111
Petersen, Paul 2, 129, 231, 261, 265, 266
Philco 283
Pigskin Palooka 322
Pirates of the Caribbean 198
Pitts, ZaSu 85, 334
The Plainsman 70, 72
Planer, Franz 59, 63
Planet of the Apes 327
Playhouse 90 269
The Plough and the Stars 193
Plummer, Amanda 101
The Plymouth Adventure 147

Pollack, Sidney 33
Pollock, Molly 57
Popular Bridge 284
Porter, Jane 342
Potter, Luce 135
Powell, Dick 180
Powell, Janie 154
Powell, William 148, 149
Power, Tyrone 198, 243
Powers, Stefanie 105
Presley, Elvis 118, 290
Prest, Patty 289
Preston, Robert 183
Price, Paul 50, 51
Prince John 242
Prince Valiant 198
Prisoner of War 287
Professional Father 297
Prouty, Jed 69
Provost, Jon 125, 233–241, 251, 257, 259, 267
Psycho 159
Public Eye 322
Pullman, Bill 119

The Quarterly 284
Queen of the Mob 42
Quillan, Eddie 90
Quo Vadis 232

Rachel and the Stranger 105–107, 109
Rains, Claude 180, 290
Ralston, Vera 165
The Range Rider 159
Ransom for Red Chief 11
Rawhide 80, 100
Rawhide Riley 222–225
Rawlings, Marjorie K. 165
The Ray Milland Show 291
Reagan, Ronald 6, 40, 109, 134, 287
Rebel Without a Cause 293
The Red Danube 227
The Red Pony 232
Red River 182–184
Redford, Robert 33, 238
Reed, Donna 115, 117, 231
Reeves, George 302
Reilly, Hugh 236
Reinhardy, Max 58
Reis, Irving 228
Remember the Day 279, 281

Remick, Lee 159
Renaldo, Duncan 197
Renegade Trail 40, 41, 43
Rennie, Michael 94–96
Rettig, Tommy 8, 11, 234, 235
Return of the Badmen 104, 105, 134
Reynolds, Debbie 126, 175, 255, 291
Reynolds, Gene 2, 242–250, 305
Rich, David Lowell 274
The Rifleman 124, 159
The Right Approach 344
The Right Man 88
Rigoletto 87
Rin Tin Tin (Dog) 6–9, 134
Rio Grande 165, 166
Rivers, Bobby 265
Roach, Hal 83, 84, 186, 187, 189
Roach, Hal, Jr. 156, 220, 221
Roaring Rangers 181
Robby Benson and Sonny Jim 281
Robby the Robot 79
The Robert Cummings Show 184
Roberts, Florence 69
Roberts, Joan 91
Roberts, Pernell 272
Robertson, Cliff 126
Robertson, Dale 159
Robinson, Frances 282
Rock Island Trail 134
Rodgers, Charles 286, 287
Rodeo 109
Rodney, Gene 64
Rogers, Ginger 283
Rogers, Roy 52, 53, 144, 158
Roland, Gilbert 178, 181
The Romantic Age 131
Romeo and Juliet 218
Room for One More 224
Room 222 246
Rooney, Mickey 4, 63, 69, 86, 118, 280, 308
Roosevelt, Franklin 25
Rosalie 90
Rosanna McCoy 228, 229
Rossner, Milt 81
Rough Ridin' Kids 48, 51, 52, 153, 156
Roughshod 164, 165
Roughly Speaking 180
Route 66 11, 212, 274
Roy Rogers Show 80
Rubin, Benny 87

The Ruggles 114
Ruggles, Charles 114
Russell, Bing 121–124
Russell, Bryan 215, 251–258, 259, 260, 264
Russell, Cathryn 258
Russell, Jeanne 259–268
Russell, Kurt 4, 217, 239
Russell, Redd 107
Russell, Rosalind 55, 180
Russell, William 260
The Russians Are Coming! The Russians Are Coming! 325, 329
Rusty's Birthday 134
Ruth, Babe 79
Ryan, Peggy 207
Ryan, Robert 160, 233
Rydell, Bobby 255

S.O.S. Tidal Wave 178
Saddle Tramp 134
Safe at Home 256
Sagal, Boris 214
Sally Jessie Raphael Show 265
Samantha (Goose) 77, 78
San Francisco 39
Sandy Gets Her Man 153
Sandy's Dreams 5
Santa Fe Trail 243
Sarafian, Richard 111
Sarandon, Chris 101
Savage Wilderness 183
Sawyer, Joe 10
Schaefer, Mandy 116
Schell, Maximilian 101
Schenck, Joseph 340, 341
Schlitz Playhouse 8
Scott, Randolph 68, 104, 165, 316
Scout's Honor 116
The Searching Wind 180
Searl, Jackie 341
The Secret of the Sacred Forest 238
See Here Private Hargrove 117
Seen but Not Heard 280
Selznick, David 173, 179
Sennett, Mack 303, 314
Sergeant Mike 219
The Seven Little Foys 98
The Seventh Cross 113, 154, 219
The Seventh Voyage of Sinbad 79
77th Sunset Strip 126

Severn, Billy 289
Shadow over the Land 272
Shamroy, Leon 61
Shane 295
Shaw, Althea 259, 262
Shaw, Glenn 251, 259, 260
Shaw, Irwin 58
She Married Her Boss 87
Sheffield, Johnny 147
Shenandoah 17, 19
Sheridan, Ann 320
Sherlock Holmes 284
Shivering Shakespeare 85
Sholdar, Mickey 128, 269–276
Shooting High 340, 341
Shore, Dinah 395
Showboat 288
Sierra Passage 97
Sigmund and the Sea Monster 330, 331
Silla, Felix 329
Silly Symphonies 336
Silver (Horse) 296
Silverheels, Jay 296
Simms, Larry 115
Simon & Simon 176
Simpson, Russell 204
Sins of Man 243
Sitting Pretty 223
Skelton, Red 140, 134, 291, 293
Skulnik, Menasha 91
Slate, Jeremy 328
Slater, Christian 119
The Sleepless 230
Slovak, Robert 137
Small, Edward 214
Smith, Bernard 255
Smoke in the Wind 128
So Big 233, 235
So Dear to My Heart 292
Some Like It Hot 98
Something Evil 329
Son of Flubber 292
Son of Lassie 289, 293
Song of Arizona 144
The Song of Love 227
Song of Norway 110
Song of the Saddle 72
Sonny Boy 38
Sons of Soldiers 58
Sorensen, Leilani 260
Sorensen, Rickie 4, 260

Sound of Music 257
Spalla, Rick 324
Sparkle Marcia Mae 176
Spearl, Connie Lee 286
Spellbound 139
Spider Baby 300
Spielberg, Steven 329
Spike (Dog) 297
Spinout 118
Stagecoach West 80
Stakeout 121, 123
Stanwyck, Barbara 10, 193
The Star 174
Star Trek 297, 298, 301
Star Wars 322
Stardust on the Sage 72, 88
The Starmaker 287
Starrett, Charles 181
Steiger, Rod 233
Stevens, Connie 31
Stevens, George 146, 302, 343, 344
Stevens, Inger 270, 271
Stewart, James 17, 113–115, 181, 182, 243, 277, 295, 316
Stockwell, Dean 4, 63, 154
Stone, Fred 39, 40
The Story of Three Loves 223
Straight Arrow 49
Strange Love of Martha Ivers 180, 181
The Story of Robert Burns 90
Street Scene 169
A Streetcar Named Desire 183
Streets of San Francisco 176
Streisand, Barbra 77
The Stu Erwin Show 158, 291
Stuart, Mary 110
Studio One 229, 283
Sturges, John 61, 62
Sugarfoot 159
Sullivan, Barry 10
The Sullivans 3, 48, 289
Summerville, Slim 193
The Sun Comes Up 140, 165
Superman and the Jungle Girl 98
Suzanne Somers Show 265
A Sweet Bird of Youth 64
Swing Your Lady 39
Switzer, Carl "Alfafa" 288, 32
Sydney, Sylvia 169

Take One False Step 148

Tales of Wells Fargo 159, 252
Talk About a Stranger 97
Tandy, Jessica 113
Taurog, Norman 85, 248, 306, 308
Taylor, Dub 328
Taylor, Elizabeth 2, 4, 92, 120, 130, 154
Taylor, Rick 330
Taylor, Robert 175, 243
Teen Beat Magazine 332
Temperature Rising 176
Temple, Gertrude 2, 173
Temple, Shirley 1, 2, 22, 26, 47, 69, 173, 174, 202, 207, 227, 316–318, 336–339
The Tenth Avenue Gang 291
Terhune, Max 196, 197
Terrell, Steve 158
Terror at Black Falls 111
Tewksbury, Peter 98, 215
Texaco Star Theater 158
The Texan 298
Thalberg, Irving 279
Thatcher, James 13
That's My Boy 180
Theatre Five 284
These Three 170, 172, 176
They Live by Night 141
They Shall Have Music 243, 247
This Is the Life 192
This Land of Ours 290
This Love of Ours 180
This Property Is Condemned 33, 34, 238
Thomas, Frank M. 277
Thomas, Frankie 277–285
Thomas, Mona 277
Thompson, Mary Ellen 153
A Thousand Clowns 274
Three Faces West 41
Three Stooges 40, 222
Three Wise Fools 103
Thriller 297, 298
Thunder on the Left 278
Thunderbirds 198
Tibbs, Casey 111
Tim Tyler's Luck 280–282
Time for Beanie 5
To Kill a Mockingbird 14–16, 18, 19, 30–33, 35, 37
To Rome with Love 326
To the Last Man 316

Todd, Thelma 84, 85
Tom Corbett, Space Patrol 283, 284
Tom Sawyer 327, 328, 330
Tone, Franchot 170
The Tonight Show 98
Top o' the Morning 134
Topper (Horse) 40
Torme, Mel 290, 291
Touched by an Angel 246
Traci, Barbara 185
Trackdown 111
Tracy, Spencer 113, 147, 248, 304, 306–308, 320,
The Treasure of Lost Canyon 148, 149
The Treasure of San Bosco Reef 215
A Tree Grows in Brooklyn 60, 61, 63, 65, 180
Tresconi, Al 118
Trigger (Horse) 53, 144
Triple Day (Horse) 125
Troubleshooters 253
True Story 284
Tucker, Forrest 163
The Tuttles of Tahiti 139, 243
26 Men 111
20,000 Men a Year 68
The Twilight Zone 36, 126
Twinkle, Twinkle Little Star 309
Two Girls and a Sailor 154, 227
Tyler, Dick 105
Tyler, Leon 180, 286–293

Ullman, George 242
Uncle Willie 91
Under California Stars 53
The Under-Pup 202, 205
Unholtz, Rudy 113

Valee, Rudy 159
The Vampire Wars 101
Van Dyke, Dick 17, 255
Vanity Fair 31
Virginia City 206
The Virginian 18, 212, 310
Vogan, Emmett 74
The Voice of Gruber Hills 118

Wagon Train 80, 125, 166, 212, 271, 272, 298
Wagons West 52
Wake Island 177

Walburn, Raymond 110
Walker, Clint 80, 215
Wallace, Richard 202
Walt Disney's Wonderful World of Color 213, 214
Wanted Dead or Alive 80, 246, 252, 253
Warner, Jack 226
Washburn, Audrey 294
Washburn, Beverly 294–302
Watson, Billy 249, 305, 314, 318
Watson, Bobs 1, 248, 249, 303–314, 318, 319, 321–323
Watson, Coy, Sr. 314
Watson, Delmar 305, 314–323
Watson, Harry 318, 320, 321
Watson, Minor 285
The Way We Were 176
Wayne, John 6, 7, 10, 41, 42, 71, 181–184, 293
Wayne, Mike 183
Wayne, Pat 7
Weatherwax, Rudd 7, 109, 235, 236, 238, 289
Webb, Clifton 115, 116, 133
Webb, Jack 50, 215, 275
Webb, Richard 18
Wednesday's Child 278, 281, 284
Weekend with Father 135, 227
Weissmuller, Johnny 13
Welles, Orson 42
Wellman, William 108, 110
Welton, Marion 290
The Werewolves on Wheels 100
West, James 218
West, Mae 334
West, Wally 10
What Became of the Children 39, 40
Whatever Happened to Baby Peggy 29
Wheeler, Bert 103
Where Are They Now 265
The Whirleybirds 244
Whispering Smith 103
Whistling in the Dark 291
Whitaker, Johnny 265, 324–333
White, Jacqueline 104
White, Jules 222
White, Samuel 222
Whiteman, Paul 169
Whitmore, James 108, 126, 183
Who Killed Doc Robbin? 156, 220–222, 224, 232

Index

Who's News 50
Wicker, Irene 57
The Wide Country 126
Wild Bill Hickok 175, 222
Wild Heritage 111
Wild Horse Ambush 156, 157
Wilder, John 167
Williams, Esther 147
Williams, John 328
Willie Wopper 336
Wills, Beverly 291
Wilson, Henry 185
Wilson, Marie 76
Windom, William 270, 271, 273
The Window 164
Wise, Robert 95
Withers, Jane 74, 170, 174, 192, 193, 263, 317, 334–345
Withers, Ruth 341
Withers, Walter 341
Witney, William 194
A Woman's Face 103
Women to Remember 283
Wonderful World of Disney 257
Wonderful World of the Brothers Grimm 253, 254
Wood, Natalie 2, 33, 34, 154, 238, 264, 293
Woods, Sam 223
Woodward, Morgan 271
Wouk, Herman 243
Wrather, Jack 236, 237
Wright, Teresa 17, 228
Wyatt, Jane 97, 98
Wyatt Earp 111
Wyler, William 77, 78, 170, 171
Wyman, Jane 163, 233, 293
Wynn, Keenan 144, 253
Wyoming 308

Yates, Herbert 51, 165, 195, 340, 341
The Yearling 161–165
Yes Sir, She's My Baby 59
Young, Alan 295
Young, Gig 9, 341
Young, Loretta 105, 297, 302
Young, Robert 64, 97, 98, 158, 180, 223, 224
Young People 207
The Youngest Profession 171, 175
Yurka, Blanche 42, 277

Zaharias, Babe 275
Zane Grey Theater 298
Zinnemann, Fred 5, 6
Zodkevitch, Dr. Ron 333
Zucco, George 221, 222

www.ingramcontent.com/pod-product-compliance
Lightning Source LLC
Chambersburg PA
CBHW051205300426
44116CB00006B/441